THE EDUCATION OF PHYSICIAN-SCHOLARS

“THE EDUCATION OF PHYSICIAN-SCHOLARS FOR LEADERSHIP IN THE HEALTH CARE SYSTEM”

A symposium on the occasion of the tenth anniversary of the establishment of the Medical Scholars Program, a joint program of the University of Illinois College of Medicine at Urbana-Champaign and the Graduate College of the University of Illinois at Urbana-Champaign

November 4–6, 1989

Beckman Institute for Advanced Science and Technology
University of Illinois
at Urbana-Champaign

Scientific Program Committee

George F. Cahill, Jr., M.D.
Howard Hughes Medical Institute

Ruth L. Kirschstein, M.D.
National Institute of General Medical Sciences

August G. Swanson, M.D.
Association of American Medical Colleges

Harold M. Swartz, M.D., Ph.D., Chair
University of Illinois College of Medicine at Urbana-Champaign

Samuel O. Thier, M.D.
Institute of Medicine
National Academy of Sciences

Organizing Committee

James E. Black, M.D./Ph.D. student
Medical Scholars Program

Michael D. Cantor, M.D./J.D. student
Medical Scholars Program

Arnold D. Curnyn, M.D.
University of Illinois College of Medicine at Chicago

Diane L. Gottheil, Ph.D.
University of Illinois College of Medicine at Urbana-Champaign

Lowell P. Hager, Ph.D.
University of Illinois at Urbana-Champaign

Paul A. Hattis, M.D., J.D.
American Hospital Association

Judith S. Liebman, Ph.D.
University of llinois at Urbana-Champaign

Ralph A. Nelson, M.D., Ph.D.
University of Illinois College of Medicine at Urbana-Champaign

Charles C. C. O’Morchoe, M.D., Ph.D., D.Sc., Chair
University of Illinois College of Medicine at Urbana-Champaign

Robert F. Rich, Ph.D.
University of Illinois at Urbana-Champaign

Harvey J. Stapleton, Ph.D.
University of Illinois at Urbana-Champaign

Harold M. Swartz, M.D./Ph.D.
University of Illinois College of Medicine at Urbana-Champaign

THE EDUCATION OF PHYSICIAN-SCHOLARS

Preparing for Leadership in the Health Care System

Edited by

Harold M. Swartz, M.D., Ph.D.

and

Diane L. Gottheil, Ph.D.

Betz Publishing Company

Rockville, Maryland

ISBN: 0-941406-41-5

Printed in the United States of America

Library of Congress Cataloging-in-Publication Data

The education of physician-scholars : preparing for leadership in the health care system / edited by Harold M. Swartz and Diane L. Gottheil.

p. cm.

"A symposium on the occasion of the tenth anniversary of the Medical Scholars Program"—P. facing t.p.

Includes bibliographical references and index.

ISBN 0-941406-41-5 : $29.95

1. Medicine—Study and teaching (Graduate)—United States—Congresses. 2. Health services administrators—Education—United States—Congresses. 3. Medical research personnel—Education—United States—Congresses. 4. Leadership—Congresses. I. Swartz, Harold M. II. Gottheil, Diane L. (Diane Levitt), date. III. Medical Scholars Program.

[DNLM: 1. Education, Medical, Graduate—congresses. 2. Leadership—congresses. W 20 E2253 1993]

R840.E38 1993

610'.71'1—dc20

DNLM/DLC

for Library of Congress 93-8340

CIP

I believe that the only practical, currently available way to guarantee the future of the American system of health care, irrespective of what financial goal is set, is through research.... The greatest national resource for the effort is not money. It is the ideas and the concepts that are the products of the minds of men and women. The interests and the activities of those minds are what is needed and what needs to be supported.

Theodore Cooper, M.D., Ph.D.
Concluding Remarks at the
Symposium of the Academic Physician:
An Endangered Species (October 1980)

CONTENTS

PREFACE

This book is written with a very specific aim: to enhance the development of physicians as scholars and leaders in the health care system. In particular, its authors try to identify the issues that are currently critical in preparing physicians for scholarship and leadership and to provide the background information needed to make realistic and effective plans for future development. With this information, we hope to be able to delineate new approaches and effectively modify old ones.

The focus on physician-scholars and leaders is based on the view that the clinical knowledge and perspective of the physician can provide unique contributions that enrich research and scholarship in fields ranging from bench science to health care policy and administration. Society stands to gain from the participation of scholarly physicians in leadership roles in all spheres of health care (1). Even academic medicine, the sector of health care most traditionally self-governed by physicians, has felt the effects of societal forces—both from within, as a result of rapid advances in medical science and technology, new perspectives on decision making, and differing views on acceptable lifestyles, and from without, as a result of demographic and economic forces and a wide array of changes in societal attitudes and expectations (2).

Although at various points in the book we briefly discuss the rationale for having physician-scholars and physician-leaders, we do not extensively attempt to justify their existence. They are an important reality on the current scene, and it is unlikely that the need for them will diminish. The fact that this book focuses on physicians should not be interpreted as undervaluing in any way the roles of other researchers and leaders in the health care system. In some sections of the book nonphysicians involved in medical research or other leadership roles are explicitly included in the discussion.

This book examines the various pathways to the careers of physician-scholar and leader, attempting to set forth the strengths and weaknesses of these routes and the likely role they will play in the future. Today, most physicians who are considered scholars or leaders have probably not completed educational programs specifically designed to prepare them for such roles. Further, the majority of physicians with specific training in research have received it in relatively unstructured programs as postdoctoral research fellows following a residency; the doctoral degree that made them eligible for a postdoctoral appointment was thus the M.D. rather than a Ph.D. Such programs are seldom comparable to the postdoctoral fellowships available to those who have received research preparation in a Ph.D. program.

Recently there has been an increased focus on the need for more specific and deliberate preparation of physician-scholars (3). Several approaches have received considerable attention as logical ways to prepare physicians to become competitive researchers in today's highly specialized and intellectually sophisticated arenas of cutting-edge research: M.D./Ph.D. programs; a number of Master's-level programs, such as the Robert Wood Johnson Clinical Scholars Program and M.P.H. and M.B.A. programs; as well as more rigorous educational programs for physicians at postresidency levels. Despite these trends, most "academic" physicians (those with at least 50 percent academic appointments or the equivalent in government or industry) have had no extensive formal preparation in research in either Ph.D. or postdoctoral programs, and most do not publish research results regularly. If greater involvement in productive research is a goal, the need for research education is evident (4).

A note on nomenclature. The terms used to describe physicians who are scholars and/or researchers are several and possibly ambiguous. We (the editors) use *physician-scholar* for physicians whose primary activities include the generation of new knowledge, usually including publications in peer-reviewed journals, and *physician-leader* for physicians whose primary activities include performing significant roles of recognized authority in the health care field. The other contributors may differ somewhat in their use of these terms and their focus on the roles; we did not try to impose a rigorous set of rules because we view our goal as inclusive rather than prescriptive.

Our interest in and knowledge of the subject of this book derive largely from our experience in the development and operation of the Medical Scholars Program, an M.D./Ph.D. program at the University of Illinois College of Medicine at Urbana-Champaign. This program is unusually broad (in the number and diversity of Ph.D. programs in which students are enrolled), and it occupies an unusually prominent role in the overall mission of the medical school. Plans for this book were initially developed along with a symposium on the same topic. The symposium was first suggested, during a discussion about the upcoming tenth anniversary of the Medical Scholars Program, as an excellent vehicle by which to review our progress and aid in the analysis of M.D./Ph.D. programs on a national scale. The focus of the symposium subsequently expanded to a much more comprehensive overview of the education of physicians for careers as scholars and leaders. This evolution was due, in great part, to the informed input we received from the symposium's Scientific Advisory Committee: George F. Cahill, Jr., M.D., Howard Hughes Medical Institute; Ruth L. Kirschstein, M.D., National Institute of General Medical Sciences; August G. Swanson, M.D., Association of American Medical Colleges; and Samuel O. Thier, M.D., Institute of Medicine, National Academy of Sciences, who pointed out that problems and opportunities in the preparation of academic physicians could be considered more effectively in the broader context. The members of the Scientific Advisory Committee not only helped in developing the content of the symposium but also provided invaluable assistance in the recruitment of many other outstanding leaders to the symposium.

The symposium was organized to bring together leading figures from the major segments of the health care system who have a significant stake in the number and type of students entering careers aimed at scholarship and leadership in medicine. The purpose of the gathering was to facilitate interaction among leading representatives of academia, government, foundations, private nonprofit agencies and associations, and corporations—sectors that work together too rarely—and enable them to discuss the type of preparation provided by various educational pathways and develop recommendations for effective future action.

Almost from the beginning we planned to develop the book in parallel with the symposium. Some of the background information and workshop discussion questions for the attendees were expanded and refined for the book and appear as Chapters 1, 2, and 5. Most of the contributed essays were developed from presentations at the symposium, selected for their unique perspectives and insights on topics most germane to the purpose of the book. We avoided the temptation to compile a straightforward proceedings, opting instead for a more comprehensive book that, like the symposium, would extend beyond the focus on M.D./Ph.D. programs. Thus, we hope to provide both a thorough background in the subject of combined degree education and other modes of research and leadership education, as well as to provide perspectives on the education of physician-scholars and leaders from the varied contributions of many of the distinguished participants.

Most of the available literature on the education of physicians for scholarship and leadership is conceptual or editorial. Few data are available on many crucial aspects of the subject, and these are often derived from data sets aimed at other objectives or from internal or otherwise unpublished sources. The chapter references constitute a list of the most pertinent publications, but certainly one of the clear conclusions from the analyses in this book is the great need for systematic data on almost all aspects of the subject, from characteristics of the pool of entering students to the outcomes of the various approaches. We have made a modest effort toward this goal in three chapters: Chapter 3 includes what we believe is the most systematic and thorough description of M.D./Ph.D. programs in the United States and Canada; Chapter 4 presents a review of all other types of efforts to prepare physician-scholars (consequently, together with Chapter 3, it provides the beginning of a compendium of pathways to leadership in health care); and Chapter 9 presents the results of a survey of the participants' backgrounds and views on education for leadership and scholarship. The material in Chapter 9 may be considered a first step in gathering the kinds of leadership data needed; we believe that the results can form the basis for a more systematic study.

The chapters that compose Part II are intended to broaden and enhance the book. The authors of these chapters were asked to provide their insights on specific topics; it remains our responsibility to make the book comprehensive and cohesive by providing appropriate content and organization throughout.

Finally, building on the literature and data, and the discussions generated before, during, and since the symposium, Part III attempts to delineate a course of future action. We hope that the materials presented in the book and the rationale for each recommendation will generate discussion and continued data gathering. Most of all, we hope that this book will lead to appropriate actions and policies to ensure the future course of medical science and health care and that these actions and policies make the wisest use of our human and material resources to fulfill a vital societal need.

References

1. Samuel O. Thier, "Clinical Investigation in the 1980's: Perspectives from the Medical Schools," *Clinical Research* 28 (Sept. 1980): 248-51.
2. D. J. Weatherall, "The Physician Scientist: An Endangered But Far From Extinct Species," *British Medical Journal* 302 (April 27 1991): 1002-05.
3. Robert S. Rhodes, "Presidential Address" (to the Society of University Surgeons), *Surgery* 102 (Aug. 1987): 115-21.
4. Joseph L. Goldstein, "On the Origin and Prevention of PAIDS (Paralyzed Academic Investigator's Disease Syndrome)," *Journal of Clinical Investigator* 78 (Sept. 1986): 848-54.

ACKNOWLEDGMENTS

The Josiah Macy, Jr., Foundation provided significant support for the development of this book. The editors particularly want to thank foundation president Dr. Thomas H. Meikle, Jr., for his encouragement and guidance in planning the book and for his role in the symposium that preceded it.

Much of the content of this book arose from materials generated by the symposium; we therefore wish to acknowledge contributions made to the symposium and those made directly or indirectly to this book by a number of individuals and organizations.

Financial support for the symposium was provided by the National Institutes of Health/National Institute for General Medical Science; Life and Health Insurance Medical Research Fund; Milbank Memorial Fund; Upjohn Company; Office of the Dean, University of Illinois College of Medicine; Office of the Vice-Chancellor for Academic Affairs, University of Illinois at Urbana-Champaign (UIUC); and the University of Illinois College of Medicine at Urbana-Champaign (UICOM-UC).

Organizational support for the symposium was provided by the Scientific Planning Committee, of which the senior editor was the chair and which included George Cahill, Ruth Kirschstein, August Swanson, and Samuel Thier. Additional organizational support was provided by Gert Brieger, Paul Hattis, Leon Eisenberg, Lee Van Lenten, Hamilton Smith, and Paul Talalay. In addition to the editors, the Symposium Organizing Committee consisted of Charles C. C. O'Morchoe (Chair), James E. Black, Michael D. Cantor, Arnold D. Curnyn, Lowell P. Hager, Paul A. Hattis, Judith S. Liebman, Ralph A. Nelson, Robert F. Rich, and Harvey Stapleton.

General support was provided by the Medical Scholars Program (MSP) Steering Committee, the governing body of the MSP, whose members represent all the academic units in which MSP students are enrolled; and the UICOM-UC and UIUC Graduate College administration. Cindi Jackson, then-coordinator of the Medical Scholars Program, participated in all phases of the symposium planning and administration and had an important role in overseeing the development of the manuscript.

The Medical Scholars Program support staff, Denice Wells, Julie Wyant, and Shirley Rademacher gave excellent and efficient secretarial support at each step of organizing the symposium and developing the book. Of particular note was the outstanding word processing of the entire manuscript by Denice Wells. As always, the Library of the University of Illinois, especially the Library of the Health Sciences, proved to be a treasure; what they lacked in their huge collection, they acquired through the magic of interlibrary loan, frequently from other medical school libraries in Illinois. We want to acknowledge, too, the MSP students for their interest and enthusiasm, in general, and, in particular, for being a constant source of inspiration.

At various points in the organization of both the symposium and the book, our research assistants played a crucial role in conducting literature searches; annotating sources; reviewing drafts; helping design, disseminate, and follow up on questionnaires; making frequent trips to the library; and providing all manner of contributions. They include Stacie Colwell, Peter Curio, Benjamin Horowitz, William King, Lawrence Lurvey, Michael Markowitz, Stephan Quentzel, Joseph Sejud, and Julia Winter, all of whom are students in the Medical Scholars Program. Beth Hahn then from the Department of Sociology assisted with computer analysis. Gail Hapke leant her considerable editorial skills to the entire manuscript and contributed greatly to its readability and coherence. Whatever faults remain are the editors alone.

This book is dedicated to the memory of Josh Gottheil in the hope that today's physician-scholars will make inroads in conquering diseases such as cancer, which took his life at age 19.

PART I
OVERVIEW: NEEDS, GOALS, PROGRAMS, AND OUTCOMES

This section provides an overview of the general concerns involved in educating physicians for scholarship and leadership in the health care system. It includes an assessment of where we stand in the early part of the 1990s in identifying concerns and issues, responding to perceived needs, defining goals, and developing programs to meet national needs and articulated goals. It thus sets the stage for more focused examinations in Part II of issues germane to the subject of educating physician-scholars and leaders.

1

Critical Concerns and Questions in Educating Physican-Scholars

Harold M. Swartz and Diane L. Gottheil

In this chapter, we attempt to delineate the principal issues regarding the preparation of physician-scholars and physician-leaders. In addressing the concerns of the various constituencies involved, we intend to provide a useful context in which to consider the data and analyses presented in succeeding chapters, which deal with more specific aspects of this topic. These concerns, of course, are often interrelated and include both short-term and long-term considerations. In some cases they may not be supported by the existing data; however, this does not necessarily diminish the need to respond to them, because regardless of the factual basis, the perception of problems may have a significant impact on behavior and policies. These issues are therefore critical to the ability of the educational process to meet the needs of the health care system for physician-scholars and leaders.

Are Enough Highly Qualified Individuals Entering Scholarship and Leadership in Medicine?

Concern about a declining supply of physician-researchers has made the topic of the education of physician-scholars especially pertinent. A shortage, whether present or impending, of clinical investigators or physician-scientists is viewed as potentially very detrimental to the quality of biomedical research. Recently the scarcity of physicians qualified to study outcomes and other issues critical to the evaluation and improvement of the health care system has added to this concern.

Expressions of concern about "supply" often refer explicitly to the number of well-qualified medical students and physicians starting research careers, but the evidence for this concern is typically derived from observations made at a later stage of the careers of physician-scholars. Supporting data refer to the number and quality of physicians awarded National Institutes of Health (NIH) fellowships and traineeships for research education. Perhaps the most familiar formulation of this argument appears in a 1979 article by former NIH director James Wyngaarden, entitled "The Clinical Investigator as an Endangered Species." (1) Other evidence cited to support this concern is the dwindling number of physicians who successfully obtain competitive research funding (2,3). Like fellowship and traineeship awards, this is a convenient criterion because it is reasonably logical and data are readily available from NIH.

Since the Wyngaarden article, a number of additional voices have expressed concern about perceived shortages of physician-researchers, both generally and in specific areas (4–8). In particular, they stress the declining number of clinical researchers, usually physicians whose principal site of research is the clinic or hospital and whose source of experimental data is the patient (9–12). Another area of perceived acute shortage is among individuals qualified to carry out clinical trials of new drugs (13). Strong arguments have also been made regarding shortages of physician-scholars in various areas of the social sciences and humanities (14–16) as well as in the basic medical sciences, particularly as they affect areas of clinical specialty (17–21). A recent article by D. J. Weatherall, based on his 1990 commencement address to Johns Hopkins Medical School, cites all these needs and expresses grave concern for the future of academic medicine if they are not met (22).

The predominant mode of formal research training for physicians entering scholarly careers is participation in postdoctoral traineeships and fellowships after the completion of a residency program (23). Yet there are concerns about whether enough postdoctoral slots are available to meet projected national needs (24) and whether candidates who enter these pathways have sufficient preparation or motivation to carry through to productive research careers. Some participants spend only one to two years in these programs before going on to the next stage of their careers; this raises questions about whether they have been adequately prepared for effective research (25,26). If they are not well prepared at this juncture and do not obtain additional training, either they will conduct research of less than optimal quality (which is unlikely to be supported by peer-reviewed funding) or, perceiving themselves as unprepared or finding themselves unable to compete successfully for outside funding, they will not participate in research at all.

Another concern is that there may be too few applicants to M.D./Ph.D. programs, a newer means of providing formal research training for physicians. Typically, those who express concern about declining applications refer to the experience of other institutions and only the *potential* for the effect to spread to their institutions in the near future. (Note, however, that few administrators indicate that their own institutions are actually having problems attracting enough qualified applicants.) Inadequate financial support for students is often cited as a factor explaining the presumed or anticipated difficulty of attracting M.D./Ph.D. applicants in this context, an issue discussed further below (6). Another source of this concern seems to have been the well-publicized decline in the quantity and quality of applicants to medical school that occurred in the mid- to late 1980s; it was argued that this trend toward declining applications would lead to a corresponding decrease in the number of well-qualified applicants for joint degree programs (8). This decline appears to have reversed itself in the 1990s; using the same reasoning, therefore, we should be able to predict an increased pool of M.D./Ph.D. applicants. While no decline in applicants to M.D./Ph.D. programs appeared to materialize in the earlier period, no data are yet available on whether such applicants have increased in conjunction with the overall increase in medical school applications of the last few years. A closely related concern is whether there are enough qualified potential applicants to allow M.D./Ph.D. programs to expand without a decrease in the quality of the students.

A final concern is the quality of individual these career paths attract. Are they "the best and the brightest"? That is, even if the entrants have sufficient talent and motivation to be successful, are we missing an even better pool of possible participants in scholarship and leadership? It is frequently asserted that the field of medicine has become less attractive in recent years as a result of rapid changes within the field that create uncertainty about the future role of physicians, as well as the lure of the quicker "pay-off" of degrees in business or engineering. It has also been asserted that within the medical profession, academic careers have become less attractive than clinical practice. The principal reasons cited are, first, that burdensome debts accumulated during the training period force graduates into clinical paths, which offer higher incomes; second, that funding for research is insufficient and undependable; and third, that financial incentives are greater even for academic physicians to focus on clinical activities (3). This final issue has emerged as a major focus of concern in regard to the increasing dependence of academic medical centers on reimbursement for patient care (18, 27–29).

In response to concerns about the number of physicians entering research, recruitment efforts are under way at all levels. These efforts include enabling premedical students to participate in medical school research activities to stimulate interest in medical science; developing or expanding research-oriented clinical residencies; and creating new opportunities for research fellowships for physicians who have completed residencies. (Activities to recruit physicians into research are considered in more detail in Chapter 4.)

Are "the Best and the Brightest" Entering the Fields Where They Are Most Needed?

Recently, efforts have been made to recruit physicians into programs focused on outcomes measurement and other aspects of health services research. This trend has arisen in response to a concern that physician-researchers be trained in areas that physicians have not traditionally pursued but that impinge greatly on medical practice. A pool of "the best and brightest" would thus optimally include students with interests outside traditional biomedical science; that is, in the social and behavioral sciences, humanities, physical or engineering sciences (such as computer science or materials sciences), or even areas of biomedical sciences not typically offered in combined degree programs (such as nutritional sciences or speech and hearing sciences). Students with interests and backgrounds in such nontraditional fields may not realize that it is possible to pursue a career of scholarship and research that relates their area of interest to the field of medicine and health care. Similarly, they may not be aware of the growing interest in facilitating such careers, in part because such interest may not be widely represented, or adequately communicated, in the medical schools.

As the relationship between medicine and society has become increasingly complex, the need for physicians to understand the forces impinging on the health care system has become more evident (14, 30). The complex environment of medicine suggests a growing need for physician-scholars with the types of backgrounds that will allow them to meet the new challenges. Is it possible, however, that we are failing to attract individuals into innovative combinations of medicine and such second fields as economics or anthropology because we lack appropriate role models? Are there also too few role models for the most traditional physician-scholar, whose research occurs primarily in a clinical setting? In addition, questions have arisen in the biomedical areas, which have typically been the domain of the physician-scholar, whether—given the nature and extent of the "biological revolution"—we are providing physician-scientists with the right kinds of skills (18, 22, 31–32).

When Should Individuals Be Recruited?

Assuming that we can determine the future need for physician-scholars and leaders and recruit talented individuals into programs that prepare them for these careers, the timing of their entrance into these programs then becomes an important issue. The costs of these educational programs—as measured by the time and effort of the participants, the investment of public funds, and the involvement of some of our most talented faculty—make it essential that the selection process be as efficient as possible. The success of a program can be gauged by its academic effectiveness and outcomes. In particular, it should minimize attrition and maximize the probability that graduates will remain in careers of productive scholarship and leadership. For these objectives to be achieved, it is essential to match sufficient numbers of the right kinds of medical students and young physicians with programs that are academically excellent and appropriate for their individual professional goals. Because of the potential for conflict among the demands of research and clinical training, questions have been raised about what is the most effective sequence or educational track (3, 33–34).

There are five principal points of entry into the scholarship/leadership career path.

1. Upon entering medical school, the student might choose a combined degree program or a school that has a reputation for producing academic physicians and thus provides opportunities for research education.
2. During the first two years of medical school, the student might enter a combined degree program to pursue formal Ph.D. education along with the M.D. or might participate seriously in an elective research program as a means of acquiring research experience.
3. Upon completion of the M.D., the physician might enter a research-oriented residency program in which research experience is required or at least encouraged and available; alternatively, the physician might choose not to do residency training but instead to enter a full-time research training program (a postdoctoral fellowship with no clinical training or responsibilities, or even a Ph.D. program).
4. The physician might enter a program after completing a residency—or after residency and subspecialty training—and perhaps board certification.
5. After entering and gaining experience in a clinical career, the physician might enter a formal program of education for scholarship and/or leadership. Such a program may be closely related to the individual's area of clinical specialization or may signal a more radical career shift.

In the following chapters, issues of timing at each of these points of entrance will be explored within the context of a detailed consideration of existing or proposed programs. For the present, note that there are questions relating to academic effectiveness raised by the point of entry issue as well as significant financial implications associated with the point at which students enter their research training. Should research training begin once the student has graduated and entered a residency, the resident's salary (~$25,000/yr), is generally considered an appropriate minimum stipend. This minimum is considerably higher than the typical stipend awarded to graduate students, and programs must have enough funding to meet these expectations. Also, increased payments on accumulated debt from student loans may become operative at this point, placing greater demands on the resources of trainees.

Are Effective and Realistic Means of Education Provided in the Needed Fields?

As the diversity of needs for physician-scholars has become manifest, there has been a concomitant increase in concern for the way in which they are being prepared. Are the traditional pathways best for all the fields now involved, or should there be distinctly different pathways, depending on the need for physician-scholars in a given field? Should the educational program for physicians who will be involved in clinical research that entails direct patient contact be different from a program for physicians who will engage in bench research (33)? Similar questions have been raised in regard to the preparation of physicians for health services research and the management of medical care in the new, complex environment of the academic medical center. The best pathway for an M.D./Ph.D. in sociology might differ significantly from that of the M.D./Ph.D. in biochemistry with respect to the sequence of studies, the appropriate residency and postdoctoral programs, and the nature of clinical training and experience.

Do Today's Programs Adequately Cover Necessary Areas of Knowledge?

Many people are concerned that successful physician-scholars, especially those who are to have effective leadership roles, require a range of skills and knowledge not provided by most training programs (35). Areas of deficiency range from biostatistics (especially as applied to the measurement of effects in clinical trials) to the organization of the health care system. However, participants in dual-degree programs may already be stretched too thin to master both medicine and a specific scholarly discipline, and it may be counterproductive to include additional topics in their training. (This issue is discussed further in Chapter 9.)

How Can High Levels of Competence Be Achieved in Both a Scholarly Field and Clinical Medicine?

It is a challenge to achieve high levels of competence in both a scholarly field and clinical medicine (33). A key question, of course, is whether such an achievement is even *possible.* And, if so, how much time and other resources will adequate preparation take, and is preparation for such a career a reasonable investment? Put simply, this is the classic issue of the cost/benefit ratio. A closely related question is whether one can be a true physician-scholar without having high levels of competence in both areas.

How then should educational programs be organized to enable the participants to achieve high levels of competence? One aspect of this question is conceptual: what do we mean by a high level of competence? Another aspect is practical, involving the need to remain current in fields that are progressing rapidly and to compete with very talented individuals who are concentrating exclusively on either clinical *or* research responsibilities. The issue of competition perhaps provides the answer to the conceptual aspect of the question: high competence will be defined by one's colleagues in the field and by one's ability to measure up on all accepted criteria of excellence. Some of these questions are raised in the survey discussed in Chapter 9; findings presented there may help us begin to provide answers.

Great demands are placed upon physicians to keep up with the literature and participate in continuing education in their areas of specialty while maintaining a patient load. Similarly, those familiar with the process of conducting cutting-edge research consider directing a research laboratory more than a full-time job.

Ongoing demands may place constraints on the range and level of activities that physician-scholars can maintain and remain fully effective. Forces from many sectors are involved; for example, the high level of accomplishment required to compete successfully for funding and the need to spend enough time in practice to be eligible for reimbursement from third parties or to obtain protection from potential malpractice complaints. As noted, the criteria of competence customarily accepted in the clinical arena and in the scholarly field delimit the individual's choices and range of participation.

Do Standard Programs of Medical Education Provide the Best Preparation for Physician-Scholars?

In considering the standard mode of medical education as a basis for preparing physician-scholars and leaders, we must ask two interrelated and quite straightforward questions: 1) are the existing undergraduate and/or graduate medical educational programs suitable for the preparation of physician-scholars? and 2) would the perturbation and/or expense caused by the use of different pathways offset any improvements in the educational process (37)? The extent and nature of these concerns are likely to be different at different institutions, but they tend to be expressed at most or all institutions at some time. Particular anxiety is evoked by the concern that physician-scholars will appear to have received a curtailed medical education in the undergraduate or graduate phase because they used some of their available time for research rather than additional clinical activities. On the other side of the argument is the assertion that typical medical educational programs emphasize many aspects of the practice of medicine that are not relevant to the kinds of clinical activity likely to be carried out by graduates of these programs. Practical considerations include the unpredictable time demands of the research portion of the educational program, with the resulting consequences for scheduling the entire program of studies, and the responsibility at virtually all institutions to educate the vast majority of their medical students and residents for strictly clinical careers. (Some interesting exceptions can be found at both the graduate and undergraduate levels. For example, the University of Illinois College of Medicine at Urbana-Champaign focuses primarily on the preparation of physician-scholars, and a number of residency programs at academic medical centers focus exclusively on the continued development of physician-scholars. These are described in Chapters 3 and 4.)

What Pathways Should Be Provided after the Formal Phases of Medical and Research Education?

A pertinent question for combined degree students and administrators is: What is the best subsequent step in career preparation? The graduates of combined degree programs go out into a world that is not institutionally prepared to utilize their special backgrounds (37). Consequently, there is great concern that much of their potential will be lost as they are forced to choose between strictly clinical or strictly research pathways. As with many of the concerns we have identified here, the problems are viewed as both practical and conceptual. On the practical side is the concern that the ability to maintain skills and knowledge in the research discipline is significantly diminished in traditional pathways, including faculty positions in academic medical centers. On the conceptual side is the concern that graduates may enter an environment in which their special capabilities and orientation are seen as *less* desirable than those acquired in conventional educational preparation in either research or clinical medicine. These attitudes may be present in both the clinical and the research arenas and may result in pressures to alter career plans to more conventional unidimensional roles. These considerations are relevant for junior faculty as well as for those in residency and subspecialty training. In fact, junior faculty may face particularly acute problems since they are expected simultaneously to assume a significant level of clinical responsibilities and to establish externally funded research programs (all while repaying student loans!).

These also are key questions for physicians who receive their primary research preparation after medical school or residency. The type of research preparation they receive, whether in the biological, physical, or social sciences, is likely to be at best the equivalent of that obtained through a rapid Ph.D. program. If they intended to pursue a scholarly career, the next steps must enable them to build effectively on this start in research so that they are not at a disadvantage compared to typical graduates of Ph.D. programs, who usually go next into full-time postdoctoral or junior faculty positions. The problem may be especially great in the shorter research training programs, because in one or two years even the brightest and best-motivated students are unlikely to develop the necessary research skills and learn the basic knowledge in their area of interest (2, 3, 36).

Similar concerns apply to educational programs for physicians at later phases of their careers. The Robert Wood Johnson Foundation's Health Policy Fellows and Clinical Scholars programs are innovative enterprises for physicians who have completed their residency. These programs address areas of great need, yet they provide, at best, a start toward the expertise and skills needed to carry out original scholarly research in fields related to health care. For graduates of such programs to fully exploit their new capabilities, they must be placed in environments where they can continue to develop their skills and/or work with individuals who have complementary skills in a team approach. Once again, the competence of these graduates will be measured against that of individuals with the best preparation in a single field—and the M.D. training will seldom compensate for inadequate research training or experience. (These and other postgraduate programs are considered in Chapter 4.)

Finally, concerns have also been voiced about the appropriate pathways for those educated in both law and medicine. Despite the rapidly increasing intersection of these two fields and the significant number of individuals possessing both M.D. and J.D. degrees, the stresses on M.D./J.D.s who attempt most effectively to exploit their dual knowledge base is due in large measure to the lack of defined pathways (38, 39).

Should Physician-Scholars and Leaders Become Board Certified?

The pressures on aspiring academic physicians to obtain board certification may have a negative impact on the progress of their careers (36). The pressure is seen to arise from the structure of medical schools, where appointments of physicians to clinical departments usually require board certification. Many specialty boards, however, do not apply time spent in research toward their board examination eligibility requirements; therefore, the resident needs to spend three to five years in purely clinical pursuits, with the consequent loss of momentum in scholarly work and extension of the training period. Further, there is a concern that public and private third-party payers may begin to link reimbursement formulas to board certification, viewing this credential as a criterion of competence and a defense against liability.

In many institutions academic physicians are under significant pressure to become further certified in a subspecialty. This pressure comes from at least two sources. In many institutions and organizations much of the power and prestige is associated with subspecialization. In many research areas one logical solution to the need to be clinically expert and still devote a majority of time to research is to have a narrow area of clinical expertise, and this is often associated with subspecialization. Thus, some physician-scholars may feel compelled to extend even further their amount of purely clinical training and their training period. Granting that for some positions of scholarship and leadership such extended training is desirable, this situation raises serious questions both about the wisdom of a structure that may create incentives for unnecessary training and about the potential attrition from research-based careers as a result.

Are Role Models Sufficient and Appropriate?

As the nature of medical research becomes more complex and technical, are today's scholars and leaders in medicine sufficient and even appropriate role models for medical students and young physicians aspiring to similar careers? Only quite recently have a significant number of graduates of M.D./Ph.D. programs or rigorous postresidency research programs entered academic medicine, and most academic faculty have therefore had much less structured preparation in research than the students they are educating. Some people even argue that the research done by many clinical faculty members is not sufficiently rigorous to make them good role models for the young, well-trained physicians now being prepared.

A related problem—more individual and perhaps even idiosyncratic rather than structural—is that the dual-degree student may be perceived as a potential threat to the mentor who has only one advanced degree. To the M.D., the presence of the individual seeking the M.D./Ph.D. implies that cutting-edge research may require the formal preparation involved in earning a Ph.D. This perception may be strengthened by arguments in favor of combined degree preparation that emphasize the more thorough nature of research education provided by Ph.D. programs, the more sophisticated nature of research being conducted, and the greater success in competitive funding support of those with a Ph.D. degree. Such perceptions may be present not only among mentors of

M.D/Ph.D. students but also among mentors in the specially designed programs that provide rigorous postresidency research training. Similarly, the M.D./Ph.D. student or young physician in a research education program can appear to be a threat to the status of the Ph.D. role model, to whom the preparation of the student may imply that having an M.D. is a requisite for effective, clinically pertinent research. In any case, can a mentor be fully effective while lacking enthusiasm for the student's program of studies or while being openly or even tacitly unsupportive? Given the tremendous challenges of the long and demanding course of M.D./Ph.D. education, the role of the mentor is crucial, and such individual attitudes can have significant consequences.

Another potential problem is that if the mentor is an outstanding scientist with either an M.D. or a Ph.D., an M.D./Ph.D. student may begin to doubt the value of pursuing both degrees. The student with a Ph.D. mentor is not exposed to the special perspective that clinical training provides and may lose sight of the value of this additional and demanding preparation. The student with an M.D. mentor may be unaware of the difficulties that individual encountered while learning research in a less-structured manner or may fail to appreciate that such a mode of preparation is becoming increasingly unrealistic. In either case, unless the mentor openly supports the value of combined degree training, the student may expect to attain the mentor's level of research skills with one degree alone. This may, of course, be a realistic assessment in some cases; however, the essential point is that students may be dissuaded from following their original plans not because of the merits of their reasoning but because of a lack of appropriate role models at a crucial juncture.

We acknowledge the fact that the overwhelming majority of today's outstanding researchers have only one degree. In presenting this particular set of concerns, we are not arguing the case for the M.D./Ph.D. but rather assuming its value. (The tensions involved in pursuing the M.D. and Ph.D. degrees are considered in Chapter 17.)

Is Adequate Financial Support Available?

Financial support is a crucial incentive for students and young physicians participating in programs to prepare for careers as scholars and leaders. Very few individuals could finance such preparation with their own resources, and the opportunity costs of participating in research education are potentially very high.

Some believe that the continued existence of formal M.D./Ph.D. programs is threatened by the high costs associated with their length (now typically greater than seven years). The principal existing method of supporting M.D./Ph.D. education, the Medical Scientist Training Program (MSTP) of the National Institute of General Medical Science, is seen as unable to support enough students to meet the national needs. Proposed remedies include an increase in the number of students supported by this mechanism or a different mode of education. The level of financial support required for M.D./Ph.D. education is also a source of increasing difficulty because of the high rates of tuition for medical school as opposed to graduate school and the longer period of time required for M.D./Ph.D. students to complete their formal education. These concerns are accentuated by the fact that many students enter the MSTP or other M.D./Ph.D. programs with appreciable debt from their undergraduate days, which continues to build as payment is deferred during the long training period. Some incur additional debt during this period.

A related area of concern is the absence of national programs to finance the education of physician-scholars outside the traditional biomedical areas. This may be the single greatest problem in preparing scholars and leaders for the health care system. Expanding the types of discipline that can be supported by the MSTP does not begin to address this concern satisfactorily because, despite a growing allocation, that program has budget constraints and presently supports only a portion of the well-qualified students in the traditional biomedical fields, fields that everyone agrees are fundamental to the progress of basic and clinical research.

There are similar concerns about the number of positions supported and the level of the support in programs that educate young physicians during or after residency. Graduate medical education is increasingly threatened with funding cuts as the federal government and teaching hospitals search for cost-reduction measures. Such cuts are likely to have adverse consequences for any research education within such programs (29).

Are We Effectively Preparing the Graduates of Existing Programs for Leadership Roles?

One of the rationales for educating physician-scholars is to develop and prepare the future leaders of medicine. Indeed, leaders may well need to be scholars if they are to be fully effective. The relationship between scholarship and leadership, however, is complex; this is discussed in more detail in Chapter 2. Some scholars are perhaps less willing to take on leadership roles than others who may lack their educational base.

Although there is no general consensus that leadership can be taught—many people argue that this is an intrinsic talent—we believe that, as in virtually all other aspects of human endeavor, at least some of the components or skills of leadership can be taught and learned. Assuming that elements of leadership are, in fact, teachable and that there is a body of knowledge that can contribute to effective leadership, the concern remains that potential leaders may not have enough time to invest in such preparation or that a particular point in a career path is not the opportune time to try to teach such skills. One dilemma is that leadership training tends to be a low priority early in a career, as leadership roles are likely to be deferred to a later stage. However, responsibilities increase at later stages and the cost of taking time for formal leadership education may be prohibitive. (See Chapters 9 and 20 for discussions of some of the issues related to education for leadership.)

How Do Personal Issues Affect the Quality of Education or Career Decisions?

A final set of issues we shall term personal or individual, as they do not relate directly to the assessment of national needs or the design of appropriate responses. We have already touched on such personal issues in our discussion of role models. Such considerations affect not only the quality of an individual's life but also the quality of his or her education or career decisions. They are therefore of concern not only to the students and young physicians in programs to prepare for scholarship and leadership but also to the faculty and staff who administer these programs. In the extreme, personal issues may limit the academic achievements of the programs and the students within them and the success of their career paths.

The most general concerns involve the ability to develop and maintain personal relationships given the time commitment and the particularly high stress involved in an M.D./Ph.D. program or an equivalent extended educational program. The source of the time commitment is obvious—both the demands on the student's time on a daily basis and the number of years involved are unusually great. Extended periods of education may require a continued period of deferred gratification, not only for the participant but for any family members involved as well. (Chapter 18 considers these questions in more detail.)

For M.D./Ph.D. students in particular, one source of stress arises from their status as the "exception" among both graduate (Ph.D.) students and medical students, which may result in isolation or lack of social and other necessary support. The stress of isolation may be exacerbated by the additional tensions that arise from the combination of two degree programs with very different attitudes, demands, and expectations in which the educational objectives and criteria of evaluation are framed, usually quite legitimately, from the point of view of each. Some students note a kind of culture shock in moving between the two worlds. Yet these students may be viewed as privileged and, to some, not particularly deserving of special consideration. In the extreme, this may even translate into hostility. (These issues are considered in Chapter 17.)

Other sources of concern include the combined effects of the length of research and leadership education and the uncertainty of obtaining a suitable position (whether initially or ultimately) in academic medicine or another appropriate environment. Similar issues arise when the research education is undertaken during or after residency. There are multiple pressures to get out of the role of a student and into a fully "adult" career position. Again, the potential exists for a "two-culture" conflict—in this case, between clinical medical care and research.

Personal and family issues also bear upon the question of the optimal time for research training or the sequencing of preparation. For example, because M.D./Ph.D. programs provide relatively low stipends, potential participants may feel some pressure to defer entry until they have completed their clinical training. However, such a delay increases the likelihood that the young physician will have family responsibilities and educational debts. This in turn may increase the perception that the training entails high opportunity costs.

Conclusion

The multitude of questions regarding the preparation of physician-scholars inevitably touches on a host of issues related to national needs and trends, curriculum design, educational and career pathways. The chapters that follow will explore each of the issues identified here in greater or lesser detail. The uneven consideration that these issues receive here reflects the early stage of our experience in educating physicians for scholarship and especially for leadership. It is hoped that the contributions to this book will mark only the beginning of our efforts to document and communicate what we have learned thus far.

References

1. James B. Wyngaarden, "The Clinical Investigator as an Endangered Species," *The New England Journal of Medicine* 301 (1979): 1254–59.
2. Gerald S. Levey, Charles R. Sherman, Nancy O. Gentile, Linda J. Hough, Thomas H. Dial, and Paul Jolly, "Postdoctoral Research Training of Full-Time Faculty in Academic Departments of Medicine," *Annals of Internal Medicine* 109 (1988): 414–18.
3. Lawrence S. Neinstein and Richard G. MacKenzie, "Prior Training and Recommendations for Future Training of Clinical Research Faculty Members," *Academic Medicine* (Jan. 1989): 32–35.
4. Committee on Medical Education, The New York Academy of Medicine, "Symposium on the Academic Physician: An Endangered Species," *Bulletin of New York Academic Medicine* 57 (July-August 1980): 411–502.
5. Gerald F. DiBona, "Whence Cometh Tomorrow's Clinical Investigator," *Clinical Research* 27 (1979): 253–56.
6. Janet W. Bickel, Charles Sherman, et al., "The Role of M.D.-Ph.D. Training in Increasing the Supply of Physician Scientists," *The New England Journal of Medicine* 304 (1981): 1265–68.
7. Gordon N. Gill, "The End of the Physician-Scientist?" *American Scholar* 53 (1984): 353–368.
8. Bernadine Healy, "Innovators for the 21st Century: Will We Face a Crisis in Biomedical-Research Brainpower?" *The New England Journal of Medicine* 319 (1988): 1058–64.
9. "A New Physician Manpower Shortage: Clinical Investigators," *The New England Journal of Medicine* 300 (May 1979): 1108.
10. Samuel O. Thier, "Clinical Investigation in the 1980's: Perspectives from the Medical Schools," *Clinical Research* 28 (Sept. 1980): 248–51.
11. James B. Wyngaarden, "Encouraging Young Physicians to Pursue a Career in Clinical Research," *Clinical Research* 31 (April 1983): 115–18.
12. David G. Nathan, "Funding Subspecialty Training for Clinical Investigators," *The New England Journal of Medicine* 316 (1987): 1020–22.
13. Theodore Cooper, "Summary and Concluding Remarks" (for the Symposium on the Academic Physician: An Endangered Species), *Bulletin of New York Academic Medicine* 57 (July-Aug. 1981): 488–92.
14. Leon Eisenberg and Arthur Kleinman, "Clinical Social Science: Is Medical Practice Impeded by 'Too Much Science'?" in *The Relevance of Social Science for Medicine*, ed. Leon Eisenberg and Arthur Kleinman (D. Reidel Pub. Co., 1980), 1–23.

15. F. M. Hull, "The Role of Socio-Behavioral Scientists in Health Care Practice," *Social Science Medicine* 25 (1987): 679–87.
16. Milton I. Roemer, "Preparing Public Health Leaders for the 1990s," *Public Health Reports* 103 (Sept.-Oct. 1988): 443–52.
17. Robert M. Glickman, "The Future of the Physician Scientist," *Journal of Clinical Investigation* 76 (1985): 1293–96.
18. Bruce Hillman, "The Inadequacy in the Number and Quality of Physician Researchers: A Perspective and Approach to the Problem," *Investigative Radiology* 20 (Nov. 1985): 767–71.
19. Institute of Medicine/National Academy of Sciences, *Personnel Needs and Training for Biomedical and Behavioral Research*, The 1986 Report of the Committee on National Needs for Biomedical and Behavioral Research Personnel (Washington, D.C.: National Academy Press, 1985).
20. Jack D. Burke, Jr., Harold Alan Pincus, and Herbert Pardes, "The Clinician-Researcher in Psychiatry." *American Journal of Psychiatry* 143 (Aug. 1986): 8.
21. S. H. Frazier, "Trends in Psychiatric Education, Services and Research in the United States," *Psychiatric Journal of the University of Ottawa* 12 (1987): 137–42.
22. D. J. Weatherall, "The Physician Scientist: An Endangered But Far From Extinct Species," *British Medical Journal* 302 (April 1991): 1002–05.
23. Lawrence S. Neinstein and Richard G. MacKenzie, "Prior Training and Recommendations for Future Training of Clinical Research Faculty Members," *Academic Medicine* (Jan. 1989): 32–35.
24. Editorial, "Postdoctoral Appointments and Disappointments," *Nature* 291 (1981): 441–44.
25. Nancy O. Gentile et al., *Post-Doctoral Research Training of Full-Time Faculty in Departments of Medicine* (Washington, D.C.: AAMC, 1987).
26. Gerald S. Levey, Charles R. Sherman, Nancy O. Gentile, Linda J. Hough, Thomas H. Dial, and Paul Jolly, "Postdoctoral Research Training of Full-Time Faculty in Academic Departments of Medicine," *Annals of Internal Medicine* 109 (1988): 414–18.
27. R. G. Petersdorf, "Academic Medicine: No Longer Threadbare or Genteel," *The New England Journal of Medicine* 304 (1981): 841–43.
28. Robert F. Jones, "Datagram: Clinician-Educator Faculty Tracks in U.S. Medical Schools," *Journal of Medical Education* 62 (May 1987): 444–47.
29. Gary Huninghake, "Maintaining the Quality of Academic Medicine," *Clinical Research* 35 (1987): 433–37.
30. Douglas J. Marchant, "Academia—An Endangered Species," *American Journal of Obstetrics/Gynecology* 156 (Jan. 1987): 185–92.
31. Janet M. Cuca, "NIH Grant Applications for Clinical Research: Reasons for Poor Ratings or Disapproval," *Clinical Research* 31 (1983): 453–63.
32. Charles R. Sherman, "Who Becomes a Physician-Researcher?" in *Biomedical Innovation*, ed. E. B. Roberts et al. (Cambridge, Mass.: MIT Press, 1981): 123–34.
33. J. W. Littlefield, "On the Difficulty of Combining Basic Research and Patient Care," *American Journal of Human Genetics* 36 (1984): 731–35.

34. Richard Wakeford, David Evered, Jennifer Lyon, and Norman Saunders, "Where Do Medically Qualified Researchers Come From?" *Lancet* 8449 (vol. 2) (1985): 262–65.
35. David A. Kindig and Santiago Lastiri, "Administrative Medicine: A New Specialty?" *Health Affairs* 5 (Winter 1986): 146–56.
36. Charles R. Sherman and T. E. Morgan, *Education Patterns and Research Grant Success of Medical School Faculty,* (Washington, D.C.: NIH Evaluation Program, AAMC, Jan. 1979).
37. Joseph B. Martin, "Training Physician-Scientists for the 1990's," *Academic Medicine* 66 (March 1991): 123–139.
38. William J. Curran, "Cross-Professional Education in Law and Medicine: The Promise and the Conflict," *Journal of Legal Education* 24 (1971): 42–72.
39. James A. Everette, Jr., "Reflections of a JD/MD," *The Pharos of AOA* 50 (Spring 1987): 10–12.

2

Scholarship and Leadership: Definitions and Data

Harold M. Swartz and Diane L. Gottheil

- Scholar and Leader: Distinctions and Similarities
- Why Do We Need Physician-Scholars and Physician-Leaders?
- Quantifying the Needs Physician-Scholars Must Fulfill
- Data on Entrants into Scholarly Careers
- Data on Outcomes of Programs
- The Effects of Programs on Subsequent Research Careers and Productivity
- Conclusion
- References

A considerable amount of the concern, doubt, and controversy surrounding the education of physician-scholars is rooted in a lack of communication over certain key concepts and the data that bear on the questions and issues identified in Chapter 1. In this chapter we address the conceptual questions regarding the scholar and leader and review efforts to provide a systematic basis for considering these questions.

Scholar and Leader: Distinctions and Similarities

Attempting to define and differentiate the roles of physician-scholar and physician-leader may seem somewhat pedantic. But the confusion of these concepts and implicit assumptions about the roles they represent have led to disagreement and misunderstanding that have sometimes had negative effects upon the development and evaluation of programs and individual careers. We will therefore try to delineate the essential attributes of the physician as scholar and as leader, and, in the process, attempt to identify the practical implications of these concepts for educational programs and professional pathways. In the balance of the chapter we will discuss data on the need for physician-scholars and on educational programs to develop scholarship and leadership.

We define a scholar as an individual who generates new knowledge that is made available to others in a particular discipline, primarily through publications in scholarly and professional journals and books. We define a leader as an individual who exerts significant authority through influence and, usually, through explicit responsibility for decision making in particular policy areas (in this case, medicine and the health care system). Most people would consider it almost axiomatic that a true leader in medicine should be a scholar. And, while they may feel a little less easy about the validity of this second assertion, they would, in general, be prepared to believe that a real scholar will inevitably be a leader. A closer examination reveals, however, that one of these roles may require certain personal characteristics and skills that the other does not and that in some situations it may be best to have a "pure" scholar or leader with none of the skills unique to the other role. (Kirschstein stresses this point in Chapter 8.)

In the real world many of our acknowledged leaders are not scholars, and vice versa. Are these situations undesirable deviations, or do they represent a functional and perhaps even desirable reality? We conclude that the truth lies somewhere between the apparent poles. In many circumstances it is desirable to combine leadership and scholarship for the most effective outcome, and it is reasonable to expect some individuals to fulfill both roles. In other situations it may not be essential to combine the attributes or to have them developed to an equal degree.

Experience tells us that the pool of potential leaders extends beyond those educated for and engaged in scholarly research, and there is little basis for arguing that it should be otherwise. Indeed the responsibilities of an increasing number of leadership positions in medicine—from the management of clinical groups to the administration of governmental departments involved in running or funding clinical services—appear to have little direct connection to scholarship. It may be desirable for such individuals to have scholarly abilities, but it is difficult to make a case for requiring them. It might even be argued that an insufficiently rigorous scholarly education can do more harm than good by imparting a false sense of confidence in one's ability to judge scholarship. It might be more realistic and more effective to offer such individuals programs that provide a realistic appreciation of scholars and scholarship than to insist that they become scholars themselves (1).

Academic medical institutions are clearly responsible for preparing physician-scholars, but what institutions should provide the formal programs needed to prepare physician-leaders? We suggest that the education of both scholars and leaders should be viewed as a responsibility of academic medicine. It is, after all, the job of educators to educate. Consequently, academic medicine needs to take a realistic view of the skills and attributes needed by potential leaders and encourage the design and development of leadership education programs, actively seeking the cooperation of organizations and individuals with experience in these areas, both within and outside the health care system (2).

Although not all physician-leaders must be scholars, or vice versa, the requisite mix of characteristics will vary from one individual to another and even within the career of a single person. For example, a leader who is not an active scholar at one particular juncture may in fact owe his or her present leadership role to previous experience in scholarly pursuits. Such experience may be the reason that he or she was selected for the position; it may provide important insights and knowledge that increase the leader's self-confidence and ability to be seen as highly competent by others; or it may provide a knowledge base necessary to the performance of the leadership role.

Similarly, some scholarly roles require at least limited leadership attributes. Although some may argue that the ability to direct or catalyze the activities of others is not intrinsic to all forms of excellent scholarship, it would be difficult to maintain that a scholar participating in the scientific enterprise as it has developed in the last half of the twentieth century could effectively sustain a research laboratory without a team of scientists and students who look to the laboratory director (i.e., the scholar) for leadership in this sense. Young scholars receiving their first NIH grants soon realize that when they add postdocs and students to the lab, they must sacrifice time in research for time in administration. And as their scholarly careers advance, they must take on the responsibility of "research leaders," protecting the research time of young scientists in their midst and maximizing the conditions conducive to productivity. Such a role clearly demands some of the attributes of leadership (3). Whether the scholar is engaged in social science research or the humanities, the nature of the demands is roughly the same; differences may be only a matter of scale.

Furthermore, there is a sense in which those who have significant accomplishments in scholarship are automatically considered leaders not only within their own particular field of scholarship, but often in all other matters relevant to medicine. The extent of this "halo effect," and the authority and influence it confers, is frequently related to the extent of the scholar's recognition within his or her own field. The scholar's personal attributes and choice of activities and venues outside the immediate area of research will also help to determine how widely the scholarly role translates into leadership.

If this "blended" concept of the scholar/leader is valid, and we believe it is, our scholars in training must clearly understand that their actions, opinions, and statements will have a special weight, and they must therefore be prepared accordingly. Preparation for scholars whose leadership is limited to the "halo effect" will naturally differ from the preparation required for scholars who will assume positions in which an explicit leadership requirement forms a significant part of their activities. Granted, the nature of responsibilities that derive from the "halo effect" are by definition rather unpredictable and appropriate formal preparation cannot therefore be defined. The leadership responsibilities that are directly related to the role of physician-scholars—such as overseeing a major research laboratory, planning and implementing national and international conferences, serving as an officer of a scientific society, chairing a department, heading an NIH study section—are more predictable, however, and preparation is not only possible but increasingly desirable. Nevertheless, the latter may involve training in specific knowledge and skills, demand a significant time investment, and appear to exact considerable opportunity costs for individuals whose career goals were not initially defined as involving formal leadership roles. Scholars in training are likely to derive great benefit from educational programs that focus on specific skills in interpersonal relations and communications and broader matters such as professional and scientific ethics, the public policy arena (particularly the actors or roles, institutions, and processes involved in decision making in health and science policy), and the array of social and cultural issues affecting the medical and scientific world. Increasingly, individuals who have had significant scholarly achievements are expected to provide leadership at various levels in their organization. This is particularly true in larger organizations and is currently the cultural norm in academic medicine and many other areas of the health care system. It therefore seems both logical and desirable for educational and training programs to recognize the roles that their graduates will most likely assume and consider how they can best prepare them for these roles.

Can leadership be taught? If one accepts the position that many skills involved in leadership extend well beyond charisma, it seems inescapable that at least some of these skills can be enhanced by appropriate education. In arenas where the demand for leadership is perhaps most overtly acknowledged, such as business, public service, and the military, evidence for the teachability of leadership is mixed. The corporate world has developed a network of educational programs to train leaders—from business schools, which provide necessary formal preparation in the knowledge and skills, to vast corporate training programs that provide leadership training on topics such as improving interpersonal skills, supervising personnel, motivating others, and communicating effectively. Corporate training programs may be offered at all levels, from entry level to middle management (often in M.B.A. programs at universities) to executive training (frequently in cooperation with university-based academic programs). In public service, formal leadership training is less available. Leaders either tend to work their way up the hierarchy of elected office, using "on-the-job training" to develop leadership ability, or else they are recruited from other arenas, typically business, academia, or the military on the basis of established records of leadership. The military traditionally provides basic skills and then subjects its leadership candidates to a "weeding out" process. At the officer level, leadership training today is likely to resemble that of the corporate world as demands on officers for high levels of expertise are coupled with a range of more traditional leadership skills (4).

Academic medicine (and academia more generally) and the health care system have tended to provide leadership development routes similar to those in public service; the more formal approach of the business world is just beginning to emerge. It is argued throughout this book that a casual approach to providing leaders for the health care system is inadequate and that a passive approach, relying upon scholars to emerge as leaders or leaders to self-select, fails to take maximum advantage of available resources.

A number of examples are worthy of mention. The American College of Physician Executives has an active program of sponsoring management training that seeks to provide necessary knowledge and skills to physicians who hold or seek leadership roles in health care institutions, as well as a publication series addressing leadership development (5–7). More recently, the Kaiser Permanente Center for Health Research in Portland, Oregon, together with the Association for Health Services Research, has sponsored a program for young scientists, developed by the Training Institute in Research Management (TIRM) and designed "to help ensure that the growth in health research is accompanied by a growth in management skills and research excellence." This effort is supported in part by a grant from the Agency for Health Care Policy and Research of the U.S. Department of Health and Human Services. The conviction of the sponsoring agencies and the individuals involved in this program that leadership can and indeed should be taught is well illustrated by the topics offered: managing for creativity, ethics and research management, managing the research culture, managing federal grants and contracts, and others (8). TIRM also offers an advanced management training program geared to those already holding leadership positions in institutions where health research is being conducted.

Data on the payoffs of such training are scarce, but it is clear that certain leadership skills are vital to success in research. For example, an article by Spangenberg and colleagues finds "the degrees of craftsmanship of the research manager" to be an important explanatory variable for predicting research productivity in clinical departments (9). We must either assume that such characteristics are innate and unteachable, or we must make the effort to provide education in leadership for physicians and examine its effectiveness. However, if such programs are to attract participants and expand, current leaders and mentors will have to instill in students and young scientists positive attitudes toward leadership training. This might require challenging some fixed ideas concerning the value of investing one's time in studying something other than the "hard" sciences.

Why Do We Need Physician-Scholars and Physician-Leaders?

Although we argued earlier that it is appropriate to assume the need for physician-leaders and scholars, it is still useful to look directly, if briefly, into the basis for this need. In all areas of human activities there will inevitably be leaders. The need for leaders is particularly great in medicine because of its importance to society and the significant share of our economic and human resources committed to it. Although there seems to be no disputing the need for leaders in medicine, the critical questions remain. Can we or should we attempt to systematically prepare physician-leaders? In particular, what is the relationship between physician-scholars and physician-leaders in any such formal preparation? (We addressed these topics in Chapter 1 and in the previous section and will provide further consideration of them later in this chapter.)

Similarly, the need for scholars in medicine should, at first glance, be axiomatic. Every scientific field needs individuals who provide new knowledge and new policies through their scholarly activity, and medicine is generally viewed as such a science. It has been argued, however, that physicians should content themselves with using information developed by others who have the technical background and skills to generate this knowledge. This is, to some extent, the way medicine is organized and practiced in some societies (e.g., the "barefoot doctor"). It has also been argued that the sophistication of modern science makes it impractical for physicians to be scholars or scientists (10). Such viewpoints are unlikely to dominate the debate, however. Despite its many limitations and constraints, medicine, throughout its history, has had strong scholarly aspects and physicians have taken a prominent role in many of the advances in the field. Also there is general agreement that research involving patients must be done under the guidance of qualified physicians.

Although most agree that physicians should take some scholarly role, there are serious questions regarding the necessity or desirability of investing the large amount of time and money needed to prepare physicians to conduct research and pursue other scholarly activities. In fact, although the view is not held unanimously, most knowledgeable observers consider medical education and the clinical activities of physicians, however challenging and important, to be professional rather than scholarly. Thus the education of physician-scholars must necessarily extend well beyond the preparation needed for clinical medicine. This would add considerable costs in time and money, costs borne by both society and the individual. The benefits afforded by such an educational venture must be weighed against these costs. Could the needs that are addressed by such a program be met as well by individuals educated only as physicians or as scholars? Could the scholarship be done better by someone who does not have the responsibilities and potential distractions associated with being a physician (11)?

More than two decades ago, Beeson argued that basic science may have already become too sophisticated for clinicians to compete successfully with basic scientists in the laboratory (12). A number of arguments, however, appear to justify the additional time expense, and potential competing responsibilities inherent in developing physician-scholars (13–15). At the purely clinical level, many research needs and opportunities can probably be best appreciated and acted on by individuals with strong backgrounds in both medicine and scholarship (16–21). At the purely scientific level, the perspectives and information provided by a clinical education can lead to the development and exploration of very cogent research questions with a high potential for enhancing medical care. Take, for example, the experimental finding that strongly oxidizing species are generated when tissues are reoxygenated after a period of ischemia. Physicians recognized the implications of this discovery, and whole new areas of clinical investigation and new therapeutic approaches have emerged for stroke and heart attack. Additionally, there are a number of areas in between the purely clinical and the purely scholarly in which the combined knowledge and perspectives of the physician-scholar can lead to very effective progress. The interplay of basic science and clinical experience for example, has been especially important is the development of new and improved drug therapy. Similarly, the interplay of clinical experience and knowledge from the social sciences has led to advances as well in health services research; for instance, this type of collaboration led to the more formal involvement of patients in treatment decisions for benign prostate disease developed by John Wennberg and his colleagues (22).

It is useful to consider the need for physician-scholars from the perspective of individual experience, however anecdotal. Many basic scientists working in medical environments testify strongly that they believe they could be more effective if they also had an M.D. Sometimes they argue in terms of organizational structure, citing the difficulties of having a full share of opportunities in a clinical environment without an M.D. Most often, however, they argue on intellectual grounds, citing the increased knowledge and unique perspectives that come with a clinical education as an obvious enhancement of research. A medical researcher with an M.D. has the advantage of knowing not only when clinical knowledge may enhance research but also when it is unlikely to do so. This enables the researcher to proceed more efficaciously. Researchers with responsibility for patient care have argued that their level of motivation in research is increased by contact with patients and direct confrontation with disease. As the roles of physician-scholars have extended to areas in the social sciences and humanities, experiential arguments for the value of formal combined education have expanded and developed further. The weight of these arguments is reflected in the actions taken by many individuals who have had seemingly successful careers but have still opted, sometimes at midcareer, to return to school to earn an M.D.

Similarly, individual experience has been the foundation of arguments that physicians need to obtain formal research education to be effective researchers (21). Professional biographies provide evidence of individuals who have altered their careers to seek research education and record discussions advocating this approach (23, 24). There is also some evidence that physicians who have obtained formal education in research have raised their productivity and experienced increased success in obtaining competitive research funding (25–27) (see Chapter 7).

Quantifying the Needs Physician-Scholars Must Fulfill

To evaluate the costs and benefits of formal preparation, it is important that we identify and quantify the needs physician-leaders and physician-scholars may be required to fulfill. Unfortunately, the somewhat intangible nature of leadership itself (as suggested in the preceding discussion), the multiplicity of social roles and arenas in which physician-leaders can and should be active, and the fact that these roles and arenas are both shifting and expanding, place any such attempt outside the scope of this book.

Similar problems arise with respect to physician-scholars. Although their roles are less diverse and their potential arenas of activities are more closely bounded by the current disciplines of scholarship that directly and indirectly relate to medicine, there does not appear to be either an existing body of data or an obvious methodology that would permit an accurate and comprehensive estimate of the overall needs to be fulfilled. However, by using the number of physicians presently engaged in activities that appear to require physician-scholars, we can begin to approximate an estimation of these needs.

The methods used to estimate the need for all biomedical scientists is briefly reviewed in Chapter 6, but as noted there, these methods do not specifically take into account the need for and desirability of scientists with an M.D. It should also be noted that, with few exceptions, compilations of data on this subject rarely take into account the need for physicians who have had rigorous research backgrounds in areas outside traditional biomedical science (such as epidemiology and biostatistics, public health, and more recently, information sciences) because it is generally assumed that the kind of scholarship needed to advance health and medicine requires people educated in the traditional biomedical sciences. The authors of this book are nonetheless deeply convinced of the need for physician-scholars in nontraditional areas (such as the social sciences and humanities). Ironically, despite the scant attention paid to these areas, demand is likely to rise. As such physician-scholars become more widely available and their credentials better understood, the perception of and appreciation for their value will change accordingly.

A potentially useful approach to estimating the number of physician-scholars needed is by looking at the data on the current primary activities of physicians in all categories except patient care, as estimated by self-reports compiled from 1963 through 1987 (Table 2.1). As these data indicate, about 39,000 physicians report that their primary activity is teaching, administration, or research. The number of physicians primarily in research varied considerably over this time period, ranging between about 16,500 and 23,000 during the most recent six years reported. Although these data indicate apparently wide, short-term swings in the numbers of physicians in research, variations may reflect changes in methodology rather than in fact (28).

Another approach is to estimate the need for physician-scholars by looking at the places they are likely to be employed. The largest employment sector for physician-scholars has been and will likely continue to be academic medicine. The 1989 report of the Committee on Biomedical and Behavioral Manpower summarized some of the available data applicable to the issue of supply and demand in the clinical sciences (28). The number of full-time faculty in clinical departments increased steadily from 1977 through 1987, reaching 48,834 in 1987 (Table 2.2). Data on the number of physicians in full-time faculty positions and in the status of trainees/fellows for 1961–1987 are summarized in Figure 2.1. The obvious upper limit of the need for physician-scholars in academia is the number of full-time clinical faculty members plus the number of M.D.s needed as faculty members in the basic science departments of medical schools. Recent figures from the Association of American Medical Colleges (AAMC) indicate approximately 55,000 full-time clinical faculty and 15,000 full-time basic science faculty in U.S. and Canadian medical schools. Assuming that 15 percent of the basic science faculty members are M.D.s, the upper limit of need is 57,500.

In reality, only a fraction of the full-time clinical faculty currently spend significant time in research. A survey of departments of internal medicine indicated, for example, that only 35 percent of the faculty could be considered active researchers (29). Traditionally, departments of internal medicine are the most research-intensive departments in medical schools; therefore, an appropriate level for active research involvement for all clinical faculty might be estimated at 25 percent. If the current activities are suitable criteria for determining the number of physician-scholars needed, the total needs are probably about 14,000 (57,500 × 25%). This estimate is similar to that of Evans, Hendee, and Loeb, (Chapter 7) for medical schools (10,000–12,000). It is somewhat lower than the report of 16,586 M.D.s listed as being "primarily in research" in 1987 (Table 2.1).

Although these data make it possible to estimate the number of individuals likely to be needed in this specific area, much uncertainty nonetheless remains because of ongoing changes in the structure and function of the academic medical center. There is currently great controversy over the amount and type of research activity that should be expected of clinical faculty in medical schools;

Table 2.1. Primary Activity of Physicians in the U.S., 1963–1987.[1]

	Total Active[2]		Patient Care		Teaching		Admin.		Research[4]		Other		Unclassified and Unknown Address	
Fiscal Year	N	%	N	%	N	%	N	%	N	%	N	%	N	%
1963	263,063	100.0	246,951	93.9	8,190	3.1	3,332	1.3	3,255	1.2	n/a	---	1,335	0.5
1964	270,885	100.0	253,543	93.6	8,869	3.3	3,512	1.3	3,627	1.3	n/a	---	1,333	0.5
1965	278,809	100.0	259,418	93.0	9,794	3.5	4,057	1.5	4,306	1.5	n/a	---	1,234	0.4
1966	287,163	100.0	266,766	92.9	10,503	3.7	4,143	1.4	4,445	1.5	n/a	---	1,306	0.5
1967	295,732	100.0	274,190	92.7	11,166	3.8	4,121	1.4	4,595	1.6	n/a	---	1,660	0.6
1968[3]	298,401	100.0	261,722	87.7	5,051	1.7	11,715	3.9	15,441	5.2	2,383	0.8	2,089	0.7
1969	305,047	100.0	270,737	88.8	5,149	1.7	12,107	4.0	12,375	4.1	2,598	0.9	5,865	1.9
1970	314,407	100.0	278,535	88.6	5,588	1.8	12,158	3.9	11,929	3.8	2,635	0.8	3,562	1.1
1971	325,435	100.0	287,248	88.3	5,844	1.8	12,076	3.7	10,898	3.3	2,633	0.8	6,736	2.1
1972	336,424	100.0	292,210	86.9	5,836	1.7	11,074	3.3	9,290	2.8	2,693	0.8	15,521	4.6
1973	343,755	100.0	295,257	85.9	6,183	1.8	11,959	3.5	8,332	2.4	2,636	0.8	19,388	5.6
1974	358,134	100.0	301,238	84.1	6,464	1.8	11,739	3.3	8,159	2.3	2,666	0.7	27,868	7.8
1975	372,293	100.0	311,937	83.8	6,445	1.7	11,161	3.0	7,944	2.1	2,793	0.8	32,013	8.6
1976	387,329	100.0	318,412	82.2	6,935	1.8	11,689	3.0	8,514	2.2	2,893	0.7	38,886	10.0
1977	392,913	100.0	332,393	84.6	6,673	1.7	11,954	3.0	9,786	2.5	2,813	0.7	29,296	7.5
1978	410,655	100.0	342,714	83.5	7,025	1.7	11,858	2.9	11,437	2.8	2,777	0.7	34,844	8.5
1979	426,226	100.0	356,783	83.7	7,523	1.8	12,118	2.8	14,515	3.4	2,790	0.7	32,497	7.6
1980	441,935	100.0	376,512	85.2	7,942	1.8	12,209	2.8	15,377	3.5	2,876	0.7	27,019	6.1
1981	450,112	100.0	389,369	86.5	7,202	1.6	13,250	2.9	17,901	4.0	3,023	0.7	19,367	4.3
1982	466,268	100.0	408,663	87.6	7,505	1.6	13,408	2.9	16,743	3.6	3,070	0.7	16,879	3.6
1983	482,635	100.0	423,361	87.7	7,783	1.6	13,828	2.9	18,535	3.8	3,290	0.7	15,838	3.3
1984[5]	500,553	100.0	437,089	87.3	7,802	1.6	13,913	2.8	22,945	4.6	3,352	0.7	15,452	3.1
1985	514,070	100.0	448,820	87.3	7,832	1.5	13,810	2.7	23,268	4.5	3,410	0.7	16,930	3.3
1986	522,325	100.0	462,126	88.5	7,721	1.5	14,399	2.8	17,847	3.4	3,657	0.7	16,575	3.2
1987	537,555	100.0	478,511	89.0	8,114	1.5	14,536	2.7	16,586	3.1	3,581	0.7	16,227	3.0

FOOTNOTES

[1] From the American Medical Association (1963-88).
[2] Excludes temporary foreign; includes unknown address and unclassified.
[3] In 1968 the AMA revised its procedures for classifying physicians, making comparisons with early years extremely difficult. One effect was to drastically reduce the Teaching category and to increase the Administration and Research categories.
[4] In 1968 includes 8,029 fellows formerly included in the Patient Care category.
[5] Although previously unpublished, these data were obtained from the AMA and are reported to be "accurate to within 100" persons.

SOURCE: **Committee on Biomedical and Behavioral Research Personnel, Biomedical and Behavioral Research Scientists: Their Training and Supply, Volume 2 (Washington, DC: National Academy Press, 1989.**

Table 2.2. Current Trends in Supply/Demand Indicators in the Clinical Sciences.

	Fiscal Year											Annual Growth Rate	Latest Annual Change	Average Annual Change
	1977	1978	1979	1980	1981	1982	1983[1]	1984	1985	1986	1987			
1. Supply Indicators (new entrants):														
a. Professional doctorates participating in NIH training grants and fellowships[2]	2,203	1,879	1,780	1,906	1,938	2,026	2,108	2,184	2,265	2,162	n/a	-0.2%	-4.5%	-5
b. MD degrees awarded	13,614	14,391	14,966	15,135	15,673	15,985	15,801	16,369	16,321	15,979	15,818	1.5%	-1.0%	220
2. Demand Indicators:														
a. Expenditures for clinical R&D in medical schools (1972 $, mil.)	$268	$282	$273	$296	$288	$295	$315	$349	$389	$420	$444	5.2%	5.7%	$18
b. Professional service income in medical schools (1972 $,mil.)	$391	$406	$441	$493	$526	$612	$740	$806	$957	$990	$1,121	11.1%	13.2%	$73
c. Total revenue (all sources), (1972 $, mil.)	$2,781	$2,839	$2,965	$3,195	$3,293	$3,488	$3,793	$4,033	$4,367	$4,681	$5,141	6.3%	9.8%	$236
d. Budgeted vacancies in medical schools:														
(1) Clinical departments	1,865	2,000	2,100	2,279	2,231	2,264	2,270	2,402	2,572	2,345	2,510	3.0%	7.0%	65
(2) Basic science departments	638	697	721	776	656	668	671	705	801	757	785	2.1%	3.7%	15
e. Clinical faculty/student ratio[3]	0.311	0.322	0.323	0.334	0.331	0.341	0.346	0.349	0.354	0.368	0.380	2.0%	3.3%	0.007
3. Labor Force														
a. MDs primarily engaged in research[4]	9,786	11,437	14,515	15,377	17,901	16,743	18,535	22,945	23,268	17,847	16,586	5.4%	-7.1%	680
b. Full time faculty in clinical departments	30,349	32,622	34,057	36,665	37,716	40,148	41,938	43,443	45,007	47,193	48,834	4.9%	3.5%	1,849
c. NIH research grants awarded to MDs:[5]														
(1) Number of competing grants	1,645	1,926	2,060	1,772	1,729	1,600	1,768	2,013	1,971	1,925	n/a	1.8%	-2.3%	31
(2) % of total competing grants	37%	33%	31%	33%	31%	29%	29%	32%	28%	27%	n/a	-3.4%	-3.6%	-1.1%
d. MD applicants for NIH research grants:														
(1) Number of competing applicants	4,184	4,302	4,239	4,182	4,301	4,281	4,313	4,621	4,865	5,080	n/a	2.2%	4.4%	100
(2) % of total competing applicants	34%	33%	31%	31%	30%	28%	28%	29%	28%	28%	n/a	-2.1%	0.0%	-0.7%
e. MD success rate:														
(1) MD awards/MD applicants	36%	41%	45%	40%	39%	35%	39%	41%	39%	36%	n/a	0.0%	-7.7%	0.0%
(2) MD awardees/all awardees	37%	33%	32%	34%	32%	29%	30%	32%	29%	28%	n/a	-3.0%	-3.4%	-1.0%
4. Enrollments														
a. Medical students	58,266	60,424	62,582	64,020	65,412	66,484	66,886	67,437	67,086	66,607	65,918	1.2%	-1.0%	765
b. Residents and clinical fellows[6]	44,795	46,444	50,188	52,491	52,871	57,504	59,138	60,442	63,507	60,875	61,539	3.2%	1.1%	1,674
c. Total	103,061	106,868	112,770	116,511	118,283	123,988	126,024	127,879	130,593	127,482	127,457	2.1%	0.0%	2,440

FOOTNOTES

[1] Financial data from the University of Washington and Mayo Medical School were included for the first time in 1983.
[2] Includes Fogarty International Center programs.
[3] Ratio of full time clinical faculty to a 4-year weighted average of total enrollments of medical students, residents and clinical fellows (WS), where $(WS)_t = 1/6(S_t + 2S_{t-1} + 2S_{t-2} + S_{t-3})$.
[4] There is some question about the interpretation of these data since they include many trainees in graduate medical programs. 1984 data are previously unpublished; AMA reports them to be accurate to within 100 persons.
[5] Data for MDs do NOT exclude those who may also have a PhD degree. As a result, the sum of percent MD awardees and percent PhD awardees (Summary Table 2), can be greater than 100%.
[6] The residents and clinical fellows reported here include only those in accredited programs affiliated with medical schools.

SOURCE: **Committee on Biomedical and Behavioral Research Personnel, Biomedical and Behavioral Research Scientists: Their Training and Supply, Volume 2 (Washington, DC: National Academy Press, 1989.**

ORIGINAL SOURCES

Item

1a. Data were extracted from the NIH Trainee and Fellow File (TFF); post-professional doctorates with activated awards were selected. FY is fiscal year of maximum time on duty.
1b. From Appendix Table A4., Total MD Graduates. Annual tabulations by the AAMC from the Medical School Faculty Roster database.

2a. From Appendix Table A7., Total Estimated Clinical R&D (1972 dollars). See Appendix Table A7 for description of method for estimating clinical R&D expenditures from AAMC annual tabulations of total R&D expenditures by medical schools, and for the implicit GNP price deflator for computing 1972 dollars.
2b. From Appendix Table A8., Total Professional Service income (1972 dollars). Annual tabulations by the AAMC.
2c. From Appendix Table A11-2., Total Revenue, All Schools (1972 dollars). Journal of the American Medical Association, annual education issues.
2d. From Appendix Table A5., Clinical Sciences Departments and Basic Science Departments. Journal of the American Medical Association, annual education issues.
2e. From Appendix Table A3., which was computed from Tables A1 and A2. All data are from the AAMC; students represent a 4-year weighted average of total medical school enrollments.

3a. From Appendix Table A6., Research. Data are from the AMA's publication "Physician Characteristics and Distribution in the US." 1984 data were previously unpublished, see Appendix Table A6.
3b. From Appendix Table A2., Full-time, All Schools, Clinical Departments. Annual tabulations by the AAMC from the Medical School Faculty Roster database.
3c. Data were extracted from the NIH Consolidated Grant Applicant File (CGAF). Research grants were defined as K, M, P, R, and U activity codes; successful new and competing applications by persons with MD or MD-equivalent degrees were selected. All grants awarded and grants awards to MDs were summed by year, MD grants/all grants were then calculated.
3d. Data were derived from the same population as in item 3c. This item represents persons (applicants) while item 3c. represents grants. MD and MD-equivalent applicants were identified and summed for each year. Percent of total competing applicants was then calculated.
3e. Data were derived from the same population as in item 3c. Awards refer to grants, applicants and awardees refer to persons.

4a. From Appendix Table A1., Medical Students, All Schools. Annual tabulations by the AAMC.
4b. From Appendix Table A1., computed sum of Intern & Residents and Clinical Fellows, All Schools. Annual tabulations by the AAMC.
4c. From Appendix Table A1., Total Enrollment, All Schools. Sum of Medical Students, Interns & Residents, and Clinical Fellows; from the AAMC.

opinions range from the conclusion that, today, real research and clinical expertise are mutually exclusive, to the position that virtually all clinical faculty members need to be actively involved in research. The outcomes of these debates will profoundly influence the number of physician-scholars needed in clinical departments and the type of research preparation they should have.

New areas of opportunity have also opened up for physician-scholars of varied backgrounds. In the site that employs the largest number of physician-scholars—the faculties of medical schools—the traditional, rather narrow range of disciplinary fields is expanding. The biological disciplines now include areas such as molecular biology, nutrition, genetics, and chemistry. New technologies (including those that support aging and disabled patients) provide rapidly expanding opportunities for physician-scholars with backgrounds in the physical sciences, including engineering, physics, and computer science. Perhaps an even greater and more challenging need is in the area of the social sciences and humanities. Expertise will be required at levels ranging from an understanding of the overall health delivery system to the ability to design comprehensive

Figure 2.1.

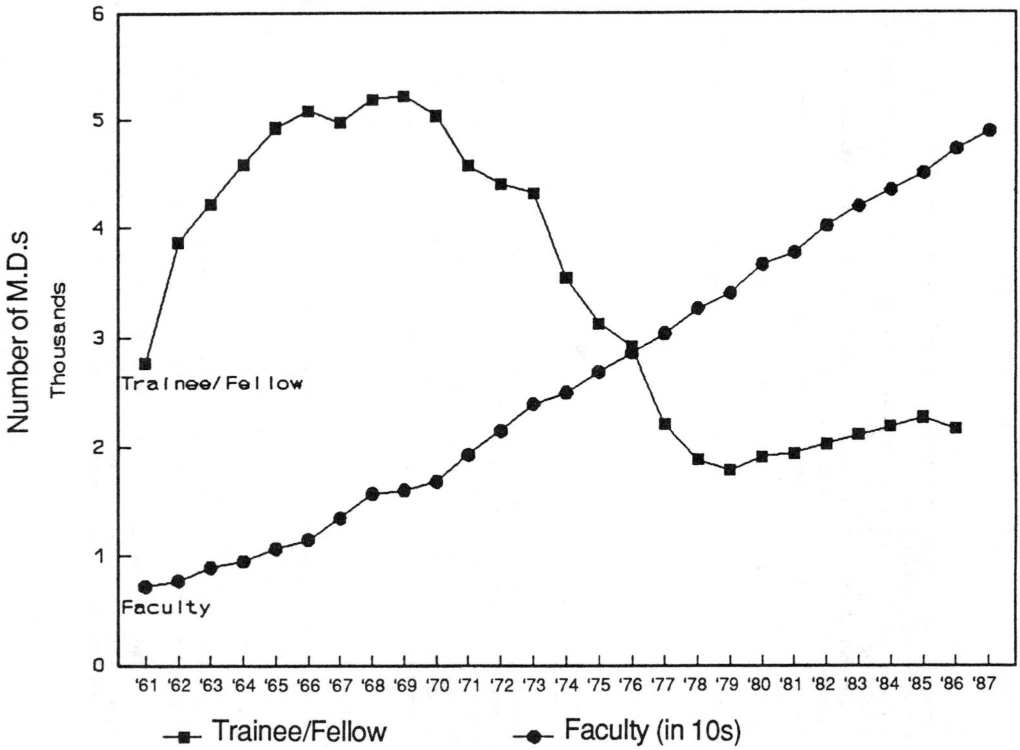

approaches to chronic diseases; in the opinion of some, this may be an especially important growth area.

In view of these kinds of uncertainties, it seems fruitless to attempt to provide a quantitative estimate of the need for physician-scholars, except to cite these possible parameters. Instead, we will summarize some of the most recent opinions regarding the types of individuals that may be needed, their likely numbers, and the sorts of positions that they will probably fulfill. The number of new employment sites seems to be increasing rapidly as roles for physician-scholars develop outside traditional academia, especially in industry, government, and not-for-profit health-related organizations (30). Existing institutions, such as NIH, are also undergoing significant expansion—in 1988 there were 1,704 M.D.s employed at NIH, including 595 in permanent positions (31). The number of potential arenas for physician-scholars might come to approximate that for physician-leaders as the demands for knowledge and technical expertise increases. Witness, for example, the technical nature of the training offered by the American College of Physician Executives (mentioned previously) in response to the increasingly technical demands on physicians in leadership roles. (At this point, the distinction between the physician-scholar and the physician-leader about which we have semantically agonized and speculated in the preceding pages becomes moot!)

The number of physician-scholars presumed to be needed, combined with rates of attrition due to death, retirement, and career change, has yielded estimates of the number of postdoctoral positions needed to provide an adequate supply of physician-investigators. Over one decade ago, the Committee on National Needs for Biomedical and Behavioral Research Personnel recommended that 2,800–3,000 postdoctoral training positions be supported annually in clinical research programs (32). This was based on a need for 1,400–1,500 entrants into the field per year and the assumption that each physician-scholar would have, on the average, twenty-four months of postdoctoral training. At about this same time, the AAMC (33) estimated a need for 1,800 entrants to postdoctoral clinical research training programs per year.

There appear to be little or no reliable data on which to base estimates of need in a number of key areas such as the emerging new fields in the social and physical sciences and areas outside traditional academic medicine (e.g., in government, industry, and not-for-profit organizations). Chapter 6 cites an American Medical Association (AMA) report that estimates an additional 6,000 positions from the latter sources, giving a total pool of 16,000–20,000.

While it is not clear how to estimate the number of physician-scholars needed, there is general agreement and concern that a shortage exists. The usual focus has been on the numbers of physician-scientists in traditional disciplines, with a particular emphasis on clinical investigators (11,34–37). The number of physicians reporting research as a primary career decreased from 15,441 to 7,944 in the period from 1968 to 1975, during which the number of full-time faculty increased by 160 percent (32). As indicated in Chapter 7, however, while the proportion of M.D.s has declined in critical areas such as NIH study sections and research grants (R01 s), the absolute numbers have remained fairly constant since 1980. The problem seems to be primarily a failure of the number of M.D. researchers to grow in proportion to the support by NIH and the size of faculties in academic medicine.

Data on Entrants into Scholarly Careers

As with most other topics in this chapter, the available data on types of new entrants into scholarly pathways are few and insufficiently specific. Some studies support the contention that the number of physician-researchers entering scholarly careers has declined as a result of decreased interest. (These studies usually focus on physician-scientists in "classical" biomedical areas.) Some of the evidence for this conclusion was summarized by ad hoc committees on the subject (33). The source of declining interest is said to begin with an apparent decrease in interest in research careers by medical students. In a survey of medical students at Harvard University, 49 percent of the respondents assigned a high priority to research in 1963 and only 2 percent in 1976 (38). This decline may have been reflected in the number of physicians in NIH research training programs, which decreased from 4,600 to 1,790 between 1971 and 1977. The decline may have been due in part to a decrease in the availability of positions, but even so, more than 650 slots were unfilled (34). The magnitude of the decline may also have been affected by a change in the philosophy of NIH for the support of physician-trainees: an increased emphasis on the need to use these trainee positions to support research rather than to provide subspecialty clinical training (Chapter 6).

It may be feasible to obtain fairly precise data on two subsets of entrants into scholarly fields: graduates of postdoctoral programs and graduates of M.D./Ph.D. programs. These data will not provide the total number of entrants as many, at least in the past, have not had formal research education or have completed Ph.D.s before or after M.D.s rather than in dual-degree programs. Such data have been reported by Bickel and colleagues: in 1980, about 850 M.D.s successfully completed a postdoctoral research program. In that same year, the number of graduates from M.D./Ph.D. programs was about 130 per year, about half from MSTPs (39).

Table 2.3 provides more recent data on the number of physicians in the major NIH-sponsored training programs. Students in the MSTPs (M.D./Ph.D. program) constitute a little more than 20 percent of the pool, with most of the trainees in the postdoctoral programs. There has been a modest growth in the number of students in MSTPs (about 10 percent) in the past decade. More recent data on M.D./Ph.D. students are cited in a Howard Hughes Medical Institute publication, which estimates 278 M.D./Ph.D. graduates in 1990. Although HHMI considers this an overestimate, it nevertheless suggests considerable growth in a decade (40). Furthermore, as indicated in Chapter 3, the number of M.D./Ph.D. students not supported by NIH appears to be increasing sharply.

As the data in Table 2.3 show, the number of physicians in the postdoctoral programs increased about 20 percent from 1980 to 1988, with the vast majority supported by institutional training grants. This contrasts sharply with the figures for Ph.D.s which shows a decrease in numbers over this period. Consistent with

Table 2.3. The Number of Appointments in NIH Research Training Programs by Academic Level and Type. Fiscal Years 1980–1988.

Academic level (est.)	1980	1981	1982	1983	1984	1985	1986	1987	1988
Predoctoral	6,343	6,682	6,533	6,648	6,589	6,356	6,083	6,237	6,188
Institutional	6,326	6,662	6,510	6,621	6,546	6,314	5,971	6,042	5,995
NRSA (T32 excluding MSTP)	4,687	4,833	4,280	4,282	4,124	3,979	3,776	3,803	3,888
MSTP	672	709	690	678	692	713	701	768	742
Postdoctoral	5,748	5,500	5,396	5,484	5,413	5,733	5,535	5,519	5,640
M.D.	2,092	2,051	2,094	2,224	2,296	2,429	2,432	2,454	2,569
Individual	283	259	272	326	367	370	349	373	376
Institutional	1,809	1,792	1,822	1,898	1,929	2,059	2,083	2,081	2,193
NRSA (T32)	1,755	1,727	1,751	1,841	1,886	2,032	2,046	2,032	n.a.
Ph.D.	3,656	3,449	3,302	3,260	3,117	3,304	3,103	3,065	3,071
Individual	1,469	1,296	1,244	1,253	1,197	1,414	1,203	1,308	1,226
Institutional	2,187	2,153	2,058	2,007	1,920	1,890	1,900	1,757	1,845
NRSA (T32)	2,118	2,067	1,966	1,930	1,857	1,830	1,833	1,718	n.a.

Source: Table 39, NIH Data Book 1989, p. 64.

the more rigorous development of their research skills, a significant proportion of the Ph.D.s in these programs were awarded individual grants. There was also an increase in the number of non-NIH-supported research training programs for physicians interested in beginning significant research training.

Another group that should be considered comprises those M.D.s on the NIH campus who are fellows or visiting scientists; in 1988 there were 1,109 such individuals (31). To some extent, they should be considered part of the pool of researchers in training, but more information is needed to determine what portion of this group should be included.

Data on Outcomes of Programs

Programs to prepare physician-scholars can be conveniently divided, for present purposes, into three principal types: M.D./Ph.D. programs, of which there are three "subtypes"; post-M.D. research experience (usually postdoctoral fellowships or traineeships); and programs for physicians in midcareer.

M.D./Ph.D. Programs in Traditional Biomedical Areas

At this time it is probably reasonable to assume that most students enrolled in M.D./Ph.D. programs are in traditional biomedical areas. In a recent report from the HHMI, data obtained from the AAMC and the MSTP were summarized on the number of students enrolled in M.D./Ph.D. programs (40). In academic year 1989–90, there were about 1,650 students listed as enrolled, about half in MSTPs. The method used by the AAMC for gathering the data are considered to overestimate the number of students in non-MSTPs because of a lack of a means to remove dropouts. (Note, however, that the data reported in Chapter 3 suggests that this is an underestimate of the number of M.D./Ph.D. students.) The MSTP probably accounts for a majority of the M.D./Ph.D. students and, for the foreseeable future, is likely to remain a dominant factor, especially for students doing their graduate work in traditional biomedical disciplines. Thus the 30 schools with MSTPs are likely to set the standards and the agenda for typical M.D./Ph.D.s.

Most of the available data on outcomes are from several of the long established MSTPs. Table 2.4 summarizes an analysis of the Duke University program on the outcomes of seventy-five graduates of these MSTPs who had completed their postgraduate training (41). Note that at the time of the study (1983), 24 percent had left academic medicine for private practice. Of the others, most (89 percent) were in clinical departments, with 11 percent in basic science departments. The academicians reported that they spent, on the average, 50 percent of their time in research.

Table 2.4. Career and Medical Specialties of 75 1970–1979 Graduates of Duke University School of Medicine Medical Scientist Training Program as of March 1983.

Specialty	Academic Medicine and Research	Private Practice
Pathology	12	6
Internal medicine	9	5
Pediatrics	8	0
Surgery	5	1
Obstetrics-Gynecology	4	1
Neurology	4	0
Psychiatry	3	2
Biochemistry	3	0
Family medicine	1	3
Ophthalmology	1	1
Other	6*	

*One academician each entered physiology, anatomy, oncology, biology, anesthesiology, and dermatology.

Source: Bradford, William D., et al, "Careers and Professional Activities of Graduates of a Medical Scientist Training Program," *Journal of Medical Education,* 61:915–18, 1986.

In 1984, the MSTP carried out an analysis of the career patterns of students who entered this program (42). They divided their analysis into two parts: graduates whose careers were sufficiently advanced to make a useful estimate of their involvement in research, and the entire cohort. This type of division points up a very significant and frustrating aspect of assessing the effectiveness of programs to prepare physician-scholars: the estimates for the former group required that they had entered the MSTP at least *fifteen years* before the analysis! As the report pointed out, approximately ten years are required for the initial pre- and postdoctoral education in the graduate and medical disciplines and five more years to complete this process and become established in the early phases of an academic position. Although some students may complete these phases in a shorter time, many will probably take even longer.

The assessment in 1984 of research status in the MSTP report was based on individuals who entered the programs at NYU, Albert Einstein, or Duke University between 1964 and 1968. Ninety-five trainees were admitted to these schools during that period; of these, sixty-four completed both degrees, twenty-nine received the M.D. only, four received the Ph.D. only, and two died. At the time of the analysis, 34 percent of the dual-degree graduates were considered to be highly involved in research (group A, Table 2.5), 34 percent significantly involved, and 18 percent involved in academic medicine but not research.

Thus, 84 percent of these graduates were in research and/or academic medicine. In contrast, of those students who completed the M.D. only, 40 percent were in research (and only one-fifth of these in group A). An additional 36 percent were in academic medicine, so a total of 76 percent were in research and/or academic medicine. This points up some of the potential problems in estimating outcomes on the basis of broad definitions of positions. The number of students involved in this study and the changed conditions over the past twenty years make it essential to exercise caution in drawing conclusions from these data, but they do appear to point out the apparent effectiveness of the MSTP in developing effective researchers.

The interim report also provided data on the status of 1,174 students who entered the MSTP between 1964 and 1968 (Table 2.6). More than 70 percent of the students earned their dual degrees, and 88 percent of those who had time to complete the postdoctoral phases of their training were in academic and research positions. These data indicate another potential problem in evaluating the outcomes of such programs: a simple enumeration of the present positions of the graduates of a program seldom shows whether the effectiveness of the program determines the outcome or is incidental to it (that is, does the program attract students who would have followed academic paths anyway?). To make an adequate evaluation, we need additional data on such factors as the level of involvement in research, the effects of completing part of the program, subsequent educational experiences, and reference to other control groups. Such evaluations require considerable effort and planning. The data on the 323 individuals who had not completed the dual degrees are also informative: 60 percent of those who had progressed past training status were in faculty and research positions.

Table 2.5. Rating of Research Activity.

Category	Characteristics
A.	Highly active in research 1. A strong publication record over at least 4 postdoctoral years, 2. A senior position (Associate Professor, Senior Investigator, or equivalent) in a university or research organization.
B.	Active in research 1. Research publications during the past 4 years, 2. Position as a research fellow, instructor, or assistant professor, or equivalent position in a research or other academic setting, 3. <u>or</u> Has research support or other evidence of research activity.
C.	Low Activity in Research Is on the staff of a medical school or research organization, but has no record of reserach publications over the past four years and no other evidence of research activity.
D.	Not in Research Is in private, clinic, or hospital practice unaffiliated with a medical school or research organization.
E.	Inactive Professionally inactive, retired, deceased, or unknown.

Source: Adapted from the National Institutes of Health Medical Scientist Training Program, NIGMS Internal Report, 1980 (unpublished), May 1980.

The students who completed the dual degrees received an average of sixty-three months of support from the MSTP, while the nongraduates ("dropouts") were supported, on average, for twenty-seven months. The report estimated that five of six dollars invested in students in the MSTP during that period went to individuals who ended up in faculty and research positions.

Data gathered in 1980 indicated the important role of both MSTP and non-MSTP support in the education of M.D./Ph.D. graduates (41). Of potential long-term import was the much higher rate of attrition for students without MSTP support: 44 percent versus 9 percent. There are no recent reports on this same topic, but the dropout rate for the non-MSTPs may no longer be much different from that for students in MSTPs.

Another possible pathway for the preparation of M.D./Ph.D.s is to have Ph.D.s enter medical school. Although most schools do not have formal programs for this, such students are often encouraged to apply. Data collected from analyses of the faculty of medical schools suggest that such students have not contributed appreciably to the pool of active biomedical researchers (39). The

Table 2.6. Current Status of 1174 Medical Scientist Trainees Entering Fiscal Years 1964–1978.

Status	Dual Degree	Nongraduates
Professor	7	3
Associate professor	43	10
Assistant professor	174	58
Instructor, etc.	41	17
Resident	322	74
Fellow/research associate	109	22
Research scientist	31	6
Industry and other active	12	2
Practice	43	63
Inactive, dead, or unknown	5	63
Subtotal	787	318
Still in training	64	5
Subtotal	851	323
TOTAL	1174	

Source: Adapted from the National Institutes of Health Medical Scientist Training Program, NIGMS Internal Report, 1980 (unpublished), May 1980.

University of Miami carried out a well-organized program for the Ph.D.-to-M.D. pathway from 1971 to 1988. This program appears to have had a fairly high yield of physician-scholars—about 30 percent have entered fields that could be considered those of physician-scholars (Chapter 12).

M.D./Ph.D. Programs in Nontraditional Biological, Physical, and Chemical Sciences Disciplines

Few available data deal specifically with entrants to nontraditional fields of scholarship that can be related to medicine, because, by definition, their numbers have been relatively small, at least until recently. Nontraditional disciplines appear to be increasingly popular for combined degree students, as it has become apparent that many very interesting and relevant areas of medically related research and academic clinical practice can benefit from individuals with knowledge and skills in these fields. Equally important, a number of medical schools have begun to recognize that these areas can attract some very strong students to their programs and that offering such a course of studies will not compromise the applicability of the training to careers in academic medicine, especially for those with long-term interests in areas such as radiology and medical imaging. At the University of Illinois in Urbana-Champaign, approximately 50 percent of the M.D./Ph.D. students and an increasing proportion of the graduates are pursuing or have pursued Ph.D.s in such disciplines (e.g., biophysics, computer science, physics, chemistry, nuclear engineering).

M.D./Ph.D. Programs in Social Sciences and the Humanities

To date, there have been only a few organized M.D./Ph.D. programs in the social sciences or the humanities, and the number of graduates and the time since graduation have been too small to permit a useful analysis of the outcomes of these programs. In 1975, Rubin and colleagues noted M.D./Ph.D. programs in these areas at six medical schools (43). We contacted these schools to find out if data were available on outcomes, but in every instance the programs apparently did not endure and no such data were available. The most successful program was at Johns Hopkins University, which eventually graduated seven individuals who earned an M.D. and a Ph.D. in a social science (44).

There are now some moderately large programs in the social sciences and humanities (at the University of Chicago, Harvard University, and the University of Illinois at Urbana-Champaign), and an increasing number of students and schools are interested in them. It therefore seems likely that in a few years enough meaningful data could be collected to show whether formal preparation in these areas leads to successful and useful careers. Anecdotal and individual comments and reports suggest that these can be richly rewarding and productive educational combinations. As noted throughout this book, these areas are important to the development of the health care system. (This type of program is discussed further in Chapter 3; Chapter 10 presents an overview program that enables medical students to pursue a Ph.D. in a field of social sciences or humanities; and Chapter 15 discusses the centrality of social sciences to medical science.)

Postresidency Research Training Programs

Few data deal directly with research training programs at the postresidency phase. As noted in Chapter 1, great concern has been expressed about the effectiveness of these programs. Chapter 13 discusses the experience of one NIH institute. It should be kept in mind that for many M.D.s, these postdoctoral experiences are the first and sometimes the only formal preparation in research; they therefore differ from the usual postdoctoral experiences of Ph.D.s.

Data obtained for a study of the research activities of faculty members of internal medicine departments provide some useful insights on the role of postdoctoral training experiences (45). Table 2.7 groups M.D.s with M.D./Ph.D.s, but because of the numerical dominance of M.D.s, the conclusions are probably applicable just to the M.D.-only part of the pool. The importance of formal postdoctoral training is clear: Faculty members without such training spent very little time in research, and only 6.9 percent were principal investigators for NIH grants. Interestingly, their other sources of grants did not differ very much from those of their peers; 25 percent were principal investigators in non-NIH grants; 10 percent were grant supported but not principal investigators; and

Table 2.7. The Role of NIH in Research Training of Physician-Faculty in U.S. Departments of Medicine: Duration of Training and Research Involvement by Source of Support.

Item	Source of Support for Postdoctoral Research Training[1]				
	NIH Only	NIH and Non-NIH	Non-NIH Only	None	Total
Number of M.D.s and M.D./Ph.D.s (row percentage)	[3]1,832 (38.6)	466 (9.8)	1,209 (25.4)	1,245 (26.2)	4,752 (100.0)
Duration of postdoctoral research training (combined experiences)					
Median months	24.0	36.0	20.0	0.0	0.0
Mean months	26.3	40.2	22.2	0.0	12.2
Effort in research					
Median percentage	40.0	40.0	25.0	5.0	25.0
Number reporting	1,804	460	1,180	1,220	4,664
Missing	28	6	29	25	x8
Research support within last two years (percentage)					
PIs on NIH grants	41.7	x4.2	24.2	6.9	28.4
PIs non-NIH grants only	29.4	33.0	37.0	24.6	30.4
Supported but not as PIs	9.0	8.4	9.8	10.2	9.4
Without support	20.0	14.4	29.0	58.3	31.8
Active researchers[4]					
Classified "Yes"	1,260	352	659	275	2,546
Classified "No"	388	75	362	439	1,264
Not classified (missing data)	184	39	188	531	942
Percentage "yes" (if classified)	76.5	82.4	64.5	38.5	66.8

Source: Special tabulation by E. Sherman of survey reported in Levey, G.S., Charles R. Sherman, Nancy O. Gentile, and Paul Jolly, "Postdoctoral Research Training of Full-Time Faculty in Academic Departments of Medicine," *Annals of Internal Medicine,* Vol. 109; Sept. 1, 1988, pp. 414–17.

[1]NIH-supported training refers to both NIH intramural and extramural programs.

[2]Numbers in this table are limited to cases where support sources and duration were fully reported for up to two separate postdoctoral research training experiences.

[3]See reference for classification rule based on research support, publications, laboratory space, and level of effort in research.

the majority, 58 percent, had no grant support. On the other hand, a substantial number of these faculty members (38.5 percent) were still classified as active researchers by fairly rigorous criteria.

Faculty members with formal postdoctoral experiences, on the average, spent at least 25 percent of their efforts in research. The level of research activity was higher for faculty whose postdoctoral support included funds from NIH, and most were classified as active researchers. Among those whose postdoctoral training came from exclusively non-NIH sources, significantly fewer were principal investigators on NIH grants (24 percent versus 42 percent), which suggests that they were not as successful in competing for the largest and most highly valued source of funding of biomedical research. If this difference is borne out by other data, it would be useful to determine whether the cause is the training itself or the qualifications of its recipients.

Special Programs in Social Sciences and Humanities

The Robert Wood Johnson Health Policy Fellows Program has been in existence since 1974 and has accepted six participants per year from academic medical centers, most of whom have been physicians. Staff evaluations have been carried out at intervals of approximately three years. Of the eighty-four fellows, seventy-two had completed the program by 1987, and subsequently an additional six per year have completed the program (46). Because of the aims of the program (see Chapter 4), the evaluations have focused on the activities in health policy of graduates who had entered the health policy sector of academia. Of the respondents in academia, 85 percent reported that they had used material from their fellowship within the previous three years. In general, both participants and higher administrators felt that the program had been very useful and had a considerable positive influence on the careers of the participants and on the institutions. About 20 percent of the fellows had left academia, but they felt that the skills and connections they had developed during the fellowship had been important in obtaining their positions and/or carrying out their duties. The responses of the individuals who met with the fellows during the orientation and the congressional staff with whom they were assigned were generally quite positive. Because of the nature of the program (principally a practical experience in working with Congress and learning about the constituencies involved in health care legislation) and its relatively short duration (one year), it is likely to have a greater impact on producing physician-leaders than physician-scholars. It would be interesting, however, to obtain data on the effect of this experience on academic productivity and subsequent leadership. The large pool of well-qualified applicants who were not accepted into the program might constitute an appropriate control group.

The Robert Wood Johnson Clinical Scholars Program has approximately 525 graduates (47). This two-year program for physicians who have recently completed their residencies provides fellowships that primarily emphasize access to coursework and pertinent experiences, but many of the participants also have some involvement in original research. There are no detailed evaluations available of the program's research productivity outcomes, but some summaries of the program have been published (48). Table 2.8 summarizes the current careers of the graduates. The largest number are internists (55 percent), and more than 80 percent of these are in academic or other careers that focus on something other than the direct personal delivery of patient care. The overall assessment by key individuals involved in the program is that the graduates are pursuing the kinds of scholarly and leadership careers that the program aims to facilitate. It would be very desirable for further analyses to focus in more detail

Table 2.8. Clinical Scholars Alumni, 1971–1989.

Career Path	Percentage
Academic medicine	60.9
Private practice	11.4
Prepaid/community health	9.5
Government	5.0
Other	13.2
TOTAL	100.0

Source: Weisfeld, Victoria (ed.), *Robert Wood Johnson Clinical Scholars Program Report,* Robert Wood Johnson Fdn., Princeton, N.J., June 1990.

on how the program has affected the careers of its graduates. The development of leaders is one of the explicit aims of the program, and some data indicate success in this regard. In 1990, sixty-four of the graduates were in leadership positions in academic health centers, in roles such as associate or assistant dean and as head of a department or division (47). Full measurements of such outcomes are difficult to make because of the time it takes to achieve such positions, but the data for the cohort of graduates since 1980 are encouraging, with twenty-seven individuals in such positions.

The Effects of Programs on Subsequent Research Careers and Productivity

Some analyses of the outcomes of particular programs and/or of cohorts of graduates of medical schools have attempted to determine what factors in educational programs and what personal characteristics are associated with the pursuit of scholarly careers and/or with research productivity (32, 49–51). Such data could be invaluable in the organization and operation of educational programs as well as in the evaluation of outcomes. However, such studies are difficult to carry out meaningfully because of the lack of good definitions of "success" and "activity" in research. It would probably be even more difficult to determine the personal and demographic characteristics likely to be associated with successful outcomes, because so much time is required to establish a record of scholarly productivity, the nature of the health care system and medical research is so dynamic, and social change has proceeded with such rapidity.

Several factors have been associated with success for active as opposed to less active former research fellows. The actives were less motivated by the desire for financial security and clinical contact; had invested more time in summer research fellowships; and had decided to enter postgraduate research training during or before internship (48 percent versus 24 percent). They had also spent a longer period in postgraduate research (3.6 years versus 2.4 years), been trained in more adequately funded laboratories, and submitted more applications for research grants in their first three years after research and clinical training (2.9 versus 0.9 applications) (26, 49).

Conclusion

It is preferable for an analysis of data on educational program outcomes to examine the number of individuals who complete formal or informal training and their subsequent involvement in scholarly activities, including the quality and quantity of their research (52). Ideally, such data would be compared with control groups to assess the effectiveness of the various paths. This review of existing studies shows, however, that the available data fall far short of enabling such analyses to be carried out. Indeed, it can only point to the difficulties of conducting rigorous program evaluation and to the need for further efforts to collect and analyze data. Further, because of the rapid and profound changes occurring in the health care system, it is quite possible that even if we are able to delineate the factors that have led to the success of students and/or programs, these may no longer be pertinent for students entering programs today.

In any event, the effort to obtain more precise knowledge about scholars and leaders in the health care system should be initiated at some point, and those concerned with the future of the health care system must recognize the need for a data base on current and projected needs and capabilities. This theme recurs in many later chapters of this book, particularly in Part III. We will try to set the stage here by describing current pathways to scholarship and leadership for physicians, including those on which there are some data (as cited in this chapter), as well as all others that have been identified.

References

1. D. J. Weatherall, "The Physician Scientist: An Endangered But Far From Extinct Species," *British Medical Journal* 302 (April 27 1991): 1002–05.
2. David A. Kindig and Santiago Lastiri, "Administrative Medicine: A New Specialty?" *Health Affairs* 5 (Winter 1986): 146–56.
3. House of Lords, Session 1987–88, Third Report, Select Committee on Science and Technology, "Priorities in Medical Research: Volume 1—Report."
4. Personal Correspondence, Executive Development Program, College of Commerce and Business Administration, University of Illinois at Urbana-Champaign.
5. The American College of Physician Executives, "Schedule of Management Education Programs," Tampa, Fla., 1991 (descriptive brochure).
6. "New Leadership for a New Era: Physician Leadership Institute, Tempe, Arizona, A University-Based Graduate Credit Certificate Program," Sponsored by Arizona State University, The Western Network for Education in Health Administration, and the American College of Physician Executives, 1989, 1990, and 1991, Western Network for Education in Health Administration, Berkeley, Cal. (descriptive brochure).
7. American College of Physician Executives, "The Physician in Manage-

ment Series: Schedule of Seminars," Tampa, Fla., January 1991 (Correspondence from Roger Schenke, Executive Vice President, and descriptive brochure).

8. Training Institute in Research Management, "The 1992 Management Training Program for Research Investigators, September 15–20, Otter Crest, Oregon." Kaiser Permanente Center for Health Research, Portland, Ore. (Correspondence from Merwyn R. Greenlick, Vice President and Director, Center for Health Research, and descriptive brochure).
9. John F. A. Spangenberg, Richard Starmans, Yvonne W. Bally, Bert Breemhaar, Frans J. N. Huhuis, and Cees A. F. Van Dorp, "Prediction of Scientific Performance in Clinical Medicine," *Research Policy* 19 (1990): 239–55.
10. G. N. Gill, "The End of the Physician-Scientist?" *American Scholar* 53 (1984): 353–68.
11. James B. Wyngaarden, "Encouraging Young Physicians to Pursue a Career in Clinical Research," *Clinical Research* 31 (April 1983): 115–18.
12. Paul B. Beeson, "The Academic Doctor," *Transactions of the Association of American Physicians* 80 (1967): 1–7.
13. Francois M. Abboud, "Investing in Excellence," *Journal of Laboratory Clinical Medicine,* 110 (1987): 3–12.
14. Paul B. Beeson, "The Development of Clinical Knowledge, With a Few Words About Targeted vs. Basic Research," *Journal of the American Medical Association* 237 (1977): 2209–12.
15. Bernadine Healy, "Innovators for the 21st Century: Will We Face a Crisis in Biomedical-Research Brainpower?" *The New England Journal of Medicine* 319 (1988): 1058–64.
16. Institute of Medicine, *Clinical Investigations in the 1980's: Needs and Opportunities* (Washington, D.C.: National Academy Press, 1981).
17. William N. Kelley, "Are We about to Enter the Golden Era of Clinical Investigation?" *Journal of Laboratory Clinical Medicine* 111 (1988): 365–70.
18. William N. Kelley, "Personnel Needs for Clinical Research: Role of the Clinical Investigator," *Clinical Research* 33 (1985): 100–04.
19. J. W. Littlefield, "On the Difficulty of Combining Basic Research and Patient Care," *American Journal of Human Genetics* 36 (1984): 731–35.
20. Frank G. Moody, "Clinical Research in the Era of Cost Containment," *American Journal of Surgery* 153 (April 1987): 337–40.
21. Joseph L. Goldstein, "On the Origin and Prevention of PAIDS (Paralyzed Academic Investigator's Disease Syndrome)," *Journal of Clinical Investigations* 78 (Sept. 1986): 848–854.
22. Michael J. Barry, Albert G. Mulley, Jr., Floyd J. Fowler, and John Wennberg, "Watchful Waiting vs. Immediate Transurethral Resection for Symptomatic Prostatism: The Importance of Patients' Preferences," *Journal of the American Medical Association* 259 (May 27, 1988): 3010–17.
23. Beverly Merz, "M.D.s in Research: A Vanishing Breed?" *American*

Medical News 3 (Dec. 1989): 35–36.

24. Harold M. Swartz, Evan M. Melhado, and Ann Barry Flood, "Thirty Years of Change in Medical Education, Money and Power: Differing Effects on Generations of Clinicians and Clinical Practice," in *Money, Power, and Health Care*, ed. Walter Feinberg and Harold M. Swartz (Ann Arbor: Health Administration Press, 1988), 263–307.
25. W. K. Davis and W. N. Kelley, "Factors Influencing Decisions to Enter Careers in Clinical Investigation," *Journal of Medical Education* 57 (1982): 275–281.
26. Michael O'Brecht and Pierre Bois, "Characteristics of Active and Less Active Researchers," *Journal of Medical Education,* 63 (April 1988): 327–29.
27. Richard Wakeford, David Evered, Jennifer Lyon, and Norman Saunders, "Where Do Medically Qualified Researchers Come From?" *Lancet* 2 (8449) (1985): 262–65.
28. National Research Council, Office of Scientific and Energy Personnel Committee, *Biomedical and Behavioral Research Personnel,* Vols. 1 & 2 (Washington, D.C.: National Academy of Science, 1989).
29. Harry N. Beaty et al., "Research Activities of Faculty in Academic Departments of Medicine," *Annals of Internal Medicine* 104 (1986): 90–97.
30. Bert Spilker, "Career Opportunities for Physicians in the Pharmaceutical Industry," *Journal of Clinical Pharmacology* 29 (1989): 1069–1076.
31. *NIH Data Book* (Washington, D.C.: Department of Health and Human Services, 1989).
32. National Research Council Commission on Human Resources, *The 1978 Report of the Committee on a Study of National Needs for Biomedical and Behavioral Research Personnel* (Washington, D.C.: National Academy of Sciences, 1978).
33. Association of American Medical Colleges, "Clinical Research Manpower: The Report of Ad Hoc Committee on Clinical Research Training" (Washington, D.C.: 1980).
34. James B. Wyngaarden, "Clinical Investigator as an Endangered Species," *The New England Journal of Medicine* 301 (1979): 1254:59.
35. Gerald F. DiBona, "Whence Cometh Tomorrow's Clinical Investigators?" *Clinical Research* 27 (1979): 253–56.
36. Samuel O. Thier, "Clinical Investigation in the 1980s: Perspectives from the Medical Schools," *Clinical Research* 28 (Sept. 1980): 248–51.
37. National Research Council, *Personnel Needs and Training for Biomedical and Behavioral Research* (Washington, D.C.: National Academy of Sciences, 1983).
38. D. H. Funkenstein, *Medical Students, Medical Schools and Society During Five Eras: Factors Affecting the Career Choices of Physicians, 1958–1976* (Cambridge, Mass.: Ballinger, 1978).
39. Janet Bickel, Charles R. Sherman, James Ferguson, Liesel Baker, and Thomas E. Morgan, "The Role of M.D.-Ph.D. Training in Increasing the

Supply of Physician-Scientists," *The New England Journal of Medicine* 304 (1981): 1265–68.

40. Howard Hughes Medical Institute, *Grants for Science Education: 1990–91* (Bethesda, Md.: undated).
41. William D. Bradford et al., "Careers and Professional Activities of Graduates of a Medical Scientist Training Program," *Journal of Medical Education* 61 (1986): 915–18.
42. National Institute of General Medical Science, "The National Institutes of Health Medical Scientist Program" (NIGMS internal unpublished report, May 1980).
43. Richard R. Rubin, Joel Elkes, Ronald W. Maris, and Park Elliott Dietz, "Medicine and the Behavioral Sciences: The Johns Hopkins M.D.-Ph.D. Program," *The Johns Hopkins Medical Journal* 136 (1975): 268–70.
44. P. Talalay. Personal communication, November 1988.
45. Gerald S. Levey, Charles R. Sherman, Nancy O. Gentile, Linda J. Hough, Thomas H. Dial, and Paul Jolly, "Postdoctoral Research Training of Full-time Faculty in Academic Departments of Medicine," *Annals of Internal Medicine* 109 (1988): 414–18.
46. Robert Wood Johnson Foundation, *Robert Wood Johnson Health Policy Fellows Program Evaluation*, (Princeton, N.J., 1987).
47. Victoria Weisfeld, (ed.), *Robert Wood Johnson Clinical Scholars Program Report* (Robert Wood Johnson Foundation) (Princeton, N.J., June 1990).
48. Annie Lea Shuster et al., "An Innovation in Physician Training: The Clinical Scholars Program," *Journal of Medical Education* 58 (Feb. 1983): 101–11.
49. Charles R. Sherman and T. E. Morgan, *A Prospective Study of Physicians and Research Careers* (Washington, D.C.: AAMC, 1979).
50. Charles R. Sherman and T. E. Morgan, *Education Patterns and Research Grant Success of Medical School Faculty* (Washington, D.C.: AAMC, Jan. 1979).
51. Charles R. Sherman, "Who Becomes a Physician-Researcher in Biomedical Innovation?" in *Biomedical Innovation*, ed. Roberts et al., (Cambridge, Mass.: MIT Press, 1981), 123–34.
52. J. Anderson and D. C. Evered, "Why Do Research on Research?" *Lancet*, 8510 (vol. 2) (1986): 799–802.

3

Existing Pathways: Combined Degree Programs

Diane L. Gottheil and Harold M. Swartz

Physician-scholars enter their careers by a variety of educational pathways. In the past, the majority probably participated in informal programs or else entered without any extended preparation beyond their medical education. At present, however, as in many other fields, there is an increasing consensus that the level of skills and knowledge that a physician-scholar or leader needs to be reasonably competent can best be achieved through systematic preparation in a formal and well-organized program. In this chapter and in Chapter 4 we provide an overview of programs to prepare physicians for scholarly careers in medicine. Most of these programs are currently in existence, and most have focused on providing formal education and other kinds of support to develop researchers in the biomedical sciences who can assume positions in academic medicine. We will also consider newer programs designed to prepare physician-scholars in other disciplines, which are increasingly seen as central to medicine and which are needed in academic medicine and the other major sectors of the health care system.

This chapter focuses on M.D./Ph.D. programs but also considers other dual-degree programs in medicine. It is perhaps a reflection of the rapidity with which M.D./Ph.D. programs have proliferated in recent years that little information about them has been systematically collected. Therefore, most of what will be reported here derives from an original data base that the authors gathered to fill the gaps, derived from a survey questionnaire sent to dual-degree program directors and medical school deans. Before examining the current status of these programs, we will discuss their origin and rationale.

Origin

An internal report prepared by the National Institute of General Medical Sciences (NIGMS) in 1980 provided some background information on the origin of the Medical Scientist Training Program (MSTP), clearly among the most significant public initiatives to date to develop physician-scientists and scholars (1). In the mid-1950s, then-director of NIH James Shannon was concerned with the need for well-trained M.D.'s in biomedical research. "The fault with the existing system, Dr. Shannon believed, was that by the time M.D.'s emerged at the postdoctoral level, it was too late to retrain them as scientists." (1)

Following some years of initial experience with an NIH program that funded periods of research for medical students, Shannon considered the amount and quality of training provided under these part-time programs inadequate. He wished instead to focus on designing a medical curriculum specifically for future scientists that would support combined training leading to the M.D./Ph.D. degree or its equivalent.

After extended discussion and debate, the MSTP began in 1964, administered by the NIGMS. (The statute under which it currently operates, PL93348, the National Health Research Service Award Act, was enacted in 1974.) The NIGMS report noted that the MSTP marked the first time the federal government "undertook support for medical school curricula, on the condition that they be adapted for the training of medical scientists in the dual degree program." The report listed other "hallmarks" that deserve emphasis. These were, in fact, operational guidelines, developed on the basis of goals and early experience, and included (1) an emphasis on selectivity to ensure the highest possible quality of program graduates, (2) an emphasis on flexibility, to encourage individualized programs and permit individualization for trainees, (3) an understanding that scientific training takes time (six or seven years for the M.D./Ph.D. rather than the five or six originally thought), and (4) stable funding, to enable programs and individuals to undertake long commitments.

Between 1964 and 1979, funding to M.D./Ph.D. programs at twenty-five medical schools was provided under the MSTP; most of the M.D./Ph.D. programs were initiated in the year this NIH support was granted. Prior to the establishment of the MSTP, medical students at some of these and other schools had pursued Ph.D. education, but usually before or after medical school rather than in an integrated fashion, and typically it was done informally, without administrative support. The MSTP therefore became the impetus to establish and expand M.D./Ph.D. educational programs that provided administrative, academic, and financial support to students, thus significantly expanding the number of medical students pursuing research training at the Ph.D. level.

Moreover, the influence of this NIH initiative reached beyond the programs it supported. Insofar as it legitimized combined degree education, it enhanced the case of those at other medical schools who sought support within their institutions for establishing such programs. The prospect of eligibility for NIH funding was also a powerful incentive to establish M.D./Ph.D. programs. If these schools could attract students into combined degree studies, they could begin to establish a track record that would bolster the strength of an application to NIH for MSTP support.

Innovations are not received without controversy, and NIGMS chose to go slowly in establishing programs. Another internal report noted, "Since only a few schools offered such combined degree programs before the founding of this NIGMS training program, the MSTP has expanded slowly with funding of only the most meritorious programs. Expansion was deliberately kept slow, but steady, to help insure the high quality of the trainees." (2)

Expansion continued throughout the 1970s, and by 1980 there were twenty-five medical schools with programs supported by the MSTP with a total of 650 trainees. The importance with which NIH viewed the program is illustrated by this increased support. Although an early evaluation suggested concern about the percentage of MSTP graduates who would enter research careers, this was overshadowed by a much greater concern for recruiting physicians into research. As discussed in previous chapters, the late 1970s witnessed a significant decline in the number of physicians receiving research training in postdoctoral (i.e., post-M.D.) fellowship programs, the other research education pathway supported by NIH (3). This alarming trend led James Wyngaarden, who shortly afterward became NIH director, to describe the clinical investigator as "an endangered species." (4)

Wyngaarden documented a decline in the number of physicians applying for training or research grants and the number reporting research as their primary activity. He attributed this to several factors, including changes in societal attitudes leading to an emphasis on primary care, the instability of federal support for biomedical research and training, the lack of laboratory experience in medical school, the additional time demands of specialty training, and a federally mandated payback provision requiring those who received support but did not subsequently engage in research or teaching to provide health care in programs for underserved populations or to repay their stipends (4). Some argued that the causes of the decline in the number of physician-scholars were so profound that the trend was irreversible; physicians were destined to be full-time providers of patient care, leaving the research enterprise to Ph.D.'s. (5). Not accepting this conclusion, Bickel and coauthors argued that federal support for the MSTP had to be expanded as one way of compensating for the failure to recruit physician-scientists through postdoctoral research fellowship training (6).

With the decline in physician-researchers, Ph.D.'s began replacing M.D.'s in applications for NIH training and research support, thus allowing important biomedical research to continue. Yet as physician-scientists played a unique and essential role in medical research, their continued involvement in scientific investigation was viewed as essential to the research enterprise. Bickel and colleagues briefly presented a case for the urgency of ensuring adequate numbers of M.D. researchers: "Only a constant influx of bright and dedicated M.D. investigators can ensure the continued development and transfer of scientific knowledge to clinical practice and the necessary clinical trials to assess the value and effectiveness of drugs, devices, and diagnostic regimens in human beings. Another responsibility of the physician-investigator is the teaching of medical students and residents.... The absence of M.D. investigator role models is likely to worsen the shortage of clinical teachers." (6) Advocating the expansion of the MSTP to deal with this shortage of physician-investigators, the authors went on to document a higher attrition rate in non-NIH-supported M.D./Ph.D. programs. As the cause of this attrition they cited a lack of adequate and stable funding for students in these programs. They then presented evidence for a qualified applicant pool beyond those accepted into the NIH-funded programs.

The discussion generated by Wyngaarden's "Endangered Species" article was joined by a group of highly distinguished academic physicians at a symposium on the topic on October 10, 1980, sponsored by the New York Academy of Medicine. The presentations from the symposium appeared in the *Bulletin of the Academy* the following year (7). In one contribution, Samuel Thier considered possible remedies for declining numbers of physician-scientists and described the clinical investigator as "a two-way conduit for research. In one direction, basic science information passes into clinical use; and, in the other direction, clinical observations go back to stimulate basic research." (8) In a 1982 address, Wyngaarden cautioned that "all clinical research involving human patients must be done by or at least under the guidance of a qualified physician." (9)

By delineating the underlying rationale and need for M.D./Ph.D. education, these discussions by leaders in academic medicine no doubt influenced the growth of M.D./Ph.D. programs. In fact, as we will show, although support by NIH for additional M.D./Ph.D. programs grew, the number of non-NIH programs grew at an even greater rate, perhaps in response not only to the clearly identified need but also to the incentive provided by the prospect of NIH funding and the perceived prestige of having such a program.

Current Status

Combined degree programs are now in place at most medical schools across the country. Most of these were initially modeled on the MSTP, but just as programs at NIH-supported schools vary, so, too, do other programs, reflecting efforts to develop a structure and procedures that would best achieve their goals in the context of the particular medical school's history and "culture." Many programs are more similar to some NIH-supported programs than the latter are to one another.

Data Collection

We sent letters to directors of combined M.D./graduate degree programs at every U.S. and Canadian medical school. When no program director was identified, we used the dean's name as the initial contact. The letter enclosed a questionnaire that sought to elicit some basic data on existing programs. The questionnaire had been developed earlier by Dr. Marlene Coleman, who consulted us in its design. Dr. Coleman, who, among her several professional responsibilities, serves as premedical advisor at Cal Tech, decided to conduct a survey after finding that easily accessed information on M.D./Ph.D. programs was not available for her advisees.

In our mailing, we also requested a brief description of each school's M.D./ Ph.D. program, so that both aggregate data and program descriptions could be provided. To obtain data that were as complete as possible, we made several follow-up mailings and phone calls. The data set appears to be complete, although some of the respondents did not provide information for several questionnaire items. Of the programs known to exist, only two did not return questionnaires, but in both cases some basic information was collected by telephone. It is possible that other programs exist but did not return questionnaires.

Sponsorship

As of the 1989–1990 academic year, there were 108 combined degree programs located at 102 medical schools, including Michigan State University College of Osteopathic Medicine, which has a D.O./Ph.D. program, and two Canadian medical schools, McGill and Toronto. The two programs at the University of Illinois College of Medicine are counted separately, as they are administratively and geographically distinct (one is in Chicago and the other in Urbana-Champaign). Four other schools have two separate programs each, and one has three, which explains the total of 108. The University of California at San Francisco has an M.D./Ph.D. program and, separately, in cooperation with the University of California at Berkeley, the Joint Medical Program, which enables students to pursue the M.D. and a master's degree in health policy fields. Students in Harvard University's M.D./Ph.D. program may pursue a Ph.D. in the departments of Harvard Medical School, Harvard University, or the Harvard-MIT Division of Health Sciences and Technology. Other students at Harvard Medical School may pursue a Ph.D. in the separately administered Harvard-MIT Division of Health Sciences and Technology. Tufts School of Medicine has an M.D./Ph.D. program and a separate M.D./M.P.H. program. Cornell University Medical College has two M.D./Ph.D. programs, one in which students carry out their Ph.D. studies in departments of Rockefeller University, and a second, separately administered program with Cornell's Graduate School of Medical Sciences. The University of Chicago has an M.D./Ph.D. program at the Pritzker School of Medicine, a separate M.D./Ph.D. Pediatric Training Program in Growth and Development, and, independent of these, the Program in Medicine, Arts, and the Social Sciences (described in Chapter 9), which enables students to carry out Ph.D. studies after their second year of enrollment in any medical school.

Several programs involve the cooperation of the medical school with other institutions that do not have M.D. programs, such as Harvard with MIT and UCSF with Berkeley. In the latter program, students complete two years of graduate study for a master's degree and the first-year basic science portion of medicine on the Berkeley campus before transferring to UCSF to complete their medical education. One of the two M.D./Ph.D. programs at Cornell University Medical College is also jointly administered, in this case with Rockefeller University. (The two programs at Cornell merged administratively since the time data were collected and MSTP support began in 1990.) The programs at the University of Pittsburgh School of Medicine and at the Baylor College of Medicine cooperate with Carnegie-Mellon University and Rice University, respectively, enabling students to carry out their Ph.D.'s in fields available only at these latter two institutions. Students in the combined degree program at SUNY Buffalo School of Medicine can pursue a Ph.D. in a department at the Roswell Park Memorial Institute, and M.D. students at Emory can pursue a Ph.D. degree in a biomedical engineering field at Georgia Tech. Northeastern Ohio University College of Medicine's program is planning three pathways in cooperation with the University of Akron, Kent State University, and Youngstown State University to expand the Ph.D. options available to students. A second combined degree program at Jefferson Medical College is in the proposal stage. It was planned to be independent of an existing M.D./Ph.D. program and to operate in cooperation with the University of Delaware, enabling students to earn master's degrees in health policy fields along with their M.D. degrees.

One other variation in program sponsorship is the M.D./J.D. program offered by Southern Illinois University School of Medicine. The law program is carried out at the School of Law at the SIU-Carbondale campus, and the basic science portion of the M.D. studies is carried out on that campus as well; the clinical portion is carried out at the medical school, which is on the SIU-Springfield campus.

Variations in sponsorship notwithstanding, the typical pathway is an M.D./Ph.D. program offered at a medical school in cooperation with that institution's graduate school. The graduate school itself may be administratively part of the medical school or completely separate from it. In some cases, the combined degree program is, in fact, administered by the graduate school, in others by a partnership of the medical school and the graduate school, and in still others by the medical school alone.

There do not seem to be any notable program variations related to these variations in administrative sponsorship; all involve both the medical school and the graduate program in one way or another. (We will describe some additional program characteristics related to administrative personnel in a later section.) This variation in administrative sponsorship is significant, first, in that it attests to the willingness of medical schools to take a creative approach to developing combined degree programs in order to maximize their ability to provide education for scholarship and leadership for medical students, and, second, in that they represent innovative responses to the variety of new needs that have begun to be identified—beyond the need for clinical investigators or physician-scientists in the biomedical fields. We will elaborate on this point later.

The fact that most medical schools sponsor M.D./Ph.D. programs reflects the value academic medicine places on Ph.D. studies for physicians who wish to become serious scholars-researchers and attests to the feasibility of this type of combined degree program.

Date of Establishment

M.D./Ph.D. programs in the biomedical sciences represent the traditional model of the combined degree program; they were the earliest to be established (with the exception, perhaps, of M.D./M.P.H. programs), and they are the most numerous. Formal M.D./Ph.D. programs appear to have originated sometime before 1960 at Columbia, Harvard, and Johns Hopkins. The 1980s saw a significant increase in the number of programs (Table 3.1).

Some schools reported that their programs were still quite small and not fully formalized and gave no date for the first entering class; hence the missing data in Table 3.1. A number of programs noted that combined degrees were

Table 3.1. Year of First Entering Class of Combined Degree Programs (N = 96).

Year	Frequency	Percentage	Cumulative Percentage
Before 1960	3	3.2	
1961-65	4	4.2	7.4
1966-70	8	8.5	16.0
1971-76	11	11.7	27.7
1976-80	16	17.0	44.7
1981-85	32	31.9	76.6
1986-89	22	23.4	100.0

sought on an informal basis before the year they cited on the questionnaire; however, no information was available on the date the first student pursued the M.D./Ph.D. informally or on the number of students involved. These respondents generally reported the year the program was administratively formalized, which was usually the date that the MSTP of NIGMS first provided funds to support students.

With the addition of twenty-two programs between 1986 and 1989, fifteen of which actually admitted their first "entering class" as recently as 1989, most medical schools now have formal programs. Another six programs, proposed at the time data were collected, may have admitted entering classes in 1990. Of the fifteen programs that received MSTP support between 1964 and 1974, all but two have continued to receive support since then. The two that did not continue their programs have reestablished them since that time, one with renewed MSTP support. Nine programs describe their administrative focus as more informal than established, but in almost every case this was viewed as the first stage in the more formal establishment of the program.

Size of Enrollment

The combined degree programs had a total of 2,307 students enrolled in 1989-1990. The majority of combined degree programs have small enrollments; about one-third have fewer than five students, and almost one-half have ten or fewer students (Table 3.2). Since students are enrolled from six to eight years in combined degree programs, total enrollments of fewer than thirty translate into only one to four students per class. Only ten programs have enrollments of more than fifty students, four of which are quite large with one hundred students (Pennsylvania) or more (Harvard, Illinois at Urbana-Champaign, and Washington University). The large programs tend to be supported by NIH—of those with more than twenty students, almost two-thirds receive MSTP support, and of those with more than forty students, 84 percent receive MSTP support. Nevertheless, not all students in programs that receive MSTP support are themselves receiving financial support from this source. This will be discussed in this chapter's section on financial support.

The role of the program within the medical school as a whole can be gauged by considering program enrollment as a percentage of total enrollment (Table 3.3). From this perspective a majority of the programs are quite small, with

Table 3.2. Total Enrollment, 1989–1990 (N = 105).

Number of Students	Frequency (MSTPs)	Percentage	Cumulative Percentage
0	1	0.9	
1 to 4	34 (1)	31.7	32.6
5 to 10	15 (2)	14.4	47.0
11 to 20	14	13.5	60.5
21 to 30	11 (4)	10.6	71.1
31 to 40	11 (6)	10.6	81.7
41 to 50	8 (6)	7.7	89.4
51 to 60	5 (5)	4.8	94.2
61 to 70	1 (1)	0.9	95.1
71 to 80	1 (1)	0.9	96.0
81 to 90	0	0.0	96.0
91 to 100	1 (1)	0.9	96.9
101 or more	3 (2)	2.9	99.8

Note: Harvard and Harvard-M.I.T. enrollments are combined.

Table 3.3. The Enrollment Size of Combined Degree Programs as a Percentage of the Total Medical School Enrollment, 1989–1990 (N = 100).

Percentage of Total Enrollment	Frequency (MSTPs)	Percentage	Cumulative Percentage
1.0 or less	44 (2)	44.0	
2.0 to 4.0	21 (2)	21.0	65.0
6.0 to 10.0	24 (17)	24.0	89.0
11.0 to 20.0	9 (7)	9.0	98.0
21.0 or more	2 (1)	2.0	100.0

Note: The University of Chicago Program in Medicine, Arts, and the Social Sciences is not included, as only a few of the students are enrolled in the medical school at that institution and the rest are from other schools. For schools with more than one program, figures are combined and included as a percentage of the total school enrollment only once.

combined degree students accounting for 1 percent or less of total enrollment of the medical school. On the other hand, in 11 percent of the programs, combined degree students account for more than 10 percent of the total enrollment. Only one program, the Medical Scholars Program at the University of Illinois at Urbana-Champaign, accounts for a majority of the medical school enrollment. Nevertheless, even when combined degree students represent a small proportion of the total medical school enrollment, the importance of these programs to the medical school should not be understated. M.D./Ph.D. programs are a highly visible, high-priority statement of the standards and academic aspirations of the sponsoring institution.

The Size of the Entering Class

In each of the past several years, approximately 480 students were admitted to combined degree programs in medicine, most for M.D./Ph.D. studies (Table 3.4).

The majority of combined degree programs have very small entering classes; one-third admit one or two students annually, and another one-fourth admit three or four students to their entering class. Only eight programs have an entering class of more than ten students, and of these only two admit more than twenty students each year. There seems to be a relationship between the size of the entering class and the year in which the program was established. This is to be expected, as a new program is likely to start with low numbers until administrators and advisors can gain some experience—not to mention the time needed to garner financial support. Also, it takes a considerable amount of time to implement a recruitment process, particularly topublicize the program to qualified potential applicants. Thus, even if the entering class is not deliberately kept small, it will tend to remain so in the beginning of any program.

Table 3.4. The Average Size of the Entering Class of Programs (N = 102).

Number of Students Entering Annually	Frequency	Percentage	Cumulative Percentage
1-2	39	38.2	
3-4	24	23.5	61.7
5-6	19	18.6	80.3
7-8	7	6.9	87.2
9-10	5	4.9	92.1
11-20	6	5.8	97.9
21 or more	2	2.0	99.9

Although the number of programs appears to be approaching the number of medical schools in the United States, the number of students entering combined degree programs annually is likely to continue to increase, because many programs intend to increase the number of students admitted annually. It is interesting and potentially significant that a number of schools have more than one program, each developed to respond to a unique need and existing set of resources. This trend could continue, especially in the area of nontraditional degree combinations (i.e., those offering Ph.D.s in fields other than the biomedical sciences).

The two factors most likely to limit enrollment are the applicant pool and financial resources available to support students and administrative costs.

The Number of Graduates

The programs reported a total of 1,703 alumni, ranging from no graduates for the relatively new programs to 143 for the Combined Degree Program at the University of Pennsylvania School of Medicine (Table 3.5). The six programs reporting more than ninety alumni all receive MSTP support and are among the older programs. The total number of graduates reported is undoubtedly an underestimate of the number of M.D./Ph.D.s produced by such programs. Several programs did not respond to this questionnaire item, and several others noted that their records of graduates were incomplete before a certain date.

It should be noted that a large proportion of individuals holding both an M.D. and a Ph.D. degree did not earn the degrees in a structured dual-degree

Table 3.5. The Number of Graduates Per Program (N = 95).

Number of Graduates	Frequency	Percentage	Cumulative Percentage
0	31	33.0	
1-10	37	38.3	71.3
11-20	5	5.3	76.6
21-30	4	4.3	80.9
31-40	3	3.2	84.1
41-50	5	5.3	89.4
51-90	4	4.3	93.7
91-143	6	6.4	100.1

program. Indeed, they frequently earned the degrees at two different institutions. Such individuals are not, of course, included in the figures presented here, nor are those holding one of these two degrees and currently pursuing the other. The increase in the number of M.D./Ph.D. programs, however, suggests that in the past decade or more, these programs have been responsible for educating an increasing proportion of those who hold both degrees, and this proportion is likely to increase steadily.

Administrative Structures

The typical combined degree program has an administrative head with the title of director whose program responsibilities are less than full-time, and a staff person with the title of administrator, coordinator, or administrative assistant who is responsible for the day-to-day administration of the program. About one-fourth of the program directors hold an M.D./Ph.D.; the rest are evenly divided among those holding the M.D. (or D.O.) and those holding the Ph.D. Most program directors devote a relatively small proportion of their time to program duties. One-fourth reported spending 10 percent or less time, and almost one-third reported spending 10–20 percent of their time on program responsibilities.

Almost 90 percent of the program directors report that they devote some time to research. In fact, about one-third of the directors devote more than half of their time to research. Fewer than one-half of those with the M.D./Ph.D. or the M.D. report that they devote time to clinical responsibilities, and no director spends more than 40 percent of his or her time in clinical medicine. Additional responsibilities of directors include teaching and other administrative work.

Almost one-fourth of the programs have associate or assistant directors, and almost one-half have a coordinator or administrator, who tends to be the number-two administrative person. Several programs, however, have all three levels of administration: director, associate or assistant director, and coordinator or administrator. Almost half of the programs have an administrative staff person with another title, and about one-fourth reported that there is a program secretary; the others presumably get clerical assistance from nonprogram administrative units. As would be expected, the larger the program enrollment, the larger the administrative staff. Clearly, medical schools and/or the graduate schools cooperating with them are willing to provide administrative support for combined degree programs.

Admission Procedures

Admission procedures can provide insights into the role of the combined degree program in the medical school. Such a program usually requires a decision concerning admission to three distinct units: the medical school, the graduate program, and the combined degree program. The rationale for requiring a separate decision for the combined degree program is based not only on financial concern, but also on a fact that becomes clear to those involved with combined degree programs. The sum of the qualifications for pursuing a dual degree as measured by aptitude and motivation is greater than the requirements for its two parts! Different programs have different priorities and allow different degrees of independence in making the three decisions (Table 3.6).

About one-fourth of the combined degree programs accept students only from those already admitted to the medical school. Some of these are small and/or new programs that lack resources to recruit more widely or do not yet have them in place, but for others, this is an explicit policy decision. This decision is often based on the express desire to have students demonstrate their ability to perform at a high level in the medical curriculum before being admitted to the combined degree program. Yet other factors must play a role as well, since

Table 3.6. Initial Steps in Admission.

Candidate Admitted First to:	Frequency	Percentage
Medical school	27	25.5
Medical school and graduate program	22	20.8
Medical school, graduate program and combined degree program	35	33.0
Medical school and combined degree program	11	10.4
Combined degree program	8	7.5
Other procedure	3	2.8
Total	106	100.0

many of these schools admit students to their combined degree program just after admission to medical school or during the first year of studies. Some schools practice another variation on the admission process, based upon the premise that applicants need a period of time to make a decision concerning the graduate program in which they which to pursue a Ph.D. They are, therefore, admitted by the medical school and the combined degree program but defer applying to the graduate program as they begin their medical studies. At some of these schools, there is a somewhat formalized process to assist combined degree students in their decision making, such as a faculty seminar series and/or laboratory rotations.

At a few schools, the admissions committees of combined degree programs have the authority to make decisions about admission both to the M.D. program and to the combined degree program. It is likely that these committees include representatives of both the medical and graduate programs and that they ensure that the applicant meets the admission criteria of both.

Most programs accept applications from medical and graduate students already enrolled at their institution. Because of the relatively small size of even the largest program and the importance of the combined degree program to many institutions, the admission processes may be more flexible than written descriptions of the process suggest. Consequently, many schools may consider qualified applicants for admission at any point in their studies.

The Sequence of Studies

Respondents for the majority of programs state that the typical sequence of studies for their students is to spend two years in the medical curriculum and two to four years in the Ph.D. studies, then complete the clinical education in medicine. However, as we found in examining the admission process, the possible sequences of studies are diverse and, like other program characteristics, reflect creative responses to an identified need and desire to establish these programs (Table 3.7).

About one-fifth of the programs have developed curricula that enable combined degree students to begin medical and graduate study simultaneously. In these programs, either the graduate courses or basic science courses in medicine are substituted for each other, or specially designed courses are available. This is feasible for those in Ph.D. programs in the biomedical sciences and even for those in bioengineering disciplines, but less so for those pursuing a Ph.D. in the physical sciences, social sciences, or humanities.

A few programs require their students to begin the graduate curriculum before beginning the medical curriculum, next complete the basic science portion of the medical curriculum, then complete the Ph.D. study, and conclude with the clinical component of medicine. One rationale for this sequence is that it permits students to spend more time participating in the graduate program, because they can remain involved in research or teaching and other graduate department activities while carrying out the basic science portion of the medical curriculum. This longer period of exposure enhances the knowledge of and effective socialization into the research field. A fair number of programs (16.5

Table 3.7. Sequence of Studies.

Sequence of Study	Frequency	Percentage
Begin in medicine/complete Ph.D./complete M.D.	65	61.3
Begin medical and graduate study simultaneously/ complete Ph.D./complete M.D.	21	19.8
Begin graduate study/begin medicine/complete Ph.D./complete M.D.	3	2.8
Program individualized (no required or typical sequence)	17	16.1
Total	106	100.0

percent) either permit students to follow an individualized program with no typical pattern or require them to begin in one or the other curriculum but maintain a very flexible policy.

However students are required to begin their sequence of studies, they typically complete their Ph.D. studies before carrying out the clinical portion of medicine. This pattern is not universal, however. Some program administrators think there is value in having some clinical perspective before completing the Ph.D. research, and quite a few are flexible enough to allow some students to complete the M.D. before the Ph.D. Nevertheless, it is generally assumed that the next phase of education for most combined degree graduates will be a residency program and therefore that the logical path is to complete clinical education as the last phase of the M.D./Ph.D. sequence, just prior to the residency.

Disciplines

Respondents for the programs reported a wide spectrum of disciplines in which students can pursue graduate degrees at their institutions (Table 3.8). The sciences traditionally considered basic to medical knowledge are, of course, offered most frequently—pharmacology, biochemistry, microbiology, physiology, and anatomy. A number of disciplines more recently seen as applicable to medical research—such as molecular biology, biophysics, or bioengineering—are also frequently available for Ph.D. studies in combined degree programs.

Only a minority of programs enable medical students to pursue a Ph.D. in the social and behavioral sciences or humanities such as philosophy, history, anthropology, political science, economics, psychology, sociology, or, despite its direct relationship, public health. These disciplines have clear and growing significance to medicine, and their importance to physician-scholars and leaders is acknowledged (see Chapter 9). Because of the relative lack of availability of M.D./Ph.D. pathways in these disciplines, we list the schools that reported that they offer such opportunities (Table 3.9).

Table 3.8. Graduate Disciplines Available in Combined Degree Programs (N = 103).

Discipline Offered	Number of Programs	Discipline Offered	Number of Programs
Pharmacology	101	Exper. pathology	35
Biochemistry	91	Biological chemistry	33
Microbiology	90	Biology	32
Physiology	88	Biomath./Statistics	27
Anatomy	77	Chemistry	27
Immunology	77	Epidemiology	23
Neuroscience	76	Philosophy	18
Molecular biology	73	Psychobiology	17
Cell biology	70	Radiology/Med. physics	17
Pathology	61	History	15
Genetics	52	Anthropology	13
Biophysics	51	Economics	13
Molecular genetics	45	Political science	13
Develop./Cell biology	41	Public health	10
Bioengineering	36	Sociology	10

Note: Some of the disciplines listed are clearly different terms for another field listed (e.g., biochemistry and biological chemistry) and some programs indicate both are available when, in fact, they may be from the same degree-granting unit.

Several programs enable combined degree students to pursue a graduate degree in any discipline offered at their institution. These programs are likely to offer degrees in more social science or humanities disciplines than those cited in Table 3.9. In addition to the disciplines in Table 3.9, the University of Illinois at Urbana-Champaign has M.D./Ph.D. students enrolled in art and design, business administration, communications research, educational policy studies, educational psychology, English, health and safety studies, law, musicology, and social work. Students in the University of Chicago Program in Medicine, Arts, and the Social Sciences may pursue graduate degrees with the Committee on Social Thought or with the schools or colleges of Business, Human Development, Law, Social Service, and Public Policy. Yale offers degree programs to its M.D./Ph.D. students in the School of Organization and Management Operations, and Georgetown was, at the time of the survey, considering enabling combined degree students to pursue a degree in business administration or philosophy.

Table 3.9. M.D./Ph.D. Programs in Social and Behavioral Sciences and Humanities.

	Anthro	Econ	Hist	Philos	PublH	PolSci	Psych	Soc
Cal/Davis	X	X		X		X		
UCLA				X				
Yale		X		X	X		X	
Florida	X	X	X	X	X	X	X	X
Emory	X							
Chicago		X			X		X	X
Chicago-(Pew) PMASS	X	X	X	X		X	X	X
Illinois-Chicago					X			
Illinois-Urbana	X	X	X	X	X	X	X	X
Indiana	X		X	X		X		X
Tulane					X			
Johns Hopkins			X		X			
Maryland					X		X	
Boston				X			X	
Harvard-MIT	X	X	X	X	X	X	X	
Tufts				X				
Michigan		X	X	X		X	X	
Mich State	X							
Columbia							X	
Cornell-Rkflr							X	
NYU		X	X		X	X	X	
SUNY-Rochester				X				X
SUNY-Buffalo	X	X	X	X		X		X
SUNY-Stony Brook	X	X	X	X		X		X
Duke	X							
Ohio State		X				X		
Oklahoma					X		X	
Pennsylvania	X	X	X	X		X	X	X
Pittsburg					X		X	
S. Carolina				X				
Temple				X				
TX-Galveston			X	X				
TX-Houston				X				
Washington					X			
McGill	X						X	

The M.D./M.P.H. program at Tufts and the M.D./J.D. program at Southern Illinois University are the only two combined degree programs known to focus on a single second-degree field. In addition to the availability of the M.D./J.D. combination at Southern Illinois University and at the University of Illinois at Urbana-Champaign, Yale, Chicago, Duke, and Penn listed the M.D./J.D. as available in their combined degree programs in the AAMC Curriculum Directory (10). In this same source, a number of schools with M.D./Ph.D. programs also reported that they permit medical students to pursue master's degrees in basic sciences, and some cited the availability of M.D./master's degrees in disciplines such as business administration or management, public policy, health administration, and, most commonly, public health.

Some disciplines available for combined degree study with medicine, such as psychology, clearly bridge biomedical sciences and social or behavioral sciences in that they employ methodologies typical of both and examine questions central to both. Fields not listed in Table 3.8 or 3.9 that may fall into this category are kinesiology, nutritional sciences, and speech and hearing sciences, all of which relate directly to clinical areas in medicine. (The Medical Scholars Program at the University of Illinois at Urbana-Champaign has students enrolled in each of these.)

Although few of the programs surveyed allow medical students to pursue a second degree in social and behavioral sciences or humanities, the figures in Tables 3.8 and 3.9 are still likely to be *over*estimates of the role of these disciplines in combined degree education in medicine. Even among programs that, in principle, offer these degree combinations, very few actually have alumni or currently enrolled M.D./Ph.D. students pursuing a Ph.D. in a social or behavioral science or a humanities discipline. The only M.D./Ph.D. programs with substantial numbers of students in these areas are the University of Illinois at Urbana-Champaign, where about 25 percent of its 123 students enrolled in 1990–1991 were in such disciplines, and the University of Chicago Program in Medicine, Arts, and the Social Sciences, where all (approximately fifteen) students are in humanities and social and behavioral sciences. Funding from the MacArthur Foundation for M.D./Ph.D. students in anthropology at Harvard University enabled some to pursue this combination for a period, but now that this funding has been discontinued, the numbers are likely to dwindle. The program at the University of Chicago also lost Pew foundation support for a period. Although this support has been restored, administrators view the long-term future of the program as dependent on obtaining a secure funding base (Chapter 10).

The University of California Berkeley-San Francisco Joint Degree Program is a master's-level program, and although any discipline may be pursued for the M.S., the focus is clearly upon disciplines related to the social context of health. This program had thirty-six students and a number of alumni.

The programs noted here have graduated only a few M.D./Ph.D.s in these disciplines each year, a rate likely to continue, and there is little indication from other programs that efforts to recruit or support such students are a high priority.

Thus, to date, we have only a small cadre of young physician-scholars in social sciences and humanities, and their numbers are unlikely to grow significantly.

In an editorial in *Clinical Research*, Edwin C. Cadman, Ensign Professor and Chair of the Department of Internal Medicine at Yale, offered a guide for the 1990s for young physicians who want a career in investigative medicine (11). As part of his prescription, he encouraged faculty and students to broaden their interpretation of the physician-scientist, arguing forcefully that research approaches beyond those of molecular biology are necessary for solving "the health care crisis that swirls around us all." Citing some major social and environmental problems, he noted, "As leaders we must encourage research in these areas as well as in the disease specific areas." Although it is doubtful that many would argue with Dr. Cadman on this point, our data suggest that medical schools are not in fact making notable gains in encouraging students to consider research training in those areas of social sciences and the humanities best suited to dealing with the health-related problems to which he referred. The reasons for this are somewhat complex and undoubtedly related to funding constraints, but the current situation suggests the need for a serious examination of the degree to which physician scholars are being properly equipped to deal with problems that presently beset health care and show every sign of growing in urgency (12, 13).

Sources of Funding

The MSTP is a significant and perhaps crucial source of support for students in combined degree programs. However, this is by no means the only source (Table 3.10). The medical schools and graduate programs themselves appear to be the most common sources of funding for students in combined degree programs. Some medical schools provide fellowship funds to their M.D./Ph.D. program from the medical service plan, some state schools use state funds as the source of fellowship support for students, and many schools rely on faculty grants to provide research assistantships and/or funds in departmental budgets to provide teaching assistantships. Graduate school funding for students is usually similar to that provided regular graduate students—research assistantships from external grants of faculty, fellowships obtained competitively from external sources, and especially fellowships or teaching assistantships from departmental budgets allocated by the institution.

Outside fellowships, awarded directly to a particular student who has applied to or been nominated by the school or program, tend to come from private foundations. One private foundation source is the Life and Health Insurance Medical Research Fund (LHIMRF), which awards several M.D./Ph.D. student scholarships annually. Students are eligible for this program after their second year of medical study and each medical school can nominate one student for this scholarship. Recipients are given a generous annual stipend, renewable until both degrees are completed. Program directors considered this a very beneficial form of support and a model that, especially if were emulated by other private foundations, could make a significant contribution to increasing the recruitment and retention of M.D./Ph.D. students. In several recent years, the

Table 3.10. Program Sources of Financial Support for Students by Percentage of Total Student Support from Each Source, 1989–1990 (N = 103).

Source	Percentage of Total Support for Students						Total # of Programs
	1-24	25-49	50-74	75-99	100	Not Known	
NIGMS-MSTP	1	7	5	6	3	7	29
Graduate school	7	9	16	4	7	31	74
Medical school	14	10	16	4	5	26	65
Outside fellowships	6	2	0	0	1	14	23
Other	8	3	1	1		12	28

LHIMRF has administered similar programs on behalf of the Lutheran Brotherhood for Lutheran M.D./Ph.D. students.

Unfortunately, some important sources of funding appear to exclude most M.D./Ph.D. students. At its inception, for example, the Howard Hughes Medical Institute (HHMI) excluded students already enrolled in M.D./Ph.D. programs from its Predoctoral Fellowships in Biological Sciences. The rationale was that the fellowship program had been designed to recruit additional M.D./Ph.D. students, but the effect was to deny a possible source of funding to those who had made the commitment to pursue both degrees. Such policies overlook the fact that retention is a serious problem related to the insufficient and unstable funding available for many M.D./Ph.D. students. Perhaps in recognition of this problem, HHMI now allows M.D./Ph.D. students to apply for its predoctoral fellowships.

The National Science Foundation excludes M.D./Ph.D. students from eligibility for Graduate Fellowships (even from its Minority Graduate Fellowships), apparently because the MSTP is available for this purpose. This policy overlooks the limits of the MSTP and the fact that many M.D./Ph.D. students may be in fields not traditionally included in MSTP funding, such as the physical and engineering sciences, social sciences, or humanities.

Some private foundations also exclude M.D./Ph.D. students. The Fannie and John Hertz Foundation, for example, provides graduate fellowships for students concerned with applications of the physical sciences to solve problems. Presumably, these could include medical and health care problems; however, M.D./Ph.D. students are explicitly excluded from eligibility (14).

A program entitled the National Research Service Awards for Predoctoral M.D./Ph.D. Fellows is a notable new effort jointly initiated by the National Institute of Mental Health, the National Institute on Alcohol Abuse and Alcoholism, and the National Institute on Drug Abuse. Beginning in 1990, up to fifteen fellowships offered annual stipends of $8,500 to support individuals in research training in specified areas of biomedical and behavioral sciences. The purpose is to help ensure that highly trained physician-scientists will be available in adequate numbers and in appropriate fields of research to meet the nation's needs in the areas of alcohol and drug abuse and mental health. The number of fellowships available was expected to increase to twenty in 1991 and twenty-five in 1992. This will clearly encourage M.D./Ph.D.'s in the social and behavioral sciences.

Several combined degree programs have been the direct beneficiaries of significant gifts from private individuals and foundations to provide support for M.D./Ph.D. students. In 1988, the University of Texas Southwestern Medical Center at Dallas announced a gift of $20 million from H. Ross Perot to allow the M.D./Ph.D. program at that institution to expand its enrollment from twenty-six to ninety. The program offered student stipends beginning at $12,000. Around this same time, Washington University Medical School received a $30 million endowment from the Spencer T. and Ann W. Olin Foundation in support of students in the MSTP at that institution, and Jefferson Medical College received a gift from an alumnus that enabled them to establish student funding for their M.D./Ph.D. program, called the Gibbons Scholars Program in honor of the donor. In 1990, Cornell University announced the receipt of a grant of $1 million from the Andrew W. Mellon Foundation to support an M.D./Ph.D. program offered jointly by Cornell University Medical College, Rockefeller University, and Memorial Sloan-Kettering Cancer Center. (This is in addition to the two programs already in existence at Cornell, mentioned earlier.)

Respondents cited a variety of other sources of funding for outside fellowships to students or as donations to programs. The programs at both the University of Oklahoma and University of Oregon receive some funding from the Medical Research Foundation in their respective states. A few respondents cited the Howard Hughes Medical Institute as supporting students in their programs, and several cited unnamed private endowments, gifts, or donations. Although several mentioned faculty research grants or departmental training grants (typically from NIH but also from sources such as the March of Dimes, Merck Sharp & Dohme, or the Denison Foundation) as sources of funding for students, most considered this source to be the graduate department, as these are generally research fellowships or assistantships available to any graduate student.

Relatively few programs have only one source of funding for students; of those reporting the proportion of total funding from each source, only nineteen cited a single source, including only three of the MSTP-supported programs. Most programs have a very diverse funding base for students, including funds from the medical school, the graduate school, outside individual fellowships, and outside programmatic sources (such as the MSTP). Of the approximately 1,350 students enrolled in programs that receive MSTP support, somewhat more than one-half receive financial support from this source. The rest are supported by funds from all other sources identified, as is the case in most programs that are not supported by NIGMS.

Types of Awards for Students

Financial support is made available to students in a variety of forms (Table 3.11). Fellowships are the most common type of award to combined degree students; about three-fourths of all programs use this type of financial support. MSTP-supported students receive fellowships, but not all students in schools with MSTP-supported programs receive their support in this form; these programs make use of teaching and research assistantships as well. Research assistantships are used by more than one-half; teaching assistantships are also awarded but are less common. Although many respondents cited loans as forms of financial support, we did not include these. Loans are typically available to all medical students, although some programs may make special loans available to combined degree students. Tuition waivers are another prominent type of support; almost one-fifth of the programs provide them. The source of a significant proportion of the research assistantships awarded M.D./Ph.D. students is NIH research grants to faculty or training grants to graduate programs, so the federal role in funding M.D./Ph.D. education is even greater than suggested by the budget for the MSTP.

Table 3.11. Types of Financial Support Award to Combined Degree Students (N = 103).

Programs Offering Type of Support	Frequency	Percentage
Fellowships	77	74.8
Research assistantship	58	56.3
Teaching assistantship	18	17.5
Other	21	20.3

Most programs provide support for students throughout the entire program of study for the combined degree. Some support students only while they are carrying out their graduate study; others begin to provide funding only after the first two years of medicine but then provide support throughout the graduate program and clinical training in medical school. Another variation is to provide only tuition waivers during the medical studies, adding a stipend during the period of graduate study.

Conclusion

Although an important beginning has been made with the establishment of M.D./Ph.D. programs in the medical humanities and social sciences, academic medicine and the federal government have a long way to go to provide the level of opportunities that those knowledgeable and concerned about this topic believe is essential to the future of the nation's health care system. One hopeful sign is that NIH has recognized the need to increase educational efforts in fields such as epidemiology, biostatistics, and behavioral sciences. This may in turn increase opportunities for pursuing M.D./Ph.D.'s in the fields of social and behavioral sciences (15).

Some programs have been established and/or have grown without significant and secure outside funding. It appears, for example, that the larger the enrollment size of a program, the more likely it is to make use of all the categories of funding sources listed in Table 3.11. This suggests that programs grow in proportion to their success in securing funding for students. This success may depend to a degree on program goals and administrative skills, but the ability to recruit qualified students is the crucial variable. If qualified, motivated students are there, dedicated faculty and program administrators can and usually will find sources of financial support within their institutions. For example, in the Medical Scholars Program of the University of Illinois, all 143 students enrolled in the 1992-1993 academic year received some financial support, a feat accomplished regularly in the past dozen years of the program's existence.

Despite the generally impressive and positive record to date in establishing combined degree programs in medicine, however, a word of caution is called for. If we wish to count upon the continued development and "good health" of these programs, growth in the amount and the predictability of financial support is necessary. If programs are to reach their full potential, additional funding sources, such as direct federal government or private foundation support, will be necessary.

Funding needs are particularly acute for M.D./Ph.D. students in the social sciences and humanities, where faculty research often fails to generate funds from external grants and research assistantships are less common.

The need for additional support can be generalized to all existing programs. It is highly probable that the financial insecurity M.D./Ph.D. students experience, even those in MSTP-supported programs, deters prospective applicants and candidates for admission. Financial concerns contribute to the attrition of students in M.D./Ph.D. programs and probably also lead some of those who complete this phase of their education to discontinue their research-oriented careers.

References

1. National Institute of General Medical Science, The National Institutes of Health Medical Scientist Program (NIGMS internal unpublished report, May 1980).
2. National Institute of General Medical Science, MSTP Evaluation (NIGMS unpublished report 79401, 1981).
3. Gerald F. DiBona, "Whence Cometh Tomorrow's Clinical Investigators?" *Clinical Research* 27 (1979): 253–56.
4. James B. Wyngaarden, "The Clinical Investigator as an Endangered Species," *The New England Journal of Medicine* 301 (1979): 1254–59.

5. Gordon N. Gill, "The End of the Physician-Scientist?" *American Scholar* 53 (1984): 353–68.
6. Janet W. Bickel, Charles R. Sherman, James Ferguson, Liesel Baker, and Thomas E. Morgan, "The Role of MD-PhD Training in Increasing the Supply of Physician-Scientists," *The New England Journal of Medicine* 304 (1981): 1265–68.
7. *Bulletin of the New York Academy of Medicine* 57 (6) (July-Aug. 1981).
8. Samuel O. Thier, "Recommendations for Remedies," *Bulletin of the New York Academy of Medicine* 57 (July–Aug. 1981): 481.
9. James B. Wyngaarden, "Encouraging Young Physicians to Pursue a Career in Clinical Research," *Clinical Research* 31 (April 1983): 115–18.
10. Association of American Medical Colleges, "AAMC Curriculum Directory, 1989–90," (Washington, D.C.: 1989).
11. Edwin C. Cadman, "The New Physician-Scientist: A Guide for the 1990s," *Clinical Research* 38 (2): 191–98.
12. Robert G. Petersdorf, "Perspective from the Medical Colleges" in *New Medical Technology: Experimental or State-of-the Art*, Mary L. Grady, ed. (Rockville, Md.: Agency for Health Care Policy and Research Pub. No. 92-0057, June 1992).
13. Robert Q. Marston and Roseann M. Jones (ed), *Medical Education in Transition*: Commission on Medical Education: The Sciences of Medical Practice (Princeton, N.J.: Robert Wood Johnson Foundation, July 1992).
14. Fannie and John Hertz Foundation, Instructions for Completing a Graduate Fellowship for 1992-93 Academic Year, (Livermore, Cal., 1991).
15. National Institutes of Health, *Review of the NIH Biomedical Research Training Programs* (Bethesda, Md., October 1989).

4

Existing Pathways: From Research Experience to Programs for New Scientists

Diane L. Gottheil and Harold M. Swartz

Chapter 3 offered a broad overview of available M.D./Ph.D. programs. This chapter describes other formal programs to educate physician-scholars. We noted in Chapter 1 that there are several key points at which one may decide to enter a path toward scholarship and leadership in medicine. Accordingly, this discussion is, for the most part, organized chronologically along the education-career path. It begins with programs at the level of undergraduate medical education, continues through residency and fellowship programs, and then considers midcareer fellowships and programs to support research by new scientists. By describing existing pathways in this chapter and in Chapter 3, we hope to begin an assessment of current efforts to educate physician-scholars.

Research Experience for Medical Students

We noted in the previous chapter that one factor contributing to the establishment of the MSTP was dissatisfaction with an earlier NIH-sponsored program, the Experimental Training Program, which enabled medical students to gain research experience (1). This program was initiated in 1956 and 1957 at thirteen medical schools. Students typically participated during summers. Although it was possible to participate during an academic year, this required temporarily "dropping out" from medical school as financial support during medical studies was not permitted. In response to those medical schools that viewed this program favorably, in 1961 it was extended to twenty-seven schools under the NIH Medical Student Research Training Program, even though the director of NIH was not fully satisfied with the amount and quality of training provided. Shortly afterward, NIH phased out this program to encourage participation in the newly established M.D./Ph.D. program it was sponsoring, then called the Clinician Scientist Program.

Despite this change in federal policy, medical students continued to participate in short-term research projects aimed at stimulating interest and beginning research education. In 1979, the president of the American Federation of Clinical Research, Gerald DiBona, cited data to support the importance of direct experience during medical school in influencing students to pursue careers in research (2). It is no wonder, then, that activities and programs to encourage medical students to pursue research careers continued. Marking renewed support for such efforts by NIH, Director James Wyngaarden, in a 1982 address entitled "Encouraging Young Physicians to Pursue a Career in Clinical Research," noted the importance of providing undergraduate medical students the time and opportunity to try research (3). Today, such opportunities are expanding and continue to be viewed as important ways of recruiting potential physician-scholars. Indeed, several studies provide evidence of the effects of research experience for medical students entering research careers (4–9). It is also becoming more widely recognized that exposure to real research experiences can be very valuable to students in college; as noted in Chapter 5, many program directors consider such experiences among the most valuable predictors of success in a research education program.

Programs Sponsored by Medical Schools

Many medical schools have programs to encourage their students to become interested in academic medicine, usually by providing opportunities for research. Some of these programs are highly structured and provide funds to support students during the period of research. Typically they provide research experiences during summers or in elective clerkship rotations. They may also employ other methods of introducing students to aspects of academic medicine, such as participation in seminar series.

One very formal program, for example, is at Bowman Gray School of Medicine, which selects six to eight students from its entering class before the start of the academic year for what it calls its Medical Scholars Program, described as an alternative to an M.D./Ph.D. program. The program was initiated in 1983 with funds from the National Fund for Medical Education and has also received funding from Burroughs Wellcome. Students in the program are assigned an academic advisor from a special faculty group identified as skilled physician-teachers who are interested in students. The students participate in a prematriculation workshop beyond the general student orientation to learn about academic and research aspects of the school and participate in luncheon seminar sessions including faculty and invited scholars who discuss academic issues and interests. The students are expected to complete one research study, are given a teaching opportunity, and are sponsored to attend scientific meetings or visit faculty scholars at other institutions (10).

Another such a program is at Morehouse School of Medicine, as described in the AAMC Curriculum Directory. Seeking to encourage students to pursue careers in academic medicine, this program provides an opportunity for qualified students to spend two years completing the second year of medical education, thereby enabling them to devote half-time to a research program directed by one of the basic science departments. Tuition and fees for students, designated Medical Student Research Fellows, are waived for the second year of medical education, and a stipend is provided (11). With Australia, facing a similar potential shortage of clinical investigators, the University of Queensland established a special degree program in which medical students spend one year in research at the end of the third or fourth year of a six-year medical course (12).

In addition to formal programs, most medical schools encourage student research, especially during summers, and offer more or less formal means of making opportunities known to students. Typically, students are expected to take the initiative in identifying a faculty member whose research is of interest and making the necessary arrangements to participate in some manner. Stipends are often available on a competitive basis. Schools frequently have research forums in which students give oral or poster presentations on research they have carried out. Many medical schools offer, and some even require, one rotation in the clinical education years to be devoted to a research project, although for many this may simply be a library project rather than experimental research. Alpha Omega Alpha, the honorary medical society, offers up to ten research fellowships annually to second- or third-year medical students who are not enrolled in M.D./Ph.D. programs or do not hold Ph.D.s. The announcement requires a one-page outline of the proposed project but does not stipulate whether the student is to continue medical studies concurrently (13).

The National Student Research Forum

The practice of holding research forums on a schoolwide or regional basis has developed into a formalized National Student Research Forum held annually for the presentation of research by medical students, residents, and graduate students in the biomedical sciences. Eighty-eight medical schools and hospitals were represented by the 194 presenters at the 1990 forum. The forum is supported by funds from the American Medical Association-Education and Research Foundation, Mead Johnson Nutritional Division, Roche Laboratories, and the American Academy of Family Practitioners and is intended to encourage and recognize medical research primarily among medical students (14).

HHMI Research Training Fellowships for Medical Students

An important and relatively new program to support research by medical students is the Research Training Fellowships for Medical Students sponsored by the Howard Hughes Medical Institute (15). This program provides fellowships for one year, with an opportunity to extend for an additional year, for medical students to conduct research at a U.S. institution chosen by the fellow. Fifty-two students were selected for the second year of the program in 1990, and each was provided a stipend of $12,900. In addition, a research allowance of $4,000 was provided to the student's mentor, and an allowance of $3,700 was provided to the fellowship institution. The goal of the program is to strengthen and expand the pool of medically trained researchers by providing an intensive year-long experience in fundamental research. It is anticipated that up to sixty fellowships will be awarded annually under this program.

The HHMI-NIH Research Scholars Program

A second program sponsored by the Howard Hughes Medical Institute brought NIH back into the business of providing research experiences for medical students, this time at NIH labs for periods of nine months to one year (15). The HHMI-NIH Research Scholars Program, also called the Cloister Program after the residential facility for program participants, provides annual salaries of $16,800. Participating students are considered employees of HHMI and receive fringe benefits. Most enter the program after the second year of medical school and choose an NIH laboratory following their arrival and a round of visits. Students are encouraged to participate in research after the NIH laboratory experience, but, of course, it is too early to evaluate the results of this or the previously described HHMI program.

Current NIH Programs

For many years, NIH has conducted clinical elective courses at the NIH campus for students from any medical school. Many of these courses tend to be research-oriented experiences, providing another opportunity to stimulate student interest in research (16). In addition, medical students may arrange for tutorials in some of the NIH research laboratories that emphasize the investigative approach to medical problems (4). A ten-week summer research fellowship enables students to conduct research under the guidance of a preceptor from one of the NIH institutes and to participate in lectures and seminars.

Another NIH program enables health professional schools to incorporate a request for a short-term research training position into a new or competing continuation institutional research training grant or for existing training grant recipients to request such positions as a competitive supplement. However, students with the M.D. or Ph.D. or students already enrolled in Ph.D. programs are not eligible for these positions (17).

An important affirmation of NIH support for predoctoral research experience is contained in the October 1989 report of a task force established by then NIH director James Wyngaarden and made up primarily of directors of NIH institutes to review the NIH Biomedical Research Training Programs. Referring to the availability of support for short-term training within the NIH institutional training grant mechanism, the T-series, the report of this task force stated: "A study of the impact of the short-term training program for health professional students (T35) showed that program participants were twice as likely to express an interest in a research career at the time of graduation as were individuals who did not have the benefit of such an experience. Additionally, T35 trainees have research goals and demonstrate a relatively greater appreciation of the value of a basic science foundation preparatory to a research career." In light of this finding, the report recommended that eligibility for short-term training on an institutional training grant be extended to medical students and other professional predoctoral students for periods of three to twelve months.

Issues

Short-term research experiences are not sufficient to produce independent investigators; however, participants may not recognize their limitations. This is clearly a potential drawback of such programs. A primary argument in support of such programs is that a significant percentage of physicians now in research careers decided to enter these careers while in medical school (4–9). It is also essential to offer undergraduate students opportunities for experience in research in order to expand the pool of those who go on to research careers. This is true in biomedical science as well as in any other field of scholarship. A number of premedical students seek research experience to enhance their medical school applications, only to find that research is something they enjoy. Their early exposure thereby increases the probability that they will participate in further training and enter research-oriented careers.

In evaluating programs for premedical and medical students, it is therefore crucial to ask, first, whether participants are more likely to consider taking more solid or sufficient research training and to pursue careers as physician-scholars and, second, whether the research experience contributed to these decisions or whether participants would have sought such a pathway even without this experience. Although it is difficult to answer such questions, they should, ideally, be asked of each type of program being reviewed.

Research Education in Residency Programs

A 1980 Report of the AAMC Ad Hoc Committee on Clinical Research Training, formed in response to growing concern about the declining numbers of physician-scientists, noted that "residency training is the time when an individual decides whether to commit an additional major block of time and effort to research training to prepare for a career as a clinical investigator." (18) The report pointed to a wide variation in the amount of emphasis given or time allowed for research experience during a residency, "with some [programs] routinely including from three months to one year of clinical research experience as an intrinsic part of the residency training program supported by the hospital."

Such research experience during a residency, the report continued, "is given not so much in anticipation of producing clinical investigators, but because it is thought to be an important part in the training of a clinical specialist." Nevertheless, this exposure is sufficient to lead some to seek the additional experience needed for a career in clinical research. Thus, just as research experience during undergraduate medical education is considered important in attracting individuals to later training in research, research experience during graduate-level medical education is considered an important means of recruiting more physician-investigators by sparking interest and providing initial education.

At the time the information for the 1980 report was gathered, research experience was more common during surgical residencies than during medicine residencies. This was attributed directly to the respective boards. The American Board of Surgery required a minimum training period of four years but encouraged hospitals to offer five-year programs. As a result, with the approval of its Residency Review Committee, five-year residency programs often included research experience as the third or fourth year. Boards of Internal Medicine and Pediatrics, as well as other primary care specialties, however, had eliminated research experience as a part of their general training requirements. One important consequence has been that, without board requirements, the usual mechanisms for residency funding have not been available, even for those programs intended to encourage research experience. Barring alternative sources of funding, involvement in research had to be deferred for three to four years. The report aptly described the resulting situation: "For most residents, and especially for those with family obligations, a heavy debt burden, and pessimism about their academic future, a four year waiting period may be the 'coup-de-grace' to an initial interest in research." (18)

Individualized Research Residency Programs

Departments concerned about this issue responded creatively with special programs to enable residents to gain research experience. One of the earliest programs, the Internal Medicine Research Residency Track, was initiated in 1972 by Harvard Medical School's Department of Medicine at Brigham (now Brigham and Women's) Hospital (19). In an interview, the program director noted that this type of program is at times referred to generically as a "hemi-doc." The Harvard program is designed to enable residents to obtain research and clinical training concurrently rather than consecutively. During the first two years of the program, time is divided between clinical training responsibilities and the lab in six-month rotations; the third year is spent on clinical services. Most trainees then complete a standard three-year fellowship and take certifying board exams in medicine and a subspecialty (20).

The Physician-Investigator Fellowship Training Program offers an approach in which students devote more time to research. Established in July 1980 in the Department of Medicine at the University of Pittsburgh School of Medicine and briefly described in *The New England Journal of Medicine* the following year (21), this program was modeled on one established earlier at Duke University School of Medicine for medical students and postdoctoral fellows. It differed, however, in two respects: it offered a fellowship to house officers who had completed at least one year of residency training, and it was designed to cover two years of research education. The authors of *The New England Journal of Medicine* article noted that the program was funded at the outset by the resources of the Department of Medicine, but they believed that external financial support would be needed to draw adequate numbers of physician-investigators on a yearly basis.

Programs such as those developed at Brigham and Women's Hospital and at Pittsburgh were called for in recommendations addressed to medical schools in the 1980 report by the AAMC ad hoc Committee on Clinical Research Training. The committee's other recommendations also called upon the specialty-certifying boards to grant credit toward primary specialty board requirements for research training. "Psychiatry, pediatrics, internal medicine and other specialties should again acknowledge that opportunities for research experience are important during the general residency period and are appropriate for the education of many qualified specialists especially those who will go on to academic careers." (18)

The Clinical Investigator Pathway

In 1984, the American Board of Internal Medicine initiated the Clinical Investigator Pathway, developed after several years of discussion and planning within the board concerning the optimal response to the widely discussed needs for clinical investigators. The pathway enables residents in internal medicine programs to complete two years of research along with two years of residency training and then be qualified to sit for the certifying examination in internal medicine (22). Interested residency program directors are expected to design the programs and submit proposals to admit a candidate to the pathway, which requires approval by the board. Between 1985 and early 1989, fifty candidates completed a Clinical Investigator Pathway in internal medicine and reached the point of the certifying examination, and in 1989 alone, thirty-nine clinical investigators sat for the certifying examination, suggesting an upward trend in participation (23).

Showing a creativity similar to that we have witnessed in the establishment of M.D./Ph.D. programs, residency directors in medicine and a variety of other fields have developed and are developing varied opportunities for research experience combined with clinical training. The Department of Internal Medicine at the University of Illinois College of Medicine at Urbana-Champaign, for example, established three separate pathways to enable residents in medicine to tailor a sequence to their specific background and interests. The Clinical Investigator Research Pathway focuses upon concomitant clinical and research activity in a four-year internal medicine residency geared to those who are completing Ph.D. research or have had other rigorous prior research experience. The Internist Scholars Pathway focuses upon education in health policy and administration, combining graduate courses and research (possibly in a degree program) with clinical training. The Faculty Development Pathway is designed to prepare individuals for a career in primary care internal medicine in an academic setting, combining clinical activities with courses and research for a master's degree in health policy and administration and in the fourth year of the program offering participants responsibilities similar to those of chief medical residents (24).

An example of a program in psychiatry is the Residency Research Track established in the Department of Psychiatry at the University of Michigan to respond to "a tremendous need for adequately trained clinician researchers in psychiatry, especially as advances are made in psychobiology and the neurosciences." (25) The goal is to allow selected, qualified residents the opportunity to combine clinical and research training in a program that adds research, and a fifth year, to their training. To be accepted, a resident must write a research proposal with the guidance of a faculty mentor, outlining a plan of study including both clinical experiences and a research project. The usual plan is for residents to enter in PGY-2 and gradually increase their proportion of time in research so that by the fifth year of the residency, they are spending 70 percent of their time in research and 30 percent in clinical activity.

Several medical schools (e.g., University of California at Davis, Washington University, Mayo) have established programs to provide research training in residencies in any of a number of participating specialties. The Mayo Graduate School of Medicine initiated the Clinician Investigator Training Program in 1981, specifically designed for M.D.s planning careers as clinician investigators. The program is available in all the subspecialties of internal medicine and in the Departments of Anesthesiology, Dermatology, Neurology, Neurosurgery, Orthopedics, Otorhinolaryngology, Pathology, Pediatrics, and Surgery. Correspondence describing this program is worth quoting at length, as it provides an example of how such a program is generally structured:

> Although each department structures its program in a slightly different way, the common theme is to combine two years of basic research with complete clinical training. In some programs, such as the Internal Medicine Subspecialties, it is constructed in such a way that the trainee can complete all of the requirements for certification in their subspecialty and two years of research within the same time frame of normal subspecialty training. For example, an internal medicine trainee with an interest in thoracic diseases for a career would have the following track:
>
> Year 1 – Rotating internal medicine training
> Year 2 – Rotating internal medicine training
> Year 3 – First six months—completion of internal medicine residency
> Year 3 – Second six months—laboratory research
> Year 4 – Laboratory research
> Year 5 – First six months—completion of laboratory research
> Year 5 – Second six months—clinical rotations in thoracic disease
> Year 6 – Clinical rotations in thoracic disease
>
> The program is not rigid and components can be rearranged to suit the individual trainee's career plans. (26)

Although the last line of this program description may appear "pro forma," those involved in research education know that flexibility is a key element of successful programs.

The University of California at Davis designed the UC-D Medical Scholars Program for residents at the PG-II level to provide an opportunity for twelve- to twenty-four-month research experiences in basic and/or clinical research. Prospective applicants may come from any department and may work under the guidance of any faculty member in the university. Up to five candidates per year may be chosen for this program, which provides funding for the resident/researcher and support to the sponsoring laboratory (27).

The Residency Program in General Internal Medicine at Rhode Island Hospital and Brown University was founded in 1980 with a built-in scholarly project and primary care focus. Unlike the typical physician-investigator track, however, this program is a three-year residency in internal medicine geared to those whose scholarly discipline is within the social sciences and humanities rather than biomedical sciences. The three components of the program are a requirement of medical rotations for board eligibility, an ambulatory curriculum unique to general internal medicine, and physician-scholar activities (such as research and guided teaching experiences). Research time increases each year and is integrated into the annual three-month ambulatory block and electives. A faculty mentor is assigned to help arrange the schedule, set goals, provide guidance, and foster research productivity (28).

Issues

This set of examples illustrates the breadth of possibilities and the flexibility that appears to be characteristic of programs designed to accommodate the needs of clinical and research education. However, as in the M.D./Ph.D. programs, any attempt to pursue two goals involves trade-offs. The director of the Internal Medicine Research Residency Track at Brigham and Women's Hospital, Dr. Marshall Wolf, has noted that it is not possible to set up a research project in the six-month block of lab time allotted by that program. Consequently, such a program generally works well only for those residents who have prior research experience and continue in that same area: six months is a sufficient period to remain productive in an area in which one has previously worked (20). This is one of several concerns voiced by Dr. David Nathan of Boston Children's Hospital in describing the pediatrics research residency being established at that institution on the Brigham and Women's model (20). Most programs have a minimum requirement of one year in research education in an attempt to provide adequate time for the completion of a research project. Although this requirement adds a year to the program, some argue that even this period of time is insufficient. The ability of residencies to offer time for research is often and increasingly constrained by financial considerations. One of the consequences of attempts at cost containment has been increased reliance on the clinical activities of residents to generate the revenues to run the department; therefore, release from clinical duties implies a loss of revenue. Simultaneously, departments, medical schools, and hospitals have less ability to provide additional funding to support research time for residents.

Residencies for M.D./Ph.D. Graduates

One obvious way to deal with the concern that a residency offers insufficient time in research to provide significant experience is to ensure that those accepted into research residencies have very strong research backgrounds. Consequently, research-oriented residency programs have begun actively to recruit graduates of M.D./Ph.D. programs. Dr. Nathan noted that Boston Children's Hospital offers its new program "particularly to attract M.D.-Ph.D.s." Several existing programs, such as the Mayo Clinician Investigator Program, have begun explicitly to point out the appropriateness of their residency for M.D./Ph.D. graduates. Others have been initiated with the growing recognition that a substantial number of M.D./Ph.D. graduates are entering the residency match each year and are very attractive candidates for residency programs because of their intellectual ability and the probability that they will become leaders in medical research and academic medicine.

Research-oriented residency programs have been initiated, and existing programs have been adapted with M.D./Ph.D. graduates specifically in mind. Examples can be found in the departments of medicine at the University of Alabama (the Academic Internist Program) and at Case Western Reserve University (the Special Internal Medicine/Basic Science Residency Program). The Department of Psychiatry and Behavioral Sciences at the University of Oklahoma Health Sciences Center, the Department of Pediatrics at the University of Rochester Medical Center, and the Department of Pathology and Laboratory Medicine at the University of Wisconsin-Madison have all informed directors of M.D./Ph.D. programs by correspondence of the characteristics of the research residencies they offer and their appropriateness for M.D./Ph.D. graduates. Since it administers one of the largest M.D./Ph.D. programs in the country, it is not surprising that Washington University School of Medicine is particularly sensitive to the need for M.D./Ph.D. graduates to move on to the residency phase of their training with opportunities for continued research involvement along with clinical education. Accordingly, a Postgraduate Medical Scientist Training Program has been established, enabling M.D./Ph.D. graduates to receive clinical training in any one of the twelve programs at Washington University while at the same time "maintaining continued access to the latest scientific developments in the physical and biological sciences." A two-year postgraduate research experience is provided along with clinical training (29).

Residency programs geared to M.D./Ph.D. graduates respond to an important question: How can graduates stay sufficiently involved in research during their residency and perhaps subspecialty training so as not to lose their skills and even motivation to pursue research-oriented careers? A long period of purely clinical training (three to seven years) raises the question of how one then initiates participation in research without some formal transitional phase. The increasing establishment of opportunities for research during residency training is therefore of particular interest to M.D./Ph.D. graduates.

For example, in November 1989, M.D./Ph.D. students initiated a newsletter intended as a vehicle for the exchange of information of particular interest to combined degree students in medicine (30). The second and third issues of the newsletter included information about residency programs in which M.D./Ph.D. graduates could pursue their research interests. The NYC M.D./Ph.D. Student Forum, organized to promote communication among the directors and students from the M.D./Ph.D. programs at seven medical schools in the New York City area, conducted a survey in 1990 of 512 residency programs in eight major specialties at eighty-one academic medical centers. The purpose was to identify research opportunities for M.D./Ph.D. graduates and develop a data file to assist in the selection of residency programs (31). As residency program administrators are made more aware of the research orientation of M.D./Ph.D. graduates, and as they learn about "what the competition is doing" to attract them, it is possible that more structured opportunities to combine clinical training with continued research involvement will develop. This will continue to be an important issue for M.D./Ph.D. program directors concerned about the next step for their graduates on the pathway toward a successful research career and for residency directors eager to attract candidates seeking academic careers.

Issues

Some have argued that effective clinical education may be compromised by incorporating research education into a residency (32). A related argument is that research experience during the residency will result in the loss of clinicians by leading some to choose research careers (33). Such concerns are a further reflection of the tension between these two arenas, a phenomenon that is not likely to disappear. (This issue is discussed in depth in Chapter 17.) Those involved in the education of physician-scholars must accept this tension as inevitable, realizing that some participants in dual-discipline education may indeed be lost to one discipline or the other. It is perhaps some consolation that those educated in both research and clinical medicine who decide to focus exclusively on one domain are likely to bring added insights or dimensionality to their work. Additional consolation might be gained from the observation that it is impossible to design a program that eliminates the difficulties of completing advanced studies in two areas or controls the complexities of human nature that result in changes in goals along the way.

The opportunity for M.D./Ph.D. graduates or other newly graduated M.D.s with strong research backgrounds to continue participation in research at some time during a residency is of significant value. Research experience during this period not only contributes to their further education but also helps ensure their continued involvement in a research-based career. This is an opportune time for many M.D./Ph.D. graduates whose thesis research was conducted in a basic science department to use their strong foundation in research to direct their research toward a clinical area and clinical problems. Most students enter M.D./Ph.D. programs with the goal of participating in clinically related research. It seems logical to capture their interest in solving problems of human disease at a time when their research skills are still strong and thereby enable them to integrate the two domains early in their careers, if this is the pathway they wish to pursue. From this perspective, notwithstanding the primary goal of residencies to ensure clinical competence, those departments interested in promoting outstanding clinical research in their field would be wise to see that such opportunities are in place for present and prospective residents with strong research orientations. As with M.D./Ph.D. programs, funding issues are likely to be a serious impediment to the expansion of such opportunities, particularly as concerns about changes in the financing of graduate medical education are heightened by federal cost-cutting moves.

Postdoctoral Fellowship Programs

Postdoctoral fellowship programs are the dominant source of physician-scholars with significant formal research education. This pathway prevents the potential difficulties of combining medical and research education by enabling

M.D.s to defer research education to the postresidency phase, when their major clinical education has been completed. A survey of physician-researchers conducted a few years ago found that the majority thought the postgraduate fellowship period, rather than the residency, was the most appropriate point for research training (7). In fact, this was the period at which research training took place for 87 percent of the respondents.

NIH Intramural Postdoctoral Research Fellowships

Formal research training for physicians today is strongly identified with NIH sponsorship. The legislation that formally established the NIH in 1930, the Ransdell Act, also authorized training as a major NIH responsibility. The NIH has grown to be one of the world's great biomedical research enterprises since its establishment and continues to be a fundamental source of support for research education. Educational activities that take place within an NIH institute and under the direction of an NIH scientist are part of what is called the Intramural Program; those that are funded by NIH but conducted elsewhere—at universities, medical schools, or other research institutions—are part of the Extramural Program.

Currently, there are two separate pathways for pursuing postdoctoral research training within the NIH. One, the Laboratory Research Pathway, is open to anyone with a Ph.D., an M.D., or another professional degree. However, the NIH catalog describing these programs notes that for non-Ph.D.s the degree is often accompanied by some previous laboratory exposure (34). Thus, while it is open to M.D.s, this pathway represents the type of research-intensive postdoctoral experience in which new Ph.D.s typically participate; geared to individuals with strong research education, and serving as an important transition to their independent careers as investigators and faculty members.

The second pathway is the Combined Clinical and Research Pathway and is open only to those with a doctoral degree in medicine or dentistry and generally two or three years of postgraduate clinical training. This involves clinical research and care in the first year and clinical and/or basic research in the second and optional third year. It may also provide credit toward or be sufficient for board certification in a specialty or subspecialty. For physicians who have some research background and wish advanced research training, the NIH Laboratory Research Pathway may be an alternative to a residency, whereas the Combined Clinical and Research Pathway is aimed at those who have finished a residency but have little or no research background. For either pathway, the participant selects from a myriad of laboratories in each of the NIH institutes.

In addition to these major pathways, NIH offers a variety of other postdoctoral research opportunities in areas identified as national needs, including computer applications in biomedical research, biotechnology information, and medical information systems, and in the areas of bioethics and epidemiology.

NIH Extramural Research Training Programs

The extramural programs of the NIH, along with the MSTP, are the major national federal efforts to train physician-scientists. Currently under the authority of the National Research Service Award Act of 1974, NIH postdoctoral research fellowships to individuals and training grants to institutions remain the most significant sources of support for biomedical research education.

Several of the chapters in Part II of this book provide an overview and report of the current status of these programs and cite the relevant literature. Chapter 6 summarizes the findings of the most recent National Research Council-Institute of Medicine committee charged with assessing the national needs and current NIH efforts to produce biomedical research personnel, including postdoctoral programs for physician-scientists. Chapter 7 updates the data that led to the concern a decade ago over the declining number of physician-scientists, providing additional discussion and literature review of NIH programs at the postdoctoral level. The types of research education support offered by NIH are described in Chapter 13.

The October 1989 *Review of the National Institutes of Health Biomedical Research Training Programs* described what its authors, a group of top NIH scientist/administrators, believe to be the optimal structure for postdoctoral research training (35). A key issue is that a minimum of two years of full-time training is required for effective preparation, and up to five years is strongly encouraged. In addition, it is clear that postdoctoral programs are most effective when those who enter them are carefully selected for their desire to pursue research interests rather than to use the fellowship as a means to obtain subspecialty training. In describing the Clinical Investigator Pathway, the American Board of Internal Medicine is careful to distinguish it from subspecialty training. Its "Policies and Procedures" document explicitly states that in addition to the four years of residency training and research in the Clinical Investigator Pathway, at least two additional years of experience are required before a subspecialty examination may be taken (22). This stipulation reflects a growing concern about the best way to fund research education and provide appropriate subspecialty clinical training for clinical investigators (36).

Fellowships from the Private Sector

Another source of support for postdoctoral research training for physicians comes from private-sector organizations, both corporate foundations and health-related not-for-profit agencies. The sponsorship of these programs is varied, but most are geared to particular research areas.

Examples of fellowships from not-for-profit organizations in disease-specific areas include the Physician's Research Training Fellowships of the American Cancer Society and the Research Training Fellowships of the American Lung Association. These fellowships carry stipends in the $20,000–22,000 range and are intended for those just completing the M.D. or residency training. The Leukemia Society of America, the Diabetes Society, the American Heart Association, and the National Kidney Foundation are among the other important sponsors of these types of fellowships.

The Pfizer Postdoctoral Fellowship Program, an example of sponsorship by a private corporate foundation, offers awards of $30,000 for up to three years to M.D.s or D.O.s with three years or less postresidency experience to conduct original clinical or basic research. Only those who have completed residency training are eligible and a minimum of 90 percent or more of the recipient's time must be devoted to research. Pfizer also administers a similar postdoctoral fellowship program in cooperation with the American Geriatrics Society for those committed to an academic career in geriatric medicine or geriatric psychiatry.

The Burroughs Wellcome Fund, like Pfizer and practically all major pharmaceutical company foundations, offers a variety of fellowships to support research and research education at various points of the career path for M.D.s and Ph.D.s, including several for postdoctoral training of one to three years. All these fellowships are administered by nonprofit organizations such as the Epilepsy Foundation of America, the American Society of Hospital Pharmacists Research and Education Foundation, or the Infectious Diseases Society of America for research in areas of their concern.

In 1987, the Howard Hughes Medical Institute initiated a Postdoctoral Research Fellowship to enable physicians who have completed at least two years of clinical training to seek additional research training with a view to becoming independent investigators. This program is geared to training in "fundamental research in the Institute's areas of interest: cell biology and regulation, genetics, immunology, neuroscience, and structural biology." Annual stipends range from $35,000 to $50,000 for up to three years. Similar to the Pfizer program, it requires that no more than 10 percent of a fellow's time be devoted to nonresearch activities. The HHMI now represents a major source of funding for medical research and research education and operates on a greater scale than any previous private-sector activity.

Aside from the HHMI, the role of private sources is relatively small in terms of total funding for biomedical research. However, it has been argued that foundations may be greater risk takers, willing to support research in areas outside the mainstream and those that may be politically controversial (37).

Fellowships from Medical School Departments

Medical school departments may also sponsor postdoctoral educational programs, drawing from a variety of funding sources to develop postdoctoral positions in their disciplines. Frequently the funding for these opportunities is, in fact, an NIH Training Grant, but grants from private foundations, gifts from other private organizations or individuals, and revenues from clinical services are among other sources used to provide postdoctoral training. The Department of Psychiatry at UCLA, for example, offers a one- or two-year fellowship for physicians who have completed their residency or for Ph.D.s to prepare for an academic research career in psychoneuroimmunology. This program is funded by the UCLA Task Force of Psychoneuroimmunology and the Bettingen Foundation (38). Two other fellowships offered by that department are funded by NIMH.

The Minority Medical Faculty Development Program

To encourage physicians who are members of minority groups underrepresented in biomedical research, the Robert Wood Johnson Foundation offers four-year postdoctoral research fellowships to physicians who are African American, Mexican American, Native American, or mainland Puerto Rican and have demonstrated superior academic and clinical skills. The program brochure notes that, at present, only 1,281 of the nation's 40,136 full-time medical faculty members are minorities. Intended for those who are committed to careers in academic medicine and biomedical research, this program provides an annual stipend of up to $50,000 along with a $25,000 annual grant toward the support of research activities. Priority is given to basic research. At the end of 1990, there were thirty active fellows in the Minority Medical Faculty Development Program and approximately ten to fifteen alumni (39).

Fellowships for M.D./Ph.D.s

Merck Sharp & Dohme Research Laboratories, in collaboration with the American Federation for Clinical Research Foundation, established a postdoctoral research training program for M.D./Ph.D. graduates. Up to five awards, renewable for three years, were made available in 1991, each with an annual $40,000 stipend, a $7,000 grant to the recipient's university for research supplies, and a $3,000 allowance for travel, journal subscriptions, and society membership. The aim of this fellowship is independent research in the basic biomedical sciences. Candidates must be accepted into a postdoctoral training program and are expected to devote 80 percent of their time to research (40).

The Merck program was initiated, no doubt, for much the same reasons that residencies geared to M.D./Ph.D. graduates were developed: that is, a recognition of the need to provide appropriate opportunities for further research education for M.D./Ph.D.s following residency training. As M.D./Ph.D.s have already completed a rigorous research education, postdoctoral positions intended to provide beginning research training are inappropriate. Moreover, a one- to two-year training period may be inadequate to produce researchers, as noted in the recent evaluations of NIH postdoctoral programs, but may be ideal for M.D./Ph.D.s who have completed the clinical phases of their education. Such a one-to-two year period provides an important transition back to research and enables the participant to launch a career as a faculty member and independent investigator.

If the attrition rate from the physician-scientist career path is to be minimized, other postdoctoral programs for M.D./Ph.D.s need to be developed. It is notable in this regard that the Markey Charitable Trust Scholar Awards in Biomedical Science, intended to "enhance the scientific development and productivity of recipients planning research careers in biomedical science," offer first-year stipends of $30,000 for Ph.D.s and $35,000 for M.D./Ph.D.s, with no mention of an award for M.D.s. This postdoctoral program also provides an annual research allowance of $15,000. As M.D./Ph.D.s tend to be somewhat older than M.D.s because of their extended programs of formal studies, the higher stipend offered by Markey and by the Merck/AFLRF award may provide an important incentive to keep them on a research-oriented track.

Issues

Postdoctoral programs will continue to be a principal form of primary research education for physicians. However, as Joseph L. Goldstein has noted in 1986: "I do not subscribe to the currently popular notion of a research fellowship that is intermingled with clinical training. Medical scientists must concentrate intensively on science in an uninterrupted fashion during their formative scientific years, and they must be equally intense about medicine during their clinical years." (41) We do not support rigid proscriptions for how any one individual combines research and clinical education, so long as quality is maintained, but recent evidence suggests that participants in postdoctoral research training programs will be more carefully selected in terms of their research commitment and will be expected to participate in longer periods of research than in the past.

The length of typical postdoctoral programs is another issue. In the section on graduate medical education in its 1986 review of medical education, the Association of American Medical Colleges noted: "There is growing recognition that this pattern of training often provides insufficiently thorough or advanced training in modern research techniques." (42) The Physician Scientist Award established by NIH, offering M.D.s support for five years of intensive postdoctoral training in research, is a further acknowledgment that a significant period of education is required to produce outstanding physician-scientists.

Nevertheless, despite efforts to improve selection and support, it may be, as former NIH director James Shannon observed, that postdoctoral training is offered too long after initial fundamental science education to be an effective way of recruiting an adequate supply of physician-scientists. Others have noted that the traditional mode of teaching science in medical schools may even decrease rather than increase the development of interest in research. We would add that, because postdoctoral programs follow clinical education in residency programs, they may be too close to the point at which young physicians are prepared to engage in clinical practice. The gratification of using one's clinical education and skills, not to mention the temptation of the marketplace, no doubt has great allure and makes programs that offer beginning research training at this point less attractive.

Fellowship Programs in Policy Related Areas

Clearly, the thrust of the education of physician-scholars has been in areas of biomedical sciences and, increasingly, molecular-level research. Without diminishing the importance and urgency of continued work in these areas, it must be noted that opportunities for acquiring expertise in the political and socioeconomic areas has not kept pace, even with growing concern for the way health services are delivered in the United States. We have pointed out that some M.D./Ph.D. programs offer degree combinations in social science and the humanities and that at least one research-oriented residency program enables young physicians to pursue studies in such fields. Similarly, some important programs for the postresidency or midcareer phase of a physician's career provide opportunities for formal education in fields broadly related to health care policy. Because of the paucity of these opportunities, however, they merit special attention here.

The Robert Wood Johnson Clinical Scholars Program

The Clinical Scholars Program, sponsored by the Robert Wood Johnson Foundation was established in 1969 with the aim of providing health care professionals with an educational background that would prepare them to identify creative solutions to problems in the health care system. The program emerged from general discussions at a number of medical education conferences in the 1960s and specific discussions among a small group of prominent academic physicians. It was agreed that the usual education of physicians did not adequately prepare them to take a leadership role in solving organizational level problems in the delivery of health care in contemporary society. With funding from the Carnegie Corporation of New York and the Commonwealth Fund, five institutions initiated programs designed to help young internists acquire competence in one or more of the disciplines essential to create a more effective medical care system. In 1972, the Robert Wood Johnson Foundation took over support of the program, and in 1978, recognizing the potential value of recruiting physicians with training outside the conventional biomedical curriculum, the Department of Veterans Affairs became a cosponsor, providing support for twelve of the fifty-two scholars (43).

Currently the program has seven training sites (UCLA; UCSF; Stanford; the Universities of North Carolina, Pennsylvania, and Washington; and Yale) and through a national competition admits twenty students per year for a two-year program. The educational programs are individualized but tend to concentrate on coursework and seminars and encourage the study of nonbiological aspects of socially important medical problems. Scholars are expected but not required to complete graduate-level research in their priority areas. Some of the priority areas that have recently been identified include care for America's vulnerable populations, leadership in maintaining the quality of medical care, chronic disease epidemiology and management, sociocultural and historical studies of health care, and the economics of health care systems. As of 1989, 524 scholars had completed the program and 50 were participating. The aims of the program continue to be education for leadership and scholarship in the academic health community (44).

The Robert Wood Johnson Health Policy Fellowship Program

The Robert Wood Johnson Health Policy Fellowships Program was established in 1973 to enable the faculty of health professional schools to participate in federal health policy processes. The goal is to "extend the public policy horizons of health professions schools and to improve the capabilities of their faculty members to study health policy and assume appropriate leadership roles in health activities at all levels." (45) Each medical school is allowed to nominate one candidate annually, and six fellows are selected by an advisory committee. Most fellows have been M.D.s, although a number of other health professionals have been selected for the program, including those with a primary background in nursing, health services research, dentistry, and veterinary medicine.

The program is administered by the Institute of Medicine, and its activities and participants' responsibilities are carried out in Washington, D.C. The first four months provide an introduction to the processes, institutions, and key individuals who dominate the health care policy-making process at the federal and other levels. Fellows are offered special seminars and presentations during this period and have opportunities to meet as a group with many of the leading figures in the field. The balance of the year is spent in active participation on the staff of a member of the House or Senate, or of a congressional committee. Although this experience emphasizes matters related to health care, the fellows are often involved in a wider range of congressional activities (46). The fellows are expected to return to academic medicine at the end of the year and serve as key sources of knowledge for their institutions in regard to the political processes affecting the health care system.

The Pew Health Policy Program

In 1982, the Pew Charitable Trusts established a program at four sites "to enable current and future leaders in health care to expand their knowledge of relevant policy issues and the policy making process." (47) Unlike the two Robert Wood Johnson programs, the Pew program is not aimed specifically at physicians or other health care professionals, but it is nevertheless appropriate for physicians who are at either the postdoctoral or the midcareer point and wish to engage in the formal study of health policy and the disciplines that bear upon policy-making. The training programs are conducted at four sites, two of which involve cooperation between two institutions: Boston University/Brandeis University, the University of California at San Francisco, the University of Michigan, and the RAND Corporation/University of California at Los Angeles. Each of the four programs is structured differently, ranging from rather traditional studies toward a Ph.D., to Ph.D. studies while continuing regular employment in a health-related profession, to one-year intensive study in courses on health policy analysis. The Institute of Medicine directs the convening and publication activities of the Pew Health Policy Program, and it administers a Career Development Fund that enables recent graduates of one of the programs to make the transition from academic study to health policy careers (48).

As of 1990, there were 50 participants in the four Pew Health Policy Programs, 5 of whom were M.D.s, and there were 132 alumni, 17 of whom were M.D.s (49). Thus, physicians represent 12 percent of those being trained for scholarship and leadership in the health care system by the Pew Health Policy Programs. The stipends or other support available are likely to make these programs less attractive to physicians than other programs described in this section.

The Kaiser Faculty Scholar Award

In the early 1980s, the Henry J. Kaiser Family Foundation established a Faculty Scholar Program in General Internal Medicine to address problems identified in the status of academic general internal medicine, particularly those generated by the increasing dependency of academic medical centers on income from faculty practice, by providing support for research activities during the "critical first five years of faculty appointment." (50) In order to target internists already on pathways of leadership and scholarship, the program required applicants to complete residency training in general internal medicine and fellowship, master's, or doctoral training in a field related to the scholar's mission. Each medical school was invited to nominate one candidate each year for an award of $60,000 per year, initially for three years but renewable for another two. Up to $40,000 per year of the faculty member's salary could be met by the award as well as any reasonable expense directly related to the recipient's scholarship. Recipients were to have at least 50 percent of their time protected for research.

Between 1981 and 1990, thirty-five physicians were admitted to the Henry J. Kaiser Family Foundation Faculty Scholar Program. Its 1990 announcement notes that preference was given to those proposing scholarly work in the areas of health promotion and disease prevention; patient functioning as a major indicator of quality and outcome of care; biopsychological concepts of health, illness, disease, and response to treatment; or ethnics and humanism in medicine (51). The authors of a review of the program completed in August 1990 called upon the field of internal medicine, and in particular the Association of Professors of Medicine, whose members chair departments of medicine at academic medical centers, to take the lead in addressing the important social issues facing medicine and to support its faculty in such efforts. The review also outlines the issues the program sought to address and the positive outcomes of its support for thirty-five scholars (50). Nevertheless, the program has been discontinued as the foundation redefined its priorities.

Other Postresidency Fellowships

Another means of educating physician-scholars and leaders in social science or the humanities is through postresidency fellowship programs. These fellowships are often aimed at physicians trained in general internal medicine, and some are degree programs leading to an M.S., M.P.H., or Ph.D. Such programs are offered, for example, by the Harvard School of Public Health (Post Doctoral Fellowships in Health Services Research), the University of Wisconsin (Fellowship in General Internal Medicine with tracks in clinical epidemiology, clinical ethics, etc.), the George Washington University (Academic Primary Care Internal Medicine Fellowship in the Department of Health Care Sciences), and the previously mentioned physician-investigator tracks at Brown/Rhode Island Hospital and the University of Illinois College of Medicine at Urbana-Champaign. These programs share a recognition of the need for physician-scholars who can provide new knowledge in fields such as health services research or medical ethics and who can bring the perspective of the clinician to bear on a search for the most effective responses to current problems and issues facing the health care system. Interest in developing programs in these areas seems to be rising. An increased emphasis on this approach at several schools of public health has been noted, and at least one major new program in this area has been established at Dartmouth.

That socioeconomic issues are germane to medical practice and the health care system is hardly a controversial matter. Federal funding of health services research, for example, has increased significantly in recent years in recognition of the growing importance of outcomes research, cost-benefit analysis, and other approaches to understanding the socioeconomic factors in health (52). Nevertheless, a recent survey of chief residents in internal medicine found residency programs sorely lacking in areas of instruction that respondents themselves consider high priorities, such as patient-physician communication, medical ethics, health care law (53). The current paucity of programs to prepare physicians as scholars in such areas means there will be too few agents of change in medical education. This in turn bodes ill for the prospect of adapting medical school curricula or residency training programs to reflect the realities of health care at the close of the twentieth century! (This topic is considered further in Chapter 9.)

Issues

The programs described in this section have some obvious advantages. First, they reach an important group of physicians that might not otherwise have as good a preparation for scholarly and/or leadership careers. Another, especially attractive, aspect of these programs is that they are aimed at areas in which trained personnel are greatly needed, but for which there are few other organized pathways to prepare physicians. They also present unusually good opportunities for physicians to interact with nonphysicians who have extensive and pertinent expertise that bears on medicine. Many participants in these programs have had opportunities to meet influential figures in the health policy process, including key individuals outside the academic health care system. Another important aspect of these programs is their availability to physicians who have already taken some major career steps and indeed may be at midcareer; such individuals may have especially useful perspectives because of their experience. And, finally, with the exception perhaps of the Pew program, the level of the stipends in these programs is sufficient to recruit outstanding individuals, allowing physicians to participate without significant financial sacrifice.

On the other hand, these programs have some potential drawbacks. The amount of time in some of the programs is clearly not adequate to allow most individuals without prior preparation in research to become competent independent researchers, yet they may be expected to have such capabilities. Some programs may be most appropriate to provide further preparation for those who have had rigorous previous education or to help physicians be effective collaborators in research programs directed by colleagues with greater research training. In response to such concerns, as we noted previously, the Kaiser Award requires nominees to have completed training in their proposed subject in addition to a residency in internal medicine. (Participation as a Robert Wood Johnson Clinical Scholar is cited as an example of such training.)

Another problem is that graduates of these programs may find it difficult to use their new capabilities because they fall outside the realm of traditional medical practice. Also, the graduate's new qualifications may encroach on areas that are considered the domain of others, including higher administrators. Program graduates may thus become "overqualified" for their previous positions and not find appropriate opportunities at their former institutions. If they then find a position that enables them to make contributions consistent with the goals of the program in which they participated, however, it would be appropriate to evaluate them as a program success.

Despite these potential drawbacks, the overwhelming problem that exists is the paucity of opportunities to participate in such programs. The demise or potential demise of the few existing programs makes the situation even more dismal for those concerned with providing physician-leaders to deal with questions that impinge so directly and critically upon health care delivery.

Clinical Education for Ph.D.s

Another creative response to the shortage of clinical investigators is to teach the clinical aspects of human disease to researchers trained in Ph.D. programs. Two programs with this goal are considered in later chapters of this book. In Chapter 11, Irwin Arias describes a program at Tufts University School of Medicine in which a course in pathobiology is taught to graduate students in the basic science departments of the school. William M. Awad, Jr., discusses the experiences of the M.D.-to-Ph.D. Program at the University of Miami School of Medicine in Chapter 12, a program, now discontinued, that enabled Ph.D. graduates to complete M.D. education in an intensive two-year curriculum.

A newer effort has been initiated at the University of Illinois College of Medicine at Urbana-Champaign. A Medical Scholars Program Fellow status has been established for individuals who have previously earned the M.D. or the Ph.D. and are pursuing the second degree in order to prepare for a career in academic medicine and research. The fellows are formally affiliated with the M.D./Ph.D. program at this medical school and thus included in all its academic and nonacademic activities. Those with the Ph.D. are expected to remain involved in research on a part-time basis while in medical school in order to maintain their interest and skills and stay abreast of scientific developments. Similarly, M.D.s pursuing a Ph.D. will carry out some clinical responsibilities either in teaching or patient care in order to maintain their knowledge and skills. The purpose is to provide a supportive environment for pursuing the second degree that enhances the educational experience and increases the probability that participants will pursue careers as physician-scientists. It is believed that other medical schools with large M.D./Ph.D. programs and significant opportunities for research could easily initiate a similar program and that a pool of prospective participants does indeed exist.

Support for Research Early in the Careers of Physician-Scholars

Physician-scientists may face considerable difficulties in making the transition to independent investigation. As noted in the 1980 Report of the Ad Hoc Committee on Clinical Research Training, "It is during the first five or so years of faculty experience that many well trained clinical investigators are lost. Problems at this level include difficulties in obtaining funding for independent research, the paperwork and restrictions that continue to increase related to grant applications, and compliance with a variety of regulations." (18) Such hurdles face all researchers, but the "lure" of clinical medicine adds to the difficulties that physician-scientists face in getting established. Moreover, some have been immersed in clinical training and may perceive, correctly or not, that they have lost significant ground in their research area. The Kaiser program, which provided support for the beginning years of a faculty appointment, was one of the few programs of its kind to place a strong emphasis on physician-scientist research in the social and behavioral sciences. As we mentioned earlier, however, it has been discontinued. A number of other such programs exist for academic physicians, especially those engaged in biomedical research, in the early stage of their careers. Physician-scientists have valuable clinical skills for which there is great demand and significant incentive to enter the marketplace. Even the institutions most likely to provide supportive settings for clinical investigators—academic medical centers—have become highly responsive to the marketplace, often placing great pressure on faculty to devote time to medical service, sometimes at the expense of research.

A graduate of an M.D./Ph.D. program recently pointed out that there is inadequate support at the completion of clinical training for M.D./Ph.D.s to resume research career development (54). Having completed three to five years of clinical training in a specialty and perhaps a subspecialty, most M.D./Ph.D.s are "out of synchrony with Ph.D. scientists who have not had a research hiatus for clinical training, making it difficult to initially compete with Ph.D.s who have completed traditional Ph.D. postdoctoral fellowships." Thus, the need for mechanisms to support research by physician-investigators at that crucial early stage is particularly acute for M.D./Ph.D.s.

NIH supports the major programs aimed at enabling newly trained biomedical scientists to launch careers as independent investigators. The NIH New Investigator Awards (sometimes called Young Investigator Awards) require the recipient to have had at least two years of research training and to be beginning independent research. This program is open to M.D.s, Ph.D.s, and M.D./Ph.D.s. There are also some private sources of funding for such programs. For example, one new investigator program sponsored by a private foundation is the Scholar Awards in Biomedical Science established in 1984 by the Lucille P. Markey Charitable Trust to "enhance the scientific development and productivity of outstanding young men and women planning research careers...by providing substantial support in the advanced postdoctoral years and the first five years of faculty service." (55) Eight awards are made annually to Ph.D.s and another eight to M.D.s or M.D./Ph.D.s. A stipend is awarded as well as research funding for up to five years. Obviously, the recipient is expected by this point to be launched on a career that makes her or him competitive for NIH funding.

Organizations dedicated to research, education, and treatment of specific diseases also have programs aimed at encouraging young physician-investigators. The American Lung Association, for example, provides a Scholar Award to physicians who have completed graduate training in pulmonary disease and are beginning a faculty track in a school of medicine. Corporate foundations, especially those of pharmaceutical firms, are another source of support for physician-scientists at the early stage of their careers. Pfizer Pharmaceuticals, Burroughs Wellcome, and Merck are among the larger such foundations offering research support specifically designed to help launch new investigators on their careers.

Issues

These types of programs fulfill an important and obvious need, but there are too few of them and many provide noncompetitive stipends. As long as a significant number of physicians educated as researchers opt for full-time clinical practice, the opportunities for research support at the critical early stage of their careers are clearly inadequate. The same can be inferred even if a large proportion of such physician-scientists are on the faculty of academic medical centers but are not devoting a significant share of their professional time to research.

The Role of Overall Research Funding

For those concerned about educating scholars and researchers, the overall level and stability of funding for medical and health care research is of direct importance in two ways. First, a significant share of the cost of research education is borne by grants to individual investigators, including funding for postdoctoral fellows and graduate assistants pursuing Ph.D.s: thus, the overall funding of biomedical and other relevant research has important and direct effects on the level of support and the kinds of opportunities available for educating physician-scholars as well as research trainees with other types of degrees.

The overall level and stability of research funding also affects the education of physician-scholars in the areas of recruitment and retention. Obviously, careers for which support is uncertain are going to be less attractive than those for which there is a fairly clear and steady demand. If research funding is, or even appears to be, increasingly competitive, it will be difficult to induce bright people thinking of careers in medicine to consider investing considerable time and other resources in research training. In addition, reductions in research funding may lead to a loss of researchers. Even those educated and experienced in the enterprise can become discouraged enough to turn to other opportunities, especially those educated as M.D.s for whom the potentially very rewarding option of clinical practice is available. Another issue related to the problem of insecure research funding is the need to provide medical schools with incentives to hire new physician-scientists in the face of increasing dependence on practice revenue (56).

In short, those concerned with preparing the next generation of physician-scholars must also be concerned with the kind of world that awaits these future leaders. Will it fully exploit their talents? It is not surprising, and perhaps encouraging, that organizations involved in supporting medical education, such as the Association of American Medical Colleges and the Pew Charitable Trusts (which is also significantly involved in funding biomedical research), devote considerable attention to the issue of research funding (42, 57, 58).

Conclusion

As this two-chapter review of the current status of efforts to educate physicians for scholarship and leadership illustrates, there are multiple points of entry to these careers. Moreover, at each stage of career development there are a variety of types of programs to encourage, recruit, educate, and/or retain physician-scientists. Although some still advocate one type of approach or another, it is likely that in this field a sound investment in human resources will require a diverse portfolio. Such diversity appears to characterize the present course, and until rigorous evaluation of existing efforts points to a sure-fire option, it is likely to be the wisest approach (59–62). Nevertheless, in some areas, notably the social sciences and humanities, programs to train physicians in scholarly research are not adequate to respond to the needs created by the scientific and social forces influencing medicine and the health care system. Moreover, all types of existing programs lack the necessary resources to respond adequately to the pool of potential applicants and support current students and trainees. The recruitment and retention problems that administrators of current programs face as a result of these and other issues are considered in Chapter 5.

References

1. National Institute of General Medical Science, "The National Institutes of Health Medical Scientist Program" (NIGMS Internal Report, unpublished, May 1980).
2. Gerald F. DiBona, "Whence Cometh Tomorrow's Clinical Investigator?" *Clinical Research* 27 (1979): 253–56.
3. James B. Wyngaarden, "Encouraging Young Physicians to Pursue a Career in Clinical Research," *Clinical Research* 31 (April 1983): 115–18.
4. Wayne K. Davis and William N. Kelley, "Factors Influencing Decisions to Enter Careers in Clinical Investigation," *Journal of Medical Education* 57 (April 1982): 275–81.
5. Mark G. Haviland, Harold Alan Pincus, and Thomas H. Dial, "Career, Research Involvement, and Research Fellowship Plans of Potential Psychiatrists," *Archives of General Psychiatry* 44 (May 1987): 493–96.
6. Michael O'Brecht and Pierre Bois, "Characteristics of Active and Less Active Researchers in a Group of Canadian Health Professionals," *Journal of Medical Education* 63 (June 1988): 327–29.
7. Lawrence Neinstein and Richard G. Mackenzie, "Prior Training and Recommendations for Future Training of Clinical Research Faculty Members," *Academic Medicine* 64: (Jan. 1989): 32–35.
8. John P. Kemph, William Sodeman, J. Russell Claybrook, and Coleen

Rand, "A Follow Up of a Program to Foster Medical Students' Interest in Research and Academic Careers," *Academic Medicine* 66 (Jan. 1991): 122.

9. Frederich L. Brancati, Lucy A. Mead, David Martin, Simeon Margolis, Michael J. Klag, "Early Predictors of Career Achievement in Academic Medicine," *Journal of the American Medical Association* 267 (March 1992): 1372–76.
10. Bowman Gray School of Medicine brochure (1989).
11. Association of American Medical Colleges, "AAMC Curriculum Directory, 1989–90" (Washington, D.C.: 1989).
12. D. G. Eaton and Y. H. Thong, "The Bachelor of Medical Science Research Degree as a Start for Clinician–Scientists," *Medical Education* 19 (1985): 445–51.
13. Alpha Omega Alpha Honor Medical Society, "Announcement," 525 Middlefield Road, Suite 130, Menlo Park, California 94025.
14. William Hope, Arvind Nana, Cathy Newman, Joel T. Patterson, and Donald Pizzo, co–directors, "32nd Annual National Student Research Forum," Abstract Packet, University of Texas Medical Branch, Galveston, Texas, April 11–13, 1991.
15. Howard Hughes Medical Institute, "Howard Hughes Medical Institute National Institutes of Health Research Scholars Program 1991–92," 1990.
16. U.S. Department of Health and Human Services, Public Health Services, National Institutes of Health, "Clinical Electives for Medical and Dental Students at the National Institutes of Health: 1990–91 Catalog."
17. National Institutes of Health, "Availability of Short Term Research Training Positions on Institutional National Research Service Awards for Students in Health Professional Degree Programs," *NIH Guide* 21 (March 1992).
18. Association of American Medical Colleges, "Clinical Research Manpower: The Report of the Ad Hoc Committee on Clinical Research Training," (Washington, D.C.: February 1980).
19. Lee Goldman, Steven Shea, Marshall Wolf, and Eugene Braunwald, "Clinical and Research Training in Parallel: The Internal Medicine Research Residency Track at the Brigham and Women's Hospital," *Clinical Research* 34 (1986): 2–5.
20. Hal Burstein, "Perspectives on Research Residencies," Fall 1990 Newsletter, Harvard Medical School M.D.–Ph.D. Program, 1(2).
21. Gerald S. Levey, Denis C. Lehotay, and Marcus Dugas, "The Development of a Physician-Investigator Training Program," *The New England Journal of Medicine* 305 (1981): 887–89.
22. American Board of Internal Medicine, "Policies and Procedures," July 1988, and Policy Adapted by the Board of Governors, February 13, 1990.
23. Muriel Horne, April 17, 1989; and Susan C. Day, M.D., January 17, 1991, private correspondence.
24. University of Illinois College of Medicine at Urbana-Champaign—Residency in Internal Medicine. "The Advantage In: Academic Excellence, Lifestyle, Clinical Experiences, Professional Opportunity," (June

1988, descriptive brochure).

25. James H. Meador-Woodruff and John F. Greden, "Clinician-Researchers in Psychiatry," *American Journal of Psychiatry* 144 (April 1987): 4.
26. Anthony J. Windebank, Chairman, Clinician-Investigator Training Program, Mayo Graduate School of Medicine, Correspondence, September 4, 1990.
27. Donald C. Walsh, Associate Dean for Curricular Affairs, University of California, Davis, School of Medicine, Correspondence, October 24, 1989.
28. Steven A. Wartman, Program Director, Residency in Internal Medicine, Rhode Island Hospital, Correspondence, September 12, 1990.
29. Correspondence and announcements from schools cited.
30. Joel Shenker, ed., "Doctor/Doctor: A Newsletter for Dual-Degree Approaches to Medicine," University of Illinois College of Medicine at Urbana-Champaign.
31. Wayne Pan and Kurt Hirschhorn, "Research 'Fast Track' Residency Survey," (NYC M.D./Ph.D. Student Forum, Mt. Sinai School of Medicine of the City University of New York, Summer 1990, unpublished).
32. Francis D. Moore, "Surgery in Academe: The Myth and the Reality: A Study in the Contrasts Between Academic Medicine and Academic Surgery," *Bulletin of New York Academic Medicine* 57 (July–August 1981).
33. J. D. Burke, Jr., H. A. Pincus, and H. Pardes, "The Clinician-Researcher in Psychiatry," *American Journal of Psychiatry* 143 (1986): 968–75.
34. National Institutes of Health, "Postdoctoral Research Fellowship Opportunities at the National Institutes of Health, Catalog: 1990–91" (draft).
35. National Institutes of Health, *Review of the NIH Biomedical Research Training Programs* (Bethesda, Md.: October 1989).
36. David G. Nathan, "Sounding Board: Funding Subspecialty Training for Clinical Investigators," *The New England Journal of Medicine* 16 (April 1987): 1020–22.
37. Zoe E. Boniface and Rebecca W. Rimel, "U.S. Funding for Biomedical Research," (Philadelphia, The Pew Charitable Trusts, 1987).
38. Department of Psychiatry, University of California, Los Angeles, "A Fellowship Training Program in the Psychobiology of the Major Psychiatric & Psychosomatic Disorders" (Undated descriptive material received December 1989).
39. Robert Wood Johnson Foundation, "Call for Applications: Minority Medical Faculty Development Program, 1990."
40. Jean M. Haddock, Executive Director, American Federation for Clinical Research Foundation, Correspondence, August 1990.
41. Joseph L. Goldstein, "On the Origin and Prevention of PAIDS (Paralyzed Academic Investigator's Disease Syndrome)," *Journal of Clinical Investigations* 78 (Sept. 1986): 848–54.
42. Association of American Medical Colleges, "Medical Education: Institutions, Characteristics and Programs—A Background Paper" (Washington, D.C., September 1986).

43. Annie Lea Shuster et al., "An Innovation in Physician Training: The Clinical Scholars Program," *Journal of Medical Education* 58 (1983).
44. Robert Wood Johnson Foundation, "Clinical Scholars Program" (Princeton, N.J., June 1990).
45. Richard L. Seggel, "Staff Evaluation Report on the Robert Wood Johnson Health Policy Fellowships Program" (March 1987).
46. Charles M. Helms, Richard E. Rieselbach, and Myron Genel, "The Robert Wood Johnson Health Policy Fellowship: The Experience and Perspectives on Its Academic Applications," *Journal of the American Medical Association* 260 (Sept. 1988).
47. The Pew Charitable Trusts, "The Pew Health Policy Program" (Spring 1988).
48. William C. Richardson, "Report to the Pew Charitable Trusts on the Pew Health Policy Program" (January 1990).
49. The Pew Charitable Trusts, "The Pew Health Policy Program: Directory of Fellows and Alumni" (1990).
50. Richard J. Reitemeier, "Review of Kaiser Family Foundation Faculty Scholars Program in General Internal Medicine" (August 1990).
51. Robert G. Petersdorf, President, Association of American Medical Colleges (Announcement, 1990).
52. Association for Health Services Research, "NCHSR's Budget Grows 50 Percent, HCFA Also Gets an Increase: Outcomes Research Funding Jumps to $32 Million," *HSR Reports* (Oct. 1989): 1, 23.
53. Peter G. Tuteur, "Resident Forum: Resident Physician Section: Internal Medicine Chief Residents Want Changes in Education," *Journal of the American Medical Association* 264 (July 1990): 175.
54. Janet H. Prystowsky, "The Attraction of MD-PhDs to Dermatology," *Dermatology* 125 (June 1989): 845–46 (Correspondence).
55. Lucille P. Markey Charitable Trust, "Lucille P. Markey Scholar Awards in Biomedical Science" (1991).
56. Matthew A. Movsesian, "Effect on Physician-Scientists of the Low Funding Rate of NIH Grant Applications," *The New England Journal of Medicine* 322 (May 1990).
57. Association of American Medical Colleges, "Federal Policy for Biomedical and Behavioral Research" (April 10, 1986).
58. Zoe E. Boniface and Rebecca W. Rimel, *U.S. Funding for Biomedical Research: A Report Prepared for the Pew Charitable Trusts* (Philadelphia: 1987).
59. Robert J. Levine, "Occasional Notes. The Future of Clinical Research," *The New England Journal of Medicine* 23 (Dec. 1979): 1295–96.
60. John N. Forrest, "The Decline in the Training of Clinical Investigators: Data and Proposals from the 1970s," *Clinical Research* 28 (1980): 246–47.
61. J. W. Littlefield, "On the Difficulty of Combining Basic Research and Patient Care," *American Journal of Human Genetics* 36 (1984): 731–35.
62. Bruce Hillman, "The Inadequacy in the Number and Quality of Physician Researchers: A Perspective and Approach to the Problem," *Investigative Radiology* 20 (Nov. 1985): 767–71.

5

Program Management and Career Development

Harold M. Swartz and Diane L. Gottheil

- Types of Programs
- Recruitment
- Selection
- Funding
- Retention
- Academic and Personal Advising of Students
- Selecting a Field and Choosing a Mentor
- Advising on Personal Matters and Life Style
- The Placement of Graduates
- Conclusion

Types of Programs

We have seen in the preceding chapters that over the past few decades a dramatic shift has occurred in the ways that physician-scholars are developed. Most medical schools now have formal programs to educate M.D./Ph.D.s; programs to provide a thorough research education for young physicians during or after residencies have proliferated; and public and private sources of financial support to prepare young physicians for research careers have increased. Given these well-established trends, what does the future hold in regard to the types of programs likely to develop physician-scholars?

Although NIH postresidency fellowships continue to fund most of the formal research preparation for academic physicians, they have not undergone any extensive changes in the past few decades. As discussed in Chapter 13, however, such programs are now being examined much more critically in an attempt to improve their effectiveness. It is likely, as a result, that these programs will produce more well-prepared physician-scholars, even though the absolute number of individuals acquiring research education through this mechanism may decrease as other opportunities become available.

It is more difficult to predict the future role of programs such as the NIH clinical subspecialty training grants, which currently provide physicians with modest research capabilities, because the role of these programs will depend on the structure of clinical faculties in the future. If the current standard is retained (i.e., virtually all clinical faculty are expected to have some research credentials and participate in research), there is likely to be a continuing need for programs that give at least some preparation for research. If, on the other hand, clinical faculty are expected to focus *either* on research that meets rigorous standards *or* on clinical activities, it is likely that fewer physicians will enter the less-structured and/or shorter research programs for clinicians, opting either for a more formal program or for further clinical training (and no research training). Although the graduates of more rigorous or formal research training programs such as M.D./Ph.D. programs do not yet account for the majority of new faculty members in academic medicine or in other leading positions in the health care system, they are likely to constitute a significant and disproportionate share of future leaders in the field. Concomitant with the development of formal programs has been a gradual recognition of ways in which such programs can increase their effectiveness in preparing physician-scholars and an increased awareness of problems likely to occur in most programs. In the balance of this chapter, we describe some key issues associated with the administration of both formal programs to prepare physician-scholars, and programs that attempt to provide research education to physicians during or after residencies. We consider "nuts and bolts" issues of importance to students and administrators as well as general organizational issues. In most sections we consider M.D./Ph.D. programs first because these programs are more uniform than post-M.D. research training programs but many of the principles of the former apply to the latter.

Recruitment

As programs have proliferated and expanded, the recruitment of eligible applicants has become increasingly important, and consequently almost all programs—even those with the most established and prestigious reputations—engage in significant recruitment efforts. It is not clear whether this is because there are too few highly qualified potential participants or because, although there is an adequate pool, the best-qualified students apply to several (or many) of the most competitive programs and thereby create the illusion that the schools they do not choose are having a low success rate in attracting some of the best students. The latter seems to be the case for the medical schools with MSTPs; the directors of these programs report that they succeed in enrolling a relatively small percentage of the students that they select as their top candidates although the number of applicants remains high. An obvious but unproven explanation is that most of the programs identify the same subset of applicants as the leading candidates.

Recruitment in Combined Degree Programs

To characterize the applicant pool to which we refer, it may be useful to consider a profile of the typical candidate for an M.D./Ph.D. program. This profile is based upon our impressions after interviewing approximately 500 applicants; it should be supplemented with the more systematically collected evidence in Chapter 13. Although this profile has been drawn from experiences with applicants to M.D./Ph.D. programs, it should apply to a considerable extent to applicants in other pathways. The typical candidate is a student in an undergraduate school who has planned for some time to go to medical school. The student may or may not be a declared "premedical student"; some schools do not have this option as a major, and some students choose to acquire a more diverse academic background than they perceive the premedical track will provide. Other popular undergraduate majors are biology and chemistry; less often candidates are declared majors in disciplines within engineering, the humanities, or the social sciences. In any case, knowing that almost all medical schools require the Medical College Admission Test (MCAT) and certain courses, all applicants will have taken basic and some more advanced undergraduate courses in biology, chemistry, physics, and mathematics.

The typical candidate became involved in research as an undergraduate, often as an honors project, sometimes as a requirement, and sometimes on the advice that such experience is looked upon favorably by medical school admission committees, as noted earlier. Whatever the reason for initial involvement—and usually the motivation springs from a simple and genuine intellectual interest in science, often reinforced by a faculty role model or advisor—for those candidates that eventually enter research training programs—interest in research is sparked or heightened by the experience.

Often, however, especially in the case of students who enter into research training pathways some time after graduating from medical school, the decision to pursue such a course occurs only after experiencing clinical medicine. The movement from clinical medicine may occur either because of the opportunities in academic medicine perceived by students who also are very satisfied by clinical medicine, or because of a dissatisfaction with the intellectual challenge of clinical medicine. These clearly are quite different motivations which result in the same type of choice and it is very desirable for administrators to take the time and effort to understand the basis of the choice for each of the students in post-M.D. research training programs. Both are valid bases for making the decision but the needs and perspectives of the students may be quite different.

Some applicants, albeit less typical ones, decide as undergraduates upon research or academic careers in the life sciences but then participate in medically related research (sometimes not until they actually begin graduate study) and recognize the value of the knowledge, clinical insights, and/or access to patients that M.D. education will provide. Applicants who were engineering majors, in particular, frequently cite their wish to become involved in biomedical engineering research as physician-scientists because, in contrast to most engineering research, it means involvement with people. Some basic science researchers pursue a medical school education because they want an opportunity to see direct, beneficial results of their research. Applicants to M.D./Ph.D. programs in the humanities or social sciences typically planned to become physicians but selected their major because of a strong interest developed from their high school courses, family background, or college classes, and/or because of the ethos of the undergraduate school. Another characteristic typical of those in the social sciences, humanities, or law is a strong concern for issues of equity in and access to health care and the wish to be involved in seeking solutions to current problems of the health care system. Increasingly, recent graduates of medical school or residencies, stimulated by the problems and/or opportunities that they see in the health care system, decide to return to formal study to become more expert in health services research with the goal of improving what is obviously an imperfect system. Applicants in the biomedical sciences express an equivalent desire to find new knowledge leading to the prevention or improved treatment of disease. Such deep and admirable motives are perhaps essential if an entering student is to have the mettle to make it through the challenges ahead.

A number of factors enter into an applicant's decision process. For students who enter M.D./Ph.D. programs, especially for those in programs without MSTP support, an important factor in recruitment success is the degree of interest that the program faculty and staff exhibit toward their current students. Interactions by applicants with students already enrolled in the program are important in recruitment, and some program directors believe that it is a major factor in determining which offer an applicant accepts. Both the amount and the security of funding for students are very important considerations and may be deciding factors in a students' decision to accept an offer of admission. Some schools whose combined degree programs are in the early stages of development attempt to compete for qualified applicants by offering higher stipends to a few. As reported in Chapter 3, the sources of funds for programs not supported by the MSTP vary, but often the combined degree program is considered a high enough priority for the institution that institutional funds, especially funds derived from clinical practice income, are made available to attract M.D./Ph.D. students.

Other factors that may have a positive role in recruitment include the institutional commitment to the program (Do the applicants perceive that it is a high priority of the school?); the degree of organization of the program (Is there a staff, a seminar series, or other program activities?); and the enrollment size (Is it sufficient to provide a real peer group?). These factors are important indicators of the program's academic and psychological support system, a feature that is particularly important to those in a long and demanding program of studies such as an M.D./Ph.D. program or a research-oriented residency program.

The perceived quality of the faculty seems to be another important factor in recruitment success, but it is not always clear that applicants have sufficient information to make accurate judgments in this regard. Some have excellent guidance from faculty and advisors at their undergraduate institution. Those already engaged in research are especially likely to have mentors who can tell them where the excellent research is being conducted in the fields in which they are interested.

For some applicants, the nature of the research problems they can address in the program may be crucial, but many students enter M.D./Ph.D. programs without having very definite ideas on the subject or even the field that they wish to pursue. The authors advise applicants and students that their primary goal should be to get an excellent research education; the topic of research is less important. Although a suitable topic is important for sustaining interest and motivation, many researchers shift the areas of their research as they move along in their educational or career paths. Even applicants to research-oriented residencies, including those with prior research training, may not know what kind of research they will engage in and will not necessarily be recruited because a particular subject is being explored by a faculty member associated with a particular program. For some M.D./Ph.D. graduates, for example, beginning a residency signals a time to shift to more clinically relevant research; the topic is sparked by clinical experience at some point during their training program.

Students already enrolled in medical school make up another pool of potential recruits to combined degree programs. Some medical students may not have been aware that combined degree programs were available or were not willing to make a commitment to such a career path before entering medical school. As discussed in previous chapters, research opportunities during medical school are considered an excellent means of arousing interest in research careers. Students may then enter academic paths through a combined degree program or obtain their research preparation during or after a residency.

The recruitment of students with interests outside the usual core of biomedical disciplines can be quite different in some respects. Two principal factors for successful recruitment in these areas appear to be 1) the ability to make such opportunities known to the appropriate pool of applicants and 2) the ability to have the graduate departments see the prospective students as desirable additions to their graduate programs. Opportunities for students to earn such nontraditional combined degrees are limited because most medical schools have few if any formal programs outside the core biomedical disciplines. Even if the school permits a wider choice of graduate fields, as is often the case, the lack of precedent makes the task of the first few students difficult, and applicants often recognize this. Recruitment into the nontraditional fields also suffers from a lack of role models, so even if the educational program seems to be well organized and the faculty are enthusiastic, the lack of a clear career path at the end of the educational program has, in our experience, led some well-qualified applicants to decide not to pursue the second degree at that time.

In our experience, applicants in nontraditional areas are more attracted to a program that is relatively large and established. This seems to be especially important for students entering a Ph.D. program that represents a very innovative combination, particularly one that no other student is known to have combined with medical studies. The presence of "kindred souls," even in other Ph.D. areas, can be a significant source of reassurance.

Some graduate programs may be reluctant to accept M.D./Ph.D. students, particularly in fields that are highly competitive at present. Largely because of the novelty of the student's proposed studies, faculty in such programs may be skeptical about the need for or feasibility of combining a degree in their field with an M.D. They may be unwilling to offer a place to someone whose future plans are not guaranteed to bring the kind of recognition to the department to which they are accustomed. That is, rather than being productive within the narrow confines of their Ph.D. discipline, graduates of M.D./Ph.D. programs are likely to make their mark in academic medicine and in interdisciplinary areas of their field. Department faculty are naturally most willing to accept M.D./Ph.D. applicants whose credentials match or excel the best of their regular applicants. In addition, the record of M.D./Ph.D. students in other similarly "atypical" departments also seems to be a reassuring factor for faculty and departmental administrators. For example, faculty in Mechanical Engineering at the University of Illinois at Urbana-Champaign were more willing to enroll their first joint-degree student when we were able to cite the academic success of an M.D./Ph.D. student in Nuclear Engineering. Similarly, Sociology became highly receptive to M.D./Ph.D. applicants after their experience with one who was among the best students to whom the department had ever granted a degree.

The availability of graduate programs in traditional university departments (familiar from undergraduate experiences) can be an attraction for some students. This has been especially noticeable among applicants who choose to do their Ph.D. studies in the chemistry department rather than biochemistry or pharmacology because they earned their undergraduate degrees in chemistry, a major field much more widely available to undergraduates. We have also found that the availability of Ph.D. programs in fields such as biophysics and nutritional sciences, which are closely linked with medicine but are presently available at fewer medical schools, is a great attraction.

A program may fail to recruit a particular student for a number of different reasons. Even the most prestigious programs usually have a recruitment success rate of less than 50 percent for the most highly rated students, since most apply to several programs and some apply to many. A significant number of students, even some who have had a long-term interest in research careers, find that when it becomes time to decide to enter such a program, they are truly unprepared to make the commitment. They will then opt for an apparently less complicated path, usually M.D. studies only, with the thought that they can enter a research path after completing medical school and/or residency. Family preferences, especially spousal, are often a deciding factor in the choice of location or even the decision whether or not to participate in a combined degree program. The nature of the family pressure is complex—relatively few parents appreciate the potential of a scholarly career, which is much less familiar to them than a straightforward career in clinical practice. The length of the program and the uncertainty of the career path after graduation are difficult matters for the applicant and for some family members to contemplate. The career aspiration of the applicant's significant other often helps him or her to determine which program to enter and, again, whether to enter a joint program at all. The applicant's ultimate choice may hinge on what may be considered relatively minor points, at times not even consciously apparent to the applicant, let alone to the program. Geography and familiarity are very powerful factors—students tend to stay in the part of the country with which they are most familiar.

Recruitment into Post-M.D. Research Training Programs

Although many of the factors discussed above apply to some of the students who enter programs at the time of residency or postresidency training, there are very significant differences in recruitment for these programs. The two most important factors probably are making the availability of opportunities known to suitable candidates and the presence of appropriate role models.

To enhance recruitment to programs that provide research education at this point in the career track, administrators need to make young physicians more aware of these opportunities and of the criteria they should use in selecting a program. It is not yet clear whether increased opportunities for students to participate in intense short-term research experiences while in medical school will increase the effectiveness of recruitment into programs of education for research careers at later points. Role models encountered during clinical medical education or the residency may be especially influential. Residents need opportunities to interact with excellent researchers, and positive attitudes toward research-oriented careers should be fostered throughout the entire faculty associated with the residency. This may be difficult, however, because the faculty who are most active clinically and who therefore interact most frequently with the residents (including the residency director, in particular) are often the least active in research. Attitudes toward the practice of clinical medicine acquired during the residency may also be a factor. Some faculty members see research involvement, consciously or not, as an unwelcome distraction to providing excellent patient care. As a result, whether actively or tacitly, they may discourage young physicians from becoming involved in research during residency training. A final roadblock at this stage is the inflexibility of residency and fellowship programs that cannot or will not accommodate research interests.

Selection

The methods by which students are selected for combined degree programs vary in the details but appear to have many elements in common. The principal criteria for acceptance usually include the GPA, scores on MCATs or GREs, and research experience. Virtually all programs also require interviews, which involve visits to the school and campus.

Interviews enable the candidate and the program administrators to exchange information that is important to the decision-making process on both sides, but in addition to this, the program's representatives expend a substantial part of their effort during the interview period in recruiting the student to the school. The interview process includes formal interviews with medical school and/or program admission committee members as well as meetings with a number of faculty members to learn more about graduate programs and research possibilities. The interviews take place over one to three days and usually include interactions with students in the program. Some schools invite their top candidates back for a second visit at the expense of the school.

There appears to be a trend for selection committees to increase the emphasis on actual research experience and recommendations from research supervisors. Certainly, it is reasonable to expect someone planning to participate in a program aimed at preparation for a research career to have a good understanding of the research process. One factor committees try to assess is how an applicant views the role of research in his or her future professional life. In some instances, an applicant may have excellent academic credentials but an unrealistic view of the demands of a Ph.D. education or the conduct of excellent scholarship. Occasionally, applicants are quite uninformed about what is involved, and the interview phase, while an important learning experience for all applicants, is the first time such applicants have begun to think seriously about the realities of research. Some applicants have an interest in a second field but an overriding goal to be a practicing clinician. At an extreme, for example, admission committee members have been told by an applicant that he or she plans to practice medicine, but "in case I tire of this activity I can fall back on research." Such applicants are obviously not good candidates for admission, as they are unlikely to have either the staying power needed to meet the demands of seven or eight years of medical and graduate education or the motivation to become a scholar in the proposed second discipline.

Another inappropriate rationale for applying to a combined degree program is the prospect of financial support through medical school. Those involved in recruitment and especially selection committees are usually sensitive to this possibility and drop such applicants like "hot potatoes." Similarly, applicants with a glamorous view of the research laboratory or a motivation that appears to spring primarily from external factors—such as an attraction to the status and prestige of the M.D./Ph.D. or perceived family expectations or pressures to achieve—are less likely to maintain the motivation to remain in a program or in a research career than those with a more realistic and self-directed view. The interview, as well as letters from a research supervisor present an admissions committee with an opportunity to assess the applicant's understanding of the potential difficulties that are the drawbacks of the research enterprise.

In view of these concerns, the interview provides an opportunity to assess not so much the applicant's level of knowledge about a particular research topic or techniques as the thoughtfulness of the applicant's goals and plans. Experience in research indicates that these goals and plans have been defined in a realistic context. A useful indicator of motivation may be the applicant's knowledge of the research interests of the faculty in the program to which the student is applying. It should be remembered, however, that applicants to M.D./Ph.D. programs often begin with a different perspective than typical graduate applicants to programs and, in contrast to the latter, may not have decided on a particular department. The latter can lead faculty who are not accustomed to such uncertainty to question the applicants' commitment.

This emphasis on accomplishments and commitment to research can lead to some discrepancies between the rating of applicants by the admissions process of the combined degree program and that of the medical school, which uses more traditional criteria. In some schools, this does not pose a problem because the admissions committee of the combined degree program has the authority to make the decision on admission. At most schools, however, these decisions remain in the hands of the medical school admissions committee, and as a consequence some candidates who would have been appropriate for the combined degree program can be lost. It is not clear whether such students subsequently gain admission to other programs.

Selection is sometimes tied to the match between a student's research interests and those of a faculty member or the department. This factor may be especially significant in programs where much of the financial support comes from the graduate department and/or the research funds of the faculty member.

Selection into research-oriented residencies is likely to be carried out within the context of the National Residency Matching Program, but in other respects it may be similar to selection into an M.D./Ph.D. program. The weight given to the research background of an applicant will vary with the program's goal and expectations regarding the balance between time in clinical and research activities. Virtually all programs will demand strong clinical ability, even of those students most likely to focus on research careers. Many residency programs make no provision for protected research time for residents but are still anxious to recruit individuals with research backgrounds and goals. They may see them as future junior faculty and expect them to participate in a postdoctoral fellowship after the residency in order to resume research. However, they may simply view their applicants' research backgrounds as evidence of their strong ability and expect nothing of them beyond clinical responsibilities.

Candidates can be selected for research traineeships or fellowships at the postresidency level in a variety of ways. Some of the positions are closely tied to interests in clinical subspecialty training rather than research, but these traineeships are under intense pressure to change or be discontinued (see Chapter 13). Selection by means of individual fellowships supported by NIH is a two-step process that usually involves an agreement between a faculty member and/or department and the applicant on a research project. This process includes the development of a formal proposal and then the selection of the proposal by an NIH study section. The latter process, while nominally conducted as an evaluation of an application for a postdoctoral fellowship, uses much different and more lenient criteria for the evaluation of proposals and applicant qualifications, reflecting the fact that, unlike a Ph.D. seeking a postdoctoral fellowship, the usual candidate with an M.D. has had little or no research education.

Currently it appears that the limiting factors in the recruitment of young physicians interested in obtaining research education are number and qualifications rather than availability of positions. Although there are few, if any, vacant positions, this is because slots are commonly filled with clinically oriented individuals with little real long-term interest in a research career.

Funding

As discussed in Chapter 3, methods to fund students in combined degree programs vary markedly from school to school and often within the same school. The goals of most schools, however, are quite similar: to provide their students with waivers or remission of tuition and adequate stipends throughout their combined degree studies. These goals are reached most effectively and consistently with the programs supported by NIH through the MSTP or through large endowments. These mechanisms support about half the students currently in combined degree programs. The rest are supported by a wide variety of mechanisms, but the level of financial support is often lower and the duration shorter. The principal additional support mechanisms are fellowship funds from the school (usually derived from earnings by the clinical departments), research assistantships (usually from faculty research grants), teaching assistantships, and training grants. Research and teaching assistantships carry responsibilities that may be difficult to fulfill when the students are in full-time medical studies, especially when they are in clerkships.

The high costs of tuition, especially at private medical schools, can also be an important limitation on the number of students who can be supported and the level of support they receive. This probably need not be a limitation, because the Liaison Committee on Medical Education will give favorable consideration to requests to expand class size in order to accommodate M.D./Ph.D. students. Funding is an especially critical problem for students in the less traditional areas, especially the humanities and social sciences, even though there is wide agreement that these are especially important areas in which to prepare combined degree students.

Specialties, such as surgery, that require research generally provide funding. Even in programs that provide support generated by the department, residents may be expected to apply for outside funding from NIH or other sources. The need to fund the research of residents may be as significant a limiting factor as the time needed to provide excellent clinical training. As noted earlier, it is becoming more difficult for residency directors in many sites to release residents for research time because the hospital is counting on the residents to carry out patient care.

Funding for research education at the postresidency level comes primarily from NIH; this source is reviewed in some detail for one representative institute in Chapter 13. Other sources include fellowships and traineeships from foundations, funding agencies such as the American Heart Association and American Cancer Society, and pharmaceutical companies.

Retention

The retention of students appears to be more of an issue in M.D./Ph.D. programs than in residency or postresidency research education programs. The overall rates of retention in dual-degree programs have not been determined systematically; the available data are reviewed in Chapter 2. Reports from individual programs and anecdotal comments indicate that the proportion of entering students who eventually graduate with dual degrees is 70 to 90 percent of those who matriculate.

It can and should be argued that a 100 percent retention rate should not be expected. Essentially no excellent graduate program expects to have all its students complete the planned program, and even medical schools have some rate of withdrawal, although relatively low. Even if no academic difficulties arise among students, it is not possible to prevent dropouts due to motivational factors, competing family and/or financial responsibilities, and, perhaps most importantly, the realization that a research career is not the correct choice for a particular individual. It is doubtful that any screening method can predict the last factor with a high degree of certainty. As noted, many programs give considerable weight in their selection process to prior experience in research. This appears to be a very important criterion for reducing the dropout rate. Although this is a less frequent occurrence, M.D./Ph.D. students may also decide to withdraw from the medical portion of the curriculum for one reason or another and to focus on their Ph.D. studies.

While dropping out of dual-degree programs may be the correct choice for some students, many students who do graduate have contemplated—and rejected—this step at some point during their time in the program. The types of pressures that lead to thoughts of dropping out are the same as for any student—academic difficulties (perceived or real), financial difficulties, personal or family issues, or a change in interests or goals. For M.D./Ph.D. students, other pressures are unique. One is simply the length of the dual-degree program and the extended period for which they must defer gratification and endure the usual problems of being students. In addition, the challenge of completing two advanced degrees is enormous and should not be underestimated simply because highly gifted individuals are involved. As discussed in Chapter 17, playing a role in two cultures is itself a source of tension, and in addition a great deal of knowledge and a high level of skills must be acquired if the participant is to succeed. While making progress in one degree program, the student is always aware that the other program is on hold. Still another source of pressure unique to dual-degree students is the knowledge that, unlike most other advanced degree students, they can drop out of one degree program, whether in the graduate field or medicine, and still have an excellent career path open in the remaining program.

Students are most likely to contemplate withdrawal from a dual-degree program at three different points. Near the beginning of a program, students may experience academic difficulties as they make the transition from undergraduate study, or they may simply lose interest as they become aware of the real demands involved. Before investing any or more time in one of the degree programs, then, these students consider withdrawing. In the middle years of progress through the program, having carried out highly demanding studies and research for a few years in each of the disciplines, students may become discouraged and consider withdrawal when they face the realization that an equivalent amount of time and effort lies ahead before graduation. Finally, near the period of completion, students may consider dropping out as a result of difficulties in completing a Ph.D. research project or disillusionment with the realities of clinical medicine.

The key to preventing an erroneous choice is to counsel the student to take time before making decisions and to delay taking steps that will lead to irreversible changes in the educational program. As administrators of programs gain experience, they can provide effective advice to students based on the experiences of other students. Direct communication with other students is often the most effective and reassuring way for a student to deal with a perceived crisis in his or her educational program. It also helps to facilitate direct conversations between the student and the graduate advisor, and others. If the administrators of the dual-degree program have good relations with the members of the faculty and good scholarly credentials, they can play very supportive roles in influencing graduate advisors and other faculty to develop constructive ways to deal with the problems. It is crucial for students to perceive the program as both strongly interested in each student's welfare and committed to the achievement of excellence in both degrees. The faculty and administration of the involved graduate department and the medical school must make the implementing decisions, not the dual-degree program. If the program administrators appear to be invading the domain of authority of the graduate or medical faculty and administrators, resentment by the latter of perceived intrusions can prevent solutions to student problems from being sought by the parties needed to participate in problem solving.

Problems of retention often occur in smaller or newer programs and among students in graduate fields not usually combined with medicine because in these situations there are few other combined degree students and thus few or no role models to provide incentives and support. In such circumstances, the lack of precedents for dealing with problems may foster a crisis atmosphere when a "novel" problem arises. For example, a student may wish to follow a sequence of studies that departs from what is recommended, or a student's advisor may take a position at another school, thus requiring the student either to follow the advisor and complete the graduate degree elsewhere or to seek a new advisor and "lose" work already completed. A crisis may be defused by drawing on the experience of other parts of the program or programs at other schools. It may be important for the medical school and/or the dual-degree program to be especially flexible and accommodating in dealing with the problems that are perceived by the graduate department, which may have little experience in the particular problems that arise and an inherent skepticism in dealing with medical schools because of apparent differences in criteria and procedures. There is nothing as useful as experience in ameliorating these concerns and thereby developing attitudes and procedures that minimize the likelihood that a student will drop out. The use of a consultant from a more established program may provide the decisive difference.

As with M.D./Ph.D. programs, there are inadequate data or reports from which to estimate the occurrence and amount of attrition in programs at the residency and postresidency levels. These programs do not have a convenient endpoint, such as the attainment of the Ph.D. in dual-degree programs, nor do they have a fixed length. The record of research productivity of some of the "graduates" of these programs, especially those who spend less than two years in research training, is a great source of concern (see Chapters 2 and 13) and might reflect the premature termination of their participation. The key elements for achieving better retention in these programs probably include more rigorous screening of applicants to ascertain their interest in research; more structure to the program including some didactic instruction in key areas; and most especially, close association between the student and an appropriate mentor.

Academic and Personal Advising of Students

The two types of guidance, academic and personal, are considered together because in the dual-degree programs, which are so long and complex, these factors become closely intertwined. Some of our more spectacular failures to provide effective advice have come from a failure to recognize this connection, while some of the most effective guidance has been possible when this connection was taken into account. Problems in graduate studies are often closely linked with problems in personal relationships at home. Inasmuch as the average time to complete both degrees is seven to eight years, it is almost inevitable that all students will experience some academic and/or personal crises during the duration of their program. This is especially likely because most students carry out their dual-degree studies during a complex and stressful part of their lives when they are completing the transition to full adulthood (or are *not* completing it because of the strenuous demands of their studies!).

The most effective guiding principle, in our experience, is to prevent students from making decisions rapidly, as already noted, especially decisions that reduce or eliminate options and opportunities. This general principle of advising is even more important in these programs because of the multitude of administrators, faculty, and systems involved in dual-degree education, which greatly increases the possibility of faulty communications.

The most effective program organization is one that maintains maximum flexibility and gives students and graduate advisors the power to decide which paths to choose. This policy position evolved as it became apparent that we did not always have sufficient information to make decisions for the students, in spite of our much more extensive experience. As a consequence, both student and advisor tend to feel more comfortable with their own decisions and tend to be more accepting of problems that may arise from those decisions. To help the student and advisor make fully informed decisions, it is very useful for the program administrators to make available any information regarding the experience of other students in similar situations and to provide strong recommendations when these seem warranted.

Once a student has started into a combined degree program, some of the principal decisions involve the methods and timing by which medical and graduate studies are to be integrated. It is important for everyone involved to realize that there is no problem-free way to combine education in both of these fields; all involved parties therefore need to examine alternatives in terms of net advantages and disadvantages to the student and the graduate advisor rather than seek an illusory "right" or trouble-free path. The problems involved in combining studies occur whether the two areas are pursued simultaneously, in sequence, or separated by a significant interval. Some paths are better for particular students or for particular kinds of research programs, and therefore flexibility and strong advising are essential ingredients of an effective program.

The administrators of the dual-degree program must effectively extend their advice to the graduate faculty and sometimes the medical faculty as well as to the student. Medical schools and graduate departments often have very different cultures and perceptions (see Chapter 17 for a more extended discussion). The administration of the dual-degree program can carry out a crucial function by helping to bridge these gaps. The most effective efforts are likely to come from individuals with credentials that both groups consider very credible. The need to "educate" faculty and administrators about the dual-degree program is likely to be a never-ending task, because the students are likely to be distributed among a large number of faculty and the programs they follow will inevitably differ from those of the "normal" students with whom the faculty usually interact.

The circumstances in which young physicians are advised during or after their residency programs differ from those of the M.D./Ph.D. programs, but the general philosophy of advising should be the same. Decisions should be made by those most directly involved, but there should be input regarding the experiences of earlier participants; decisions that remove options should be discouraged and delayed; and the experiences of peers should be taken into consideration.

Selecting a Field and Choosing a Mentor

Many directors of research training programs consider the choice of a mentor to be one of the most crucial decisions to be made. In graduate education, the relationship between the thesis advisor and the student is often the dominant factor in the educational process of obtaining a Ph.D., and similar considerations apply to the relationship between the young researcher and the research mentor in postdoctoral programs. Compatibility in outlook and procedures is often more important than the details of the research problem to be pursued. We strongly advise students to recognize the complex nature of the relationship between a graduate student and her/his advisor and, especially, to take into account that the "power" resides very much with the advisor. Students should be counselled to try to adapt to the procedures and needs of the advisor rather than try to change or "reform" the advisor. The student should understand that although potentially appearing submissive, such behavior, in the long run, leaves the student with the most options for control of his/her destiny. Similarly, students should be advised of the advantage of becoming viewed by the faculty of the department as an academically and socially "good citizen." Although such advice applies to all graduate students, it may be especially important to M.D./Ph.D. students because they may be more assertive than many typical graduate students, often feel more pressure to complete their graduate studies rapidly, and often are viewed with initial concerns by many faculty. It may be helpful to point out to M.D./Ph.D. students that their very existence is a challenge to many of the faculty who have a single doctoral degree but feel that they are fully competent without the need to have dual degrees.

Programs differ significantly in the time and manner in which the mentor is chosen. In some instances, the thesis advisor is chosen before the student enters the program; in other instances, the decision is delayed until up to three years after the student has entered the dual-degree program. The latter variation is especially common in programs where M.D.\Ph.D. students spend the first two years primarily in their medical studies.

The choice of a graduate program may or may not be a critical one. In principle, it should not be particularly crucial because the subject of the research topic is less important than the rigor of the research experience. In practice, however, this choice can be very important because in some programs the graduate department has a significant role in the financial support of the student.

Perhaps more importantly, departments will inevitably differ in their attitudes toward dual-degree students. In departments that view such students as desirable additions to the graduate program, problems tend to be solved smoothly and effectively, whereas in departments that are not strongly committed to the combined degree program, problems may not be as easily solved. Administrators of dual-degree programs need to provide appropriate advice to students but avoid antagonizing departments or individual faculty—this is a task that sometimes would challenge Solomon. Advisors can facilitate this process by spending time with the graduate departments before a crisis occurs, incorporating the needs of these departments into the structure of the dual-degree program, and conveying a commitment to excellence and rigor in the joint program.

In programs for young physicians, there is likely to be less potential for conflict with the graduate department, but the assignment of a mentor is probably even more critical. Again, the research topic is not as important as the rigor of the experience, and it is essential that the research topic be of high priority to the faculty member. The faculty member needs to have the time and interest to interact effectively with the student and to recognize that physicians starting their research training at this point are likely to differ significantly from typical postdoctoral or graduate students. Young M.D.s come into the research arena from the clinical arena where they have gradually become relatively authoritative figures. Yet their research skills at best are quite rusty and may be essentially nonexistent. Further, some of the characteristics that lead to good results in the clinical setting, such as the ability to make judgments and take action on the basis of incomplete information, may be in direct opposition to the habits needed for excellence in scholarly endeavors.

Advising on Personal Matters and Life Style

Personal and life style issues can be critical for students in all types of programs. Although the student's choice of the career path seems very reasonable and desirable to the faculty and administrators in the program, this is not the case for virtually everyone else with whom the student interacts. Parents, relatives, peers, and "significant others," while superficially expressing admiration for the choice of an academic pathway, often do not really understand it. This choice of career appears to involve more time and more effort and in return the participant faces a less certain future with less financial award but will work much harder! It therefore is very desirable to provide these students with strong support and advice and, especially, to promote opportunities for the participants to interact with others who have made a similar career choice. Probably the most important group to provide positive reinforcement is their peers. It also is very helpful for students to have frequent opportunities to talk with those who have completed similar training and now are at various points in their careers. Many programs provide such opportunities by means of periodic meetings which have both an academic and social purpose and by less frequent but more prolonged "retreats," often in a setting away from the institution. There is nothing as reassuring to a student facing an insolvable crises than to talk to others who encountered similar crises and emerged from them with little or no damage.

There are some principles that may be very useful for the program administrators to stress to students and to strive to incorporate into the ambience of the program. Perhaps the most important is to encourage the student to see this period of education as an important part of their life which should be enjoyed and integrated in to normal activities, even if this means that they may take a little more time to complete their studies. The need for the student to emerge as a real human being is great and cannot be over stressed. Another useful principle is for the student to consider choices from the point of view of what will give her/him the most flexibility for future opportunities. This principle sometimes can convert an apparently undesirable option into a much more acceptable one. Another important principle is to continue to reinforce the desirability of obtaining a quality education in both fields; this provides the student with the best return for the very considerable effort that is involved and provides an excellent basis for taking the time needed to complete the program successfully and with one's humanity intact. Finally, again it is worthwhile to stress the desirability of avoiding premature decisions which restrict one's options. While it certainly can be carried to an unproductive extreme, in retrospect it becomes clear that often the most valuable advice that an advisor can give most often is to postpone a decision that will result in a significant change. Even short periods of giving time to consider such decisions—or even to put them to rest for this period—often leads to considerable re-evaluation of the value of the proposed change.

The Placement of Graduates

Choosing the step that will follow the primary phases of combined degree education is one of the most important decisions that a student can make. It is also one for which effective advising is often critical, for two reasons: the lack of clear-cut descriptions or directories of appropriate residencies and postdoctoral options for graduates of dual-degree programs, and the strong tendency for dual-degree graduates to be influenced by the factors and procedures followed by the vast majority of medical school graduates who are not seeking scholarly careers. As noted in Chapter 4, residency programs that are particularly suited to graduates of dual-degree programs are becoming more available, and in time these should help resolve the problem. In the near term, graduates must be vigorously advised to seek positions where they can continue to develop their scholarly careers. Further, the administrators and faculty of the program may need to intervene actively on behalf of their graduates to ensure that prospective employers gain a full appreciation of their potential. This may be especially important for graduates who are seeking careers in specialties with highly competitive residencies, such as radiology or neurosurgery. The directors of these residency programs, and especially the chairs of the departments, may need to be informed about the special attributes of the applicant. In the absence of such intervention, graduates of dual-degree programs may not get past the screening done by clerical staff, which may be based on criteria that are appropriate for regular graduates but not for combined degree students. The involvement of department heads may be especially important because they are more likely to want to build the academic reputation of the department and more appreciative of the value of research experience and ability. The director of the residency program may, on the other hand, be more concerned with the smooth running of the clinical services and thus see research-oriented residents as a potential problem. For this reason, as well as for more fundamental academic reasons, it is important for M.D./Ph.D. students to build excellent credentials in the clinical portion of their education.

The placement of young physicians who complete their traineeship or fellowship is also a critical step. A premature move into a position with high clinical responsibilities can thwart further development of research capabilities. Fortunately, there is increased recognition of the need to provide an effective environment at this stage of a young physician's career (see Chapter 13). Programs have been developed by NIH, medical schools, and a number of other sources to provide the support young physicians need to stay active in research until they can compete successfully for external funding of research proposals. Appropriate advice and information on these opportunities is an essential component of an effective program.

Conclusion

Program administrators must be keenly aware that issues of recruitment, selection, funding, retention, and advising are crucial parts of their responsibilities. The success of programs to prepare academic physicians, whether they are M.D./Ph.D. programs or postresidency research training programs, depends on organizational structures and procedures that maximize the effectiveness of each of these elements. It is also important for programs to engage in an ongoing evaluation of their experience and to consider new policies and procedures as difficulties are identified. Students, faculty, administrators, and perhaps even outside consultants, should be involved in program assessments. Ideally, the data that are collected should be shared with other programs in order to enhance the way all programs educate physician-scholars. More specific recommendations on these and other aspects of program development are considered in Chapters 19 and 20, but the most important elements for effective advice are clear and quite simple: to maintain maximum flexibility, to avoid steps that prematurely terminate options, and to use the experience of other students and program participants to provide guidelines.

PART II
CRITICAL ISSUES IN THE EDUCATION OF PHYSICIAN-SCHOLARS

The chapters that follow enlarge on themes established in Part I and provide a more in-depth look at many of the questions raised. Chapters 6 and 7 consider questions related to the supply and productivity of physician-scientists. Chapter 8 reinforces earlier points concerning combined degree education and reflects the author's direct experience as a leader in the policy process. Chapter 9 provides preliminary data on specific factors in the preparation of physician-scholars and supports a major argument of this book, that education for leadership in the health care system must expand research training to encompass additional essential attributes of future leaders. The remaining chapters, 10 through 18, look at specific programs, providing depth to the coverage given in Chapters 3 and 4, and examine specific themes, giving further consideration to issues identified in Chapters 1, 2, and 5.

PART I
CRITICAL ISSUES IN THE EDUCATION OF PHYSICIAN-ETHICISTS

6

Biomedical Research Scientists: Issues of Labor Supply and Training Quality

Joe G. Baker, Gerald S. Levey, and Robert McGinnis

- Future National Needs for Biomedical Research Personnel
- Considerations Specific to Physician/Scientists
- Existing Research Training Mechanisms
- Foreign Scientists and Biomedical Research
- References

Since the Congress passed the National Research Service Awards (NRSA) Act in 1974, the National Research Council (NRC) and the Institute of Medicine (IOM) have conducted studies of training needs for biomedical and behavioral research personnel. The most recent NRC/IOM committee was formed in November 1988 and concluded its meetings in 1989. The conclusions reached by this committee were recently published (1). The purpose of this chapter is to highlight some of the major areas of discussion and recommendations made by the committee with regard to biomedical research. The present chapter is not a comprehensive review of the committee's work; the interested reader should consult the entire report for a more detailed exposition of the problems and needs in biomedical research, as well as behavioral research, health services research, and NIH training mechanisms.

Future National Needs for Biomedical Research Personnel

The demand for new scientists comes from two sources: 1) job openings created by growth in total employment and 2) job openings created by scientists who die, retire, or leave science for other activities. The total number of job openings thus varies with changes in health R&D expenditures, general economic growth, wage rates, retirement rates, and other labor market factors. The supply of new scientists is based ultimately upon decisions to enroll in graduate school; factors that affect graduate enrollment include current student support, starting salaries, expected future earnings, earnings available in alternative careers, and student attitudes concerning science.

To project the future demand for biomedical scientists, the committee developed assumptions about the level of demand for goods and services that biomedical scientists produce, such as the level of public and private health-related R&D to be conducted and the levels of undergraduate and graduate enrollment. New public health efforts in areas such as AIDS research and mapping the human genome could significantly increase the demand for health research personnel. Austerity in the federal budget could reduce future public health expenditures and demand for scientists. Research in the private sector, especially in the emerging biotechnology industry, has the potential to add significantly to demand and command an increasing portion of limited biomedical scientific resources. Demand for teaching faculty depends upon university enrollment; graduate biomedical enrollment has grown in the late 1980s after steady declines from the late 1970s to 1983. As the biomedical scientist work force ages, the need to replace scientists who retire and die will increase.

Based upon assumptions described in the full report (1), total Ph.D. biomedical science employment is projected to increase from 76,300 in 1987 to 102,500 in 1995 (an average annual employment increase of 3,300 scientists). The number of biomedical scientists engaged primarily in R&D or the management of R&D is projected to grow faster than the biomedical work force in general. This is because private industry, in which a high percentage of biomedical scientists are engaged in R&D, is projected to grow faster than the other employment sectors (universities, government, hospitals, etc.).

Figure 6.1 summarizes the estimated annual number of openings from death, retirement, net out-mobility, and growth for historical and projected periods. Openings due to death and retirement are projected to increase from approximately 1,200 per year in the mid-1980s to 1,650 per year for the 1987–1995 period. Workers who leave biomedical science for other occupations

Table 6.1. Annual Job Openings and new Ph.D.s.

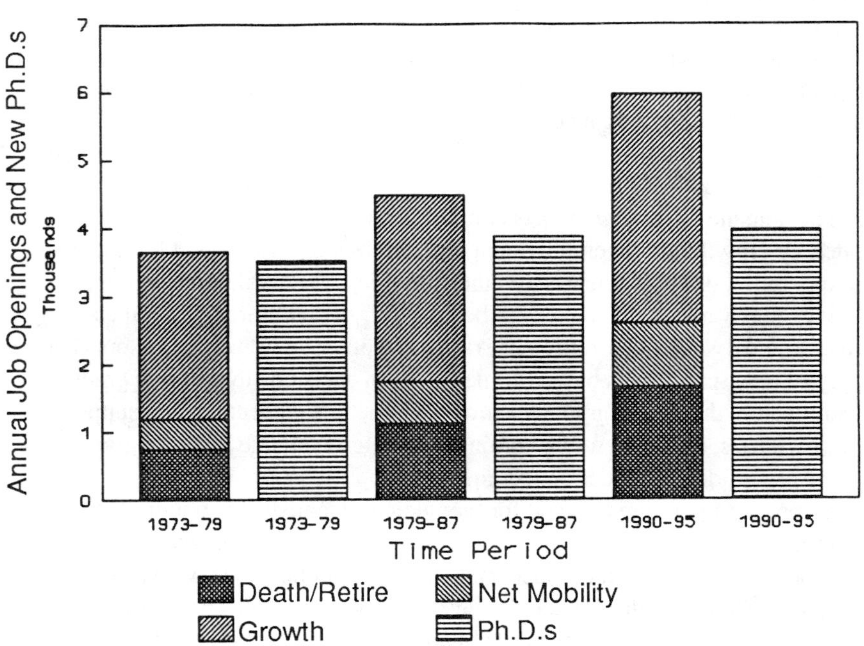

created approximately 650 job openings annually in the 1980s; this is projected to increase to 950 per year for the 1987–1995 period. Thus, for the 1987–1995 period, approximately 2,600 new scientists will be required annually just to maintain current employment levels. An additional projected average of 3,300 openings due to growth gives an average of 5,900 new biomedical scientists needed annually for the period 1987 to 1995. New Ph.D.s in the biomedical sciences numbered approximately 4,000 annually in the 1980s; and based upon historical enrollments little change in Ph.D. output is projected through the mid-1990s. According to the committee projection, the 1990s labor market for biomedical scientists will be characterized by an increasing imbalance between job openings and new Ph.D.s. Because the need to replace Ph.D.s lost through death and retirement is expected to double in the next decade, and because most of the openings created by retirement will be in academe, competition between academic institutions and the emerging biotechnology industry for scarce scientist labor will intensify.

Although distant projections become more uncertain, the committee also attempted to characterize the labor market of the year 2000 based upon the assumption that the key variables would continue on paths established in the 1980s. Projections based upon recent employment growth (4.1 percent per annum) and attrition yield annual job openings in excess of 8,000 in the year 2000 or twice the current Ph.D. production.

Because of the increasing imbalances between demand for and supply of new Ph.D. biomedical scientists, the committee recommended substantial increases in the number of predoctoral traineeships and fellowships to be awarded by NIH in these fields. If this recommendation is implemented, it will be at least a decade before a corresponding increase in the supply of new Ph.D.s occurs. The committee has made a supplemental recommendation that, if implemented soon, could accelerate the process. There appears to be a massive leakage from graduate schools in biomedical training fields, to the extent that 50 percent or more of each entering cohort fails to receive a doctorate. None of the major data sets in use today are sufficient to explain or control these apparent losses. For this reason, the committee recommended research that would investigate cohorts of entrants to graduate school in fields covered by the NRSA act. The focus would be on the careers of the cohorts both in graduate school and beyond. Such research could serve several purposes including a major input to the evaluation of training programs. It could also provide the information needed to more effectively control leakage from the graduate academic pipeline.

Considerations Specific to Physician/Scientists

Because there are no accurate survey data of physicians involved in science and because of difficulties in defining a "physician/scientist," it is difficult to provide estimates and projections of the labor market. Recent evidence indicates that the level of demand for physician/scientists may be lower than previously estimated.

The American Association of Medical Colleges (AAMC) Faculty Roster indicates that 69.6 percent of academic physicians are engaged in research activity. More recent evidence indicates that this overstates the number of medical school physician faculty involved in research (2–4). This new evidence indicates approximately that 20 to 25 percent of all clinical faculty members would be properly classified as "physician/scientists." Given the AAMC's total estimates of 48,800 full-time medical school clinical faculty in 1987, a statistic of 20 to 25 percent would indicate that between 10,000 and 12,000 physician/scientists were employed in medical schools. Using data from the American Medical Association and figures from the NIH, the committee estimated that approximately 6,000 additional physician/scientists were employed outside of medical schools, giving a total of between 16,000 and 18,000 physician/scientists in 1987.

What of the future demand for physician/scientists? Because the committee projects growth in future health research, demand for physician/scientists should also grow. This increased demand is expected in both academic and industrial settings and in both traditional areas of clinical investigation and areas of new or renewed interest such as health services research, outcome assessment, epidemiology, and occupational and environmental health. These latter topics would require the participation of M.D.s in areas where medical training has traditionally given little emphasis.

The supply of new physician/scientists is produced mainly through postdoctoral training and combined degree (M.D./Ph.D.) programs; the postdoctoral training of physicians often differs from that of Ph.D.s because most of the physicians have not had extensive research training. In 1987, NRSA provided research training for physician/scientists in approximately 2,500 postdoctoral positions and 700 M.D./Ph.D. degree (Medical Scientist Training Program) positions.

Existing Research Training Mechanisms

The NRSA program is the primary vehicle for research training within the National Institutes of Health (NIH) and the Alcohol, Drug Abuse and Mental Health Administration (ADAMHA). In 1987, approximately 7,000 predoctoral and 6,200 postdoctoral students received $262.2 million in support under the NRSA program. Approximately 90 percent of this training was in biomedical or clinical science; the remaining 10 percent was in the behavioral sciences. Fellowships, which are awarded to individual scientists on the basis of a national competition, numbered approximately 2,100 in 1987; the remaining support came in the form of training grants awarded to institutions that then select individual trainees.

While there can be little doubt that the NRSA program has increased the quantity of scientists, it is more difficult to measure the effect on quality. The following section surveys recent literature that attempts to evaluate the effectiveness of NRSA training (5).

Are persons who receive NRSA research training more productive? As measures of scientific productivity, recent studies have focused upon whether graduates are engaged in health-related research (including postdoctoral support), how much they are publishing and having work cited, and to what extent they are applying for and receiving research grants. Most of these studies attempt to compare NRSA-trained scientists with a "comparison group" who did not receive NRSA training but are similar in other respects to the NRSA group. The construction of the comparison group is the "Achilles' heel" of these studies; it is extremely difficult to develop groups that closely match the NRSA group, and this difficulty weakens any conclusions drawn from the studies.

Ph.D. Research Training

Employing the measures of scientific productivity we have outlined, almost all the evaluation studies found that NRSA-trained scientists performed better than non-NRSA-trained scientists. In a study of predoctoral support, Coggeshall and Brown compared NRSA scientists with two comparison groups: age-matched Ph.D.s who received their degrees from departments that had received an NIH training grant but who had not received NIH support themselves, and scientists trained in departments that had no NIH training grants and who had not received NIH support themselves (6). The NRSA scientists' productivity was moderately superior to that of the first group and substantially superior to that of the second group. Because the first comparison group could be assumed to receive a graduate education similar to that of the NRSA group, this finding implies that the better Ph.D. students are receiving NRSA support.

Garrison and Brown examined NRSA postdoctoral training by comparing NRSA postdoctorates with 1) Ph.D.s who indicated that they planned to take a post-doctoral appointment that was not funded by NIH and 2) Ph.D.s who had no postdoctoral plans (7). They found that the NRSA postdoctorates had superior performance in most of the productivity measures; these performance differences were much greater in comparison with the group that had no postdoctoral plans.

M.D. Research Training

The construction of comparison groups is even more problematic for physician/scientists because research is an atypical career goal for M.D.s. The research training of M.D.s is supported by foundations, volunteer health agencies, and other non-NRSA sources; this makes it difficult to separate M.D.s who received research training from those who did not. Also, M.D.s involved in "hands-on" research on patients are less likely to apply for and receive NIH research grants, a standard measure of research productivity in NRSA evaluation studies.

Garrison and Brown studied the performance of M.D.s who received NRSA postdoctoral research training (7). Postdoctoral NRSA fellowships are awarded to individual M.D.s on the basis of national competition and numbered approximately 370 in 1987; another 2,100 M.D.s received NRSA postdoctoral traineeships (grants made to institutions, which then select individual M.D.s as research training postdoctorates). Postdoctoral NRSA M.D. fellows and trainees were compared to 1) all M.D.s and 2) a subset of M.D.s who later went into research or teaching as primary work activities. The research productivity of NRSA postdoctoral M.D. fellows was superior to that of both comparison groups; a surprising finding of the study was that the research productivity of NRSA postdoctoral M.D. trainees was superior to group 1 but lagged behind group 2. The reasons for this are unknown.

NIH administers two programs unique to physician/scientists—the Medical Scientist Training Program (MSTP) and the Physician/Scientist Award program. The MSTP is a predoctoral NRSA program that supports exceptional students who pursue a combined M.D./Ph.D. degree. The Physician/Scientist program supports newly trained physicians nominated by their institutions for the development of research skills and experience; this program is not under the NRSA. Because both programs provide intensive research training to physicians, they may yield high levels of research productivity, yet neither has been adequately researched. These programs are also costly in comparison to other forms of research training.

Former NIH director James Wyngaarden stated that research training and career development programs have a priority for NIH "virtually equal to the support of research project grants." (8) Wyngaarden made this statement with the knowledge that NRSA training, particularly the training of physician/scientists, has variable success rates. According to Wyngaarden, too few of the M.D.s who receive their research in traineeships apply for and receive research grants, and some of the training programs simply provide support while the physician pursues subspecialty clinical training. These issues prompted Wyngaarden to call for a comprehensive review of NIH research training programs, including those tailored for M.D.s.

Wyngaarden's position accords with remarks made by Joseph Goldstein in his 1986 address to the American Society for Clinical Investigation (9). Goldstein stated that intelligence, curiosity, and drive are necessary but not sufficient for the productive physician/scientist; there must also be technical skill and the ability to reduce a complicated clinical phenomenon to a manageable biochemical problem. Given the complexities of modern biomedical research, a clinical investigator must have a sophisticated understanding of the fundamental sciences, a mentor in the sciences to direct development, the opportunity to learn techniques, and uninterrupted time in the laboratory to conduct the research. The committee concurred and recommended the establishment of systematic, credible evaluations of NIH training programs, including MSTP.

Given these concerns, the committee considered the following potential changes in postdoctoral institutional training programs, which serve as the primary research education mechanism for physician/scientists:

- The establishment of a true consortium between the clinical and preclinical departments of the institution, with shared responsibility for the design and administration of the program
- The selection of trainees on the basis of some previous experience in research and overall promise
- Sufficient formal coursework in the physical and biochemical sciences to give graduates a theoretical background comparable to that of individuals with graduate degrees in the biological sciences

- Not less than three years of research training, primarily in direct research experience under the supervision of a mentor
- Modules of instruction, specifically tailored to the needs of the physician-trainee, in such areas as basic laboratory techniques, chromatography, radioimmunoassay, protein purification, advanced instrumental techniques, fundamental principles of enzymology and molecular biology, subcellular fractionation techniques, computer technology, evaluation of experimental data, epidemiology, and statistics and data base management, as well as grant and manuscript writing

A 1986 survey of full-time faculty in departments of medicine made similar recommendations regarding postdoctoral research training (2). The survey identified several common features of the training experiences of faculty members who were currently active researchers. Among these features are the following:

1. Most postdoctoral training occurred in medical schools, and the primary source of funding was NIH.
2. Faculty members with an M.D. degree were more likely to be active researchers and principal investigators for peer-reviewed research grants if their period of training was longer.
3. The average length of time between the end of postdoctoral research training and the first peer-reviewed research grant was twenty-four months, regardless of the length of training, source of training support, training site, or type of academic degree (M.D., M.D./Ph.D., or Ph.D.).
4. Active researchers incorporated formal coursework, particularly in the basic sciences and statistics, into the structure of the postgraduate training programs, allocating less time to patient care.
5. Contributing factors include the following: two or more years of postdoctoral research training, including formal coursework in the fundamental sciences pertinent to biomedical research; two to three years of full research funding from an academic institution until the first extramural grant is obtained; and a time commitment of at least 33 percent to research activities.

The former trainees, upon reflection, favored changing the curriculum to include more formal coursework and training in fundamentals, particularly mathematics/computer science, statistics, research techniques, grant administration, and medical writing. Of equal interest, the vast majority (65 percent) wanted less time devoted to clinical medicine during the training program. The committee found merit in these suggestions and recommended that NIH establish a committee, conference, or study to consider whether changes should be made in the program of study in postgraduate institutional training grants for physician/scientists.

Foreign Scientists and Biomedical Research

Foreign participation in U.S. graduate education and science has grown in recent years. In the biological sciences, foreign students earned 20 percent of all

Ph.D.s awarded by U.S. institutions in 1989; in 1980, this statistic was 12 percent. The 20 percent of U.S. doctorates awarded to foreign students in 1989 went to students with permanent visas (4.6 percent) or with temporary student visas (15.4 percent). Foreign students who have permanent visas when they receive their doctorates exhibit labor market behavior similar to that of U.S. citizens: virtually all tend to stay in the United States to work.

Biological science Ph.D.s awarded in the U.S. to foreign students with temporary visas has grown from 7.9 percent of all U.S. biological science Ph.D.s in 1980 to 15.4 percent in 1989. The behavior of these temporary visa holders is markedly different from that of the permanent visa holders: Only about one-fourth are still in the United States for work or study within two years after receipt of the doctorate, and they tend to emigrate from the United States at faster rates than U.S. citizens (10). This overall "stay rate" of one-fourth is heavily concentrated in postdoctoral appointments; foreign nationals composed 42 percent of all life science U.S. postdoctoral appointments in 1988, up from 30 percent in 1980 (11).

What is the overall contribution of foreign nationals to the Ph.D. biomedical science work force in the United States? Recent estimates indicate that U.S.-educated foreign nationals from all sources (those who stay after graduation and those who leave and then return) constitute approximately 6 percent of the new entrants into the life science work force (12). While this contribution is significant, it is small in relation to engineering (36 percent) or physical sciences (15 percent). This estimate does not include immigrant scientists who were educated outside the United States; nor does it take into account emigrant U.S. citizens who were educated in the United States. Although recent data on these categories are nonexistent, they were minor during the 1970s (12).

In light of the committee's projected imbalance between Ph.D.s and job openings in biomedical science, the issue of foreign nationals as a potential supply source arises. Currently, approximately 15 percent of biomedical science Ph.D.s awarded in the United States go to foreign nationals with temporary visas; if these scientists all stayed in the United States to work, Ph.D. output available for domestic employment would increase by a maximum of 15 percent annually. However, some of these scientists are already staying; also, some may not wish to stay even if the opportunity existed. The 15 percent increase represents an upper bound; but even half that would be a significant (and virtually costless) increase in labor supply.

Other factors should be considered. If a firm or university wishes to hire a foreign national with a temporary visa, it must obtain certification from the U.S. Department of Labor (DOL). This certification, which requires proof that no qualified U.S. citizen scientist is available, is costly and time-consuming and must be done on a case-by-case basis. An alternative to this approach is a "blanket" designation by DOL based upon a petition by employers; currently, physicians represent the only occupation with such a blanket designation. However, both Ph.D. engineering and Ph.D. physical sciences have successfully relied on foreign nationals with temporary visas hired on a case-by-case basis as a supplement to shortages of U.S. citizen Ph.D.s.

The hiring of foreign nationals is not without costs. If the domestic hiring of foreign nationals were to increase, talented foreign nationals might enter U.S. graduate schools in biomedical science as a means of immigration to the United States, and foreign graduate enrollment and influence would grow. In engineering, where foreign nationals make up a large percentage of the Ph.D. work force, there have been negative effects on universities that employ large numbers of faculty and teaching assistants who are separated from their students by culture and language barriers; it is possible that this could happen in the life sciences. Also, if the immigration of experienced scientists increased, this might cause contention between foreign countries and the United States over the "brain drain" of scarce scientific talent needed and trained in their native country.

References

1. Committee on Biomedical and Behavioral Research Personnel, *Biomedical and Behavioral Research Scientists: Their Training and Supply*, Vols. 1, 2, and 3 (Washington, D.C.: National Academy Press, 1989).
2. Gerald S. Levey et al., "Postdoctoral Research Training of Full-Time Faculty in Academic Departments of Medicine," *Annals of Internal Medicine* 109 (1988): 414–18.
3. Charles R. Sherman, "The NIH Role in Training of Individual Physician Faculty: A Supplementary Analysis," NIH memorandum dated March 30, 1989.
4. Institute of Medicine, *Medicare and Medicaid Reimbursement Policies Study* (Washington, D.C.: National Academy Press, 1976).
5. For a critical survey of this literature, see Georgine M. Pion, "Evaluating the National Research Service Award Program: A Review and Recommendations for the Future," *Biomedical and Behavioral Research Scientists: Training and Supply* Vol. 3: 1–40 (Washington, D.C.: National Academy Press, 1989).
6. Porter Coggeshall and Prudence Brown, "The Career Achievements of NIH Predoctoral Trainees and Fellows" (Washington, D.C.: National Academy Press, 1984).
7. Howard Garrison and Prudence Brown, "The Career Achievements of NIH Postdoctoral Trainees and Fellows" (Washington, D.C.: National Academy Press, 1986).
8. James B. Wyngaarden, (memorandum to BID Directors and OD Staff), "Review of NIH's Biomedical Research Training Program," April 19, 1989.
9. Joseph L. Goldstein, "On the Origin and Prevention of PAIDS (Paralyzed Academic Investigator's Disease Syndrome)," *Journal of Clinical Investigation* 78 (1986): 848–54.
10. Michael G. Finn, "Foreign National Scientists and Engineers in the U.S. Labor Force, 1972–1982" (Oak Ridge, Tenn.: Oak Ridge Associated Universities, 1985).

11. National Science Foundation, "Science and Engineering Indicators 1989" (Washington, D.C.: U.S. Government Printing Office, 1989), 55.
12. Michael G. Finn and Sheldon B. Clark, "Estimating Emigration of Foreign-Born Scientists and Engineers in the United States," (Working paper, Oak Ridge, Tenn.: Oak Ridge Associated Universities, 1988).

7

Physician-Researchers: An Endangered Species?*

R. Mark Evans, William R. Hendee, and Jerod M. Loeb

More than a decade ago, several respected members of academic medicine expressed concern about what they perceived as a decline in physician-conducted research (1–3). An analysis of National Institutes of Health (NIH) grants (2) suggested that physicians were steadily losing ground to their Ph.D. colleagues as recipients of traineeships, fellowships, career development awards, and individual project awards. Over subsequent years, these data have become the yardstick for measuring the relative competitiveness of the physician-researcher.

This chapter examines NIH awards for research training and support for M.D.s and Ph.D.s over the decade of the 1980s. Trends in the data are identified to help characterize the present status of physician-researchers. This approach underestimates the total number of physicians who receive research support, because an unknown number are supported by foundations, volunteer health agencies, and industry. But the data do provide one important information base for assessing the well-being of physician-researchers in academic institutions today.

Physician Research Traineeships and Fellowships

Research training and fellowship awards are the principal mechanisms by which the NIH supports the development of new researchers. The number of awards is one indicator of the number of young physicians pursuing a research career.

---

*We thank Mary Look, Quantum Research Corporation, for the preparation of the graphs; Charles Sherman, Ph.D., and Walter T. Shaffer, Ph.D., of the National Institutes of Health for their comments and suggestions; and Mary C. Taylor, Maggie Gasparac, and Diane Gillan for the preparation of the manuscript.

Research training grants are allocated by academic departments based on faculty evaluations of the research potential and career goals of applicants. From 1961 to 1973, the NIH provided support for 1,700 new physician-trainees annually (Figure 7.1, top). From 1974 to 1979, the number of first-time trainees declined to less than half. The intersection of the lines for Ph.D. and M.D. trainees in 1978 was an early indication that biomedical research has begun to be perceived as more suitable for Ph.D.s than M.D.s.

The mid-1970s decline in research training grants awarded to physicians in part reflected a new philosophy in research training. No longer were research training grants to be used to support clinical training in a medical subspecialty. When training grants were converted into National Research Service Awards (NRSAs) in 1974, a public health service requirement was imposed on recipients who subsequently chose not to pursue research careers. An NRSA recipient who refused this service obligation had to repay the cost of research training. This payback provision appears to have had minimal influence on research career decisions (4). However, it sent a message to academic medicine that NRSA grants were to be used exclusively for research training.

With the increasing costs of NRSAs, it is unlikely that the number of grants awarded to physicians will ever again approach the level of the 1960s and early 1970s. Nevertheless, the number of physician-trainees has increased over the past decade and, since 1982, has exceeded the number of Ph.D. trainees.

A companion NIH postdoctoral training program provides NRSA support through research fellowships. Their fellowships are a more direct signal of the intent to pursue a research career, because they are awarded following approval of a peer-reviewed research proposal. In the 1950s, the number of research fellowships awarded annually to physicians was comparable to that for nonphysicians (Figure 7.1, bottom). After 1968, the number of new Ph.D. fellows exceeded the number of physician-fellows and contributed to the fear that physician-researchers were an endangered species (2). Over the past decade, the gap between the number of nonphysician and physician fellowships has narrowed as the result of a gradual increase in the number of M.D. fellows since 1982 and a steeper decline in the number of Ph.D. fellows since 1975.

A 1986 study, which evaluated the effectiveness of NIH training grants and research fellowships from the perspectives of subsequent grant success, academic position, and publication rate (5), revealed that these indicators are all influenced by the length of research training. The longer the training period, the greater the subsequent success in obtaining grants, academic rank, and scientific publication. Evaluation of the absolute effectiveness is complicated by the difficulty of identifying control groups for comparison with NRSA trainees and fellows (6).

The NRSA program includes support for individuals seeking a combined M.D./Ph.D. degree through the Medical Scientist Training Program (MSTP). This program, initiated in 1964, provides participants with the advantage of a formal curriculum of research training early in their educational experience (7). MSTP graduates are highly competitive in securing research funding and academic advancement (Figure 7.2). Compared with physicians who received

Figure 7.1. (top) M.D. and Ph.D. Postdoctoral Trainees Supported by NIH. (bottom) M.D. and Ph.D. Postdoctoral Fellows Supported by NIH.

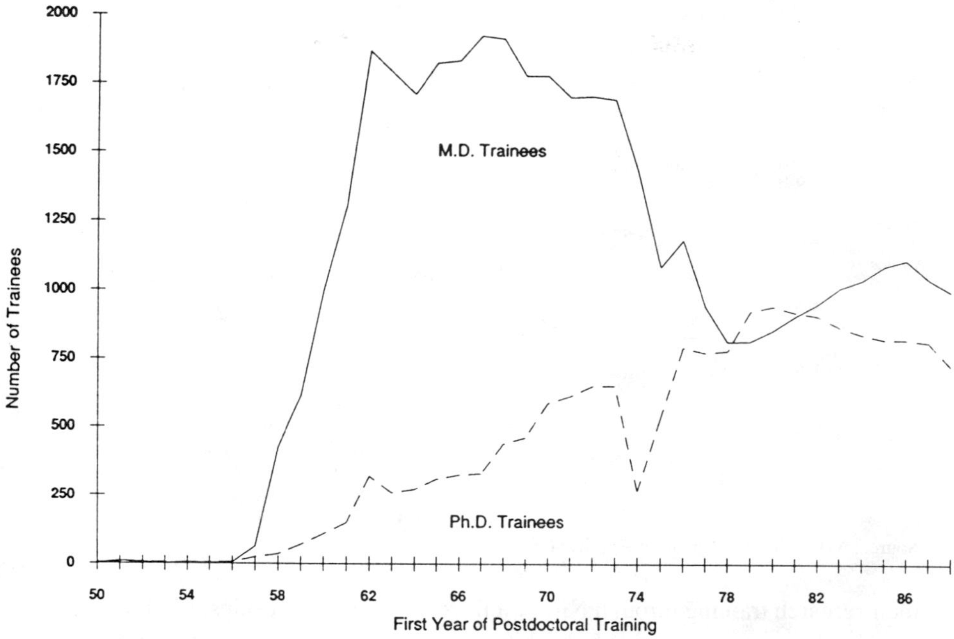

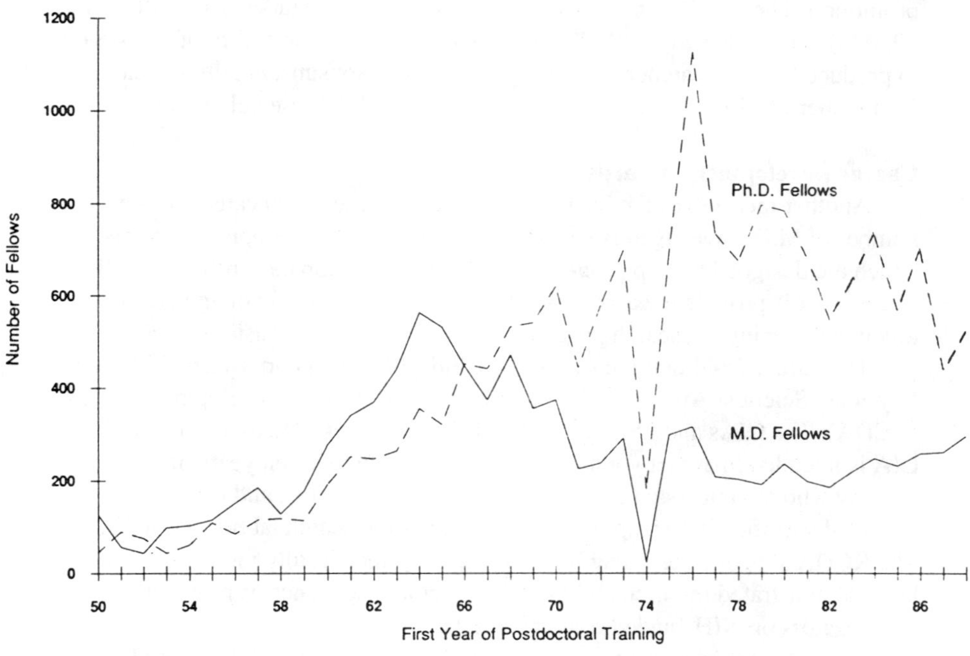

Data includes fellows with at least nine months of support.
Source of data: NIH Trainee and Fellow File.

Figure 7.2. Competing and Noncompeting R01 Awards to M.D./Ph.D.s, FY 1975-88.

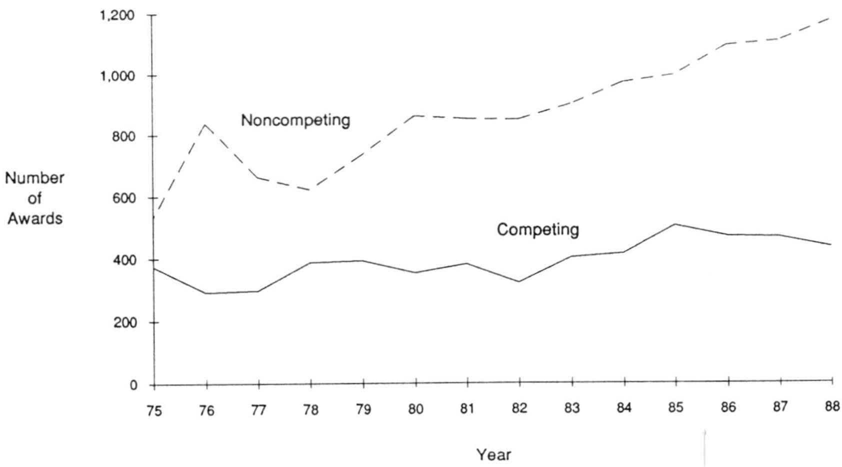

Source: NIH Consolidated Grant Applicant File.

their research training through NRSA fellowships and traineeships, M.D./Ph.D.s have been more successful in publishing research results and attaining academic promotion. The MSTP has supported approximately 700 students annually since 1980 (8) and graduated 150 M.D./Ph.D.s each year (7). The ability of the MSTP to produce M.D. researchers, while significant, has not substantially increased the number of M.D./Ph.D.s who receive competing NIH research grants.

Career Development Awards

Another measure of the interest of physicians in research careers is the number of M.D.-investigators supported by NIH career development awards, which are designed to help promising researchers develop their research skills. These awards provide released time of up to five years to aid young investigators in developing a research program, usually in an area of basic science.

They are offered in three forms: the Clinical Investigator Award (CIA), the Physician Scientist Award (PSA), and the Research Career Development Award (RCDA). The CIAs and PSAs are offered almost exclusively to physicians. The CIA is intended to attract young physicians with two to seven years of clinical training who are interested in developing research skills (9), and the PSA is provided specifically to help investigators develop research laboratory skills. The RCDA supports the career development of junior faculty members who have demonstrated research ability and project independence as principal investigators on NIH-funded research grants.

In 1979, concern was expressed about the gap between the number of M.D. and Ph.D. recipients of career development awards (2). Since 1984, the gap has shifted greatly in favor of physicians (Figure 7.3). The number of physicians

Figure 7.3. M.D. and Ph.D. Recipients of NIH Career Development Awards.

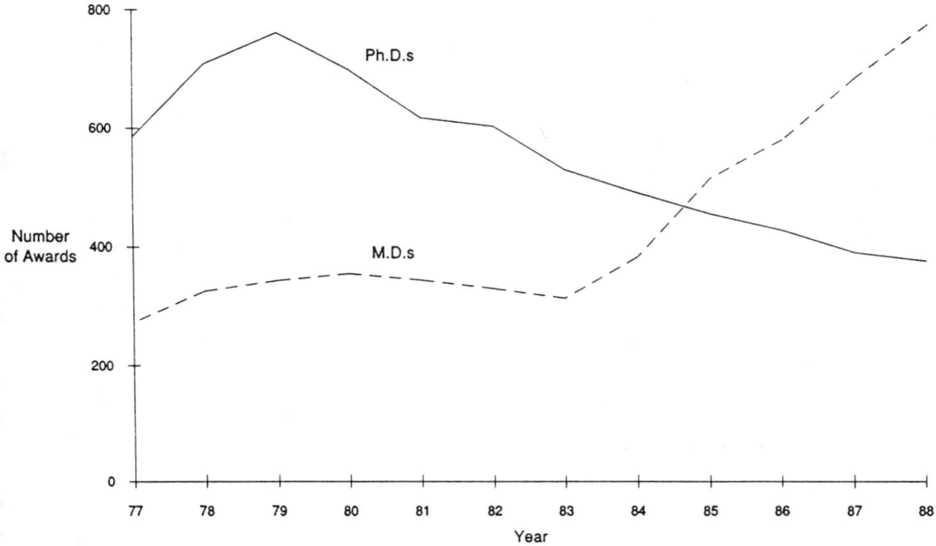

M.D. data include M.D./Ph.D.s.
Career Development Awards are Research Career Development Awards (1977-1988); Clinical Investigator Awards (1977-1988); and Physician-Scientist Awards (1984-1988).
Source of data: NIH Data Book.

receiving CIAs has increased more than tenfold since 1977 (8). In 1988, approximately 425 physicians were supported by this program, four times the number supported by RCDAs. The PSA program has been growing at a rate of approximately fifty new M.D. recipients annually since its introduction in 1984. In 1988, 246 physicians were supported by PSAs (8).

Individual Research Awards

Investigator-initiated NIH research grants (R01s) are the primary measure of the involvement of physicians in biomedical research. Wyngaarden cited the number of physician recipients of R01 grants in 1979 in support of the contention that the number of M.D.-researchers was declining (2). Expressed as a percentage of total R01 awards, competing and noncompeting R01 grants to physicians decreased from 25 percent to 19 percent and 31 percent to 20 percent, respectively, from 1975 to 1988. From 1977 to 1988, the percentage of grant applications filed by M.D.s and M.D./Ph.D.s declined from 36 percent to 30 percent. (For data from 1979 to 1988, see Figure 7.4.) In absolute terms, however, the number of R01s awarded annually to physicians over the past decade held relatively constant at about 1,000 competing and 2,300 noncompeting awards (Figure 7.5, top and bottom).

Recipients of first-time R01s and FIRST (First Independent Research Support and Transition) awards (or R29s) constitute an important subset of applicants for research funding because they represent the initial entry of investigators into peer-reviewed research funding. With the exception of a small

Figure 7.4. Percentage of M.D. R01 Applicants and Recipients, and Percentage of M.D.s on NIH Study Sections.

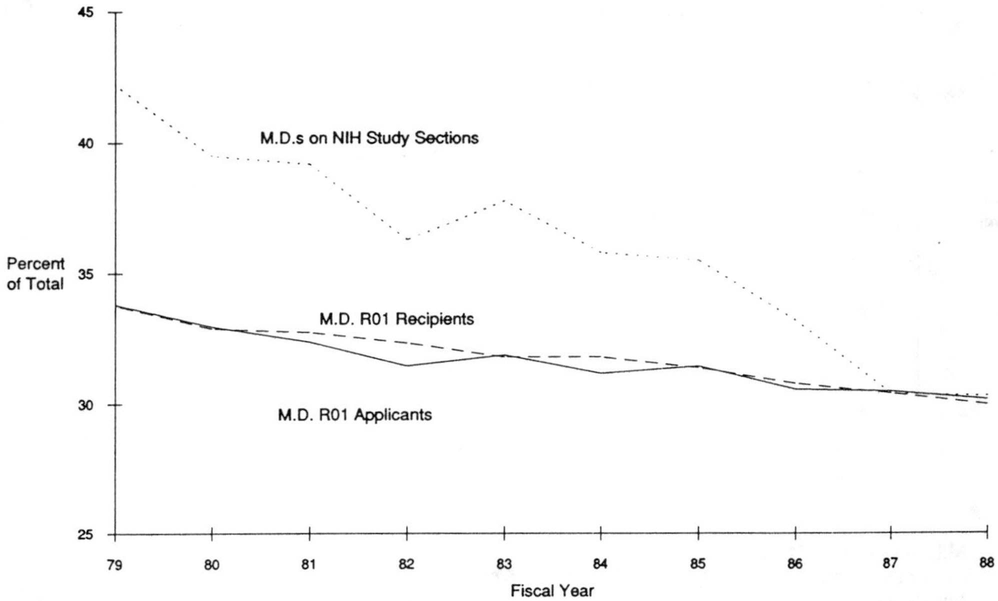

M.D. data include M.D./Ph.D.s.
Source of data: NIH Consolidated Grant Applicant File (R01 applicants and recipients) and NIH Division of Research Grants.

increase in 1979 and a small decrease in 1982, the number of physicians receiving their first research grant remained relatively constant from 1974 through 1988 (Figure 7.6). The gap between physicians and nonphysicians who receive first-time R01s has not widened during the past decade, and the competitiveness, as measured by the award rate, for M.D. and Ph.D. applicants is about the same.

FIRST awards, which are relatively new, provide funds for five years to permit a newly independent investigator to establish an independent research program. The longer period of funding provided by a FIRST award, compared with that of an R01, is intended to provide greater opportunity for creative research to succeed. Although the FIRST award program is too new for trend analysis, over 500 M.D.s and M.D./Ph.D.s were supported by R29s in 1988. R29s went to physicians in the same proportion as R01 awards (10).

The Representation of Physicians on NIH Study Sections

The participation of physicians in NIH study sections declined significantly during the 1980s, at least in part as a reflection of changes in the researcher pool. In 1979, 42.2 percent of study section members had M.D. degrees. By 1988, this

Figure 7.5. (top) Competing R01 Awards by Year and Degree of Recipient. (bottom) Non-Competing R01 Awards by Year and Degree of Recipient.

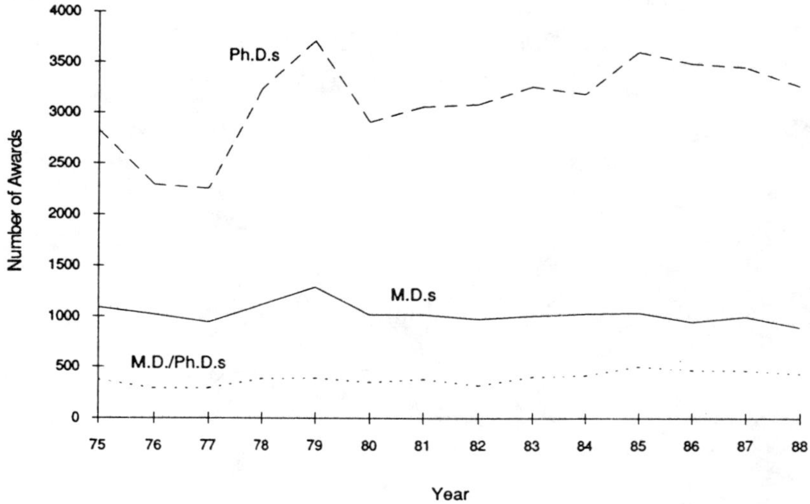

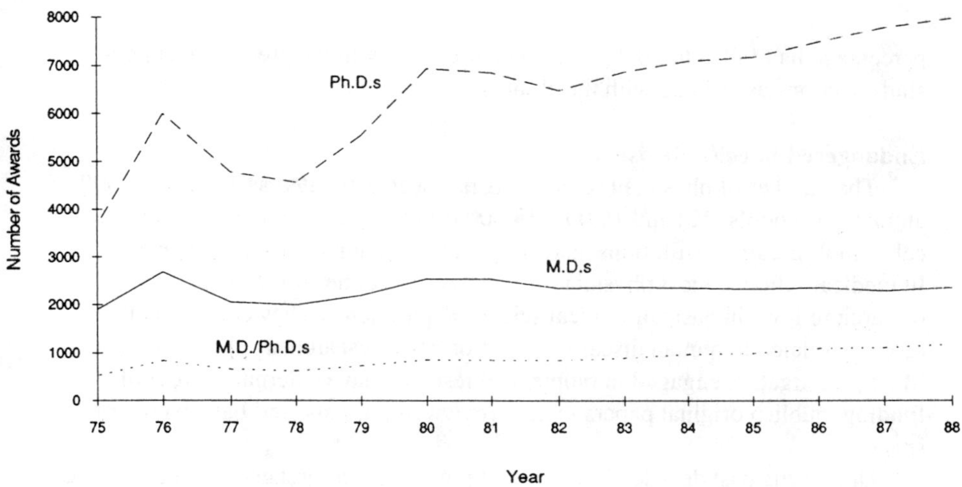

Source: NIHConsolidated Grant Applicant File.

Figure 7.6. First-Time R01 Awards by Year and Degree of Recipient.

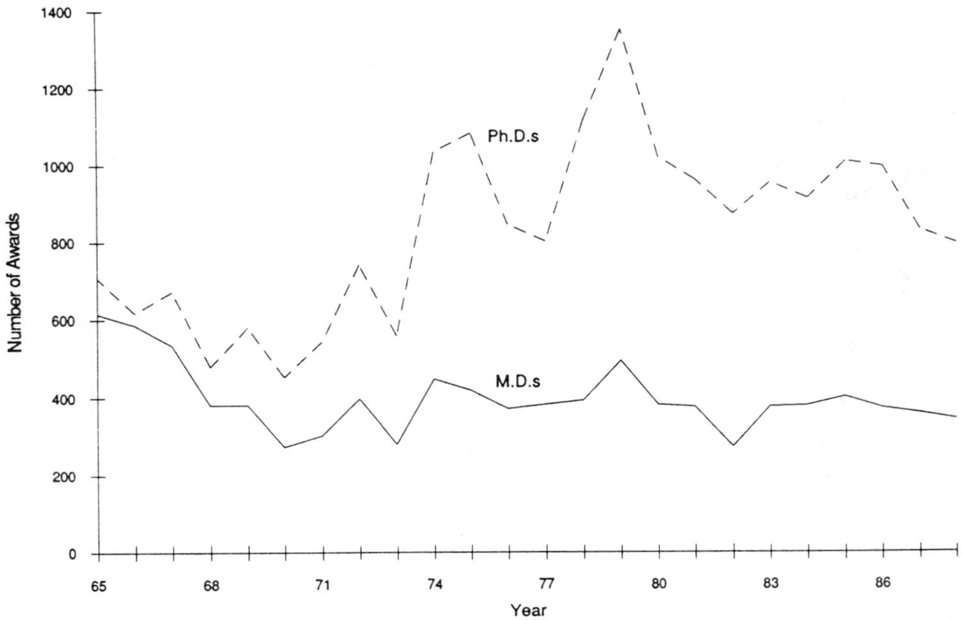

M.D. data include M.D./Ph.D.s.
Source of data: NIH Consolidated Grant Applicant File.

percentage had fallen to 30.3 percent (Figure 7.4), with the greatest decline in study sections associated with the clinical sciences (11).

Endangered Species Revisited

The number of physician researchers has been estimated as 10,000–12,000 at medical schools (12) and 16,000–18,000 if investigators at the NIH, nonmedical school research institutions, and commercial organizations are included (13). In medical schools, most physician-researchers are either full-time faculty or research fellows in basic or clinical science departments. They conduct bench research related to human disease, patient-oriented research, or clinical trials (6). Most investigators engaged in biomedical research have external sources of funding, publish original papers in peer-reviewed journals, and have laboratory space.

During the past decade, the supply of physician-researchers has been a topic of concern within academia, organized medicine, and the public health service (1–3, 6, 14–22). In absolute terms, however, the number of physician-researchers appears to be remaining steady rather than declining. There has been essentially no growth in the number of R01s awarded to physicians over a period that has witnessed significant expansion in the total physician pool and an increase in the percentage of graduating medical students who indicate a preference for research careers (i.e., 22 percent to 30 percent from 1981 to 1989) (23).

Opportunities have never been greater for physician-researchers to contribute to advancement in medicine, public health, and personal health care. Knowledge accumulated over the past decade in the biomedical sciences invites imaginative new approaches to clinical medicine. The emergence of new medical challenges such as HIV disease and drug-resistant tuberculosis, and new insights into established diseases such as cancer, cardiovascular disease, dementia, and diabetes are compelling reasons for physicians to become involved in research. Improved preventive measures, diagnostic methods, and therapeutic approaches are a direct result of past contributions to medicine by M.D. scientists. In many cases, these contributions have occurred because of the unique perspective of physicians, who are oriented toward the use of laboratory findings in the development of new approaches to preventing, diagnosing, and treating disease. A lack of growth in the number of physician-researchers at a time when biomedical knowledge is advancing at an unprecedented rate could well lead to delays in technological innovations and missed opportunities in the preventive, diagnostic, and therapeutic arenas.

The static number of R01 grants awarded to physicians can be attributed to several causes. Redirection of the mission of physician faculty, especially younger faculty, away from research and toward clinical care is undoubtedly an important factor. Academic medical centers now rely heavily on patient revenues to support salaries and expand clinical faculties. In 1976, income from clinical service represented 18 percent of the total annual revenue of academic medical centers. By 1988, this percentage had increased to 38.5 percent, and the trend is clearly upward (24). Clinical services have evolved into "profit-sharing" plans for medical school faculty, with salaries and bonuses tied directly to patient-generated revenue. Under this system, incentives favor more time in patient care and less time in other academic duties, including research.

Academic physicians usually find their professional time divided among three missions: teaching, research, and patient care (25). Some have argued that this "triple threat" mission compromises the ability of physicians to compete in biomedical research (22). In some cases, a physician can attain a balance among these duties, emphasizing certain activities that reflect personal talent, interests, and career goals. But in other situations, personal or institutional expectations to pursue all three missions exceed the physician's available time and energy. Under such conditions, productive biomedical research often becomes the first casualty.

With the expansion of clinical services at academic centers, the role models of medical students and residents are more frequently physicians with clinical rather than research orientations. Medical practice provides immediate gratification from the act of helping patients, whereas rewards from research are delayed and less predictable. Also, societal changes affect the expectations and attitudes of medical students toward research. For example, the additional period of training required for a research career may be incompatible with an individual's commitment to obligations such as marriage, family, and personal lifestyle.

Traditional medical education does not attract students into research careers. Laboratory courses during the first two years of medical school are the first exposure many students have to an educational process that encompasses anything resembling research. Some academic leaders believe that these courses may deter rather than stimulate interest because they emphasize existing knowledge rather than new frontiers (20). Medical students (and residents) may view the requirements for success in academic research as almost unattainable, especially during the limited time they have to establish a record of research productivity and support before being considered for promotion.

Excessive debt also has a negative effect on involvement in research. Earlier surveys suggested that debt was not a major reason for rejecting a research career (7, 26); however, student debt has increased significantly over the past decade. In 1988, 83 percent of graduating medical students reported loan debts, with an average debt of $31,370 for students in public medical schools and $48,068 for those in private schools. Of these students, 24 percent had debts of $50,000 or more (24). In 1988, the average "premedical debt" was $7,283 for students entering medical school.

Conclusion

In part because of the attention paid to the status of physician-researchers over the past decade and the money spent on research training and career development, the number of peer-reviewed R01 grants awarded to physicians has not diminished. However, the total number of R01 grants has increased over this period, and the percentage of R01 grants awarded to physician-researchers has decreased slowly since 1980. The targeting of the physician-investigator as an endangered species may no longer be appropriate. Nevertheless, the challenge remains to encourage a greater number of physicians to pursue research careers, and to identify additional ways for these individuals to succeed within the modern academic environment.

References

1. J. V. Warren, James B. Herrick Award Response, Presented at American Heart Association Meeting, November 1976; Miami, Fla.
2. J. B. Wyngaarden. "The Clinical Investigator as an Endangered Species," *The New England Journal of Medicine* 301 (1979): 1254–59.
3. G. F. DiBona. "Whence Cometh Tomorrow's Clinical Investigator?" *Clinical Research* 27 (1979): 253–56.
4. *NIH Program Evaluation Report on the Status of Medical School Faculty and Clinical Research Manpower, 1968–1990*, (Bethesda, Md.: U.S. Department of Health and Human Services, National Institutes of Health, 1981), 215–21.
5. *The Career Achievements of NIH Postdoctoral Trainees and Fellows*, (Bethesda, Md.: National Institutes of Health, 1986). (Program Evaluation Report).

6. Committee on Biomedical and Behavioral Research Personnel, *Biomedical and Behavioral Research Scientists: Their Training and Supply,* Vol. 1 (Washington, D.C.: National Academy Press; 1989).
7. J. W. Bickel, C. R. Sherman, J. Ferguson, et al. "The Role of M.D.-Ph.D. Training in Increasing the Supply of Physician-Scientists," *The New England Journal of Medicine* 304 (1981); 1265–68.
8. *NIH Data Book 1989* (Washington, D.C.: Department of Health and Human Services; December 1989).
9. R. E. and C. M. Balch, "The NIH Clinician-Investigator Award: How to Write a Training Grant Application," *Journal of Surgical Research* 46 (1989): 1–3.
10. Briefing on FIRST Awards (R29), ICD Directors Meeting, Division of Research Grants, National Institutes of Health, June 28, 1990.
11. Information Systems Branch Division of Research Grants, *DRG Peer Review Trends. Member Characteristics: DRG Study Sections. Institute Review Groups, Advisory Councils and Boards, 1988* (Bethesda, Md.: National Institutes of Health).
12. *Physician Characteristics and Distribution in the U.S.*, Survey and Design Department (Chicago, Il.: American Medical Association, 1989).
13. R. Penchansky, J. R. Landis, and M. B. Brown, "Education for Clinical Research: An Experiment at the University of Michigan," *Clinical Research* 36 (1988): 21–32.
14. J. V. Warren, "The Evolution of the Clinical Investigator," *Journal of Laboratory Clinical Medicine* 101 (1983): 335–50.
15. R. S. Ross, "The Next 30 Years: Will the Progress Continue?" *Circulation* 62 (1980): 1-7.
16. G. D. Whedon, "Further Analysis of Research Support at NIH," *Perspectives in Biological Medicine* 23 (1980): S34–S43.
17. S. O. Thier, "Clinical Investigation in the 1980s: Perspective from the Medical Schools," *Clinical Research* 28 (1980): 248–51.
18. R. S. Ross, "Boundaries of the General Clinical Research Center in Academic Medical Centers," *Clinical Research* 33 (1984): 105–10.
19. J. L. Goldstein, "On the Origin and Prevention of PAIDS (Paralyzed Academic Investigator's Disease Syndrome)," *Journal of Clinical Investigation* 78 (1986): 848–54.
20. M. Saffran, "Rx for M.D.-Researchers: Back to the Lab," *Scientist* (February 1988).
21. J. W. Littlefield, "The Need to Promote Careers that Combine Research and Clinical Care," *Journal of Medical Education* 61 (1986): 775–89.
22. B. Healy, "Innovators for the 21st Century: Will We Face a Crisis in Biomedical-Research Brainpower," *The New England Journal of Medicine* 319 (1989): 1058–64.
23. *AAMC Data Book*, Table B10, Association of American Medical Colleges (Washington, D.C., 1990).
24. L. Taskel, P. Jolly, and R. Beran, "U.S. Medical School Finances," *Journal of the American Medical Association* 262 (1989): 1020–28.

25. R. G. Petersdorf, "The Evolution of Departments of Medicine," *The New England Journal of Medicine* 303 (1980): 489–96.
26. J. Bickel and T. E. Morgan, "Research Opportunities for Medical Students: An Approach to the Physician-Investigator Shortage," *Journal of Medical Education* 55 (1980): 567–73.

8

Meeting the Challenge of the Future

Ruth L. Kirschstein

First and foremost, all physicians should, ideally, be scholars—which is to say, they should be erudite. Second, all physicians should be humanitarians. And third, all physicians should be concerned with the social issues that affect medical care, biomedical research, and society's approach to the ills of mankind. With these criteria in mind, let me set the themes that I believe need emphasis as we look ahead to the year 2000. Some of these were sounded by Lewis Thomas, recipient of the Albert Lasker Public Service Award, in an interview published in *The Washington Post,* and I shall quote liberally from it (1).

Theme 1: The Integrated Approach

The medical scientist, as defined by the National Institute of General Medical Sciences, is an individual who has received rigorous education in an integrated curriculum designed to earn two doctoral degrees, one of medicine and one of science, as a single combined entity, the M.D./Ph.D. Such an individual thus has the background and discipline, breadth and depth, to be both "healer" and "investigator."

When asked, as he looks ahead, what issues should concern us in medicine and health, Lewis Thomas answered:

> Our main worry ought to be to maintain good basic research. We're learning more about several central areas of basic biomedical sciences than ever before. Research is going at top speed. We're really beginning to see one revelation after another, things such as understanding how cells work. If we keep it up, the questions that need to be asked about such things as Alzheimer's disease, rheumatoid arthritis, cancer, AIDS, and all the rest will begin to pop into our minds and we will be able to pursue leads (1).

More than twenty-five years earlier, then-director of NIH, James Shannon, had the vision to realize that the preparation for a medical degree did not *necessarily* provide the background required to prepare one for biomedical research. Dr. Shannon was the father of the Medical Scientist Training Program at NIH, started in 1964. His vision then was that research is complex, taxing, and hard. Today, the truth of this insight is clearer than ever: Research requires not only enormous creativity but also discipline in reasoning, and discipline and skill in methodology—characteristics not *necessarily* taught in the medical school curriculum. At the same time, Dr. Shannon also understood—as we do today—that clinical research, even using molecular biological techniques, must be based on clinical understanding and diagnostic and therapeutic skills. It is therefore imperative that we take an integrated approach to the preparation of physician-scholars.

Theme 2: A Diversity of Pathways

Not all medical students, not all physicians, not all members of the health professions will or should follow the same path. Society has great need for practitioners, clinicians, providers of health care, counselors in disease and its prevention, nurturers, and those who provide support systems for persons who are acutely or, even more important, chronically ill. But society also needs biomedical research, and to fulfill this need it must markedly increase the number of physician-researchers or medical scientists.

The paths that medical students take to reach the goal of a research career need to be multiple and flexible. No one way can provide the numbers of researchers we need. No one way can meet the needs of individual students. The path that the National Institute of General Medical Sciences has chosen to offer is the integrated M.D./Ph.D. curriculum in basic and clinical studies. Its advantage is that the coursework and clinical training are admixed with the rigor of graduate studies and the preparation of a thesis that must meet the standards of the graduate school faculty at a university and be defended as all Ph.D. theses are.

It should be noted that this MSTP model has been more and more emulated and more and more sought after. For years, the number of schools supported by NIGMS was between twenty-two and twenty-five. Now, there are twenty-nine, and others may well follow. More important, appreciation for the value of these programs has grown, the medical schools that have MSTP grants have begun to provide fiscal and institutional support for more students than the NIGMS grant permits, often doubling the number of such students.

For example, at Washington University in St. Louis and the University of Texas Southwestern Medical Center in Dallas, funds from private sources greatly expand the M.D./Ph.D. programs. H. Ross Perot, the benefactor of the Dallas program, viewed these funds as a way "to create a new generation of Joe Goldsteins and Michael Browns." Yet to illustrate the multiple career pathways a medical scientist may pursue, neither Joe nor Mike has the combined degree. They had what Joe called "the equivalent—a period of time (minimum of two years) spent at the NIH." For many years, this was considered, as stated in *Science*, "de rigueur" for the country's brightest M.D.s (2).

Theme 3: "Selling" Science to the Country's Youth

About this theme I, and many others, have a deep concern that goes beyond the problem of just the physician-scholar or physician-scientist. The process of instilling the desire to "do science" must start very young and must be nurtured carefully by mentors at all stages of life, mentors who are exciting and enthusiastic role models.

At a colloquium on physician-scientists in May 1989, Dr. James Wyngaarden, then-director of NIH, gave a presentation entitled "Quo Vadis the Physician-Scientist?" I, in turn, said that the issue of "turning our youth on" must be addressed or the "quo vadis" would need to be asked not of the physician-scientist but of the scientist in general. When asked how to get young people excited by science, Dr. Thomas said:

> I think the main problem in just the last few years is that the youngest and brightest people at the university level are trying to decide whether to go into science, science of any kind—physics, mathematics or biological science—but they become discouraged by what they hear about the difficulties in the generation that is ahead of them, the instability of the research support, the intense competition for grants, and the low stipends. They are a little bit turned off, as well, by the things they read in the press that tend to suggest too often that we almost know everything about everything (1).

While this issue cannot be addressed here, it must be considered in the near future or this country will be in serious trouble.

Theme 4: The Limits of Leadership

Physician-scholars can take on a variety of roles, and as leaders in each of these roles they can make a different and important contribution. To be serious, dedicated, creative researchers, however, medical scientists must garner their energies and time, have a goal, and pursue research relentlessly without much in the way of diversion. Yes, they are leaders in the sense of being mentors, teachers, visionaries regarding possible research outcomes, but their enormous talents must not be diversified or their roles will be diluted. We must protect these researchers and teachers for the benefit of future societies.

Theme 5: The Value of the NIGMS-Supported Medical Scientist Training Program

Some have stated that since the funds for the MSTP are very scarce and the expense per student is very high, the program has outlived its usefulness. Is this conclusion valid? Quite the contrary: it seems to me that what is happening is that the vital nucleus (albeit sometimes small) of an energetic and successful combined M.D./Ph.D. program is the core MSTP, NIH-supported grant. It sets the tone, ensures the standards, and, in some cases, allows an institution to start a program that might not otherwise be possible. But for all schools, the newest as well as those that have had programs for more than twenty-five years, the NIH peer review process and support form the core of what the MSTP is all about.

There are now more than 100 M.D./Ph.D. programs throughout the country (many call themselves MST programs). A number apply for training grant support each year. Four new NIH-supported programs were started in the last two years. Obviously, with resources as tight as they are, expansion by NIH, even if warranted, can be expected to be very limited.

Is this model for developing research physician-scientists worth the cost? To this, my answer is a resounding yes! Eighty-eight percent of the MSTP graduates who have also completed postgraduate training are in academic or research positions.

The success of MSTP graduates in competing for NIH grants is significantly greater than that for all applicants, M.D.s or Ph.D.s. (Table 8.1). Anecdotes abound concerning the contributions and successes of MSTP graduates.

Table 8.1. NIH Research Project and Research Career Applications FY 1981-1985 (MSTP vs NIH-at-Large).

Applications	Percent of Applicants	
	All NIH	MSTP Graduates
Approved	85.6	94.6
Award rate	37.6	47.7
Success rate	32.4	45.2

Conclusion

Given the importance of physician-scientists—and of stable, available funding for their training, the question is, What resources will be available for the training of physician-scientists in the future? Clearly, a multiplicity of sources and resources are needed, and it is important to take advantage of all possible avenues. But certain hallmarks must be emphasized. First, some rules, written or otherwise, must be changed. For example, in setting up the MSTP in 1964-1965, the federal government, for the first time, changed its rules and undertook support for medical school curricula on the condition that they be adapted for the training of medical scientists in the dual-degree program. It is now necessary to change the "rules" that govern residency training and qualifications for specialty boards to permit research to be counted, ideally on a one-for-one basis, toward accreditation. Recently the internal medicine and pediatric boards have modified their requirements—a welcome change.

Other criteria also must be set and adhered to:

- Selection of the best and the brightest individuals and the best institutions must never be compromised.
- Continued flexibility is needed so that programs can be modeled to suit institutional and individual needs.
- Of essence, however, is the fact that there must be no compromise regarding not only the quality, but the rigor and length of training. Research in modern molecular medicine requires a deep and lengthy commitment. It cannot be learned overnight or on a part-time basis.

Finally, while all resources and many sources of funds should be used, in my view, the stability of a nucleus of funding is absolutely required. Perhaps this is one of the MSTP's most significant accomplishments.

References

1. "Poet Laureate of 20th Century Medical Science," *Washington Post Health* October 17, 1989.
2. "Perot to Fund Scientist-Physicians," *Science* 239 (1988): 554.

9

Developing Leadership in the Health Care System

Diane L. Gottheil and Harold M. Swartz

The topic of leadership development has been extensively and actively examined in a number of academic disciplines, yet there are remarkably few studies on education for leadership in the health care system, and these do not appear to bear directly on the questions addressed in this book. Therefore, we surveyed leaders in the health care system regarding their views of the factors affecting their own preparation and that of other leaders.

Leadership and scholarship are related in a complex way. As noted in Chapter 2 and elsewhere, scholars in the health care system are very likely also to be leaders, and it is desirable that leaders be scholars. We use the term leader broadly to indicate individuals in the health care system who exert significant influence on others, usually in formal roles such as heads of public or private organizations or institutions, programs, and departments but also individuals whose scholarly reputations make their actions and recommendations carry considerable weight with their peers and others.

Although an important set of personality factors is undoubtedly involved in leadership, the complexity of health care argues that to a significant degree, successful leadership in the health care system is based on the depth and breadth of knowledge that the leader possesses (1). Knowledge about clinical medicine and the delivery of health care is of course primary, but, increasingly, leaders have been called upon to develop policy to respond to political, economic, social, and cultural issues and to perform as high-level administrators and managers. Many of the present leaders in health care acquired their knowledge of second, related fields by experience, but our major concern lies with formal educational programs. Thus, the questionnaire developed for our survey primarily focused on the areas of competence and fields of knowledge that are prerequisites for leadership in the health care system. The aim of this survey was to define present needs and develop programmatic recommendations. We include in the term health care system all health-related organizations, especially the institutions and processes of clinical medicine, medical research and education, and health care delivery; health-related industries (e.g., pharmaceutical or biotechnology firms); and agencies that develop public policy on health care.

The fact that leadership in health care is indeed knowledge-based makes us more comfortable with the term physician-scholar than the term physician-scientist. The former is meant to encompass the latter, as a scientist must be a scholar in his or her field of study. The term physician-scientist usually refers more narrowly to those engaged in bench research in the biomedical sciences, whereas we include physicians with expertise in other fields as well, particularly the social and behavioral sciences, including management and administration, and in the humanities. By scholar we mean to include only those whom others consider expert in a shared discipline.

Methodology

The population that we studied was drawn from individuals who chose to participate in a symposium on the education of physician-scholars for leadership (2). We prepared a questionnaire to obtain information on the respondents' leadership roles and their opinions on aspects of leadership, including background, educational preparation, needed skills and knowledge, and professional activities. The questionnaire inquired about respondents' background and experience, their perceptions of other leaders, and their opinions on what was ideal. The questionnaire was field-tested and revised accordingly. It was distributed to all the approximately 140 eligible individuals attending the Symposium on the Education of Physician-Scholars for Leadership in the Health Care System. The criteria for eligibility were designed to garner the responses of a sample of health care leaders to a set of questions about leadership (in other words, this is a survey of experts); all symposium participants were included except students and those from the host institution.

The symposium participants eligible for the study were drawn from an invitation list that included medical school deans and associate deans; directors and administrators of combined degree programs, research-oriented residencies, and fellowship programs at all U.S. and Canadian medical schools; and CEOs or other high officials of major health care organizations (including academic health centers, foundations, federal agencies, corporations, professional societies and associations, and others). Although all these segments of the health care system participated, the topic was most pertinent to those directly involved in the scholarly education of M.D.s and therefore the majority of those attending were academicians. The survey responses no doubt reflect this bias, and we will consider this in our discussion of the results.

Following the collection of survey responses at the symposium, we made two follow-up requests by mail to all nonrespondents. We received completed questionnaires from 100 of the 140 eligible respondents, a response rate of 71 percent. The responses were coded and analyzed by machine.

The size and method of selecting the sample prevent this from being a thoroughly representative cross-section of leaders in the health care system. The sample is of sufficient size and diversity, however, to provide useful data, especially in view of the paucity of other sources. We view the study as exploratory and the results as indicative rather than definitive. We anticipate that the results may be a useful first step in designing a more definitive study to be carried out with an appropriately selected sample and a refined survey instrument.

Characteristics of the Sample

If we keep in mind the high representation of academicians in our sample, an analysis of characteristics of the respondents can tell us something about leaders in the health care system, while serving as a note of caution about our ability to generalize our findings. The respondents were overwhelmingly white (93 percent) and male (90 percent) (Table 9.1). There is little reason to believe that these figures are not representative. Although women have begun to enter medicine and science in greater numbers, such recent trends are unlikely to be reflected in a survey of leadership positions (3). There is also evidence that

Table 9.1. Sex of Respondents, by Race or Ethnic Background (N = 99).

	Race/Ethnic Background				
Sex (N)	White	Black	Hispanic	Asian	Total %
Male (89)	84.8%	2.0%		3.0%	90%
Female (10)	8.1%	1.0%	1.0%		10%
Total (99)	92.9%	3.0%	1.0%	3.0%	100%

women who entered medicine at the beginning of the past few decades did not get promoted to leadership positions at the same rate as men (4). Racial and ethnic minorities have been historically underrepresented in medicine, and although this has improved in recent years, notably among Asians and some Hispanics, these trends are likely to be too small and too recent to have made a notable difference in the leadership strata (3).

Table 9.2 presents the age and income distributions of the respondents. In view of the extended educational paths and the need to acquire experience in order to attain a leadership position, the small percentage of sample members in the youngest age category is not surprising. Seventy percent of the respondents were fifty years of age or older—which is likely to be a good reflection of the actual age distribution of leadership in the health care system.

Table 9.2. Age of Respondents, by Income (N = 77).

	Income						
Age (N)	$30,000 to $59,000	$60,000 to $89,000	$90,000 to $119,000	$120,000 to $149,000	$150,000 to $199,000	$200,000 or more	Total
30-39 (3)	33.3%	33.3%	33.3%	---	---	---	100%
40-49 (20)	20.0%	20.0%	30.0%	10.0%	15.0%	---	100%
50-59 (36)	-----	11.1%	55.5%	19.4%	11.1%	.03%	100%
60-69 (18)	-----	16.6%	33.3%	11.1%	16.6%	22.2%	100%

As would be expected, the younger members of the sample tended to be in the lower income groups, whereas the average income for those fifty years of age or older was approximately $120,000. On the whole, incomes are high relative to the general population, which is not surprising in light of the average income figures for physicians in the United States. Our respondents, however, are most likely not among the higher income brackets of physicians in full-time clinical practice. It should also be noted that the sample included respondents who held the Ph.D. degree and no M.D. degree, and who were typically at a somewhat lower pay scale than M.D.s. The data in the sample suggest that leaders in the health care system are well remunerated and that this is, in part, a function of age and therefore experience.

Table 9.3 shows the educational profile of the respondents by age. Because of the nature of the symposium, it is reasonable to expect M.D./Ph.D.s to be more heavily represented in the sample than in the general population of leaders in the health care system. This characteristic may be a significant factor in the interpretation of the data. Nevertheless, since a primary purpose of this study was to raise questions about educating physicians for leadership, this strong representation of M.D./Ph.D.s may be considered an advantage. The M.D./Ph.D.s among the respondents were somewhat younger, probably because this pathway has only recently become prominent.

Table 9.3. Degree Category of Respondents, by Age (N = 81).

Degree (N)	30-39	40-49	50-59	60-69	Total %
M.D./Ph.D. (25)	20.0%	28.0%	40.0%	12.0%	100%
M.D. (35)	----	22.9%	45.7%	31.4%	100%
Ph.D. (21)	----	38.1%	38.1%	23.8%	100%

Table 9.4 presents, by degree category, the data on the types of institutions at which sample members have their primary employment. As expected, the vast majority in each degree category were employed in academia; fully 95.8 percent of the M.D./Ph.D.s, 70.7 percent of the M.D.s, and 91.7 percent of the Ph.D.s cited an academic institution as their employer. While some other sectors of the

Table 9.4. Primary Site of Employment, by Degree.

Site of Employment	M.D./Ph.D. (N=24)	M.D. (N=41)	Ph.D. (N=24)
Academia	95.8%	70.7%	91.7%
Government	---	4.9%	4.8%
Health care delivery institution	4.2%	---	---
Other nonprofit organization or institution	---	9.8%	---
Professional organization or association	---	4.0%	4.2%
Pharmaceutical corporation	---	7.3%	---
Other private sector organization	---	2.4%	---
Total	100%	100%	100%

health care system were represented, they tended to employ the M.D.s rather than the M.D./Ph.D.s or the Ph.D.s. It is likely that the strong commitment to research of these latter two groups ties them more closely to academia. The Ph.D.s may also have fewer opportunities in other sectors of the health care system where clinical experience, and thus the M.D., are often perceived as important qualifications. A fair proportion of the M.D.s (18.7 percent) were employed in government and other nonprofit organizations or institutions and professional organizations. A somewhat smaller percentage (9.7) were employed by pharmaceutical or other private-sector firms. (It should be noted that the number of empty cells in this table reflects the effects of a small sample size. We can assume, for example, that M.D./Ph.D.s are employed at NIH and thus that a representative sample would include a greater than zero proportion of the M.D./Ph.D. respondents in the government category. This is no doubt true in any tables with many cells; interpretations of the data should therefore take into account the potential artifacts of sample size.)

In fact, the representation of other sectors is broader than the data in Table 9.4 suggest. Members of the sample were also asked to give multiple positive or negative responses on a list of types of institutions of employment, on the assumption that many had professional responsibilities associated with more than one type of employer. The results are presented in Table 9.5.

Table 9.5. All Principal Sites of Employment.

Site of Employment	Percentage of Respondents Employed
Academia	88%
Government agency	7%
Health care delivery institution	6%
Other nonprofit organization or institution	9%
Professional organization	2%
Pharmaceutical company	4%
Other private firms	1%
Research institute	4%

While an even larger proportion (88 percent) listed academia when they identified more than one employer, all the other employer categories increased as well, with the exception of private firms. Health care delivery organizations were represented by 6 percent of the sample, and although this is likely to be low for physicians as a whole, it may be more accurate for physician-leaders. Data from the American Medical Association show that approximately 90 percent of U.S. physicians cite patient care as their major professional activity, the rest citing administration, teaching, research, or another activity (5). Clearly our sample is drawn from an atypical subset of physicians as a whole; nevertheless, it is probably representative of leaders in the health care system.

Professional Activities

Many of the most critical questions about physician-scholars relate to the time spent in various professional activities. These considerations should bear on the types of educational programs developed and on the feasibility of "triple threat" as well as "double threat" careers.

Several trends are quite clear from the data summarized in Tables 9.6 and 9.7. Most of the respondents have spent a major portion of their career time in research. The M.D./Ph.D.s and M.D.s both spent only about one-fifth of their career time in clinical medicine, which is consistent with other indications that this type of career path results in substantially "atypical" activities for physicians. Compared to M.D.s, M.D./Ph.D.s spent more time in research and less time in management and administration. Probably because of their lack of involvement in clinical medicine, Ph.D.s spent somewhat more time in manage-

Table 9.6. Mean Estimated Percentage of Career Devoted to Major Responsibilities, by Degree.

Responsibilities	M.D./Ph.D.	M.D.	Ph.D.
Research	49	36	43
Clinical medicine	19	20	1
Management/administration	15	25	33
Teaching	17	18	23

Table 9.7. Mean Estimated Percentage of Total Career Time Devoted to Area of Responsibility, by Age.

	30-39	40-49	50-59	60-69	Difference between youngest and oldest age groups
Research	57	51	41	41	-16
Clinical medicine	2	15	14	16	-4
Management/ administration	10	22	27	33	+23
Teaching	12	14	18	18	+6

ment/administration and teaching than either of the M.D. groups and more time in research than the M.D.s. Clearly one's educational preparation affects distribution of career time or major areas of responsibility.

The data in Table 9.7 indicate the relationship between age and professional activities. The amount of time devoted to research decreased with age but, in this sample, remained substantial even in the oldest group. The amount of time in management/administration increased gradually, while the time devoted to clinical medicine and teaching changed little.

Knowledge Base: Areas of Responsibility

If students are to be properly prepared for leadership in the health care system, it is crucial to know the areas of responsibility in which they must be competent and the fields in which they should have knowledge. Respondents were asked to rate the importance of various areas and fields from the perspective of their own experience. To tap the respondents' views more deeply, we also asked them what they thought *should* be important in an ideal health care system.

Respondents were asked to rate the importance of competence in a number of areas in which leaders in the health care system have responsibilities. Ratings were done on a four-point scale (1=very important, 2=somewhat important, 3=not very important, 4=not at all important). The mean ratings that respondents provided for themselves and for those in an ideal system are shown in Table 9.8. Respondents considered almost all listed areas important, with skills in communication and research of prime importance both for themselves and for those in an ideal system. Although the high ratings for competence in research was obviously expected, the emphasis on communication and interpersonal skills was somewhat more surprising and suggests the need for formal leadership education, as discussed in Chapter 2. It can be assumed that all medical schools stress communication and interpersonal skills in the doctor-patient relationship and in case presentations during clinical training, but it is not clear that these skills are systematically taught rather than simply evaluated in students. Moreover, the perceived meaning of communication and interpersonal skills in this study must be viewed broadly, since the item was not explicitly linked to the doctor-patient relationship in the questionnaire but to an "area of competence" of leaders in the health care system. Clearly, communication and interpersonal skills are required for competence in all the other areas of responsibility—research, clinical medicine, management and administration, teaching, and public policy and the political process.

Respondents gave a lower rating to skills in clinical medicine and public policy than to the other areas, particularly for themselves. In principle, clinical skills are obviously important for a leader in the health care system, but in reality may be less important to the responsibilities of a research-oriented physician. It is notable that the respondents considered competence in public policy and the political process only somewhat important for themselves in an ideal world. A significant shift in ratings of the importance this area of competence is likely to have taken place since just after this study was conducted as issues related to health care emerged in 1990 and since as increasingly important on the public policy agenda.

In contrast to the similarity with which all three degree groups rated communication and research, there was a tendency for Ph.D.s to give a slightly lower rating to competence in the other four areas than did their colleagues with M.D.s. The most marked difference is in clinical medicine, which is to be expected, as non-M.D.s would have no direct involvement in clinical practice. It is interesting, however, that this rating is nevertheless in the range of the "not too important" category rather than the "not at all important" category and that the mean rating in the ideal system is similar to the ratings made by M.D./Ph.D.s. This suggests that leaders in health care who are Ph.D.s still consider the knowledge base of clinical medicine of some importance for themselves and supports the value of programs such as that described in Chapter 11.

Knowledge Base: Fields of Knowledge

Again using a four-point scale, respondents were asked to rate the importance of knowledge in a number of fields related to health care as that knowledge pertains both to themselves and to those in an ideal situation. The results are presented in Table 9.9. These specific fields are not generally considered as central to the professional activities of health care leaders as the areas of responsibility summarized in Table 9.8. It is notable, however, that although few items received very high ratings, none were very low. This result suggests that all the fields of knowledge listed are of some importance to leaders of the health care system. The tendency of ratings to be higher in an ideal system is clear and contrasts with the pattern in Table 9.8.

Table 9.8. Mean Ratings of Importance* of Competence in Areas of Responsibility, by Degree.

	Self/Ideal		
	M.D./Ph.D.	M.D.	Ph.D.
Research	3.92/3.68	3.80/3.84	3.79/3.92
Communication/interpersonal skills	3.84/3.62	3.91/3.65	3.88/3.76
Management/administration	3.60/3.33	3.41/3.33	3.31/3.16
Teaching	3.56/3.24	3.55/3.49	3.25/3.28
Clinical medicine	3.24/3.35	3.55/3.63	2.14/3.28
Public policy/political process	2.96/3.30	2.95/3.33	2.83/3.08

*4 = very important, 3 = somewhat important, 2 = not too important, 1 = not at all important.

The high rating the respondents gave to the knowledge of bioethics confirms the media attention given to the ethical problems faced by the health care system in recent years. On the other hand, respondents placed health care financing, health law, and nutritional sciences on the low end of the rankings for themselves, despite the great deal of attention devoted to these fields in recent years. They placed them somewhat higher in an ideal system, however, suggesting that health care leaders may not directly face the issues associated with these fields of knowledge, yet they may recognize that colleagues do face them and that in an ideal situation leaders of the health care system would have knowledge of them. In fact, for all twelve fields, the ideal level is higher than the personal level. This result may well reflect an understandable conflict between what leaders view as ideal and what is achievable.

The lower ratings for the importance of a knowledge of medical sociology and anthropology suggests that the leaders in this survey disagree with their colleagues who argue for the importance of these fields (see Chapter 15). Once again, however, these ratings are close to the mean score for importance, they are slightly higher for an ideal system, and the differences among all ratings are small.

Table 9.9. Mean Scores of Importance* of Knowledge of Fields Related to Medicine, by Degree.

	Self/Ideal		
	M.D./Ph.D.	M.D.	Ph.D.
Statistics	3.28/3.60	3.11/3.48	3.20/3.17
Bioethics	3.12/3.33	3.20/3.38	3.08/3.26
Epidemiology	2.72/3.20	2.98/3.53	2.70/3.17
Health economics	2.71/2.90	2.91/3.35	2.42/2.90
Public health	2.64/3.30	2.72/3.40	2.57/3.04
Medical history	2.56/2.70	2.41/2.73	2.39/2.65
Medical sociology	2.56/2.75	2.32/2.75	2.04/2.30
Health care delivery system	2.52/2.90	2.93/3.33	2.29/2.87
Health care financing	2.44/2.70	2.74/3.28	2.08/2.74
Medical anthropology	2.44/2.65	2.18/2.60	1.96/2.39
Health law	2.40/2.85	2.43/3.03	2.29/2.65
Nutritional sciences	2.40/2.79	2.27/2.85	2.38/2.78

*4 = very important, 3 = somewhat important, 2 = not too important, 1 = not at all important.

M.D.s tend to give these fields of knowledge a slightly higher rating than do M.D./Ph.D.s and Ph.D.s. M.D.s rated seven of the twelve fields as more important to themselves than did M.D./Ph.D.s or Ph.D.s, and M.D./Ph.D.s rated the other five higher for themselves than did their M.D. or Ph.D. colleagues. M.D.s rated ten of the fields as more important in an ideal system than did M.D./Ph.D.s or Ph.D.s. The differences are not great, but the pattern is clear. The largest differences between M.D.s and M.D./Ph.D.s occur in evaluations of the importance of health economics, health care financing, and health care delivery systems. This may be explained by the greater and more diverse experience of the M.D.s, who tend to be somewhat older than the other two groups and to have worked in administration and other health-related institutions where knowledge of these fields might be more pertinent.

All three groups considered statistics, bioethics, epidemiology, and public health among the four most important of the twelve fields, with public health usually ranked third or fourth. The public attention to bioethics noted earlier may affect the high rating of the importance of knowledge of this field, and the fact that statistics and epidemiology are traditionally part of the medical school curriculum may explain the high ratings of these fields. These explanations are somewhat problematic, however, when we consider the lower rating of nutritional science, which is also a topic of much media attention and also traditionally part of the medical school curriculum.

The Ph.D.s rated the knowledge of statistics slightly higher for themselves than for those in an ideal system. This is the only exception to the respondents' pattern of rating knowledge of these items higher for those in an ideal system than for themselves.

The Triple Threat: Physician-Scientist-Teacher

Physicians take on a mighty challenge when they have responsibilities for patient care, research and teaching. Indeed, as noted in Chapter 1, questions have been raised as to whether these so-called "triple threats" can be expected to attain true competence in all these areas. In particular, can they achieve excellence in both clinical medicine and research? To gauge views on this topic, we asked respondents how important it is for them, personally, to achieve high levels of competence in both a scholarly field and clinical medicine. We also asked them how important they feel it *should* be to achieve high levels of competence in both (that is, in an ideal health care system). Table 9.10 shows the results by degree.

Table 9.10. Ratings of Importance* of Both Scholarly and Clinical Competence, by Degree.

	Self	Ideal
M.D./Ph.D. (25)	3.04	2.78
M.D. (43)	3.35	3.53
Ph.D. (21)	1.90	3.16

*4 = very important, 3 = somewhat important, 2 = not too important, 1 = not at all important.

The data indicate that M.D./Ph.D.s place less importance upon a high level of dual competence than do M.D.s. This is somewhat surprising as the M.D./Ph.D.s have gone through the demanding process of completing two formal degree programs to achieve high competence in both. Interestingly, the M.D./Ph.D.s rate dual competence as less important in an ideal situation than it is for themselves, whereas the M.D.s consider that ideally it should be even *more* important. Perhaps, the M.D./Ph.D.s are more secure in their competence in both research and clinical medicine and with that perspective have made a choice to emphasize one or the other, a choice they think ideally should be even more available. The importance the M.D.s place upon high levels of competence in both most likely is heightened among our respondents compared to any national sample as they are involved in M.D./Ph.D. education and undoubtedly place high value on it (even higher than their colleagues who have undergone it!). Not surprisingly, the Ph.D.s believe competence in both is not very important for themselves but, like their M.D. colleagues, rate it as more important ideally. We might speculate that M.D./Ph.D.s feel greater pressure to have high levels of competence in both research and clinical medicine and thus believe that, both for themselves and ideally, this is not and should not be the case. They might believe that expectations are too great whereas their colleagues, trained in one area or the other, but involved in M.D./Ph.D. education for others, do not personally see the gap between high expectations and the reality of what is demanded. If this interpretation is correct—and it is offered quite tentatively—it suggests that board certification, subspecialty training, and other measures viewed as indicators of clinical competence should perhaps be de-emphasized as necessary steps following M.D./Ph.D. education. This issue was explored in Chapter 1 and is taken up again below.

We sought a somewhat different perspective on the qualifications for leadership by asking respondents to review a list of areas of responsibility in the health care field and indicate what skills (if any) they think are generally most lacking among leaders and scholars in these areas (Table 9.11). A notable proportion of the respondents indicated that they believe leaders in the health

Table 9.11. Lack of Skills in Leaders, by Degree.

	Percentage Indicating Leaders Lack Skills		
Area of Responsibility	M.D./Ph.D.	M.D.	Ph.D.
Research	23.8	21.4	23.8
Clinical medicine	4.8	23.8	4.8
Management/administrative	61.9	61.9	47.6
Communications/interpersonal	33.3	59.5	28.6
Public policy/political process	76.2	64.3	66.7
Teaching	14.3	19.0	23.8

care field lack skills in major areas of responsibility. The three areas about which there appears to be the most concern are management/administration, communications/interpersonal skills, and public policy/political process. Almost two-thirds of the M.D./Ph.D.s and M.D.s and almost one-half of the Ph.D.s cited a lack of management/administrative skills. In the area of communications and interpersonal relations, there was some disparity among the three groups: a majority (59.5 percent) of the M.D.s believed that leaders lack skills in this area; a smaller, but still notable proportion of the other two groups (33.3 percent of the M.D./Ph.D.s and 28.6 percent of the Ph.D.s) agreed. More than three-fourths (76.2 percent) of the M.D./Ph.D.s and about one-third (64.3 percent) of the M.D.s and the Ph.D.s (66.7 percent) thought that leaders lack skills in the public policy/political process area.

By contrast, respondents did not appear to consider the areas of responsibility within the triple threat role to be as problematical. Fewer than one-fourth of the respondents in each of the three degree groups (23.8 percent, 21.4 percent, and 23.8 percent, respectively) believed that leaders lack research skills. There is disagreement among the three degree groups with respect to clinical skills: Nearly one-fourth of the M.D.s cited a lack of clinical skills, but the vast majority of M.D./Ph.D.s and Ph.D.s (95.2 percent for each group) did *not* cite a lack of skills in this area. There is more agreement among the three groups with respect to teaching: 14.3 percent of the M.D./Ph.D.s, 19 percent of the M.D.s, and 23.8 percent of the Ph.D.s believed that leaders are deficient in teaching skills. Although the proportion of respondents expressing concern in these areas was not inconsiderable, it was notably less than the proportion expressing concern in the other three areas of responsibility: management/administration, communications/interpersonal relations, and public policy/political process.

These three areas of most concern are not customarily included in curricula for medical or research education, most likely because they are not considered germane to the educational effort. Nevertheless, our respondents' belief that skills are lacking in these areas would suggest that training is needed. This conclusion is reinforced by the data presented earlier on respondents' views of the importance of competence in these areas, particularly in communication and interpersonal skills, as well as by several recent journal articles that call for education and training for physicians in these and related areas (6–9). If existing programs and efforts to develop new programs of education for leadership in health care are to reach their full potential, it is clear that more emphasis should be placed upon these areas. Moreover, if physicians seek to participate in current and future planning for health care system reform, knowledge of the policy process is crucial.

Finally, the perceived lack of skills in the areas of management/administration, communications/interpersonal relations, and public policy/political process should also be viewed in light of the figures presented in Tables 9.8 through 9.10. The M.D./Ph.D.s and Ph.D.s among the respondents indicated less concern for high competence in the triple threat areas, but their expectations concerning these other areas suggest that they believe leaders should receive a broad education rather than a narrow, exclusively research-oriented one.

Pathways to Leadership

Another focus of the study was to gather data on career path options for physician-scholars by surveying the respondents' career decisions and opinions about the importance of various alternatives. The questionnaire items dealing with this topic did not apply to the Ph.D.s; some applied to both the M.D.s and the M.D./Ph.D.s, and others only to the M.D./Ph.D.s.

Scheduling options are a matter of concern to all those involved in combined degree and other programs for educating physician-scholars/leaders. We asked respondents to indicate at what point in their medical education they decided to embark on a scholarly/leadership track (Table 9.12). As might be anticipated, the majority of the M.D./Ph.D.s (54.2 percent) decided to enter a

Table 9.12. Timing of Decision to Enter Scholarly/Leadership Career Track, by Degree.

Timing of Decision	M.D./Ph.D.	M.D.
Before medical school	13 (54.2%)	9 (20.9%)
During medical school	5 (20.8%)	13 (30.2%)
During residency or immediately after	4 (16.7%)	16 (37.2%)
Midcareer	2 (8.3%)	4 (9.3%)
Total	24 (100.0%)	42 (100.0%)

scholarly/leadership career track before entering medical school, yet 25 percent did not make the decision until after graduating from medical school. Those with only the M.D. tended to make this decision later; one-fifth (20.9 percent) indicated that they decided on a scholarly/leadership career before medical school. More typically, the decision was made during medical school, or during or just after the residency. The proportion of M.D.s that made this decision in midcareer (about 9 percent) is similar to that of the M.D./Ph.D.s. These data confirm that there are multiple decision points, a finding that reinforces the arguments put forward earlier and in Chapter 14 about the role of the undergraduate and medical schools and the residency in recruitment to academic medicine and leadership roles in the health care system.

The respondents were also asked to what extent they integrated their scholarly/leadership pursuits with the practice of medicine throughout their careers. The data in Table 9.13 indicate that the M.D.s are more likely to have integrated their scholarly/leadership pursuits with the practice of medicine than the M.D./Ph.D.s. This is consistent with the data in Table 9.6, which showed that M.D./Ph.D.s tend to devote a larger portion of their career time to research responsibilities than M.D.s, whereas the M.D.s tend to devote a larger portion of their career time to management/administrative responsibilities. This finding suggests that research is less likely to be integrated with clinical practice than are administrative and management responsibilities.

Respondents were asked to rate the importance of several educational options—residency, board certification, primary care or specialty residency, fellowship training, and postdoctoral research. As with previous questions, respondents were asked whether each pathway was important to themselves and whether it *should* be important for achieving a position as a leader and scholar in the health care system; that is, in an ideal system. Table 9.14 indicates several

Table 9.13. Integration of Scholarship Leadership with Practice of Medicine, by Degree.

Extent of Integration	M.D./Ph.D.	M.D.
Very integrated	9 (36.0%)	23 (52.3%)
Somewhat integrated	9 (36.0%)	13 (29.5%)
Not too integrated	4 (16.0%)	5 (11.4%)
Not at all integrated	3 (12.0%)	3 (6.8%)
Total	25 (100.0%)	44 (100.0%)

Table 9.14. Mean Ratings of Importance* of Pathways for Obtaining Position as Leader/Scholar, by Degree.

Pathway	Self			Ideal		
	M.D./Ph.D.	M.D.	Ph.D.	M.D./Ph.D.	M.D.	Ph.D.
Residency	3.16	3.66	NA	3.48	3.59	3.26
Board certification	2.28	2.91	NA	2.70	2.98	2.91
Primary care specialty	1.96	2.75	NA	2.32	2.63	2.52
Fellowship	2.44	3.64	NA	3.05	3.70	3.42
Postdoctorate	3.44	3.82	3.74	3.48	3.89	3.71

*4 = very important, 3 = somewhat important, 2 = not too important, 1 = not at all important.

interesting and perhaps even unexpected results. The perceived value of a residency was high, although M.D./Ph.D.s rated it as less important for themselves than did M.D.s. All categories rated board certification lower than might be expected, but M.D./Ph.D.s gave this career option an especially low rating for themselves. M.D./Ph.D.s and M.D.s seem to have given a primary care specialty a particularly low rating for positions as leaders or scholars both for themselves and—along with Ph.D.s—ideally. M.D./Ph.D.s differ from M.D.s in the value they attribute to a fellowship; this may reflect the fact that this may be the M.D.s primary research experience. All groups placed a high value on the postdoctorate experience; M.D.s gave it the highest rating, which again may reflect its potential as their primary source of research education. (The NIH treats postdoctoral positions for clinicians and Ph.D.s differently; the Ph.D.s are expected to carry out more sophisticated research, but the M.D.s may use this as their first real research experience.) Some of these findings may suggest that faculty members could be advising students who are completing their M.D./Ph.D. programs and contemplating the next phase of their careers to pursue board certification out of a sense of "realism," as a kind of insurance policy, rather than because the advisors found it personally valuable or legitimately of importance. This reflects the continuing tension concerning the question of "how much" clinical acumen is necessary for physician-scholars/leaders.

The respondents were asked to rate the importance of several factors involved in obtaining both their first professional position and their current position (Table 9.15). The factors rated most important are the M.D. or Ph.D. degree itself, no doubt because these are requirements of professional positions by definition, and surprisingly, except for M.D./Ph.D.s, their mentor. All three groups gave more weight to the importance of a mentor for obtaining their first positions as opposed to their current ones, but the M.D.s gave this factor a much higher mean rating than did the M.D./Ph.D.s. All categories gave professional experience the highest rating for their current position and one of the lowest ratings for their first position.

Table 9.15. Mean Ratings of Importance* of Educational and Other Factors in Obtaining Positions, by Degree.

	First Position			Current Position		
	M.D./Ph.D.	M.D.	Ph.D.	M.D./Ph.D.	M.D.	Ph.D.
Professional contacts	3.32	3.19	3.30	3.64	3.57	3.39
Professional experience	3.08	3.19	2.61	3.72	3.93	3.87
Mentor	2.88	3.42	3.30	2.21	2.29	2.14
M.D. education	3.66	3.40	NA	3.52	3.54	NA
Ph.D. education	3.74	NA	3.61	3.65	NA	3.79
Combined degrees	3.29	NA	NA	3.29	NA	NA

*4 = very important, 3 = somewhat important, 2 = not too important, 1 = not at all important.

Current Policies and Programs

A final set of items in the questionnaire sought to elicit evaluations of programmatic, professional, and personal factors that may affect decisions to follow academic career paths. As these have some direct bearing on how existing programs to educate physician-scholars/leaders might be improved or new programs shaped, we consider them here in the context of current policies and programs.

Respondents were asked to evaluate the quality of a number of characteristics of the combined degree programs at their institutions, where applicable, and then to evaluate the same set of characteristics of combined degree programs nationally (Table 9.16). The respondents rated the various elements of the programs at their own schools with moderate enthusiasm and consistently evaluated their own schools' programs more favorably than national programs. The areas of greatest concern overall were financial aid and other support

Table 9.16. Mean Ratings of Quality* of Characteristics of Combined Degree Programs.

	Own Program	(N)	Nationally	(N)
Medical curriculum	3.22	85	3.00	74
Graduate curriculum	3.47	85	3.01	74
Integration of medical and graduate curricula	2.87	84	2.32	74
Flexibility in scheduling	3.05	86	2.29	72
Time required to complete	3.04	84	2.56	71
Availability of role models	2.94	86	2.55	74
Availability of mentors	3.27	85	2.89	73
Financial aid	2.71	83	2.18	74
Other support services	2.73	81	2.09	71

*4 = very important, 3 = somewhat important, 2 = not too important, 1 = not at all important.

services and, at other sites only, flexibility in scheduling and integration of curricula. These results suggest that there may be rather negative attitudes toward the overall status of dual-degree programs. It would clearly be desirable to obtain more comprehensive and detailed information on the actual quality of existing programs to make more informed decisions regarding national needs. If the respondents' evaluations of their own programs are accurate, the national picture is brighter than generally realized, although concern about financial and other support is widespread.

Another area of concern for existing and proposed programs is recruitment; that is, ways to increase the number and the quality of applicants to combined degree and other programs to educate physician-scholars/leaders. Because research education is assumed to be the most demanding mode of preparation for a scholarly and/or leadership career, one item in the questionnaire asked leaders about factors that might significantly assist in motivating young physicians to enter research (Table 9.17). The respondents' ratings indicate clear directions to pursue to enhance the recruitment of excellent applicants. It would be very valuable to obtain similar data from prospective applicants for such

Table 9.17. Factors Motivating Young Physicians to Enter Research (N = 99)

Possible Motivating Factors	Percentage Selecting
Funds to finance education	81.8
More flexible programs	53.5
Higher salaries in workplace	48.5
More appropriate residencies	44.4
More programs/more diverse programs	40.4
Shortened time to complete programs	28.9

careers. Interestingly, one characteristic that drew considerable attention in the early development of educational programs for physician-scholars—the need for a "fast track"—is not rated as an important factor by this set of respondents, who are active in the field.

If the ratings of these respondents are accurate, they provide effective guidelines for policy within the academic community, such as support for opportunities for research education, flexibility in scheduling for prospective trainees, and residencies geared to the interests and abilities of physician-scientists. If funding needs are to be met, resources within academia must be allocated to support research training programs and possibly to provide increased salaries for productive researchers. In addition, the academic community must make an organized effort to seek increased public support. If sufficient opportunities exist, young physicians may be more willing to devote the time and effort required to become researchers and thus increase the supply of physician-scholars/leaders.

A final consideration of this study was the effect of one's personal life on decisions to undertake a scholarly/leadership career in the health care system, a topic considered from a student's viewpoint in Chapter 18. Respondents were asked to rate the importance of family and personal life in the formulation of various career decisions. The findings are presented in Table 9.18. It appears that family and personal life are a very important factor in decisions to accept or reject a job offer. Given that the processes involved in job offers are usually quite explicit and that job choices imply a relatively long-term commitment, the high mean rating of the importance of family and personal life in such decisions is not surprising.

The ratings for each of the other items fall below the average, suggesting that the respondents tended to make decisions about these important career options on primarily professional criteria, with less regard for personal or family considerations. This may reflect the traditional view (discussed in Chapter 18) that to do well professionally is to do well for oneself and one's family. Another interpretation is that it is realistic to make decisions about such career options on primarily professional grounds. Whatever interpretation one prefers, the system does not appear to accommodate personal or family considerations. Since the questionnaire did not include an item about the role of such considerations in an "ideal" situation, as was done for items related to the knowledge base of leaders in the health care system, we do not have data on leaders' attitudes about the appropriateness, desirability, or legitimacy of their own decision processes. Nevertheless, the figures in Table 9.18 raise questions about the extent to which social changes—particularly the increasing proportion of women in medicine and other leadership pathways in the health care system, and the increasing number of two-career couples—might affect the responses to questions on this topic.

Finally, to gain more insight into the personal demands of their professional lives, we asked the respondents to indicate the extent to which the pressures and time demands involved in pursuing a career of leadership or scholarship in health care adversely affect their family lives. Respondents were also asked to indicate how stressful they found the task of pursuing both medicine and a second field. As Table 9.19 shows, respondents indicated that their family lives had been affected somewhat adversely (mean rating, 2.76) by pressure and time

Table 9.18. Mean Ratings of Importance* of Family and Personal Life in Career Decisions.

	Mean Rating	N
Accepting/rejecting job offer	3.21	86
Postdoctoral training	2.46	76
Fellowship training	2.42	59
Combining research with clinical practice	2.42	55
Choice of residency	2.35	65
Pursuing a degree in addition to the M.D.	2.29	40
Board certification	1.86	57

*4 = very important, 3 = somewhat important, 2 = not too important, 1 = not at all important.

demands, and that it had been somewhat stressful (mean rating, 2.66) to pursue both medicine and a second field. (The latter item was not applicable to respondents with only the Ph.D.) Given what we know about the pressures of achievement, these figures suggest that we are not asking the impossible of our leaders in the health care system. In addition, these figures, and perhaps all the previously cited data on attitudes and beliefs, should be interpreted in light of what is

Table 9.19. Mean Ratings of Career's Adverse Effect* on Family Life and Stress Level.**

	Mean Rating	N
Extent career pursuit adversely affects family life	2.76	85
Degree of stress pursuing medicine and second field	2.66	62

*4 = very adversely affected, 3 = somewhat adversely affected, 2 = not too adversely affected 1 = not at all adversely affected.
**4 = very stressful, 3 = somewhat stressful, 2 = not very stressful, 1 = not at all stressful

known about the high self-expectations of high achievers. As with the data in Table 9.18, however, today's patterns are not necessarily completely applicable to the future.

Conclusion

The data collected from a sample of health care leaders offer few surprises but mark the beginning, we hope, of an attempt to examine the areas of knowledge and competence and the possible pathways that will provide more deliberate and effective preparation of future leaders. Earlier chapters have argued for more rigorous research education in order to enhance retention and productivity. The percentage of career time that the respondents devote to research reinforces this argument. In earlier chapters, we have also stressed the need for programs to educate physician scholars in social and behavioral sciences and the humanities. The importance of management and administrative ability is demonstrated by the time that leaders devote to these responsibilities and by their assessment of the importance of competence in this area as well as in communication and interpersonal skills and public policy and the political process. All these areas of knowledge can be taught and should be introduced into programs to prepare physician-leaders.

The problem of introducing new material into already crowded curricula should not be underestimated. Surveys conducted by residency programs, for example, provide evidence that alumni believe many areas of clinical medicine need more emphasis in residency programs, not to mention additional training in procedures (10). It may thus be unrealistic to call for significant new areas of education, even for those in programs designed to prepare physician-scholars and leaders. Short courses or master's degree programs such as those referred to in Chapter 2 may be the only formal training that can be expected from our current system of medical education in those areas that our survey cited as necessary for more effective leadership.

On the other hand, current programs, though few, will soon result in a cadre of individuals armed with M.D./Ph.D. education in social sciences and humanities who may represent the agents of change in the near future. That is, one way in which physician-sociologists, physician-anthropologists, physician-economists, and the like, may have important effects on the health care system is by introducing into the medical school curriculum and graduate medical education programs approaches to teaching their fields to future physicians. Developed by physician-scholars in the social sciences and humanities, these aspects of the curriculum will have the clinical perspective that makes them as important to the standard knowledge base of physicians as molecular biology or electrocardiographic interpretation. Physicians whose education includes such knowledge will be better prepared to participate in the changing health care system and to accept and help develop a system that meets current and future needs and expectations. The following chapter discusses one of the current programs to prepare M.D./Ph.D.s in social sciences and humanities.

References

1. Peter F. Drucker, "The Coming of the New Organization," *Harvard Business Review* (Jan.-Feb. 1988): 45–52.
2. Held at the University of Illinois at Urbana-Champaign, November 1989. See the Preface and Chapter 19 for further discussion.
3. Diane W. Lindley and Park Randolph, *Trends in Medical School Applicants and Matriculants 1981–1988* (Washington, D.C.: AAMC, 1989).
4. Janet Bickel, "Women in Medical Education: A Status Report" *The New England Journal of Medicine* 319 (1988): 1579–84.
5. *Physician Characteristics and Distribution in the U.S.*, Survey and Design Department (Chicago, Ill.: American Medical Association, 1989).
6. Allan Hillman, "Sounding Board: Managing the Medical-Industrial Complex," *The New England Journal of Medicine* 315 (1986): 511–13.
7. Douglas J. Marchant, "Academia—An Endangered Species," *American Journal of Obstetrics and Gynecology* 156 (1987): 185–92.
8. John Bernard Henry, "Letters. M.D.-M.B.A.: A Dual Degree Whose Time Has Come," *Journal of American Medical Association* 257 (1987): 1727–28.
9. Floyd E. Bloom, Ruth Ellen Bulger and Mark A. Randolph, "Funding Health Sciences Research: A Strategy to Restore Balance," *Clinical Research* 38 (1990): 671–85.
10. Roger L. Nelson, Lee Ann McCaffrey, Fred T. Nobrega, et al., "Altering Residency Curriculum in Response to a Changing Practice Environment: Use of the Mayo Internal Medicine Alumni Survey," *Mayo Clinical Procedures* 65 (1990): 810–17.

10

The Program in Medicine, Arts, and the Social Sciences* at the University of Chicago

Stanley Yachnin, Roberta Siegel, and Godfrey S. Getz

The enterprise we call "medicine" sows the wind and reaps the whirlwind. Medical science, the biotechnology of molecular genetics, and complex arrays of computers connected to powerful supercooled magnets or diagnostic X-ray beams continue to propel the capabilities of the medical profession past new thresholds. As dramatic as these advances are, however, public focus seems to concern itself with questions addressed less to what medicine can do than to what it should do. The economics of health care has emerged as one of the most vexing aspects of the politics and public policy debate in our contemporary life. Complicated questions of access to health care as a "right" challenge our society's commitment to social justice. Ethical questions confront physicians, families, and often the courts as we grapple with complex life support systems, definitions of brain death, autonomy for patients, and substituted judgment for incompetent or comatose persons. Euthanasia hovers offshore. Philosophical and even theological considerations inform public policy debate on many health care issues and challenge all of us to probe and judge abstruse problems: When does life begin? Should old people receive expensive hi-tech medical care? What about the choice between one liver transplant for a child as against prenatal care for two hundred women when resources are limited? Is AIDS a personal, civil rights, or public health matter?

These problems at the nexus of medicine and its societal framework have outstripped the biomedical scientific paradigm. One could frame the following analogy: If war is too important to be left to the generals, then surely medicine is too important to be left to the doctors. Those of us involved in the Program in Medicine, Arts, and the Social Sciences at the University of Chicago would *not* support such a premise. Indeed, we believe that properly trained physician-scholars, equipped with the intellectual tools acquired during the pursuit of their nonmedical doctoral degrees, can make important, perhaps even crucial, contributions to the solution of the overlapping social, economic, scientific, ethical, legal, and humanistic problems which medicine as an enterprise and as a profession faces today. In a personal communication, Carlos F. Gomez, one of the first cohort to receive a doctoral degree made possible by the support of the Pew Program, has this to say about the role such persons may play:

---

*Funded with a grant from the Pew Charitable Trusts; until 1992 known as "the Pew Program in Medicine, Arts, and the Social Sciences."

> One way of thinking about the potential of the Pew Program is to consider what might happen with a group of physicians who also understand the languages and ways of thinking of other disciplines. That we might act as interpreters between the different professional segments of society is obvious. That we might help shape the debates over health policy—without acting as apologists for one professional group or another—might in itself be a significant contribution.

The Pew Program in Medicine, Arts, and the Social Sciences was funded with a grant from the Pew Charitable Trusts in 1985; in 1992, a renewal grant was awarded by the Pew Charitable Trusts and the name of the program was changed to the Program in Medicine, Arts, and the Social Sciences at the University of Chicago to indicate the intention of the university to institutionalize the program. The program presents a unique opportunity for medical students to pursue a doctoral or professional degree at the University of Chicago. We encourage students to focus on one of three major areas: the organizational settings for medical practice; the social responsibility of the physician; and public policy and health care.

The program began with a national recruitment policy and continues to contact all schools in the Association of American Medical Colleges for prospective students. It also advertises in *The New Physician.*

The application process requires students to submit a preliminary "statement of purpose" by November 15 of the academic year. They are then asked to apply directly to the degree-granting unit of the University of Chicago in which they wish to pursue graduate or professional studies. Opportunities for doctoral programs are offered by the Graduate School of Business, the Divinity School, the Law School, the Irving B. Harris Graduate School of Public Policy Studies, and the School of Social Service Administration; the Division of the Humanities: Committee on the Conceptual Foundations of Science, Department of Philosophy; the Division of the Social Sciences: Departments of Anthropology, Behavioral Sciences/Psychology, Economics, History, Political Science, Sociology, and the Committee on Social Thought. Research can be undertaken at the Center for Health Administration Studies, the Morris Fishbein Center for the Study of Science and Medicine, or the Center for Clinical Medical Ethics.

The Faculty Advisory Committee, which serves as the selection committee, considers those medical students accepted for graduate or professional study by the university schools or divisions for program support and selects students in the spring. The committee established the policy of considering all applicants who have completed at least two years of medical school eligible for an award, providing that they have not gone beyond their postdoctoral clinical training. The faculty inserted this last qualification in order to avoid "second-career" applicants.

Since beginning our student recruitment and the enrollment of our first class of Pew Program students in 1986, a total of seventeen students have been supported by the Pew Program in Medicine, Arts, and the Social Sciences. Five students enrolled in the Irving B. Harris Graduate School of Public Policy

Studies; four in the Division of the Social Sciences: Anthropology, Behavioral Sciences/Psychology, Sociology, and Committee on Social Thought; three in the Division of the Humanities: Philosophy and Conceptual Foundations of Science (2); three in the Divinity School; and one each in the Law School and the Graduate School of Business.

At the time they entered the Pew Program, twelve students had completed two years of medical school, and three students had finished their third years. One student, with both M.D. and M.P.H. degrees, had completed one year of internship. A student who began his doctoral studies in 1989 has completed a psychiatric residency training program and obtained a masters' degree in the history of medicine at Cambridge University.

Three Pew Program students are from the University of Chicago Pritzker School of Medicine. Two other students are from the Harvard Medical School. In keeping with our goal of being a program of national scope, our other students (and applicants) are from a broad and representative sampling of U.S. medical schools.

In 1991, the Pew Charitable Trusts renewed the grant which allows the program to support eleven additional students. During this second phase of support from the Pew Charitable Trusts, the program will be known as the Program in Medicine, Arts, and the Social Sciences at the University of Chicago. The university and its development office will work with the program administration to identify private sources of restricted funding to endow the continuation of the program after the grant expires. This underscores the University of Chicago's commitment to continued support of at least two new medical students/scholars each year in doctoral programs such as those described earlier.

Two program evaluations have been made comparing Pew Program students with other medical students. In the first study, the initial cohort of five Pew students was compared to medical students who were admitted to doctoral programs at the University of Chicago but not to the Pew Program and therefore did not matriculate (control group I), and to students at the Pritzker School of Medicine with comparable years of medical education (control group II). In the second study, the Pew students were compared only to Pritzker medical students with equivalent years of medical education. Both surveys indicated that the Pew students are a self-selected group who are more deeply concerned with the broader societal issues confronting medicine as well as with the ethical consequences of medical practice.

Future program evaluations will need to examine the career development of the Pew students, including an assessment of the contributions they make to creative scholarship in their chosen doctoral areas of interest. The faculty committee will consider the program a success only if its graduates assume leadership roles in academic research; in teaching designed to illuminate hitherto arcane or murky areas of the medical universe; and in the world of public policy, health care reform, and evolution in our society. In this regard, it should be pointed out that three of our first four graduates have already assumed important teaching responsibilities in the medical schools and undergraduate programs of two universities and have made significant contributions to the literature in their chosen fields. Another graduate is the associate investigator for a National Institute of Alcohol Abuse and Alcoholism study.

In designing and implementing the program, the Faculty Advisory Committee needed to answer two fundamental questions: 1) Should the scope of disciplines students are allowed to study be broad or narrow? and 2) If graduates choose a career path that leads them away from the core of patient-related clinical medicine, can they still make important contributions to the range of issues confronting medicine now and in the future? The consensus was, first, that the scope of disciplines should be as broad as the divergent enthusiasms of potential students require and our university's programs can support and, second, that program graduates who did not pursue careers at the traditional heart of medicine could nonetheless make contributions of the highest value.

Students accepted into the program receive tuition support for up to four years and a guaranteed stipend for three years. This decision was based upon our hope that students might complete their degree programs in three years and thus be separated from their required medical studies for little more than this period. While we still believe that certain highly motivated program students will be able to complete a Ph.D. program in three years and that those who complete their doctorates in this time will have less difficulty in resuming their medical studies, our experience has taught us that some students may find it impossible and may require a fourth or even a fifth year.

We perceive that the heart of the program is the sense of fellowship and community that has developed amongst the students. In addition to several social activities each quarter, and at the very core of the program's success, is our seminar series. Seminars, at first held three times each quarter and subsequently increased to five, are presented either by participating faculty, guest lecturers from outside the university, or students in the program. In a personal communication, another of our Pew students, Richard Gunderman, has described the value of these meetings as follows:

> Those [students] who present papers have the opportunity to think through their work, to gain experience presenting it to peers, and to receive helpful suggestions on how it might be improved. Others learn to think critically about the work of their colleagues and to bring their perspectives to bear on problems somewhat beyond the bounds of their own disciplines. The seminars keep everyone in the program abreast of their colleagues' work, adding to every fellow's education. The greatest resources of the program are the fellows themselves, and the program has done an admirable job of tapping them for the benefit of all. . . . I suspect that acquaintances are forming now through the program that will be important twenty years from now in medicine and social policy.

A few medical students pursuing degrees in the humanities or social sciences under other auspices have also participated in and enriched this special seminar series. Some of these students have later joined the program.

It is apparent that the inception of the Pew Program in Medicine, Arts, and the Social Sciences in 1985 was well timed with respect to the emerging trends in medical ethics. The basic legal and policy tensions facing modern medicine arise from an effort to reconcile four powerful institutional pressures that simultaneously work their effect on the medical system: cost containment, quality assurance, universal access, and the structure of the health delivery system. In principle, these always work at cross-purposes. Nonetheless, in the 1980s there was major legislation on all fronts: the DRG system, the COBRA rules that require hospitals to treat at their own expense emergency patients and women in active labor; the Health Care Improvement Act of 1986 with its national peer review system; and the Massachusetts and New York universal insurance proposals. The pressing agenda of the 1990s is how the many demands on the health system can be reconciled, and today's Program in Medicine, Arts, and the Social Sciences with its interdisciplinary focus offers medical students the opportunity to master the collateral disciplines necessary to make intelligent choices on these issues.

The importance and scope of the problems medicine faces overwhelm the resources of any single institution or program. Nonetheless, we at the University of Chicago and others have felt compelled to address them. The students supported by the program in Medicine, Arts, and the Social Sciences will be equipped to initiate collaborative leadership for the medical profession. But, clearly, more physician/scholars are necessary for the sustenance of humanistic scholarship in medicine and for the continuous nurture of informed and multidisciplined physicians as policymakers and leaders in the profession and in the public domain of the twenty-first century.

11

Training "Double-Threat" Basic Scientists*

Irwin M. Arias

Society increasingly demands that long-standing disease-related problems be solved, but who will solve them? The opportunity is greater today than in the past because of the amazing conceptual and technical advances that have occurred in basic biologic science, and all indications are that these advances will continue at an increasing rate. However, as science has become more complicated, applications to disease-related problems have begun to exceed the ability of the traditional clinical scientist and call for the expertise of basic scientists, whether alone or in collaboration with clinicians. Unfortunately, most basic scientists have little knowledge of pathobiology or clinical medicine. The thesis of this chapter is that, because most clinical scientists can no longer be expected to function as basic scientists, basic scientists must learn enough pathobiology to attack disease-related problems.

Concern about research physician manpower is reaching crisis proportions (1–3). Factors responsible for the steady decline in the number of physician-scientists include the financial indebtedness of medical graduates, lengthened postgraduate training periods for specialty certification, decreased emulation of the physician-scientist professor as a role model, uncertain long-term institutional support, and increasing competition for research funding. Competition for research grants applies to Ph.D. as well as M.D. graduates; however, there has been a progressive decline in the proportion of research grants awarded by the NIH to physician-scientists. In 1970, 37 percent of NIH grantees had an M.D. degree; the proportion steadily decreased to 26 percent by 1987 (4). In comparison, 57 percent of 1970 NIH grantees had a Ph.D. degree, and the proportion increased to 64 percent by 1987 (4).

Another reason why clinical investigators frequently have difficulty in remaining scientifically competitive is the inadequacy of their postgraduate medical research training. The goal of NIH-supported training programs is to provide the trainee with sufficient research training to become an independent scientist and successfully compete for research funding. Of NIH-supported medical research trainees who began training in 1982 or 1983, however, only 20 percent submitted research grant proposals to NIH by 1988 (5). Few medical specialty training programs include obligatory basic science courses, and basic scientists rarely serve as preceptors; this no doubt contributes to the apparent lack of subsequent applications for NIH research support.

---

*Most of the statements presented here were originally published in *The New England Journal of Medicine* 321 (1989): 972-74. (See note 5.)

Many programs have been created to bridge the increasing gap between advances in basic biology and their application to human disease. Most notable are combined degree (M.D./Ph.D.) programs, the NIH program for physician-scientists, and foundation programs directed at students at every level of the academic tree. However, all these programs have a common premise and objective. The premise is that "biomedical research is tightly linked to physician manpower." (1) The objective is to recreate the proverbial "golden era" of the 1950s and 1960s, when an academic physician could be a "triple-threat" clinician, teacher, and biomedical scientist. At present, this objective is neither as enthusiastically sought nor as frequently attained. The major reason is that each component has become a full-time job, largely as a result of the increasing complexity of medical practice and the rapid pace of biomedical research.

Should our efforts be directed exclusively toward the recreation of the proverbial "triple-threat" medical academician? Are we missing other opportunities to bridge the gap between biological science and medicine? I believe that the answers are "no" to the first question and "yes" to the second.

Almost every basic science department in our medical schools has a graduate program. There is usually no difference between research activities and graduate programs in the basic science departments in medical schools and those in universities. Graduate students in medical schools spend approximately six years studying in the shadows of major medical centers. At the onset of their training, many graduate students are interested in human disease and health-related research. In interviews I conducted with fifty-one randomly selected graduate students in medical school basic science departments, thirty-nine stated that an interest in research related to human disease was an important factor in their decision to enter a basic science program in a medical school rather than in a university. At the conclusion of their training, graduate students rarely understand what takes place in clinical departments, and their interest in pathobiology largely disappears. The major reasons are that few graduate programs teach pathobiology and many thesis advisors in basic science departments have little interest in or linkage to clinical problems. Occasionally, basic science faculty express negative attitudes toward physician-scientists, and these attitudes are acquired by their students. For these reasons, it is not surprising that most Ph.D. graduates seek careers in academia or industry and do not seriously consider biomedical research in clinical departments.

In addition, appointments in a clinical department are often believed to confer second-class citizenship on a basic scientist, mainly because scientific independence and academic tenure are frequently restricted. Consequently, as a graduate student remarked, "You work for, and not with, a physician."

Graduate students, Ph.D. postdoctoral fellows, and thesis advisors can, however, learn sufficient pathobiology to be able to work *with* physicians rather than for them. Toward this end, four years ago, we created a novel course in pathobiology, which has been completed by fifty-four graduate students, seven postdoctoral fellows, and five faculty members. The course is based on analysis of twenty major human diseases. Students experience gross and microscopic pathology, observe major diagnostic procedures (e.g., MRI, NMR, CT scanning, cardiac catheterization) and specialized patient care activities (e.g., transplantation, dialysis) and participate in patient presentations. These activities are accompanied by detailed analysis of the major biological processes involved in each disease. It is surprising but reassuring that our objectives can be attained in a one-semester course that meets only twice weekly for 150 minutes per week.

To avoid overcrowding in clinical activities, we limited attendance to fifteen participants. Students or fellows from any basic science graduate program are accepted; approximately one-third are first-year students.

The format is best illustrated by an example. The topic for the first week is liver failure and regeneration, and the basic biology counterpart is growth control. Students meet in the Pathology Department with an experienced pathologist and the course director, who is a physician-scientist. A few questions usually reveal that the students have little knowledge of the anatomy or function of the liver and cannot accurately describe inflammation, necrosis, or fibrosis. CT scans, gross liver specimens, and histologic sections are examined in such a way that students quickly learn the rudimentary but essential aspects of liver function and disease. A clinically related activity follows. A suitable patient, diagnostic procedure, or therapeutic modality is demonstrated and discussed. Students are given up to six selected reprints related to the topic. Two days later, the group meets with the course director and a basic science faculty member who is an expert in the biologic process being considered. The format is Socratic: question, answer, more questions. Students consider mechanisms, hypotheses, and experimental approaches to the basic problem. The faculty members are facilitators, not lecturers.

The following representative diseases have been considered in parallel with their associated basic biologic processes:

Primary cancer of the liver—DNA viruses and cancer
Osteoporosis—mineralization
Transplantation—immunobiology
Atherosclerosis, gallstones—cholesterol metabolism
Inflammation—mediators
Lysosomal diseases—intracellular trafficking
Leukemia—cell proliferation
Cystic fibrosis—regulation of ion transport
Acromegaly—hormonal control of growth
AIDS—retrovirology
Aging—molecular and cellular mechanisms
ITP—autoimmunity
Liver failure, regeneration—growth control
Hepatitis B virus liver cancer—parasitism
Pathobiology of hunger—malnutrition

In each case, the presentation of gross and microscopic pathology is followed by a selected clinical experience. In this manner, the class eventually becomes acquainted with all major clinical activities in the medical center. Patients are briefly presented by the course director to illustrate major disease manifestations and problems. Reprints are distributed and the associated basic biology session follows the format described.

Because the course has been in existence for only four years, there has been no long-term follow-up. Students select the course voluntarily; however, it is oversubscribed, which suggests that many students in our graduate programs seek training in pathobiology. Annual questionnaires and, when possible, interviews have been conducted with 82 percent of the students and fellows who have taken the course. Almost all have sustained an interest in pathobiology and encouraged other colleagues to take the course. Five students indicated that their choice of thesis research was influenced by the course. Most important is the realization by all but four students and one fellow that an academic career in a clinical department has desirable features and should not be automatically excluded. The number of Ph.D. postdoctoral fellows and faculty who request the course has increased steadily. In 1989, eight Ph.D. postdoctoral fellows and five faculty members made such requests.

Conclusion

A major challenge in bridging the gap between important advances in basic science and their application to medicine is how to create a group of scientists who share knowledge of pathobiology and basic science. Programs designed to recreate the "triple-threat" physician-scientist are an important part of this effort. Less well-recognized is the need to create "double-threat" basic scientists who are knowledgeable about human disease and who will become major participants in scientific bridge-building.

References

1. B. Healy, "Innovators for the 21st Century: Will We Face a Crisis in Biomedical-Research Manpower?" *The New England Journal of Medicine* 319 (1988): 1058–65.
2. J. B. Wyngaarden, "The Clinical Investigator as an Endangered Species," *The New England Journal of Medicine* 301 (1979): 1254–59.
3. B. Healy, and G. A. Keyworth, II, "The NIH and Numbers: A Vital Concern's Concern," *The New England Journal of Medicine* 312 (1985): 1450–52
4. J. Moskowitz, NIH, July 6, 1988, Internal communication from Associate Director for Science Policy and Legislation to the Director of NIH.
5. I. M. Arias, "The Sounding Board," *The New England Journal of Medicine* 321 (1989): 972–74.

12

The Ph.D.-to-M.D. Program of the University of Miami School of Medicine

William M. Awad, Jr.

After nineteen years, the Ph.D.-to-M.D. Program of the University of Miami School of Medicine came to an end with the graduation of its eighteenth and last class on June 3, 1990. This chapter describes selected aspects of this special course of study.

The program was conceived and implemented at a time of both a perceived significant shortage of physicians and a lack of professional opportunities for many Ph.D. scientists. Reports on manpower needs gave little indication that the maldistribution in these professions would be short-lived; indeed, they implied a possible steady state of significant duration. In response to this apparent long-term need, the School of Medicine set about to create a career shuttle, through an accelerated medical curriculum, which would resolve the dearth in one professional group by tapping the surplus in the other. Initially, it was anticipated that the less successful scientists would be the interested candidates, that a shortened curriculum could be developed to take advantage of the scientific backgrounds of the candidates, and that no meaningful contribution to manpower requirements could result from the efforts of a single school. The curriculum was therefore designed to be sufficiently attractive to be adopted by several other institutions.

The setting in Miami was an extremely favorable one for this new venture in medical education. From conception to implementation, the process took less than eight months, an extraordinarily short interval, largely because the principals in the School of Medicine (1) were in close agreement on the goals, philosophy, and plan of the program. During this time, the approval and support of individual departments were obtained, a course of studies was defined, the appropriate academic bodies of the school and university reviewed and approved the curriculum, the state licensing authority and national accrediting agencies provisionally accepted the validity of the credentials that future graduates would present, the program was announced, and finally the review and selection of candidates were completed. In 1971, from a pool of 130 applicants, 20 individuals were admitted to the first class. Despite the uniqueness of the curriculum and the fact that an inaugural class was being constituted, a daring complexity was added to this educational experiment: four nonbiologists (two physicists, a metallurgist, and an organic chemist) were included in this first group of students.

The first class had a schedule of eighteen months: six for the basic sciences and twelve for ward experiences. It was soon apparent that very few courses could be used from the regular four-year curriculum. Most of the basic science presentations were developed into special courses. The majority of students in the first class completed the curriculum without difficulty in time to start house-staff appointments on January 1, 1973. Because this was distinctly out of cycle with the usual start of internships, the appointments could be arranged only through supplication by several faculty members to colleagues throughout the country, a procedure that would be difficult to undertake on a yearly basis. It soon became clear that students would need both an integrating course in the basic sciences as an introduction to the clerkships and some clinical work beyond that experienced in the usual junior year, and the curriculum was extended to twenty-four months with the third entering class (2). Thereafter, the curriculum remained largely unchanged, with six months of basic science courses, two and one-half months of courses in introduction to medicine and mechanisms of disease, twelve months of core clerkships identical to the junior year of the regular curriculum, and, finally, approximately two and one-half to three months of elective clerkships, including an almost mandatory subinternship. The latter requirement was adopted in response to the near-universal recommendations of the graduates of the first few classes. Virtually every time period was accounted for, with up to forty hours per week of coursework. Because examinations were frequently scheduled on Monday mornings, weekends were generally needed for study and review. Only three two-week periods of vacations (one during the intervening summer, and one during each Christmas) provided any respite during the two years, and a few individuals occasionally required even these short holidays for remedial work.

After the fourth year of operation, only minor changes beyond those relating to schedules were introduced (a three-week clerkship in family and community medicine and a lecture series in the behavioral sciences). Since the four nonbiologists in the first class completed the curriculum with a record indistinguishable from that achieved by their life-scientist peers (3), all future classes were selected without any attempt at quotas or proportions of different disciplines. After the first year, it had become evident that only a very few courses from the regular curriculum could be adopted for the students in the program and that the applicant pool included a large number of individuals with strong academic credentials. This realization led to a change in perspective. Rather than pursue the populist goal of satisfying a national shortage of physicians, the program naturally developed into an elitist experience in the best possible sense, introducing the best young scientists to the theory and practice of medicine. This was a fortunate development in view of the great change in the national perspective on the shortage of physicians. With the increased enrollment in medical schools, the institution of new schools throughout the country, and the increasing number of American graduates from foreign medical schools, the indications were that the nation would soon face a surfeit of physicians (4).

Table 12.1 lists the prior professional disciplines of all matriculants. About 53 percent came from life sciences; chemists, engineers, and physicists constituted 44 percent of students. The procedures for the selection of candidates were described earlier (2). As stated then, three features were considered in evaluating individuals: academic distinction, professional achievement, and

Table 12.1. Disciplines of Ph.D. Degrees of Matriculants in University of Miami M.D. to Ph.D. Program.

Discipline	Number	Percentage
Biochemistry	87	16
Biological sciences	196	37
Chemistry	82	15
Engineering sciences	74	14
Mathematics	17	3
Oceanography	4	1
Physics	77	14
TOTAL	537	100

motivation for a medical career. How these elements were to be weighted was never defined, and obviously members of the program committee, the body in charge of all aspects of the curriculum including admissions responsibilities, wrestled individually and collectively in the selection process. The composition of individual classes within a representative three-year period attests to the fact that no other preconceived selection standards were entertained. Indeed, class composition varied from 80 percent life scientists to only 15 percent life scientists and 35 percent physicists. It should be noted that the latter class achieved the highest scores on National Board examinations in the history of the program.

Class composition changed significantly as the years passed. For example, where physicists constituted 24 percent of all students for the first eight classes, their numbers dropped to a little more than 8 percent for the last ten classes. Several factors contributed to this change. First, when the program started, Ph.D. physicists and other nonbiologists lacked the credentials for admission to regular four-year programs (5) and thus were frequently denied any opportunities elsewhere for medical qualification. We believe that these impediments to admission were dropped by an increasing number of prestigious institutions because of their awareness of the achievements by graduates of the first few classes of the Miami program. Second, the number of doctoral candidates in physics nationwide dropped significantly, and this phenomenon, together with increasing professional opportunities in industry, led to a reduced interest in medicine as an alternative career. Third, and this was true for all disciplines, the poor press that the practice of medicine was receiving, especially with such issues as malpractice insurance and litigation, diagnosis-related groups, and the increasing requirements for documentation of clinical activities, led to a reduction of interest in medicine as a profession. As a result, the number of applications in general dropped from more than 1,000 in 1972 to less than 250 in 1988, but the drop in the number of physicists who applied was steeper. There was always a disproportionate number of outstanding physicist applicants compared to applicants from other disciplines, and this discrepancy was reflected in the composition of the different classes. For instance, the class with 35 percent physicists was selected from a pool of applicants in which less than 12 percent came from that discipline.

Table 12.2 summarizes the progress of all matriculants. Approximately 95 percent of the students graduated within a two-year period; another 3 percent graduated eventually. Twelve students delayed graduation for nonacademic

Table 12.2. The Progress of All Matriculants in the University of Miami M.D. to Ph.D. Program.

Status	**Number**
Graduates	525
On time	508
Academic delay	5
Nonacademic delay	12
Withdrawals	10
Academic	3
Nonacademic	7
Dismissals	2
TOTAL	**537**

reasons: two because of illness, one because of personal issues, and nine because of concerns about fulfilling future licensure requirements in California. This last group were all members of a single class, during a time when the program was contesting an adverse change in policy toward licensure of graduates in that state. Three students withdrew from the program because of academic reasons: Two declined to repeat the first year after an initial unsatisfactory performance, and the third transferred to the regular four-year curriculum after encountering difficulties with the intensity of the basic sciences courses. Seven students withdrew in good academic standing: two because of poor health, one because of financial reasons, three who believed that they had made an error in changing from successful positions in their previous professions, and one who was overwhelmed by the intensity of the curriculum. Two students, one in each of the first two classes, were dismissed because of unsatisfactory performance.

In the fall of 1988, a survey was made of the graduates of the first ten classes of the program. Table 12.3 provides an overview of the results. A little more than 30 percent of those who had completed house staff training had full-time faculty positions, the overwhelming majority of which were in schools of medicine. About 64 percent were in private practice. Some of the latter

Table 12.3. Graduates of Classes I–X in the University of Miami M.D. to Ph.D. Program.

Status	Number
Full-time faculty	75
Schools of medicine	73
Other	2
Industry	7
Federal and state government	7
Private practice	156
In training	25
Deaths	

individuals had experienced full-time faculty positions before entering private practice; a few had part-time positions in clinical departments. Of the seven graduates in industry, six were in administrative positions and the seventh was undertaking basic research in molecular biology. Of the seven in governmental positions, most were undertaking research, for example, at the National Institutes of Health. No survey has yet attempted to discover why some graduates chose academic careers and others selected private practice. It is clear that a few individuals have become productive clinical scientists in the setting of group private practice where the opportunities for patient-based research are broader than those afforded by a school of medicine. This was especially true for a few physicists who became radiologists and found that as junior faculty members they had insufficient access to state-of-the-art equipment compared to full-fledged members of well-equipped group practices. In view of the high cost of equipment in some fields of physics and the very limited access to that equipment for junior researchers, those individuals may have felt that they were repeating, as medical faculty members, earlier unsatisfactory experiences.

The Ph.D.-to-M.D. program was a bright experiment in American medical education. It showed that a talented young individual with a strong background in a basic science could become well educated in medicine through an accelerated course of study. The termination of the curriculum was due largely to forces beyond the control of the school: the rising costs of the educational experience, the reduced interest of Ph.D. scientists in medicine, and, most important, the increasing difficulties in gaining licensure in several states as a result of the very success of the graduates. The graduates were uniformly licensed without difficulty until about six years ago through the discretionary powers of the state regulatory agencies, which recognized the contributions of the prior educational experiences of the students. However, graduates from foreign medical schools raised the issue of a discriminatory practice when they were denied licensure because of inadequate credentials, while the graduates of the program, with fewer years in medical school, had no such difficulties. Licensing authorities were faced with the difficult problem of meeting these challenges in court. Needless to say, almost all who participated in the curriculum regret its demise.

References

1. W. J. Harrington, W. J. Whelan, B. J. Fogel, and E. M. Papper, "Alleviating the Shortage of Physicians," *Science* 172 (1971): 1109–11.
2. W. M. Awad, Jr., W. J. Harrington, and E. M. Papper, "The Ph.D.-to-M.D. Program: The Seven-Year Mark," *The New England Journal of Medicine* 301 (1979): 863–67.
3. K. H. Muench, W. M. Awad, Jr., W. J. Whelan, "The Experimental M.D. Program for Ph.D.s: An Evaluation at the Three-Year Mark," *Journal of Medical Education* 49 (1974): 649–59.
4. R. J. Smith, " Carter Attempt to Limit Doctor Supply Faces Tough Going in Congress," *Science* 203 (1979): 630–32.
5. E. M. Papper, " University of Miami School of Medicine M.D.-Ph.D. Program," *Journal of Laboratory Clinical Medicine* 85 (1975): 351–54.

13

The Research Training of Physician-Scientists

Charles H. Rodgers, Phillip Gorden, and Gary E. Striker

The health care needs of the citizens of the United States require a continuing source of qualified basic and clinical biomedical scientists who can develop the necessary data for increasing the ability to diagnose, treat, and prevent disease. The role of sound research training in the development of qualified scientists is widely recognized as a critical element in the advancement of biomedical science. As the pace of scientific change accelerates and international competition for scientists and scientific progress intensifies, the availability of proper training becomes a factor of considerable significance. Continued progress can be ensured only if sufficient numbers of appropriately trained individuals pursue careers in biomedical research.

Some of the existing training programs are producing either too few scientists or scientists who are incapable of conducting modern research. One difficulty may be a lack of knowledge of the many types of support available to M.D. and Ph.D. trainees. Another problem is that some institutions may not have the appropriate type and number of faculty to provide proper research training in the basic sciences and subsequent application to the clinical arena.

This chapter will highlight current and projected programs offered in support of research training by the National Institute of Diabetes and Digestive and Kidney Diseases (NIDDK) and some of the special programs initiated at the local level by universities. In addition, we will present an evaluation of the Institutional Training Program of the Division of Kidney, Urologic and Hematologic Diseases (DKUHD) of the NIDDK. Finally, we will present the findings and recommendations on research training developed by the National Kidney and Urological Diseases Advisory Board.

NIH Manpower Development Programs

As an important part of its mission, NIH sponsors programs designed to help ensure that highly trained scientific personnel will be available in sufficient numbers and in appropriate fields to meet the nation's biomedical research requirements. Research training and career development opportunities are supported by the NIDDK for all stages of professional development from the pre- and postdoctoral levels to the senior investigator level. These awards are designed to support specific stages of career development and can be awarded for a particular stage or in sequence to provide as many as nine years of continuous support for research training. Initial training experiences are often supported by the National Research Service Award (NRSA).

An NRSA Institutional Training Grant (T32) enables the directors of training programs to recruit and select trainees for their pre- and (or) postdoctoral research training positions. Experience suggests that trainees who are accepted for predoctoral training in basic science research laboratories are most likely to choose research careers early in their professional development. The most common profile of a postdoctoral fellow supported on an NIDDK institutional training grant is an M.D. who has just finished clinical training in a specialty of medicine and seeks to use this support mechanism as a bridge between clinical/academic training and full-time research training.

The NRSA Individual Postdoctoral Fellowship (F32) is another type of NRSA award, which can be utilized by either M.D.s or Ph.D.s to obtain initial research training. This fellowship award may also be granted after the individual has received the M.D., Ph.D., D.D.S., D.V.M., or equivalent degree. Individuals may have had prior support for one or two years on an institutional training grant. In contrast to the institutional research award, the NRSA fellowship requires the applicant to submit an application to the NIH. An Initial Review Group (IRG) at the NIH reviews the application for its scientific merit and training potential. It is ranked in relation to the applications submitted by a national pool of competing applicants.

Although NRSA-supported training is limited to thirty-six months, a waiver of the limit may be requested. Waivers are usually granted by the director of NIDDK if they are well justified.

There are three types of Career Development Award, whose purpose is to provide advanced research training in support of career development in scientific research: the Physician Scientist Award, the Clinical Investigator Awards, and the Research Career Development Award (RCDA). The first two awards are meant to provide additional supervised training opportunities for physicians who are not yet independent investigators. The third award is for the final development of those who have demonstrated their ability as independent investigators. M.D.s may apply for all three types of awards; Ph.D.s have access to the RCDA. M.D.s who possess Ph.D.s in nonbiomedical or behavioral sciences or M.D./Ph.D.s who require two or more years to update their basic science skills may request special consideration by the IRG for a Career Development Award.

An M.D. who has had little or no research experience, and ordinarily has completed at least one postgraduate year of clinical training, may choose to apply for the Physician Scientist Award (K11). This program, like the NRSA, has both individual and institutional components. There are two general phases of research training. In Phase I, the trainee must be involved in a specific research project and follow a course of study to gain increased knowledge in the basic sciences. The length and rigor of this phase may be sufficient to qualify the candidate for an advanced graduate degree. After two to three years in Phase I, the trainee enters Phase II to spend full time in a clinical or basic science research project designed to provide for successful entry into a full-time academic research career in a clinical or basic science department. In both phases, the trainee is under the direction of one or more sponsors. The K11 is normally a five-year training program, but a trainee who has had several years of NRSA training may apply for three years of support on the K11.

The Clinical Investigator Award (K08) is another career award program available to young physicians in pursuit of research training. In contrast to the applicant for the Physician Scientist Award, the applicant for this program must have had several years of research training. This award also requires the submission of an application to NIH, where it is reviewed in national competition. The applicant must present evidence of research potential, a defined research proposal, and a credible sponsor. The Clinical Investigator Award, therefore, often serves as a bridge between the institutional training grant and an independent research career for the M.D. investigator. Like the K11, the K08 is normally a five-year award but may be given for three years if the trainee has received two years of support as an NRSA awardee.

At the time of application for a Physician Scientist or Clinical Investigator Award, an applicant cannot be a principal investigator on an NIH grant. However, recipients of these awards are encouraged to apply for either a First Independent Research Support and Transition (FIRST) Award (R29) or a Research Project grant (R01) before finishing the fellowship support. This ensures an orderly transition into a full-time research career.

The Research Career Development Award (K04) also requires an application to NIH. This award provides salary support for young M.D. or Ph.D. scientists who have demonstrated their ability as research scientists. The salary support provides for at least an 80 percent time commitment for research activities. The accepted evidence of research ability is a reasonable bibliography and the presence of existing research grant support. The research grant support must be funded by the NIDDK. The K04 is a five-year award.

Illustrative Manpower Development Programs at Academic Institutions

In the past, programs originated and supported by academic institutions tended to be informal and limited in number and scope. Interest in developing and expanding these programs appears to be increasing.

Johns Hopkins University

The Clinician Scientist program at Johns Hopkins University, developed and funded by the School of Medicine, promotes the research careers of young M.D. faculty by providing financial support so that they can spend additional time on research activities. The source of this salary is a fund generated by the School of Medicine from foundation support, pharmaceutical companies, endowments, and clinical earnings. Recipients of this award are selected by a competitive application process tied closely to concurrent efforts to obtain external research support. This program has been developed to lessen the pressure on young clinical faculty to generate salary support from patient care activities.

Candidates for this program must meet the following requirements: They must possess an M.D. degree; have a full-time primary appointment as an instructor or assistant professor in a clinical department, salaried by the university at the time of initiation of the award; be nominated by a department director, who will protect at least 75 percent of the applicant's time for research if an award is made; have a funded, pending, or draft application for external research support (e.g., NIH R01) or Career Development Award (K08) obtained through a competitive review process (federal or nonfederal); be active as a clinician; and provide evidence that the award will in fact result in the protection of research time normally devoted to clinical practice.

Successful candidates for this program must have demonstrated potential for, and commitment to, a career as an independent investigator; capability to spend at least 75 percent of their time on research during the period of the award; adequate research training (training in a different field is allowable, but initial research training should not be concurrent with the Johns Hopkins Clinician Scientist Award); an acceptable research plan, as assessed by review of an existing (funded), pending, or draft application to an external sponsor; and completion of a satisfactory interview (promising candidates are interviewed by one or more members of the selection committee).

The awards provide as much as $50,000 per year for a maximum of two years to support up to 75 percent of salary and benefits. Research support from external sources is deducted from the 75 percent, since the award is not intended to supplement external support and thus enable the applicant to devote more than 75 percent effort to research. Funding of the second year depends on continuing in the program and receiving a satisfactory progress report. Support is limited to salary and fringe benefits; a maximum of $25,000 per year will be allowed to those with concurrent external support. Funding for the second year is usually no higher than the level for the first year and depends on demonstrating sufficient progress and a continuing need for salary up to 75 percent. To monitor the program and its usefulness, the committee requires awardees to provide reports on their research, publications, and funding for several years following their award.

The program at Johns Hopkins provides an excellent and flexible complement to the programs supported by the NIH. If adopted by other institutions, this type of program could significantly expand the amount and efficacy of research education support for physician-scientists. For physicians with thorough research training (e.g., through an M.D./Ph.D. program), the Johns Hopkins model can provide an effective means to generate significant preliminary data as the basis for a successful application for an R01 or FIRST award. For physicians with less complete research training, this type of program may assist in obtaining one of the research career awards.

University of Washington/Fred Hutchinson Cancer Research Center

At the University of Washington/Fred Hutchinson Cancer Research Center, a pilot program was developed in response to the shortage of physician-investigators capable of exploiting the rapid growth of biologic research topics and the recent advances in new techniques in cellular and molecular biology. The program is especially designed for physicians seeking training in modern biology. Program administrators believe that this field offers an undeveloped potential for the enhancement of human health.

The need for such a program is quite apparent. Although there are physician-investigators working in the basic sciences who are capable of training young investigators in modern research, including the most recent techniques, there are too few similarly trained clinical investigators with a degree of commitment and sophistication in molecular biology proportional to the potential opportunities for clinical applications. Scientific training is clearly lacking at the postdoctoral level for physician-investigators in this field due to the relatively small number of clinical faculty in postresidency clinical research training programs who are familiar with modern research techniques. Training opportunities in other programs, such as M.D./Ph.D. programs, are not large enough to meet the current and future needs in this area.

The joint training offered by the University of Washington and the FHCRC provides training opportunities across the full range of concepts, technical approaches, and experimental systems that characterize modern biology. The faculty is a broad-based group of about thirty established basic biologists, skilled in cellular and molecular techniques, who have volunteered to accept physician postdoctoral trainees.

Of the approximately 102 postdoctoral fellows in basic science laboratories at the FHCRC, 21 are physicians who have made a commitment to advanced modern biology training with individual mentors. One-fourth are M.D./Ph.D.s seeking further research training, and the remainder are M.D.s from subspecialty training programs. The program is supported in part by NRSA Institutional Training Grants awarded by the NIDDK and the National Cancer Institute.

Most trainees have completed their residencies and are in subspecialty training programs. The purpose of providing this type of research training program at this stage in the clinical training of physicians is to increase the likelihood that the trainees will follow a research career in the clinical sciences rather than in a basic science discipline.

The admissions committee is composed of staff members from the University of Washington and the FHCRC. Candidates are solicited by many means, including national advertising. Successful candidates are admitted to an appropriate subspecialty program at one of the two training centers and remain associated with that program throughout their training. Each has a clinical mentor responsible for helping him or her meet specialty requirements and develop clinical proficiency. Clinical responsibilities are assumed toward the end of research training. The opportunity to integrate research and clinical interests prepares the trainees for a position in a research-oriented academic clinical department in their specialty.

Trainees are required to commit three years to the overall program. The faculty requires a full-time commitment to research, especially for those trainees who have not received in-depth training in modern biology. Flexibility is allowed for individuals with earlier partial training experience sufficient to meet program requirements.

The good response to this program and the perceived shortages in trained faculty and physician-scientists in fundamental biology raise several questions about the feasibility of establishing training programs with similar goals at an earlier point in the career path: Is there a need for such training programs in molecular medicine during medical school? If so, can such programs provide a different pathway than existing M.D./Ph.D. programs by offering sufficient training in fundamental biology in conjunction with the clinical sciences but requiring less time? Will the number of trainees necessary to meet the national needs in molecular medicine be willing to commit the time required to become competent in modern fundamental biology? This would necessarily prolong the period during which the student would be dependent on financial aid. It would also extend the medical school curriculum to more than the current four years, but probably not as much as the seven- to eight-year M.D./Ph.D. program.

An Evaluation of NRSA Institutional Training Grant Programs

Continuing concern about the decline in the number of M.D. applicants for NRSA individual fellowships and Research Career Development Awards (1) and about the apparently decreasing interest among senior medical students in research careers (2) has caused the NIH to encourage the recruitment of more physicians into research careers and to allow the prolongation of the NRSA appointments to NRSA Institutional Training Grants in an attempt to enable physician-scientists to become competitive for NIH research funds.

An NIH Evaluation

As director of NIH, Dr. James Wyngaarden commissioned a task force on physician scientist training in 1989 to review and make recommendations concerning NIH research training programs. The task force found that

1. Fewer than 20 percent of all M.D. trainees apply for grants, and of these, 10 percent receive NIH research grants.
2. A study of eleven fiscal years showed that more than 50 percent of physician trainees spent twelve months or less on NRSA Institutional Training Grants. This figure exceeded 60 percent during several fiscal years during the study period.
3. Examination of the cohort of postdoctoral M.D. trainees supported by NRSA Institutional Training Grants from fiscal years 1972 to 1982 revealed a direct correlation between the number of months of training and the percentage of trainees who submitted grant applications. For instance, when the length of training was twelve months or less, about 27 percent applied; of those in training for thirteen to twenty-four months, about 37 percent applied; and if the training period was twenty-four months or more, about 44 percent applied.

4. Postdoctoral positions on NRSA Institutional Training Grants are not always used to support individuals committed to a career in biomedical research. Some NRSA Institutional Training Grants have been particularly ineffective in producing physician-scientists.

In view of these findings, the task force made specific recommendations, including 1) a requirement for a minimum of two consecutive years of training for those supported on NRSA Institutional Training Grants and 2) individual tailoring of research training for M.D. scientists.

Individual tailoring can be accomplished by combining the training and career programs in various ways. For instance, a trainee can be supported on an NRSA Institutional Training Grant for a period of two to four years (the fourth year requires a waiver of the thirty-six-month limitation on NRSA training), then receive further training as a recipient of a Clinical Investigator Award. Alternatively, several years of research training can be combined on each of the NRSA programs (Institutional Training Grant and individual postdoctoral fellowship) before the Clinical Investigator Award. Some may find it more appropriate to utilize an institutional NRSA for one year and then apply for a Physician Scientist Award. This sequence enables the trainee to take advantage of the Phase I and II components of the Physician-Scientist program. To provide further aid to trainees taking this path, the task force on physician-scientist training recommended that applicants be allowed to apply for three years of support on either the K08 or K11. Until now, the length of these awards has been five years. It is also possible to insert a year of clinical training between the NRSA programs or between the NRSA and the research career programs as long as clinical training is not supported by any of the NIH program awards. Using various combinations of NIH research training and career programs in conjunction with clinical training now allows the director of the training program to be more flexible in meeting the particular needs of physician-scientist trainees. Program directors, or trainees, are encouraged to contact the NIH manpower program director in the institute appropriate to their research interest(s) to take advantage of these and other opportunities.

A DKUHD/NIDDK Evaluation

An evaluation of NRSA Institutional Training Grants in nephrology and hematology during fiscal years 1977 through 1981 was made by the Division of Kidney, Urologic and Hematologic Diseases of the NIDDK (3). The data demonstrated that of the 330 trainees (229 M.D.s, 101 Ph.D.s) supported on NRSA Institutional Training Grants, 105 (32 percent) applied to the NIH for research support. Sixty-eight of the applicants received at least one regular research grant or equivalent award, and twelve received one of the career awards (K08, K11). Sixty-six M.D.s submitted 151 applications, of which 84 were funded (56 percent), and 39 Ph.D.s submitted 95 applications, of which 54 were funded (57 percent). There was no correlation between the length of the training period and the presence or absence of applications for research support among the M.D. trainees. The proportion of M.D. applicants supported on training grants for twenty-four months or more (50 percent) was no greater than that for applicants supported on training grants for twenty-three months or less (50 percent). As was the case for M.D. trainees, there was no correlation among Ph.D.s between the duration of support on a training grant and the number who made application for research support. However, a slightly higher proportion of Ph.D. applicants were supported on training grants for twenty-three months or less (52 percent) than for applicants supported twenty-four or more months (48 percent).

In the DKUHD study, we sought evidence other than NIH support (RO1) to determine whether trainees subsequently pursued careers in research. For instance, we attempted to determine whether trainees were responsible for subprojects on General Clinical Research Center grants and whether they were contributing to peer-reviewed research literature. The following method was used: Fifty-five individuals without a record of applying to the NIH were randomly selected. Of these, twenty-seven (49 percent) were found to have had at least one research publication in the literature for the years 1986 through 1988. An additional six were responsible for one or more subprojects on NIH-supported General Clinical Research Centers. In total, 42 percent of the former trainees met the criteria for being active in research, including those who applied to the NIH for research project support, those who had publications in the research literature, and those responsible for subprojects on General Clinical Research Center grants. These data are very conservative in that they do not take into account other sources of research support, many of which (such as the Department of Veterans Affairs) employ the peer-review process. Further, the data do not consider individuals with primary research responsibility in a medical facility or in the pharmaceutical industry.

Since the number of trainees who obtain positions in industry or private research facilities was thought to be large, we utilized the data base generated for fiscal years 1977 through 1981 to obtain related information on trainees who did not apply for NIH research support. Directors of NRSA Institutional Training Grant programs were sent a list of individuals who had been supported on their training grants during this interval and asked to update their research support/activities. The data obtained from this survey (Table 13.1) indicate that the proportion of former trainees who can be considered active researchers is 53.9 percent. It is clear that physician-scientists obtained support from other agencies as well as the NIH and that some are quite successful in other efforts. Further, the data show that M.D.s who were supported on NRSA Institutional Training Grants for twenty-four months or more (63 percent) were the most likely to be engaged in research activities. Ph.D.s tended to be supported for a longer period of time on an institutional training grant, but a large number who are active in research spent lessthan twelve months on a training grant. These data support the general statement that individuals active in research are more likely to have had longer periods of training on an NRSA Institutional Training Grant (Table 13.1). The data do not support the converse, since 46 percent of the M.D.s and 49 percent of the Ph.D.s active in research were supported for less than twenty-four months on an NRSA Institutional Training Grant. These

Table 13.1 Activities of Former Trainees (N=330) Supported by DKUHD Institutional Training Grants Between 1977-1981, by Degree and Duration of Training.

Degree	N	Months of Training				% Totals
		1-11	12-23	24-35	36+	
MD						
Research	118	7 (06%)	47 (40%)	53 (45%)	11 (09%)	100
Nonresearch	111	7 (06%)	64 (58%)	35 (31%)	5 (05%)	100
PhD						
Research	60	13 (22%)	16 (27%)	25 (42%)	6 (10%)	101
Nonresearch	41	7 (17%)	15 (37%)	14 (34%)	5 (12%)	100
Overall						
Research	178[1]	20 (11%)	63 (35%)	78 (44%)	17 (10%)	100
Nonresearch	152	14 (09%)	79 (52%)	49 (32%)	10 (07%)	100

[1]Rate of active researchers: 178/330 = 53.9%.

conclusions may be complicated by the fact that the research training of the individuals surveyed may not have been acquired entirely on NRSA Institutional Training Grants.

An examination of NRSA Institutional Training Grants in nephrology and hematology reveals that not all training sites are equally effective in developing active physician-scientists. In our study, we reviewed several programs whose graduates more often pursued scientific careers and attempted to ascertain if their content and organization appeared different from those of programs that had fewer graduates active in research. The conclusions must be considered tentative, but the following factors appeared with regularity in the more effective programs: a strong program director, institution, and faculty; broad-based recruitment with careful and systematic screening of candidates; and a carefully structured program, the elements of which appeared to be less important than the presence of a specified program. Another necessary element was the expectation that each trainee would reach a high level of performance in the academic and research program. Finally, a strong collaborative relationship with basic science departments appears to relate to the number of successful trainees. The National Research Council 1989 study of training suggested that more exposure to basic science and scientists might have value in the training of physician-scientists (4).

These criteria are only approximate and quite incomplete. Although they were present in most successful programs, for instance, their presence was not very useful in predicting the success of programs. Therefore, other elements must contribute to success. The presence of active NIH research programs is most likely a requirement for an adequate research environment, but it does not ensure a proper training environment. Another feature of the more successful programs was the presence of both M.D. and Ph.D. trainees. Unfortunately, few

NRSA Institutional Training Grants in nephrology and hematology have both M.D. and Ph.D. trainees.

Future Directions in Training

The National Kidney and Urologic Diseases Advisory Board submitted its long-range plan after a three-year study of the resources needed to fight kidney and urologic diseases (5). The board determined that there were significant shortages in the following areas of training: highly qualified researchers; trainees who spend the four to six years needed for optimal training in the biomedical sciences; postdoctoral training programs in pediatric nephrology and pediatric urology; training in pathology and health services research (e.g., epidemiology, sociology, psychology, statistics).

The advisory board as well as the National Research Council (4) recommended significant increases in appropriations to support graduated increases in trainee stipend levels, as well as to support more trainees for longer periods of training (6). Levels of funding specific to nephrology and hematology NRSA awards in the DKUHD/NIDDK remained relatively static during the 1980s (3). These recommendations would require substantial additional funds.

An increase in resources must be coupled with an increase in the efforts of the medical academic community to recruit medical students and residents into research careers. The data clearly show a decline in medical student and physician interest in research careers. This is reflected in a decline in the number of applications for individual postdoctoral research training (1, 2, 3, 7). Regardless of the undoubtedly multiple reasons for this phenomenon, the fact represents a critical condition for the U.S. research community, which must put forth its best efforts to foster an interest in, and motivation for, a career in research. Those responsible for medical student training programs should make every effort to allow time and opportunities for students to become involved with ongoing research projects early in their training. The ability to formulate questions capable of resolution by experimentation and the joy of discovery are powerful motivators for research careers. Of all the factors that led them to choose a career in research, the M.D. and M.D./Ph.D. scientists surveyed in 1989 American Association of Medical Colleges study most frequently identified a professor or mentor as the most influential (8).

References

1. J. B. Wyngaarden, "The Clinical Investigator as an Endangered Species," *The New England Journal of Medicine* 301 (1979): 1254–59.
2. J. B. Wyngaarden, "Encouraging Young Physicians to Pursue a Career in Clinical Research," *Clinical Research* 31 (1983): 115–18.
3. C. H. Rodgers and M. J. Scherbenske, "An Evaluation of Postdoctoral Research Training and Trainees Supported by the NIH in the Division of Kidney, Urologic and Hematologic Diseases," *American Journal of Kidney Disease* 16 (1990): 147–53.
4. *Biomedical and Behavioral Research Scientists: Their Training and*

Supply, Vol. I: Findings, Committee on Biomedical and Behavioral Research Personnel, Office of Scientific and Engineering Personnel, National Research Council) (Washington, D.C.: National Academy Press, 1989).

5. The National Kidney and Urologic Diseases Advisory Board, 1990 Long-Range Plan. NIH Publication 90–583, March 1990.

6. G. M. Pion, "Evaluating the National Research Service Award Program: A Review and Recommendations for the Future," in *Biomedical and Behavioral Research Scientists: Their Training and Supply, Vol. III: Commissioned Papers*, Committee on Biomedical and Behavioral Research Personnel, Office of Scientific and Engineering Personnel, National Research Council (Washington, D.C.: National Academy Press, 1989), 1–40.

7. G. F. DiBona, "Whence Cometh Tommorow's Clinical Investigators?" *Clinical Research* 27 (1979): 253–56.

8. N. O. Gentile, G. S. Levey, P. Jolly, and T. H. Dial, *Post-Doctoral Research Training of Full-Time Faculty in Departments of Medicine* (Washington, D.C.: Association of American Medical Colleges 1989), A35.

14

The Role of College, Medical, and Graduate Medical Education in the Development of Clinician-Scientists

DeWitt C. Baldwin, Jr., Beverley D. Rowley, and David Babbott

> The most important event in the life of a young scientist is the personal contact with a great scientist.
>
> —Otto Warburg, Nobel laureate

Although many of the factors contributing to the development of clinician-scientists are unknown at present, there can be little doubt that the educational environment plays a significant role. Conventional wisdom and the available data would suggest that a continuous learning environment which favors the development of inquiry and scholarly accomplishment provides the greatest opportunity for the development of future clinician-researchers. At the same time, some researchers appear to develop in spite of, rather than because of, their environment.

Students develop an interest in science and research at different times in their lives and progress at different rates. As yet, we do not know how many students decide at each level to abandon or commit themselves to a scholarly career. The work of Sherman and Morgan (1979) suggests that many researchers decide early to pursue a career in research and that others come to it much later (1). The prevalence of early decisions is confirmed by the fact that on their Medical College Aptitude Test (MCAT) questionnaire, 2.2 percent of premedical students have already stated an intention to enter a career in basic science or clinical research (2). Further questions on the MCAT survey inquiring specifically as to the entering student's major area of interest in medicine indicate that some 10 percent have a primary interest in biomedical research. It, therefore, seems useful to look at three learning environments in which interest in research can be stimulated; first, the prebaccalaureate institution; second, the undergraduate medical school; and third, the graduate medical education or residency training program.

Prebaccalaureate Education

It is clear from the evidence that some colleges and universities provide more medical school applicants and matriculants than others. Studies by the AAMC in the 1960s indicated that colleges such as Harvard, Michigan, Columbia, Cornell, and Yale supplied the largest individual numbers of students entering medical school at that time (3). Indeed, twenty-five schools (only 3 percent of institutions supplying at least one student) provided nearly 30 percent of the entering class. Since these universities tend to be among those best known for high scholarship and scientific achievement, it can be assumed that students entering such environments may be stimulated to go on to further scientific careers. What is relatively unstudied is the role that preselection and self-selection play.

In an earlier study, Sherman and Morgan (1) carried out a prospective study of 2821 students who entered 28 selected medical schools in 1956. In reviewing their careers in 1977, they separated their sample of physicians into five groups based on the students' previously stated career intentions and records of research participation: "consistent researchers," "latecomers to research", "dropouts from research," "specialty practitioners" and "general practitioners." In examining the prebaccalaureate origins of these groups, they found that 73.4 percent of the "consistent researchers" had attended private colleges, while only 57 percent of "latecomers to research" had attended such schools. Since "dropouts" as a group had originally committed to research careers, it is consistent that 70.5 percent of them also had gone to private schools. On the other hand, only 55.0 percent of "specialty practitioners" and 46.9 percent of "general practitioners" had attended such schools. While this study clearly shows a close association between private school background and future research careers, it does not address for the effect of pre or self-selection, or of socio-economic background.

In the same study, these same investigators showed that graduation from one of the 50 leading universities in terms of federal support and production of Ph.Ds annually, (Carnegie Classification Research Universities I) was highly associated with a future research career for all three of the identified research groups, with private liberal arts colleges next. Physicians with early research intentions ("consistent" and "dropouts") were more likely than others to have attended leading liberal arts colleges. Of note in their study was that over half of the physicians with early research ambitions did not fulfill them.

In 1985 there were 3388 institutions of higher education in the United States. Of these 115 were called universities and 1943 were four-year colleges. Nearly half (45 percent) of the four year colleges (866) had total enrollments of less than 1000 students and 83 percent (1616) enrolled less than 5000 students each. The great majority of these schools (1365) were privately operated. These 1616 schools (including one university) enrolled a total of 2,112,824 students nationwide, while the remaining 442 universities and colleges enrolled nearly three times as many total students (6,261,470). Only 113,960 total students attended schools with less than 500 students each, while those enrolling less than 1000 students were educating 325,011. It is easy to see that while there are four times as many small (especially private) four year colleges than there are large ones (over 5000 enrollment), these small schools account for less than one-third of the total number of students. Thus, if the number of future scientists was equally distributed, one would expect the larger schools to produce greatly superior numbers. This apparently is not the case.

The work of Hall (4) and Fuller (5, 6) is of primary importance in this regard, since both have demonstrated that certain schools, especially the smaller liberal arts colleges, appear to contribute a greater percentage of their graduates to science and other doctorates than do larger institutions. Indeed, Fuller has found that among institutions ranking among the most productive in future doctorates (percentage of graduates that complete Ph.D.s) in the humanities, as well as in the empirical, life, and social sciences, only Harvard and the University of California-Riverside can be considered even modestly large; the rest are mostly well-known small liberal arts colleges with under 500 graduates annually. This is not to say that larger universities do not contribute greater total numbers of persons who progress to the doctoral level. Institutions such as the University of California-Berkeley, the City University of New York (CUNY), and the Universities of Illinois and Michigan lead the list in total numbers of Ph.D.s in all fields conferred during the period from 1951 to 1980. However, based on proportion of awarded doctorates to the total number of graduates, the productivity ratios for M.I.T. (21.1), Harvard (16.2), and Columbia (10.8) lead the way.

The same large universities also lead in the number of doctorates in science awarded to graduates, with U.C. Berkeley and M.I.T. at the top of the list, although once again the highest productivity ratio (percentage of awarded doctorates to baccalaureate graduates) is achieved by M.I.T. (19.9) and Harvard (10.3). Although total numbers are obviously much lower, the smaller liberal arts colleges appear to have an even higher percentage of graduates with doctoral degrees compared to larger institutions, with Reed, Chicago, and Swarthmore boasting productivity ratios of 25.3, 24.4, and 20.9 respectively for awarded Ph.D.s in all fields (excluding technical institutions, such as Harvey Mudd College (40.7), the California Institute of Technology (40.0), and M.I.T. (21.1) which tend to have the highest ratios of all). Indeed, Fuller's studies show that the top forty rankings are almost exclusively occupied by smaller private, liberal arts schools.

In terms of science doctorates alone, once again adjusted for size, with the exception of Cal Tech, Harvey Mudd and M.I.T., these same small liberal arts colleges occupy nearly all of the top 30 positions, with Reed, Chicago, and Swarthmore having adjusted ratios of productivity of 20, 16.0, and 14.4 respectively.

It has not been shown whether this success is primarily due to selection factors, including those of previous education or socioeconomic background. However, it can be safely assumed that if one is looking strictly at percentages, these smaller colleges contribute proportionally more than their expected quota of future scholars and scientists.

To test the hypothesis that these small liberal arts colleges produce a disproportionate number of medical scientists and faculty, in 1986, the first author studied a random list of full-time faculty members of departments of internal medicine secured from an AAMC study of faculty in medical schools (7). This list of 369 full-time members was matched with the institutions where they received their baccalaureate degrees as seen in Table 14.1.

Table 14.1. Baccalaureate Institutions Attended by Random List of Full-Time Faculty in Internal Medicine, 1983 (N = 369).

BACCALAUREATE GRADUATES PER YEAR*					
<500	501-1000	1001-2000	2001-3000	3001-4000	4001+
104 (28%)	78 (21%)	89 (24%)	41 (11%)	46 (12%)	11 (3%)
182 (49%)		187 (51%)			

Source: *American Universities and Colleges,* 12th Edition 1983.

It is clear that approximately half of this random sample of full-time faculty members in internal medicine departments have graduated from colleges with fewer than 1,000 graduates per year, 14 percent of them from colleges with fewer than 300 graduates per year, thus providing some suggestive support for the hypothesis.

As most of the smaller schools are privately controlled, it was decided to examine the distribution of this sample of faculty with regard to the public or private designation of their baccalaureate institution. Of the 369 full-time faculty members, 229 or 62% had attended private colleges or universities, while 140 or 38% had gone to public schools.

In addition to the 369 faculty members, the AAMC sample identified an additional 18 full-time researchers on internal medicine faculties. Of these, 14 or 78% had attended private schools, as opposed to only 4 from public schools; five of the 18 attended schools graduating less than 500 students annually. Thus, even in this selective faculty sample, persons who attended private colleges and universities (predominately smaller) tend to be found more often in academic and research careers.

The potential impact of small institutional size plays another role in that the larger the institution, the more likely it is to have graduate or ancillary programs which tend to divert resources and focus from undergraduate baccalaureate programs. It is of interest that most schools with graduating classes of less than 500 tend to place their entire emphasis on the undergraduate curriculum and, thus, beginning students are taught by senior faculty, instead of junior faculty or graduate or teaching assistants. The percentage of awarded baccalaureate degrees to total enrollment can vary from 1 in 4 in the smaller liberal arts colleges to 1 in 10 in the larger schools.

At an anecdotal level, in 1986, the senior author was privileged to attend a banquet in the United States honoring a number of Nobel laureates and was able to determine the baccalaureate origins of those who had attended college in this country from the printed program. Nearly 50 percent of these distinguished scholars had graduated from institutions with fewer than 1000 graduates annually, 4 of the 22 from colleges graduating less than 300. It is of note that in this small group, there were 3 graduates from City Colleges of New York, and 2 each from Swarthmore, Chicago, and Columbia.

What is it that the smaller colleges seem to provide? For one thing, their small size. Second; their commitment to excellence in teaching, exclusively at the baccalaureate level. Third, their generally high faculty to student ratios (1 to 10 to 1 to 13). Fourth, their tradition, often rooted in religious origins, of high scholarship and achievement (8, 9). All of these seem to favor increased personal and scholarly contact between students and their teachers. As the lead quotation of this chapter suggests, such personal contact often strives to ignite the sense of inquiry which seems to presage a scholarly research career (10, 11). If so, such opportunities need to be provided more often throughout the course of secondary, (perhaps even earlier) and higher education if we are to assure a continuing supply of bright young scholars and scientists. Much remains to be studied about the effect of mentoring and role-modeling in the development of future physician-scientists.

Before any conclusions are drawn, further research needs to be done, further testing the hypothesis that on a percentage basis smaller liberal arts colleges are more likely to produce future M.D./Ph.D.s than are large undergraduate universities and, if so, examining the reasons for this. As yet such a study has not been done and would require the ability to identify the prebaccalaureate institutions of entering medical students and tracking them through to their eventual careers.

Undergraduate Medical Education

As noted above, a small percentage of premedical students indicate on their MCAT questionnaires that they are interested in a career in full-time basic science or clinical research and/or in positions on basic science and clinical science faculty. It is not currently known how many of these go on to achieve both an M.D. and a Ph.D. or actually meet their career research goals. However, it is possible to examine the changes in the numbers of such persons from the time of application to medical school (MCAT) to the senior year of medical school (Graduation Questionnaire). Utilizing the AAMC's Student and Applicant Information Management System (SAIMS) database, Babbott and colleagues were able to examine specialty and career choice for the medical school class of 1983 as expressed on their MCAT and GQ surveys (2).

Answers to the MCAT questionnaire indicate the distribution of initial student interest in different aspects of medicine. Pre-medical students destined to receive their M.D. degree in 1983 (N=15,826), were asked to indicate their area of greatest interest in medicine from among the following five choices: social aspects of disease, psychological aspects of disease, patient management, pathophysiology, and biomedical research. Ten percent of the respondents in 1979 indicated that their primary interest was in biomedical research (1,575 of 15,826); 39.6 percent expressing a primary interest in pathophysiology, 16.9 percent in patient management, 11.9 percent in the psychological aspects of disease, and 8.0 percent in the social aspects of disease. Asked for their area of least interest, the proportions tended to be reversed, with 27.9 percent (4,419 of 15,826) claiming that they were least interested in biomedical research. In the same survey, however, 30.8 percent of women and 26.9 percent of men ranked research as the most important factor in their choice of a medical career.

In an earlier study, Babbott and colleagues (12) used chi-square analysis to relate the interest areas designated by entering students on the MCAT questionnaire to the following variables reported on the Graduation Questionnaire (GQ) administered a few months before graduation from medical school:

1. Expected career research involvement: >25%, <25%, limited, or none.
2. Did the student plan a research fellowship: yes or no.
3. Did the student author or co-author a paper while in school: yes or no.
4. Was the student an investigator in a research project in medical school: yes or no.
5. Research classification of the medical school attended: high, medium, or low.

The medical school research classification was determined by the amount of research funding received by each school. These included federal funding on R01 grants, foundation funding for research, and institutional funds. These amounts are totaled and the schools ranked from highest to lowest in amounts of funding received. This list can be roughly divided into thirds, with categories for the top forty schools, the middle forty, and the lowest forty-seven.

Not surprisingly, the most outstanding difference among students who expressed different primary areas of interest was that those who were originally interested in biomedical research tended to be significantly more research-oriented than students interested in the other four areas. Specifically, students expressing an interest in biomedical research were more likely than those with other primary interests to attend medical schools with a higher level of research funding ($p=<.002$), to plan on a higher level of career research involvement than other students ($p=<.001$), to have plans for seeking research fellowships ($p=<.001$), to have authored or co-authored a scientific paper while in medical school ($p=<.001$), and to be planning to become research investigators ($p=<.001$).

On the other hand, students who expressed a primary interest in patient management tended to be the least research-oriented. Compared to students primarily interested in social, psychological and pathophysiological aspects of disease, they projected for themselves a lower level of career research involvement ($p=<.001$), were less likely to plan for research fellowships ($p<.001$), and were not as likely to plan to become research investigators ($p<.005$). In these same three respects, those students primarily interested in social, psychological and pathophysiological aspects of disease were quite similar (p=.534, p=.312, p=.740, respectively). Students expressing interest in areas other than biomedical research also attended schools with similar research funding levels (p=.127) and had comparable levels of student authorship (p=.584).

In summary, then, students' expressions of primary interest areas are in fact related to their research orientation as measured by the five outcomes previously listed. Students thus can be placed into three groups according to their interests: those interested in biomedical research are most research-oriented; those interested in patient management are the least research-oriented, and those interested in social, psychological, or pathophysiological aspects are in between.

In another analysis, relationships among career choice, medical school level of research funding, and research orientation of students were tested for statistical significance using loglinear modeling techniques. Career choices were separately identified from MCAT (taken before medical school) and from GQ information (taken late in the senior year of medical school). Students' research orientation was measured by 1) claimed authorship or coauthorship of a scientific paper during medical school, and 2) research activity during medical school. Four combinations of the variables were analyzed:

1. MCAT career choice by research funding level of medical school by whether the student authored a paper.
2. MCAT career choice by research funding level of medical school by whether the student participated in research during medical school.
3. GQ career choice by research funding level of medical school by whether the student authored a paper.
4. GQ career choice by research funding level of medical school by whether the student participated in research during medical school.

In each case, the following relationships were statistically significant: 1) Students interested in different careers chose different types of schools. Students expressing interest in fee-for-service occupations at the time of the MCAT were least likely to attend high-level research institutions. Those who attended high-level research schools were most likely to choose administrative careers and least likely to choose fee-for-service careers by the end of medical school. 2) Students expressing a research-oriented career goal, such as full-time faculty, on either the MCAT or the GQ, were more research-oriented. Students who chose fee-for-service were least likely to participate in research or author a paper. 3) Students at higher research institutions were more likely to do research.

In the case of MCAT career choice, there was no significant interaction of these three. That is, the effect of medical school level of research funding on student level of research did not vary between career choices. In the case of GQ career choice, there was a very slight difference in tendency to do research at the higher research funded institutions from career to career. The lack of strong three-way interaction and the difference in results for MCAT and GQ career choices suggest that students seem to choose medical schools with their career goals in mind, but once they have chosen a medical school, the research level of the institution will affect the likelihood that they will do research, whatever career they had planned.

Because men and women in the study differed from each other in the choices they made, the above analysis was repeated, controlling for gender. The following differences between men and women were significant:

1. Women were proportionately more likely to attend highest-level research institutions; men were more likely to attend those at the medium level. Both were equally likely to attend institutions at the lowest level.
2. At the same time, men were more likely than women to have participated in research or to have authored a paper in medical school.

As premedical students, men and women did not differ greatly in their career choices. However, by the senior year of medical school, women were more likely to select salaried practice positions, and men were more likely to choose fee-for-service occupations. Despite gender differences, the basic relationships between career choice, research level of medical school, and the student's research orientation remained the same.

Graduate Medical Education

While it is clear that research interest and experience must be fostered throughout premedical, medical, and graduate education, relatively little attention has been paid to the role of residency training and graduate medical education in fostering research careers. Utilizing the American Medical Association's Medical Education Research and Information database (MERI), which supports the AMA-FREIDA system, it was possible to determine which residency programs offer optional or required research rotations over the length of the training program and to calculate the number of weeks required for such rotations (13).

Table 14.2 shows that optional research rotations were offered by all specialties. However, there were vast differences between them, ranging from anesthesiology, in which 71 percent of the programs (104 of 146) offered optional research rotations, to pediatric subspecialties, in which only 3 percent offered such rotations (6 of 184). The top five specialties in this regard were anesthesiology, followed by psychiatry (70 percent), pediatrics (66.3 percent), pathology (65.8 percent), and internal medicine (64.1 percent). The number of residency programs offering an optional research rotation was 2,178, or 40.3 percent of all surveyed programs.

Perhaps more pertinent to this chapter are the number of graduate medical education programs offering required research rotations (Table 14.2). To a large extent, the relationship between required and optional research rotations is reciprocal and there is frequent overlap. For example, whereas only 3 percent of pediatric subspecialty programs offer optional research rotations, 80.4 percent *require* a research rotation that averages out to be some sixty weeks long over the length of the program. The specialties most likely to require research rotations include pediatric subspecialties, geriatric family practice, preventive medicine subspecialties, and preventive medicine. Throughout the list, it is clear that the subspecialties are more likely to require research rotations than are the general disciplines. This observation is demonstrated in internal medicine, where the subspecialties are nearly ten times as likely to require research rotations. This is also true for anesthesiology, where the same relationship is four times more likely, and for surgery, where surgical subspecialties are twice as likely to require such rotations.

The length of required research rotations also varies widely between the specialties, ranging from a high of 60.3 weeks in the pediatric subspecialties to a low of 3.6 weeks for family practice. Other specialties requiring lengthy

Table 14.2

	Research Rotation Optional			Research Rotation Required			Average # Weeks Required Research
(Sub)Specialty	Yes	Total	%	Yes	Total	%	Rotation
Internal medicine	254	396	64.14	19	396	4.80	11.07
Int. med. subspecialty	447	1476	30.28	656	1476	44.44	30.53
Anesthesiology	104	146	71.23	7	146	4.79	13.00
Anesthesiology subspec.	13	20	65.00	4	20	20.00	16.50
Emergency medicine	31	72	43.06	22	72	30.56	5.50
Family practice	203	331	61.33	25	331	7.55	3.63
Family practice subspec.	1	13	7.69	8	13	61.54	31.57
Obstetrics/Gynecology	71	257	27.63	62	257	24.12	9.58
Pathology	125	190	65.79	19	190	10.00	20.35
Pathology subspecialty	49	124	39.52	38	124	30.65	28.10
Pediatrics	132	199	66.33	12	199	6.03	4.89
Pediatrics subspecialty	6	184	3.26	148	184	80.43	60.25
Physical med. & rehab.	32	60	53.33	10	60	16.67	7.43
Preventive medicine	5	24	20.83	12	24	50.00	26.00
Preventive med. subspec.	5	37	13.51	21	37	56.76	11.90
Psychiatry	126	180	70.00	18	180	10.00	16.86
Psychiatry subspecialty	52	95	54.74	12	95	12.63	15.60
Radiology	92	194	47.42	24	194	12.37	7.88
Radiology subspecialty	82	163	50.31	37	163	22.70	11.34
Surgery	143	269	53.16	52	269	19.33	28.87
Surgery subspecialty	164	824	19.90	289	824	35.07	18.88
Transitional year	41	149	27.52	2	149	1.34	4.00
Total	**2178**	**5403**	**40.31**	**1497**	**5403**	**27.71**	**17.74**

research rotations include subspecialties in family practice (geriatrics), surgery, internal medicine, and pathology.

In summary, the data in Table 14.2 suggest that there is a wide variation among the specialties in the number of programs offering both optional and required research rotations and the length of these rotations. Physicians in graduate medical education are thus likely to have a varied experience in this regard. Less than half of the specialties require a research rotation, the average length of which is less than five months.

In Table 14.3, we attempted to look at these same data according to state and region. Although there are wide variations between some of the states (not shown here), it is notable that regions are surprisingly similar in the percentages of programs offering an optional research rotation: some 40 percent of all programs (2,179 of 5,437) for all regions.

The same cannot be said for required research rotations. Certain regions are more likely than others to have programs requiring research rotations. The

Table 14.3. Research Rotation in Residency Programs by Region

	Research Rotation Optional			Research Rotation Required			Average # Weeks Required Research
Region	**Yes**	**Total**	**%**	**Yes**	**Total**	**%**	**Rotation**
New England (CT, ME, MA, NH, RI, VT)	179	402	44.53	111	402	27.61	35.91
Middle Atlantic (NJ, NY, PA)	538	1336	40.27	400	1336	29.94	28.95
East North Central (IL, IN, MI, OH, WI)	389	933	41.69	245	933	26.26	28.09
West North Central (IA, KS, MN, MO, NE, ND, SD)	146	378	38.62	204	257	79.38	23.05
South Atlantic (DE, DC, FL, GA, MD, NC, SC, VA, WV)	311	830	37.47	252	588	42.86	27.13
East South Central (AL, KY, MS, TN)	108	253	42.69	95	191	49.74	28.85
West South Central (AR, LA, OK, TX)	191	472	40.47	112	351	31.91	27.95
Mountain (AZ, CO, MT, NM< UT, WY)	81	185	43.78	150	185	81.08	26.94
Pacific (AK, CA, HI, ID, NV, OR, WA)	228	587	38.84	159	420	37.86	38.94
Territory (PR)	8	61	13.11	42	49	85.71	13.40
Total	**2179**	**5437**	**40.08**	**3180**	**5437**	**58.49**	**27.92**

highest percentages were recorded for the mountain states, where 81.1 percent of the programs (150 of 185) require such a rotation; for Puerto Rico, where 85.7 percent of programs (42 of 49) require such a rotation; and in the West North Central region, where 79.4 percent of the programs require such a rotation.

Similarly, the regions differ in the number of weeks of required research, with the greatest average length (38.9 weeks) being in the Pacific region, followed by New England, with 35.9 weeks. The rest of the programs in the country seem to offer an overall average of 27.9 weeks of required research rotation. Four of the regions record lower lengths of time than this average, and six exceed it. Data on the individual states, while available, were felt to be less useful, since residency programs are not distributed evenly, nor are they evenly distributed by specialty across states.

While it is clear that the period of graduate medical education is important, if not essential, for the stimulation and nurture of scientific careers and the production of clinician-scientists, it seems evident that graduate medical education has not fully met this challenge. The wide variation between the specialties as well as between states and regions indicates that opportunities are not equally distributed and that students and recent graduates must choose carefully if they are to preserve their interest and inclination toward research. Although it is obvious that the choice of a scholarly research career is still limited to relatively few graduates and that the bulk of trainees seek mainly to perfect their clinical skills during residency, it would seem important that certain residents be enabled to pursue research during their residency training so as to preserve the motivation and enhance the opportunities of those few students who graduate with such a career in mind.

Conclusion

Because of the paucity of data in the field, this chapter has been relatively short on research data and long on speculation. Indeed, one of the frustrations in undertaking this task has been the lack of information and data on this important topic and on this phase of student research development. Many of the speculations raised here are at an early level of exploration and do not provide the answers we need. They do, however, clearly suggest that there is an urgent need to examine more closely the nature of the learning environments of premedical, medical school, and graduate medical education if we are to further support the need for clinician-scientists.

References

1. C. R. Sherman and T. E. Morgan, "A Prospective Study of Physicians and Research Careers," *Association of American Medical Colleges Report* (1979), 151 pp.
2. D. Babbott, S. O. Weaver, and D. C. Baldwin, Jr., "The Research Interests of Medical Students in the Class of 1983 as Expressed on Their MCAT and GQ Questionnaires," 1989, (unpublished manuscript).
3. W. F. Dube, "Undergraduate College in Relation to Medical School

Application and Enrollment," *Journal of Medical Education* 42 (1967): 83–84.

4. A. E. Hall, "Starting at the Beginning—The Baccalaureate Origins of Doctorate Recipients 1920–1980," *Change* 16 (1983): 40–43.
5. C. H. Fuller, "An Analysis of Leading Undergraduate Sources of Ph.D's, Adjusted for Institutional Size," *Report prepared for the Great Lakes Colleges Association*, 59 pages, August 1986.
6. C. H. Fuller, "Undergraduate Origins of Women and Men Who Received Ph.D.s, 1961–1980," *Report prepared for the Great Lakes Colleges Association*, 120 pages, 1987.
7. N. O. Gentile, P. Jolly, G. S. Levey, T. H. Dial, "Research Activity of Full-time Faculty in Departments of Medicine," Final Report. *Association of American Medical Colleges Publication*, 1987.
8. K. R. Hardy, "Social Origins of American Scientists and Scholars," *Science* 185 (1974): 497–506.
9. M. E. Tidball and V. Kistiakowsky, "Baccalaureate Origins of American Scientists and Scholars," *Science* 193 (1976): 646–52.
10. H. A. Krebs, "The Making of a Scientist," *Nature* 215 (1967): 1441–45.
11. K. S. Mangan, "Undergraduates, Professors Collaborate on Research at More and More Colleges," *The Chronicle of Higher Education*, (May 27, 1987).
12. D. Babbott, D. C. Baldwin, Jr., P. Jolly, and D. Williams, "The Stability of Early Specialty Preferences Among U.S. Medical Graduates in 1983," *Journal of the American Medical Association* 259 (1988): 1970–75.
13. B. D. Rowley and D. C. Baldwin, Jr., "Research Opportunities in Graduate Medical Education," (1990) Unpublished manuscript.

15

The Social Sciences Are Among the Sciences Basic to Clinical Medicine

Leon Eisenberg

Let me be up front about it: I want to persuade you that the social sciences are no less basic to clinical medicine than are the natural sciences. Let me warn you: That premise may be hazardous to the health of our laboratories. For, if MSTPs assign tuition support and stipends for graduate training in social science, that will inevitably curtail the number of students in the biological sciences, because finite resources must be spread over a larger number of fields.

We can, of course, and should, join in a common effort to increase the total funds awarded to MSTP. But that really won't solve the problem. Most programs have more good applicants than they can support. Therefore, when I ask you to acknowledge the legitimacy of graduate education in the social sciences, I am in effect asking you to forego positions that could have been used for additional recruitment into biological fields.

What will make it difficult for programs to assent is that the enthusiasm for maintaining the current thrust of the MSTP is primarily altruistic. That is, molecular biology, neuroscience, genetics, and immunology are intellectual arenas of enormous potential, not only for obtaining new knowledge about fundamental questions in biology but also for providing direct benefit in the treatment and control of disease. Further, that potential is not now being fully exploited for two reasons: research funding is inadequate, and too few physician-scientists are being trained for fundamental research. Why, then, divert even modest funds from a highly successful effort to support one that has less of a track record?

That question is the same as the one involved in arriving at national policy decisions on science funding. Should large sums be devoted to building the superconducting supercollider or to carrying out the Human Genome Project when each will be funded at the expense of investigator-initiated research? This is not the forum for a reexamination of those decisions. What I wish to emphasize is that an opportunity cost is inevitable when resources are allocated from a fixed budget. The challenge is to fashion rational priorities across scientific fields, because resources are certain to be insufficient to support everything that is worthwhile.

It is unrealistic to expect that biological scientists will cheerfully cede funds to the social sciences. The response would be no different were the situation reversed—although it takes a vivid imagination to conceive of social scientists having enough funding to make it worthwhile for biologists to try to pry some loose! The problem is unavoidable so long as the fox is set to guard the chicken coop.

A few years ago, I asked each of the directors of NIH-supported MSTPs about policy on doctoral studies in the social sciences in their medical schools. All twenty-four responded. Only four had ever enrolled such students, and one school had already discontinued the option. Fourteen stated that no formal decision precluding a social science track had been taken; thus far, no student with such interests had applied; most added that candidates for social science programs would not fare well in the selection process because of a strong bias in favor of biologists. The remaining six stated flatly that they would not accept such students, four because they were dubious about the quality of the social science departments in their universities.

That set of responses will explain why I place no great faith in the therapeutic efficacy of my sermon even before a controlled clinical trial. Nevertheless, it remains the case that the social sciences are essential to the resolution of certain key problems in medical care. The impact of those problems on the viability of the medical enterprise demands that resources be devoted to preparing physician-scholars in the relevant disciplines. The methods of the biological sciences, for all they can contribute to the understanding of disease, are orthogonal to the psychosocial and organizational problems behind the current crisis in medical care.

Let me summarize my argument before trying to defend it. First, much of today's morbidity and mortality stems from the effects of behavior on health status (habits of eating, sexuality, substance use, driving, drinking, smoking, exercise, and so on); the unmet challenge in prevention is to develop effective means to promote health-enhancing behavior throughout the population. Second, one-quarter to one-third of patients who consult physicians bring complaints that either have no ascertainable biological basis or are disproportionate to the pathology detected. Third, psychosocial skills well beyond the competence of most practitioners are required for the efficient management of chronic illnesses, which constitute an ever-increasing proportion of medical morbidity precisely because of the success of medical science in postponing death. Further, a cadre of physicians skilled in economics, ethics, political science, and management is essential if we are to answer the demands for containing the costs of care without sacrificing equity of access and quality of service by making mindless budgetary cuts. Fifth, physicians knowledgeable about population and environmental factors will be required to respond to the interaction of disease and the ecosystem and to think globally.

Challenge 1: High-Risk Behavior

High-risk behavior contributes substantially to morbidity and mortality. The years of life lost because of violence (accidents, homicides, and suicides) account for 37 percent of the years of potential life lost (YPLL) before age sixty-five from *all* causes of death (1). Total YPLL from violence is about the same as that from heart disease, cancer, and stroke *combined.* Some 30-40 percent of the 700,000 annual deaths from cancer and coronary heart disease and about 80 percent of the 45,000 deaths from chronic obstructive pulmonary disease are attributable to cigarette smoking (2,3). In 1986, for the first time in U.S. history, the death rate for lung cancer in females exceeded the rate for breast cancer (4), a macabre triumph for the Virginia Slim [sic] slogan "You've come a long way, baby." Drunk driving is responsible for about half of all fatal traffic accidents (that is, for some 20,000 to 25,000 deaths each year) and alcoholism for the bulk of the deaths (20,000) from cirrhosis. It is hardly necessary to remind anyone of the toll exacted by HIV infection secondary to intravenous drug abuse and high-risk sexual behavior.

Nor is the link between behavior and disease limited to industrialized nations. In the Third World, now in the midst of the "health transition"—a stage of national development in which "diseases of affluence"—that is, First World diseases—have been added to the health burden while "diseases of poverty"—massive infection and malnutrition—persist (5); patterns of behavior vis-à-vis water use, food preparation, and waste disposal are major factors in perpetuating endemic diseases (6). In addition, cultural barriers impede the implementation of biomedical therapeutics. Effective remedies, such as oral rehydration therapy for diarrhea or maternal immunization with tetanus toxoid to prevent neonatal tetanus (7, 8), have not been well accepted by local populations despite efforts to make them accessible. Learning how health beliefs are embedded in the world view of each culture and discovering the ways in which modern therapeutics can be made compatible with those health beliefs constitute a key research area in medical anthropology. The findings will be equally crucial in our own society, with its growing multiethnic composition.

It is, of course, possible to imagine scenarios in which bench science can make a difference in behaviorally transmitted diseases. Because not all smokers develop lung cancers (and some nonsmokers do), identifying the source of variance in biological vulnerability might make it possible to target education primarily at individuals at highest risk; for example, those who inherit a gene for the inducible form of aryl hydrocarbon hydroxylase, a member of the family of cytochrome P 450s (9, 10). Enthusiasts for science fiction may foresee "treating" susceptibles with an aryl hydrocarbon hydroxylase inhibitor, but that is likely to prove a dubious tactic in view of the role of P 450 enzymes in detoxifying foreign chemicals. I dare say that social strategies to discourage smoking are more likely to pay off in the near term and are far more sensible than a Rube Goldberg scheme to permit smoking (and the acquisition of chronic obstructive pulmonary disease!) by neutralizing carcinogens.

Challenge 2: The Social Psychology of Doctor Visits

Deciding to see the doctor is a social process in which the biological component is decisive only when disease is severe. Community surveys regularly identify many more individuals with symptoms and abnormal physical findings than are under medical care, even when there are no financial barriers to care (11, 12). Life stress increases the number and severity of symptoms an individuals will experience and makes it more likely that a physician will be consulted (13, 14). Moreover, one-fourth to one-third of patient visits are for complaints without an ascertainable physical basis (15). Those complaints are physiological expressions of personal distress or represent somatized equivalents of depression. Most physicians begin with an exhaustive diagnostic workup and end with the prescription of drugs despite their inability to arrive at a diagnosis; both the workup and the "therapy" contribute to iatrogenic toxicity and add substantially to costs. Research to uncover the pathophysiology of somatization, to develop more effective screening measures for the detection of somatized diseases, and to equip physicians with psychosocial skills is urgently needed.

Challenge 3: The Management of Chronic Disease

The number of people aged sixty-five and older, about 3 percent of the population at the beginning of the twentieth century, will rise to 20 percent in the third decade of the next century. Even more striking is the fact that the cohort of those aged eighty-five and older has experienced the largest proportional increase of any age group in the United States and by the year 2030 they alone will add up to almost 3 percent of all citizens (16). The issues at stake in successful aging and in coping with progressive functional limitation go well beyond biological questions. Agreed, hope of more effective care for some diseases of later life, such as senile dementia of the Alzheimer type, rests on progress in the neurosciences. In the meantime—likely to be a long time—the task of the clinician is primarily in the psychosocial arena.

Whatever successes are achieved in the laboratory, it is illusory to expect that biomedical research will obliterate all the ills the flesh is heir to. In the words of the microbiologist René Dubos, "Complete and lasting freedom from disease is but a dream remembered from imaginings of a Garden of Eden designed for the welfare of man." (17) Fashioning a meaningful social role for the later years of life, assessing the quality rather than mere quantity of life, and reassessing the appropriateness of interventions to perpetuate vegetative existence require an analysis of the social and ethical context of longevity in our society.

Challenge 4: The Cost of Care

The fourth set of problems shouts out at us from every day's newspapers. Concern over the costs of care has become a preoccupation of government, business, and labor, to the point where cost controls have been imposed with little thought about their effects on the quality of care (18). The organizational arrangements for health care delivery are being driven primarily by cost considerations. Only belatedly has there been any discussion of the impact of incentives for greater dollar "efficiency" on how well the needs of the patient are met. If this situation is to be remedied, it will require physicians trained in epidemiology, economics, and management to attend, at one and the same time, to health outcomes *and* cost consequences rather than, as has become the custom, to cost containment alone.

Medicine, as Rudolf Virchow, the father of modern biomedicine, recognized, is applied social science as much as it is applied biological science (19). But the tradition has been more honored in the breach than in the observance. What I am proposing are early steps in a courtship between medicine and the social sciences (marriage and progeny are still off in the distance). The best and the brightest should be encouraged to pursue anthropology, psychology, demography, economics, epidemiology, sociology, political science, history of science, and philosophy. The earlier outbreeding with the biological sciences enriched the medical species; I am confident the proposed new crossings will be no less fertile.

Some may argue that educating physicians in the social and behavioral sciences is unnecessary because specialists in these disciplines have contributed and are continuing to contribute to research and education in medicine by collaborating with physicians. There will continue to be a role for social scientists per se, but a cohort of individuals with combined training can make a special contribution to education and research. As teachers, they bring an integrated presentation to medical students which is more readily assimilated because they can speak knowledgeably about both medicine and social science. They provide role models for medical students, who are all too often skeptical about the relevance of nonphysician faculty. In research, familiarity with both terrains (biological and sociobehavioral) enables the doubly trained individual to identify problems that may otherwise escape attention. Indeed, one of the besetting difficulties in interdisciplinary research is the limited knowledge each set of collaborators has about the methods (and the limitations) of the other. The integration of the biological and the social sciences permits the investigation of problems where pathological outcomes result from the interaction of biological and social variables when neither set alone is decisive.

Challenge 5: The Environment

I wish to make a final point about the importance of having joint degree programs with the population sciences and the environmental sciences. Simply put, the extent and distribution of disease in human populations is a function of *where* people live and *how* they live; that is, of the characteristics of the environment they inhabit and of their interaction with that environment and with one another. Crucial determinants of those interactions include modes of production, political and economic structures, cultural beliefs that govern behavior, and, ever more decisively, relationships between nations.

Human populations are part of the terrestrial ecosystem. If humans have pride of place, it is only because our aggregate impact, given our numbers and our technologies, outweighs by far that of any other component. Eugene Odum stated the general problem of the human role in the dynamics of the ecosystem in the following words:

> Until recently mankind has more or less taken for granted the gas-exchange, water-purification, nutrient-cycling, and other protective functions of self-maintaining ecosystems, chiefly because neither his numbers nor his environmental manipulations have been great enough to affect regional and global balances. Now, of course, it is painfully evident that such balances are being affected, often detrimentally. The 'one problem, one solution approach' is no longer adequate and must be replaced by some form of ecosystem analysis that considers man as a part of, not apart from, the environment. (20)

Historically, diseases infectious only in the acute phase, such as measles, mumps, rubella, or poliomyelitis, could not have been endemic in neolithic populations (21). It was only when the food surplus generated by the agrarian revolution permitted the large-scale aggregation of human groups that these infectious agents had a host reservoir sufficient for them to become endemic. The penetration of a virus into a small hunter-gatherer community of several hundred behaves today as it did hundreds of thousands of years ago; it rapidly kills or immunizes so high a proportion of the population that the virus is unable to continue propagating itself. Human culture thus created the conditions necessary for infectious diseases to exert selective evolutionary pressures on human biology (22).

To carry the measles example a step further, the outcome of infection with the measles virus, as with other infections, is a function of co-morbidity. Malnutrition increases vulnerability to infection; in turn, infection increases nutritional demands. Whereas the case fatality rate for measles in the United States had fallen to less than 1 in 100,000 *before* vaccination was introduced, it remains as high as 10 per 100 in infants in tropical African urban areas (23). That devastating mortality rate stems from (a) crowding, which enhances transmission; (b) co-infection with other agents; and (c) malnutrition and dehydration, which increase vulnerability (24).

The marked reduction in mortality and morbidity in the industrialized world between the mid-nineteenth and the mid-twentieth centuries has been credited to the advent of scientific medicine. The fact is that the downward trend began well before effective treatments were introduced. For example, mortality from tuberculosis in the United Kingdom had fallen by half between 1840 and 1880, two years before Koch discovered the tubercle bacillus; it fell to one-sixth of the 1840 figure by 1940, a decade before the introduction of effective chemotherapy (25). Similar data exist for diphtheria, scarlet fever, pertussis, and measles (26). The observed improvement in health resulted, on the one hand, from lessened exposure to pathogenic bacteria through the provision of pure water, sanitation, and the reduction of crowding via better housing and, on the other, from improved host resistance secondary to better diet and, in the case of women, lower reproductive rates. These changes were made possible by the economic gains of the industrial revolution, the growth of democracy, and universal public education. While the benefits from chemotherapy, once it was introduced into medical practice, are indisputable, changes in the mode of life of ordinary citizens were far more decisive in producing the observed decline in mortality from infectious diseases.

Let us also remember that disease control is not always an unmitigated blessing. Pastoral peoples have long subsisted by exploiting domestic livestock in extensive areas of Africa where rainfall is insufficient for agriculture. The traditional pattern of energy utilization by pastoral peoples has promoted ecological stability (27). The forces of modernization intervened with the introduction of control measures for the sleeping sickness of humans and nagana of cattle, both caused by trypanosomes (28). In the Sahel desert margin, successful chemoprophylaxis against nagana permitted a sizable increase in the cattle population. During the same period, three other forces were at work (29). Farmers began extensive cultivation of the land that had been used for pasturage, and many newly independent African countries refused to allow pastoralists to cross national borders in their traditional patterns of migration. International aid projects, oblivious to ecological considerations, drilled bore holes to provide water; nomadic peoples were encouraged to settle around the new water supplies (30). These developments led to the overgrazing of areas of grassland barely able to support the smaller herds of the past. So extensive did this overgrazing become that it altered the reflectivity of the earth to the sun's light, a factor in determining patterns of rainfall.

High reflectivity (as from desert surfaces) reduced rainfall by as much as 70 percent, further contributing to the Sahel drought and the tragedy of human starvation. As the herds began to die of starvation, so did the population of herders. The introduction of a Western technology, done with the best intent, disrupted a marginally balanced ecological cycle, with severe consequences for life and health. It is not enough to mean well; it is necessary to *do* well.

My reason for recounting this cautionary tale is to emphasize that the science base needed to enhance human health, the ultimate goal of medicine, must include the sciences that deal with humans in society. Molecular biology is making and will make enormous contributions to theory and practice in medicine. Powerful as it is when applied appropriately, reductionistic science is simply irrelevant to health problems that stem from social and organizational pathology.

References

1. Centers for Disease Control, "Years of Potential Life Lost before Age 65, United States, 1987," *Morbidity and Mortality Weekly Reports* 38 (January 20, 1989): 27.
2. Centers for Disease Control, *Reducing the Health Consequences of Smoking: A Report of the Surgeon General*, DHHS Publication No. (CDC) 89-8411, (Rockville, M.d.: 1989).
3. Centers for Disease Control, "Chronic Disease Reports: Deaths from Lung Cancer, 1986," *Morbidity and Mortality Weekly Report* 38 (1989): 501-05.

4. National Center for Health Statistics, *Health, United States, 1988*, DHHS Pub. No. (PHS) 89-1232, Public Health Service (Washington, D.C.: U.S. Government Printing Office, March 1989).
5. Advisory Committee for Medical Research, *Report on Health Research Strategy for HFA/2000*, EB77/Inf. Doc./8 (Geneva: World Health Organization, 25 November 1985).
6. L. Eisenberg and N. Sartorius, "Human Ecology in the Repertoire of Health Development," *World Health Forum* 9 (1988): 564-68.
7. M. Rahman, L. C. Chen, J. Chakraborty, et al., "Tetanus Toxoid: I. Reduction of Neonatal Mortality by Immunization in Rural Bangladesh," *Bulletin of the World Health Organization* 60 (1982): 261-67.
8. M. Rahman, L. C. Chen, J. Chakraborty, et al., "Tetanus Toxoid: II. Factors Related to Immunization Acceptance," *Bulletin of the World Health Organization* 60 (1982): 269-77.
9. E. W. Nebert, "The Ah Locus, a Gene with Possible Importance in Cancer Predictability," *Archives of Toxicology* Supplement 3 (1980): 195-207.
10. J. L. Marx, "The Cytochrome P 450's and Their Genes," *Science* 228 (1985): 975-76.
11. K. K. White, T. F. Williams, and B. G. Greenberg, "The Ecology of Medical Care," *The New England Journal of Medicine* 265 (1961): 885-92.
12. J. G. Ingham and P. M. C. Miller, "The Concept of Prevalence Applied to Psychiatric Disorders and Symptoms," *Psychological Medicine* 6 (1976): 217-26.
13. R. Demers, R. Altamore, H. Mustin, et al., "An Exploration of the Depths and Dimensions of Illness Behavior," *Journal of Family Practice* 11 (1980): 1085-92.
14. R. Tessler, D. Mechanic, and M. Dimond, "The Effect of Psychological Disease on Physician Utilization: A Prospective Study," *Journal of Health and Sociological Behavior* 17 (1976): 353-64.
15. L. Eisenberg and A. Kleinman, "Clinical Social Science," in *The Relevance of Social Science for Medicine*, ed. L. Eisenberg and A. Kleinman (Boston: D. Reidel, 1981), 1-23.
16. D. P. Rice, "Demographic Realities and Projections of an Aging Population," in *Health Care for an Aging Society*, ed. S. Andreopoulos and J. R. Hogness (New York: Churchill Livingstone, 1989), 15-45.
17. R. Dubos, *The Mirage of Health: Utopias, Progress and Biological Changes* (New York: Harper and Brothers, 1959), 2.
18. L. Eisenberg, "Health Care: For Patients or for Profits?" *American Journal of Psychiatry* 143 (1986): 1015-19.
19. L. Eisenberg, "Rudolf Ludwig Karl Virchow, Where Are You Now That We Need You?" *American Journal of Medicine* 77 (1984): 524-32.
20. E. P. Odum, "The Strategy of Ecosystem Development," *Science* 164 (1969): 262-70.
21. F. L. Black, "Infectious Diseases in Primitive Societies," *Science* 187 (1975): 515-18.

22. J. B. S. Haldane, "Natural Selection in Man," *Acta Genetics and Statistical Medicine* 6 (1956/7): 321-32.
23. Editorial, "Vaccination Against Measles," *Lancet* 2 (1976): 132-34.
24. J. A. Walsh, "Strategies for Control of Disease in the Third World: IV Measles," *Reviews Infectious Disease* 5 (1983): 330-40.
25. T. McKeown, *The Role of Medicine: Dream, Mirage or Nemesis?* (London: Nuffield Provincial Hospitals Trust, 1976).
26. E. H. Kass, "Infectious Diseases and Social Change," *Journal of Infectious Disease* 123 (1971): 110-14.
27. M. B. Coughenour, J. E. Ellis, D. M. Swift, et al., "Energy Extraction and Use in a Nomadic Pastoral Ecosystem," *Science* 230 (1985): 619-25.
28. W. E. Ormerod, "Ecological Effects of Control of African Trypanosomiasis," *Science* 191 (1976): 815-21.
29. A. R. E. Sinclair and J. M. Fryxel, "The Sahel of Africa: Ecology of a Disaster," *Canadian Journal of Zoology* 63 (1985): 987-94.
30. N. Wade, "Sahelian Drought: No Victory for Western Aid," *Science* 185 (1974): 234-37.

16

Mentoring

Robert G. Petersdorf

- Student Attitudes
- M.D./Ph.D. Training
- Housestaff Training
- Fellowship Training
- Ultimate Career Planning
- References

It is widely assumed that too few of our medical school graduates have scholarly qualities and that too few of these have the opportunity to develop their talents. The prevailing view is that attaining an M.D. degree and completing a residency does not provide the knowledge needed to participate in scholarly discourse about biology, medicine, and health care or, more important, to pursue original research.

For a profession that has nearly doubled the length of its educational requirements while increasing the size of its academic faculties fourfold, this state of affairs suggests that something is amiss in the way we go about developing scholarly talent. Yet the bulletins of virtually all our medical schools include a statement alluding to the development of scholarly physicians as one of their missions. Faculty feel the need, at least rhetorically, for students to develop critical analytical skills, to be independent learners, and to be creative thinkers. Surely, if the practice follows the preaching, there would not be a shortage of scholarly physicians prepared to assume leadership in research in both biomedicine and health care. There is a disjunction between what is stated and what is done. We need to ask why this disjunction exists and how it can be corrected.

Students can develop scholarly attributes only if they are able to associate personally with scholars. Attitudes of inquiry and healthy skepticism are not learned in lecture halls or in hurried attending rounds. The experience of discussing and reflecting on ideas and questions with a scholarly faculty member is essential for opening students' minds to the exciting challenges of research and scholarship.

Unfortunately, there are no hard data on the frequency with which students have such experiences. Because of the common and continuing complaint that a student may complete medical school and never really get to know a single faculty member well, I suggest that these experiences are few and far between. Whether that is the fault of the students or the faculty is arguable. But whichever it is, such interactions are needed if students are to develop scholarly attitudes.

Student Attitudes

Some students graduate from medical school intent on pursuing a career in research. The AAMC's graduation questionnaire asks, "How extensively do you expect to be involved in research during your medical career?" (1) In 1988, 44 of the 10,379 respondents answered that they would engage in research exclusive of other activities, and 1,557 (15 percent) answered that they expected to be involved extensively. If 15 percent of medical school graduates actually pursued research careers to the degree indicated by the responses of the 1989 seniors, there would probably be no need to research these issues. Indeed, I doubt that we could absorb 2,500 researchers into our biomedical research enterprises annually, but we certainly could use a significant fraction of those 2,500.

Why are these graduates unlikely to fulfill their expectations for research careers? I want to emphasize one reason: the lack of relationship between students (and I include here interns, residents, and fellows) and their faculty mentors.

M.D./Ph.D. Training

The proportion of each class expecting extensive involvement in research remains relatively constant at 14–15 percent year after year. Among these, some are graduating with combined M.D./Ph.D. degrees. The proportion of each graduating class attaining M.D./Ph.D. degrees is also remarkably constant—about 1–1.5 percent annually. In 1988, approximately 200 combined degrees were granted. Of these, between 100 and 120 came from NIH-sponsored medical science training programs, and the balance were supported by other sources. One characteristic of Ph.D. education is the close association with one or two faculty mentors over an extended period of time. Many who are in leadership positions of joint degree programs support the view that students from these programs are more likely to have productive scholarly careers than their peers, probably because M.D./Ph.D. candidates are more likely to select a more lengthy and challenging educational curriculum. Speaking pragmatically, the opportunity to develop skills in research techniques accounts for most of this productivity. However, the nurturing that M.D./Ph.D. students receive from their mentors accounts for more of their ultimate success than does the mere mastering of technology. After all, techniques change and skills must be adapted, but a prepared mind is essential to identify opportunities for investigation and scholarly leadership.

There is no question that having an M.D./Ph.D. helps to ensure a future academic career. For example, in the competitive atmosphere of NIH funding, M.D./Ph.D. investigators generally compete better than M.D. investigators and as well as Ph.D.s. In the Pfizer fellowship competition, two-thirds of the successful candidates hold M.D./Ph.D.s.

The preparation afforded M.D./Ph.D.s must be provided to a larger number of physician graduates if we are to replenish our faculties and continue the present rate of advance in biomedical science. To be sure, during medical school many students have some research experience. In 1988, 46 percent of the graduates reported being involved in research, and 25 percent were named as authors on published papers. These exposures, however, are usually limited to brief periods of two or three months, and even if there is a close association with a faculty mentor, the time is too short. Sustained involvement is needed. There is sufficient talent among our students to allow a doubling or trebling of joint degree programs.

Changes may eventually provide more candidates for scholarly leadership in medicine. AAMC data show that during the past few years the excessive number of scheduled hours in medical school curriculums has been decreasing somewhat. Lecture hours have decreased by 10 percent, while conference hours have increased by 20 percent. Schools are introducing problem-based learning tutorials either in a separate curriculum track for a portion of the class or as a complementary sequence for the entire class. This trend toward greater faculty-student interaction needs to be accelerated. As we move further in this direction, let us hope that our faculties will take advantage of the opportunity to make medicine a more scholarly profession by involving students in research to a greater degree.

Housestaff Training

Many directors and faculties involved in residency training fail to establish the mentoring relationships with their residents which are essential to the further development of scholarly pursuits. When residency programs were smaller and senior physicians were less distracted by the complex demands on their time and energy, the close relationship that was characteristic of the apprenticelike mode of training predominated. Today many residency programs in internal medicine are so large that the residents rarely see the senior physicians who should be models of scholarly inquiry. In many institutions, the responsibility for the programs is entrusted to junior staff members who are more coordinators and schedule makers than leaders. Service demands on residents have increased as academic center hospitals provide increasingly complex services to very ill patients, and requirements to document reimbursement have subtracted from the time faculty members spend with residents. These increased service demands on both residents and faculty members are often most severe in the very institutions to which potential scholars are recruited. I do not advocate requiring research experience during residency, but those who have evinced a desire to be involved in research should be stimulated to pursue research careers during the course of their clinical training. Residency programs that recruit candidates with research talents are obligated to nurture and not to stultify their residents' aspirations.

The debates about residents' working hours and supervision are relevant to the development of physician-scholars (2). Residents who are stressed and fatigued by excessively demanding schedules and who are inadequately supervised are unlikely to maintain their curiosity and creativity. While excessive working hours are undesirable, even more undesirable is a lack of close association with experienced faculty mentors. The excitement of being involved with a stimulating clinician-teacher can ameliorate fatigue and enhance dedication to the profession of medicine.

I also want to consider briefly the phenomenon of "certifimania" in the development of physician-investigators (3). We are witnessing a veritable explosion of subspecialty certification by the various specialty boards. As certificates of special competence and of added qualifications are layered onto primary certificates, additional years of clinical training are required. A resident who is interested in pursuing research in an area that has been recognized by a subspecialty certificate is almost forced into obtaining the "union card" typified by such a certificate for the area of special interest. This additional clinical training will almost surely come at the expense of research skill development. The boards need to be more flexible in giving credit for research training to prospective faculty members who wish to pursue a career in clinical investigation.

A related, but antithetical, development is the move by the American Board of Pediatrics to force research experience on candidates for its clinical subspecialties by requiring sixteen or more months of research during a thirty-six-month subspecialty training. The Accreditation Council for Graduate Medical Education declined to include research in the special requirements for the accreditation of pediatric subspecialties, on the grounds that training for board certification is designed for clinical training and that Residency Review Committees are not prepared to judge the quality of research training. As a result, the American Board of Pediatrics intends to require evidence of research experience as a requirement for certification. Pediatric subspecialty programs will not be required to provide such experience to gain accreditation by the Residency Review Committee in pediatrics and the ACGME. It is not clear how the board will determine the research qualifications of its subspecialty candidates. The career development of future pediatric subspecialists should be analyzed to determine whether a research requirement leads to the development of more physician-scholars in that specialty. I doubt it, particularly as the required sixteen to twenty months is probably not sufficient to train a competent investigator and may detract enough from the time allotted to clinical training to weaken the candidate's clinical expertise.

Fellowship Training

Mentoring in clinical postdoctoral fellowships is, by and large, inadequate. What is the basis for such a harsh indictment?

First, fellowship programs are too large. It is not unusual in clinical departments to have entering classes varying from three to six fellows. Since most fellowship programs are now three years in duration, this means that a faculty mentor may have as many as eighteen individuals under his or her tutelage. Assuming that at least one-third of these are engaged in clinical pursuits, this still means twelve people in the laboratory, and that is far too many.

Second, as a consequence, some fellows must be assigned to more junior faculty. Often these individuals are recently out of fellowship themselves and have had little experience in mentoring. Moreover, they are still bent on advancing their own careers and often consider the fellow assigned to them as a competitor who will be at their level in the not too distant future rather than as an individual who needs to be brought along and nurtured.

Third, there is excessive absenteeism. Faculty mentors spend most of their time presenting their research to audiences other than those at their home base. The pernicious habit of presenting research at medical grand rounds—even if that research is unrelated to any of the clinical topics that should be the subject of grand rounds—keeps more people in the air than at home. There are also far too many national and international meetings, usually consisting of the same people talking about the same things. The result is excessive absence from the laboratory by the mentor and weeks of unsupervised activity by the trainee.

Fourth, the subject lacks definition. All too often, novice fellows are given a research project with the admonition to go to it, but little time and effort is expended on showing them how to do research. The assumption is that somehow everybody knows how. This leads to excessive floundering. Also, too little attention is given to measuring interval progress. For many fellows, the time to determine whether a project should be chucked, or indeed if an entire research career should be abandoned, should come much sooner than is usually the case.

This brings me to a fifth thesis, which is that for most fellows, a research career is planned backward. In departments of medicine, at least, most fellows come to the laboratory after three or even four years of general clinical training. The first year of specialty training is usually a clinical fellowship, and individuals spend that year running around the wards seeing consults or doing clinically oriented laboratory procedures such as reading bone marrows or doing blood-clotting tests. At the end of this year, the individual enters the laboratory. At that time, he or she is usually over thirty years old and is just beginning a research career. It would be preferable for individuals to begin their fellowships in the laboratory to see whether they like research and are good at it. The advanced clinical training could be scattered throughout the research experience or used to top off a successful stint in the laboratory. The same principle should be applied to residency training. Those people who want to try their hand in the lab and who seem to have the talent should perhaps do so after the first two years of residency training. If they are successful, they can always top off their clinical training with a senior or chief residency or a clinical fellowship.

The vagaries of the research training environment have led to a large-scale abandonment of the field by research trainees. As a by-product of this, research training programs furnish an excessive number of clinical subspecialists.

Ultimate Career Planning

Even for the individual who completes the course, which from the time of entry to medical school until the completion of fellowship is often ten to twelve years, the future is uncertain. Graduating trainees do not get very good advice about jobs. In their last year, they often set about writing a grant application, which on the first go-around, at least, is unlikely to be funded. It is not nearly so well known, however, that the success rate can be improved considerably by a second and third application. What this strategy requires, however, is the backup of an academic home in which to spend an additional year or two until funding becomes available. Often that academic home and the financial infrastructure to support it are not available. Neither, for that matter, is the proper faculty mentoring, which, in my experience, does not improve with age.

It is little wonder, therefore, that so many research careers end on the academic scrap heap. Indeed, if we as faculty took a closer look at how we recruit trainees, how we train them, how we support them, and how we counsel them, we could easily attract, retain, and launch the successful investigators of the future. I hope some of the issues that I have raised here will receive careful consideration.

References

1. Association of American Medical Colleges, *Graduation Questionnaire* (1988).
2. R. G. Petersdorf and J. D. Bentley, "Residents' Hours and Supervision," *Academic Medicine* 64 (1989): 175–81.
3. R. G. Petersdorf, "From the President," *Academic Medicine* 65 (1990): 96.

17

The Two Cultures of M.D./Ph.D. Programs: Conflict or Evolution?

Frances Degen Horowitz

- Two Cultures
- Conflicts of Cultures
- Prescriptions and Remedies

In the last years of the nineteenth century, Thomas Huxley and Matthew Arnold were principal protagonists in a debate that echoes still today. They argued about whether or not training in science could ever result in real knowledge of the world. Huxley believed that science would lead us to the fullest understanding of the beauty of nature; Arnold felt that science could never replace what was to be learned only through humanistic endeavors. This "two-cultures" debate has enjoyed periodic resurgence. F. R. Leavis and C. P. Snow had their go at it in the 1960s. As we approach the twenty-first century, the debate continues, though sometimes in variant forms and with respect to different topics. One form involves the very specialized "two-cultures" issues related to patterns of training for the M.D. and the Ph.D. When individuals participate in both M.D. and Ph.D. programs in an integrated or dual-degree program, there is a potential for cultural confusion and conflict that can create problems for the students and tensions in the programs. It is my intent here to examine the cultural context of M.D. and Ph.D. training, to identify some of the forces that can result in cultural conflict, to suggest how such conflict might be minimized, and to indicate some of the benefits that might result from a program that is sensitive to cultural conflict and committed to reducing it.

Two Cultures

There are many definitions of "culture," but most would agree that it represents the overriding, subtle and not-so-subtle organization of environment and experience that shapes the individual events and relationships affecting the people who live in it. Cultures work their effects on an individual through persons (usually older and more experienced) who serve as behavioral models; through the organization of time and space; through interrelated symbols; and through rituals, rites, traditions, and all manner of repetitious patterning of experience.

Strong and cohesive cultures exert powerful influences on their youngest and most inexperienced members. Such cultures tend to absorb and adapt new cultural forces only if they are viewed as compatible with the existing culture; they tend to reject strongly those that are not. Most strong cultures remain strong, however, only when their patterns of cultural transmission across generations are well established and continually reinforced even as they evolve over time. Weak and diffuse cultures are more easily influenced by new cultural forces; their members are more likely to lose their sense of identity and cohesiveness. This loss sometimes results in confusion and feelings of disconnection and frequently creates the conditions by which the culture itself becomes easy prey to other, stronger countercultures.

How strong cultures and weak cultures interact with each other or with like cultures depends on many factors. The age of the cultures, their relationship to and tolerance of difference and change, the rate of internal and external change, and the specific nature of that change can all help us understand what happens when two cultures come into contact. One of the most important variables involves the leadership figures in each culture—who they are; their standing within their communities; and their backgrounds, visions, and skills. Another variable is the degree to which the values of cultures are inherently conflicting or compatible.

This discussion can be easily applied to many educational cultures, which, in the process of forming their students, adopt practices designed to transmit specific and general understandings along with sets of skills and values. These educational cultures define their tasks in terms not only of the particulars of instruction and training but also of their responsibilities to socialize their students into the culture of the field or area. They are replete with all the trappings necessary to define a culture and to ensure cultural transmission across generations of students. In previous eras, guilds served such functions; in our era, the professions often fulfill these roles. The longer the educational/training program and the more demanding the criteria for admittance into the profession, the stronger the cultural conditioning/socialization forces are likely to be.

Degree programs leading to the M.D. and the Ph.D. represent two of the clearest examples of education as culture. It is true that across the whole array of Ph.D. programs there are as many cultural variations as there are fields and subfields within the enterprise of doctoral-level education. There are also cultural variations within M.D. programs, especially since different philosophies of medical training may be found in different institutions. Yet the variations *within* M.D. and Ph.D. programs are smaller and less significant than the cultural differences *between* them.

To understand the cultures of M.D. and Ph.D. programs and the forces that define them, we must discuss similarities and differences. There are a number of basic similarities. Both M.D. and Ph.D. programs require, in this country, graduation from an accredited baccalaureate program, usually involving four years of undergraduate study. The undergraduate program can be quite directly focused on the intended postbaccalaureate work or not. Students heading for the M.D. may take a heavy "premed" curriculum, eschewing any electives not seen as related to getting into medical school and becoming a physician. These students often major in fields considered close to medicine—chemistry or the biological sciences. Other students come to medicine with minimal premed prerequisites, from majors as far flung as philosophy, psychology, and economics.

A similar pattern can be seen in students entering Ph.D. programs. Some have been very focused almost from their first year—majoring in physics and pursuing doctoral work in physics, majoring in history and pursuing doctoral work in history. Others make large, sometimes quite significant, shifts from undergraduate to graduate work.

The faculties of both M.D. and Ph.D. programs, however, are typically unconcerned about the differences in backgrounds as long as the students beginning their respective programs have the requisite entry skills to take up the prescribed course of study. The M.D. program is, in many instances, a replay of some of the patterns of undergraduate study, only more intense, more focused, and more narrowly defined. Students are accepted as part of a class, not by an individual faculty member or a faculty committee. The faculty do not see themselves as individual mentors for particular students. This is quite different from the entry patterns for many Ph.D. programs, in which students have chosen the program because of the presence of particular faculty members or faculty research interests and in which the faculty, in turn, regard themselves almost immediately in some sort of individual mentoring role to particular students. For the M.D. student, such individualized choices will await the residency period or the fellowship period. For Ph.D. students, the individualized study pattern may well continue past the Ph.D. program to a postdoctoral program—especially in the sciences.

The four years of medical school, like the four or more years of graduate school, have certain rhythms. For the medical student in most programs (though some of this is changing), the first two years involve intensive coursework and the memorization of a vast amount of factual material, punctuated by periodic lengthy and exhaustive examinations. While the Ph.D. student's program may also be heavily loaded to courses in the first two years, in many programs and disciplines students may become involved early in research, working quite personally with selected faculty and postdoctoral students. The socialization process that begins very early for many Ph.D. students is heavily weighted toward encouraging independent thinking and toward research and the identification of the area of work that soon will be the student's "own" to develop or expand.

Unlike the medical student, who feels very fully part of a cohort or a class of students, a Ph.D. student may be working immediately with second- and third-year graduate students (especially in the lab sciences, where team research is more the norm), with postdoctoral students, and with faculty members. In the first two years, medical students typically see faculty not as senior colleagues but as teachers imparting knowledge to help prepare them for the criteria examinations that are necessary for entrance into the clinical years and ultimately for licensing.

For both M.D. and Ph.D. students, faculty model expected behaviors. They impart the criteria by which students will be judged, and they communicate what is expected of someone who is fully a professional in the field. This modeling ranges all the way from how one dresses to the form of inquiry one is expected to adopt, from deference or lack of deference to the kinds of aspirations that are proper for students in the program.

A major difference in the training cultures of M.D. and Ph.D. programs involves faculty expectations. In many medical programs, students are expected to complete the four years, go on to take a residency, and then practice medicine in some office, community, or hospital setting. The typical medical student is not being groomed to take a place in an academic setting and become a junior colleague in the field. Just the opposite occurs in Ph.D. programs: The Ph.D. student is expected to take a place in the academic world, to be seen again at professional meetings, and ultimately to be doing elsewhere what faculty members are now doing. In some fields, Ph.D. students who elect to go into clinical and industrial settings are sometimes seen as having made the lesser choice. In the field of psychology, a major disjunction has occurred because so many Ph.D. students in clinical psychology *just go into private practice* and never again do research, even though the Ph.D. is a research degree. The development of the "Doctor of Psychology" resulted from the feeling that an alternative training program was needed for clinicians exactly because clinical students were being given so negative and unreinforcing a message in some Ph.D. programs. When academic jobs were scarce in many different fields, faculties of Ph.D. programs were often unable to provide the counseling and mentoring that students needed to help them look at alternative careers.

The feelings of faculty toward students in M.D. and Ph.D. programs, while neither more nor less humane, caring, or concerned, differ to a large extent over this issue of expectations. Faculty from the basic sciences who might teach medical students do not see them as "their students." They do not expect these students to use their teachers' behavior as a model and eventually take their place as bench scientists. Similarly, the M.D.s who teach medical students in didactic classes and clinical settings may expect these students to use some of their teachers' behaviors—especially in diagnostics and patient care—as models, but they do not expect most medical students to end up as junior colleagues on medical school faculties. The inclination to begin socializing medical students to the roles expected in academic medicine is reserved only for those in the M.D./Ph.D. programs, where academic medicine is the intended destination. However, since the number of M.D./Ph.D. students is typically a very small fraction of the total class of medical students, the faculty may not perceive the responsibility to play such a socializing role as dominant, although this can vary greatly according to the strength with which particular faculty are identified with the M.D./Ph.D. program and with individual M.D./Ph.D. students. For the most part, however, there tends to be a relatively large personal distance between most medical students and the faculty who teach them.

Faculty who train Ph.D. students, especially individual advisors and faculty committees, are very conscious of their responsibility to socialize students into an academic role. As the years of the Ph.D. program pass, students and their graduate school mentors often develop close personal relationships. Indeed, this can be an occupational hazard when the need to pass a negative judgment results in a strong emotional conflict as a result of the personal friendship between a student and a faculty member. For medical faculty, such personally close relationships with students may come only in the years of residency and fellowship and are much less likely to occur during the time the students are pursuing the M.D.

Other cultural differences exist between Ph.D. and M.D. programs. The Ph.D. is a research degree designed to emphasize the discovery of new knowledge and to enable the student to become an independent researcher. Although the modes of inquiry differ vastly depending upon whether the Ph.D. program is in the bench sciences, the humanities, or the social sciences, the basic context of the graduate school experience remains fundamentally consistent across disciplines, in that the student is expected to master skills and information for the eventual purpose of becoming established as an independent scholar or investigator. The Ph.D. experience also lacks a "life-and-death" context: Few Ph.D. students are being groomed to take their place in the decision-making arena where they must handle, and handle expeditiously, issues related to life, quality of life, and death. Some students in Ph.D. programs may be closer to these issues than others. Students in environmental studies or in the chemical and pharmaceutical sciences may be doing work that relates to risk and toxicity with "life-and-death" implications. However, this does not usually occur in the context of individual patient care, nor is the student being trained to act on an individual basis and in a personal decision-making role. The need to act professionally in a crisis or an emergency is theoretically always possible but not highly probable.

The M.D. degree is a clinical degree. It is designed to enable the student to become an independent clinician (although, increasingly, the new graduate might really be considered semi-independent, since he or she is expected to undergo a period of residency in which supervision is the norm). Much of the information acquired during medical school is intended for use in clinical situations. While the notion of an independent clinician may be not unlike the idea of an independent investigator, the context of that independence is quite different. Ever present are the issues related to patient care, to illness and disorder, and to life, quality of life, and death. Medical students are trained to understand that there is a high probability that they will need to act professionally in a crisis or emergency.

Conflicts of Cultures

Bringing these two cultures together in M.D./Ph.D. programs can produce feelings of discordance at best and serious conflict at worst for both the M.D./Ph.D. students and the faculty training them. The years of evolution of the M.D. and the Ph.D. cultures have produced two strong and resilient cultures. The members of each culture recognize the members of the other and are well aware of their differences. Students often consciously choose one culture or the other exactly because of these differences. Members of the two cultures do not interact frequently, with the exception of the M.D.s and the Ph.D.s who are on the same medical school faculties. In such settings, Ph.D.s who teach medical students reserve their most involved teaching for their own Ph.D. students and M.D.s who teach Ph.D. students do not usually become extensively involved either with them or, as I have pointed out, with M.D. students. M.D. faculty do become involved with residency and fellowship students, sometimes in the same manner that Ph.D. faculty become involved with Ph.D. students although this is more likely to occur in areas involving empirical research and bench science research—especially if the M.D. faculty member is also a Ph.D. and/or heavily involved in research.

Both M.D. and Ph.D. faculty members may have a difficult time with the M.D./Ph.D. student. The Ph.D. faculty mentor in the student's Ph.D. program expects him or her to become a full-fledged, card-carrying member of that Ph.D. culture. The mentor is about the business of "cloning" his or her professional self, with the expectation that, when fully credentialed, the student will take a place as an academic doing research in the same field—even if this entails going off in a somewhat different direction or pursuing further training in a postdoctoral fellowship. While treating the student as a future academic colleague, the mentor may have little appreciation for the student's clinical interests. Furthermore, the Ph.D. faculty members at medical schools are accorded a lesser status. The possibility of conscious and unconscious resentments toward students who will hold not only the Ph.D. but also the M.D. and thus be eligible for a more elevated status ought not to be discounted as part of the dynamic of the relationships between the Ph.D. medical school faculty and the students in the M.D./Ph.D. program.

The M.D. faculty member is concerned with cloning his or her clinical self or at least helping the student acquire the minimum level of diagnostic clinical skills that he or she will need to act as an independent M.D. and respond in the case of an emergency or crisis with life-and-death implications. The faculty member may or may not be sensitive to the fact that medical students who are also pursuing the Ph.D. are future academic colleagues and may fail to treat them as such.

Cultures condition their members by communicating subtle and not-so-subtle messages about what the culture does and does not value. Esoteric research, research for the sake of research, and research divorced from application can be considered a luxury and not one that the world of medicine or society ought to indulge. Medical students may hear this message in many ways throughout medical school. On the other hand, research driven by application and clinical concerns, research too quickly forced to be related to real-world issues, and research designed to solve the practical problems of the here and now can be considered shallow, less important, and worthy of only weaker students or lower-status Ph.D. fields and/or departments. The culture of the Ph.D. is saturated with these kinds of messages, and Ph.D. students clearly understand them. Indeed, those in the more "applied" fields or those who gravitate to the more applied areas within a discipline are often apologetic and believe they hold positions of lower status than those who are not doing applied work within the Ph.D. culture.

The student who is in both an M.D. and a Ph.D. program can bear the brunt of these conflicting messages and expectations from the faculties in both programs and sometimes from fellow students who are not pursuing the two degrees. Relationships with Ph.D. faculty mentors may become strained if they do not feel that the Ph.D. cultural conditioning is "taking" as fully as expected. The more nonapplied the nature of the Ph.D. program and the orientation of the faculty, the greater may be the risk of strain.

M.D. faculty may see the M.D./Ph.D. student as being sidetracked by the Ph.D. program and not serious enough about clinical responsibilities. They may also be inclined to envy the close personal relationships that they see developing between Ph.D. faculty mentors and the M.D./Ph.D. student, since the relationships between M.D. faculty and medical students tend to be more distant. If the M.D. faculty can be encouraged to see the M.D./Ph.D. student as a future academic colleague, they will be more likely to encourage him or her, especially if they can also see how the student's Ph.D. work will eventually be brought to bear upon clinical problems. If the M.D./Ph.D. student is seen as veering off toward basic and nonapplied research, the M.D. faculty may regard their investment in the student's clinical training as a waste of scarce resources. This may be especially true when the Ph.D. program is in a field like history or philosophy or very advanced basic science.

The student in the M.D./Ph.D. program can feel very pressured by these conflicting messages and expectations. It is not always clear who the models are, nor is it easy to identify all the elements of those models the student is expected to emulate. The student may feel that he or she is being pulled toward one or the other culture and, at the same time, perceive that he or she is cutting a different path and receiving little reinforcement for doing so.

The M.D./Ph.D. student may also become aware that fellow students not in the dual-track program differ from students in the M.D./Ph.D. program in terms of values, expectations, and relationships. Among the differences in expectations is the matter of income. Even in an academic setting, an M.D. will likely receive a larger salary than a Ph.D. But an academic M.D. with a Ph.D. will likely command a lower income than a nonacademic M.D. without the Ph.D.

In many areas where the research is heavily supported by federal resources, Ph.D.s know they will be competing with M.D.s, who have often had little formal research training or have received it in the context of a fellowship rather than an organized Ph.D. program. Ph.D. students often devalue medically driven research that does not meet what they consider the high standards practiced by those with a great deal of formal research training. They may learn from their Ph.D. mentors to resent the fact that M.D.s often compete quite successfully for federal research support when, as the Ph.D. faculty believe, their success is due more to the critical importance of the problems they are studying than to the validity of their research designs. Students pursuing only the Ph.D. may consequently adopt attitudes that communicate a lesser valuing of their fellow Ph.D. students in the M.D./Ph.D. program. On the other hand, medical students not pursuing the Ph.D. may regard those who are as headed for a career that will not really solve the important problems of the field and at the same time not really committed to patient care.

The most pervasive aspect of this culture conflict for the M.D./Ph.D. students is to be found in the basic difference between the manner in which the M.D. and the Ph.D. define what is really important in research. If the research has no foreseeable application of the research to diagnosis, to treatment, to cures, or to patient care, most M.D.s, even if they also hold the Ph.D., will not value the research as highly as they would if the application of the results were clear. The basic conflict for M.D./Ph.D. students is that just when the entire set of possible research futures ought to be available on the horizon, the M.D. part of them is attempting to constrain that horizon to clinical relevance and application. Without individuals who are sensitive to this conflict and able to help students deal with it, the combined M.D./Ph.D. programs can be more stressful than one or the other alone—and not only because of the time demands on the student.

Prescriptions and Remedies

There are a variety of reasons for establishing and supporting M.D./Ph.D. programs. One is to bring the Ph.D. program's focus on research training into stronger relationship with the M.D. program's focus on clinical training and ultimately to improve the quality of medically oriented research. (It has not been lost on many that a significant percentage of the fraud in science involves investigators in medical schools, many of whom do not have the formal Ph.D. research training background.) Another reason is to nurture a cadre of individuals obviously destined to take their place on the faculties of medical schools. Interestingly, the reverse reason is rare—to bring more clinically oriented research into Ph.D. programs or to increase the number of medically trained individuals qualified for academic posts on nonmedical faculties. The impetus for an M.D./Ph.D. program is more likely to begin with medical faculties except in those instances where basic science faculty in a medical school see the M.D./Ph.D. program as helping them attract better graduate students into the Ph.D. programs. Still another reason for the development of some M.D./Ph.D. programs is to foster leadership, particularly in medicine. Much change is anticipated in medicine, if it is not already upon the field. Many expect the M.D./Ph.D. students now being trained to provide important leadership for shaping change and dealing with important societal issues in medicine.

Both Ph.D. and M.D. programs have highly selective admissions policies. Admission to an M.D./Ph.D. program is generally more selective than to either program alone. Obviously, M.D./Ph.D. programs are for highly motivated and intellectually strong students. However, if the analysis of the two-culture situation and the resulting conflicts and pressures has any validity, it must also be recognized that M.D./Ph.D. programs are probably better suited to students who have the personal abilities to handle the cultural conflicts with some equanimity and perspective. What is required is a kind of psychic stamina that permits a student to negotiate between the two cultures. If the student can take the best of both cultures, given his or her goals, and ignore or put in personal perspective the negative messages, the chances are that he or she will perceive the stresses as less intense.

The proper selection of students is only half the picture for program success. The other half must be found in what faculties do to sensitize themselves to the cultural conflict, in how actively they help students understand and deal with the conflicts, and in how willing they are to see themselves as part of the process of change. To accomplish these things (or to keep them going where they already exist) will require a commitment of time and effort on the part of the faculty involved in training the M.D./Ph.D. students. This time and effort must be expended in helping to create a community of association for the M.D./ Ph.D. student cohort and to include in that community key faculty members from both the medical and the nonmedical faculties involved. To do this also requires an institutional commitment of resources to enable one or more persons to focus some significant portion of time on many of the nonacademic or extracurricular aspects of the M.D./Ph.D. program that relate to the establishment and maintenance of the "community."

How an institution makes the commitment to fostering the M.D./Ph.D. community depends on the nature and structure of the academic aspects of the program. Where there is an identified cohort of new M.D./Ph.D. students perceived by both the faculty and the students themselves as a group, the community is a ready-made concept. In some settings these students are identified as "medical scholars"; in others they might be called "medical scientists." Most M.D./Ph.D. programs limit the Ph.D. possibilities to bench sciences. Some permit students to pursue a Ph.D. in the computational sciences or the social and behavioral sciences. A few have permitted students to take a Ph.D. in business, education, or the humanities.

The broader the spread of Ph.D. disciplines permitted in an M.D./Ph.D. program, the more defined will the effort need to be to create a community for M.D./Ph.D. students. But, in addition, the greater the diversity of areas the students are pursuing, the richer are the possibilities for that community. In programs where M.D./Ph.D. students are not admitted as a cohort or as an identified group, where there is a much more individual declaration of intent and students enter at various points in academic time, the creation of a community will be more difficult and require even more institutional effort. Indeed, these students are probably at highest risk for feeling the conflicts in cultures and experiencing stress.

As has been noted, M.D./Ph.D. programs are for a very select group of students and also for a relatively small cadre of students in the universe of M.D. and Ph.D. aspirants. If a reasonable number of M.D./Ph.D. programs flourish and attract very talented students, a number of results can be expected. We will have developed a good pool of candidates with important strengths in research to fill posts in academic medicine. They will be committed to medicine and able to take their place on Ph.D. faculties in and out of medical schools. Perhaps most important, we will have fostered a new breed of leaders in medicine and in research who can participate constructively in the processes of change that are now upon us and that will remain with us for the foreseeable future. To achieve all these results, however, will require that each M.D./Ph.D. program develop an understanding of the issues of cultural conflict and the will to address them forthrightly and creatively.

18

In Praise of Families

James E. Black

- Baptism by Fire
- Introducing the Family
- An Older Model of Professional Training
- The Modern Dilemma
- Exempting the Student from the Adult Role
- Women Physician-Scholars Choosing Not to Be Adults
- Is It Possible to Have Both a Career and a Family?
- Why Bother to Have a Family at All?
- The Price of Not Supporting Family Life
- Conclusions
- References

Professional socialization can have an enormous impact on private life, and vice versa. While that statement seems trite, the actual consequences rarely escape the pages of student handbooks, confidential files in the dean's office, and journal editorials lamenting the state of medical education. A frequent condition of the medical education of physician-scholars is the denial of family life: denial that family life can be of vital importance to the student and that the family can be harmed by M.D./Ph.D. training. In one of the perennial reviews of what's wrong with the medical profession, McCue lamented, "Even physicians with reasonable working habits often praise colleagues who abandon their personal lives to their profession." (1) This chapter addresses the consequences of abandoning oneself to the career of academic physician and the costs of such abandonment to persons near and dear.

Instead of a parade of statistics about M.D./Ph.D. suicide, divorce, and drug abuse, I'll rely on human voices. I quote from medical students, graduate students, and physician-scholars—from a variety of sociological studies and autobiographical accounts. In the interest of full disclosure, I should tell you that I have a personal interest in this topic, since I was a child in a doctor's family and now am myself an M.D./Ph.D. student with a family.

Baptism by Fire

First, let's consider the origins of this trend in professional socialization. M.D./Ph.D. programs are designed to produce model professionals with superior autonomy, commitment, motivation, judgment, and skills. Everything in the pedagogy pushes the student toward total involvement in the training. Graduate school similarly offers the hard-working "winner" the rewards of extra money, more publications, and less involvement in the tedium of undergraduate teaching. Some aspects of training are considered absolutely nonnegotiable by the faculty. Some essential features of clinical work (such as its inherent uncertainty and its proximity to life and death) also demand the student's complete attention. Peer pressure and the proximity of demanding role models complete the full circle of pressures on the student. This is an overwhelming inundation of young adults, a "baptism by fire." (2)

All too often the compassionate and sensitive students get discouraged from this career path, leaving behind a population of students enriched with obsessive-compulsive behavior and egocentrism and thoroughly dedicated to the "fast track" of M.D./Ph.D. stardom. However, not all the negative traits of M.D./Ph.D. students have fixed, premedical roots. Most of these qualities reflect the adaptations of relatively normal people to an extremely demanding training system. While such adaptations can be temporary and even essential for survival, if the pressures are intense enough and persistent enough, the student's maladjustments in character and behavior may become permanent.

Introducing the Family

The period of M.D./Ph.D. training typically overlaps with other intensely stressful tasks of adult development, particularly forming an intimate and nondependent relationship with another adult and becoming a parent. The importance of finding a "soul mate" is evident in the heartbreaking struggles so many young adults undertake to start and maintain romantic relationships, as well as the consistently high ranking of marriage on a list of lifetime priorities.

Raising children is also a very high priority, but it requires sacrifices in terms of effort, time, money, and intimacy in the marriage. For example, marital satisfaction drops significantly with the arrival of the first child (3). Family life may be very desirable for many students, but is also inherently very demanding. Regardless of how an M.D./Ph.D. student arranges his or her priorities, there will be an inevitable conflict that can be intensely stressful and painful for everyone involved. It's a tug-of-war between medical/graduate training, which demands *all* of the student, and the other, equally demanding tasks of adulthood. Listen to this medical student describe her life:

> When I'm involved in training, the house goes to hell, my husband complains that his needs are not being met, the kids complain. And the experience of tending to a lot of pressure at school, and then coming home and finding a lot of pressure there—I just feel like everywhere I turn I'm inadequate. (2)

Note that *everyone* is under pressure here, not just the medical student. In a systems theory approach to this issue, one can describe the family as adjusting to the self-preserving changes in the student, so the structure of medical education elicits adaptive responses from the spouse and children as well. Here is an (unfortunately rare) example of a positive adaptation, which ironically is presented as a complaint by a resident:

> I worry about my own kids and what they're getting from me these days. Most nights, when I get home the two little ones are in bed already, although they are waiting up for me and we have a chance to talk for awhile. The thing about my kids, though, is that they have learned to be squeaking wheels and get the grease. If I neglect them too much they let me know in no uncertain terms. (4)

The "squeakiness" of these kids is probably maintained because this parent *really* listens to them. That pattern is healthier than what is found in some other families, where the student has completely disengaged from the family and the children have long ago become resigned to the loss of this parent.

An Older Model of Professional Training

Not so long ago, the typical first-year medical or graduate student was a white, middle-class, unmarried twenty-two-year-old male. Medical scientist training in the last decade evolved to take full advantage of the characteristics of these students. In turn, these adaptations served to restrict the participation of students with different backgrounds, hence the "complaints" of administration officials that they just cannot find enough qualified minority or women candidates for their programs. In particular, single students could be expected to study during all of their nonlecture time, to work 120-hour weeks, to take frequent night calls away from home, and to put their clinical duties above all else. (It is worth noting that in the recent past young men drafted into the military were similarly required to put their service above all else and to disengage completely from their families.) When single men put medicine first in their life, making use of cafeterias and laundry services, and letting their rooms go to hell, they are expecting exemptions from the adult role: Somebody else is feeding and clothing them; money is borrowed, not earned; and other basic chores of adult living have been deferred until semester break.

Although these men often became fathers during medical school or residency, the top priority and long hours of medicine could still be reasonably demanded of them by old-fashioned M.D./Ph.D. program directors. This was justified by the beliefs that these men would undoubtedly be the primary wage-earners in the family (so it was important for them to make the sacrifice) and that the father's contribution to child development is minor (so their absence from the family would not be harmful). These M.D./Ph.D. students were among the best and the brightest, and other members of the family were expected to defer to their meteoric careers.

The Modern Dilemma

The population of medical students is now changing: They are older on average, they are more likely to be women, more of them are from dual-career families, and more are managing single-parent families. (Consider also that gay and lesbian students frequently have long-term relationships, so they share many of the problems and stresses of heterosexual couples.) Another recent trend is that more students are getting pregnant during their training because more of the student population is female and because they are generally older and "their clock is ticking." Male students are affected by recent changes as well, because in an aging student population they are more likely to be married and to be fathers, so they also have substantial components of their lives outside of medical school. There are also demands imposed on male students by dual-career marriages, primarily because the old expectation that the wife would do all the housework is no longer realistic and much less likely to be tolerated (at least, not without a fight). A growing awareness of how important fathers are in child development also discourages men from neglecting their families (5).

Exempting the Student from the Adult Role

Unflagging commitment to an M.D./Ph.D. program must be maintained for a very long period, often as much as ten years, and there may be additional trials of postdoctoral and residency positions at the end. During this period, a student might expect a new marriage to mature, or even to watch an infant grow into an adolescent. An unflagging commitment to medicine that requires disengagement from the family therefore requires an enormous sacrifice from the student—a sacrifice that is rarely mentioned in student handbooks or residency brochures. Broadhead succinctly described this adaptation of the entire family unit to one single goal: "Attending medical school becomes a 'master plan' for the family as a whole, a key to immense security, status, and success, and a chance to share in a highly honored tradition and purpose." (2)

A university mental health counselor, Michele Scheinkman, described a similar pattern among graduate student families, in which the entire family pathologically focuses itself on helping the student succeed.

> At the clinic, many graduate students came to us when their marriages were falling apart, often around a transition point like orals, preliminary exams, or graduation. The stresses in their relationship stay buried until these milestones come along that bring a couple to a crisis.... Most modern couples expect their marriage to involve a sense of companionship, reciprocity, and equality, but the inequality that graduate school imposes on their relationships makes it difficult for them to sustain their egalitarian ideals. (6)

When "push comes to shove," the other areas of a student's life give. Part of this tendency lies in a rigid educational system that will tolerate little deviation and rarely concedes to personal concerns. For example, many medical schools do not have standard policies for medical students requesting leave, so already harried students must undergo a humiliating and seemingly capricious process of begging the administration for it and hope that it will not be held against them.

The traditional role of the father as the family breadwinner can be fulfilled in large part by doing well in medical and graduate school, and that essentially requires devoting oneself completely to it and neglecting everything else. Male students who accept this older definition of the family do not see a contradiction between almost completely disengaging from the family and being a good husband and father.

As you might guess, the spouse may not agree with this perspective. Here are three examples:

> I had all these demands at school, and I would come home and the only way that Mary would be willing to stay at home was if I would do more work at home. I felt that was totally impossible. I just had to get home and study, and she was demanding that I not do that, and that I help with the kids…and I felt she was very unreasonable. (2)
>
> And I would come home feeling, wow! I'd really put in a hard day's work. And as far as my wife was concerned, I'd put in zero for her and the kids. And I just felt wronged. And when I was confronted with this attitude, I'd come home and the house would be a mess, and I thought, what the hell have you been doing, having coffee with the neighbors all day long! (2)
>
> If he wants medical school, fine, but help me also. And when I did say, "I really need help, come home, I can't take it any more," he'd come home and he was like, "God damn, look what you're doing. You're sabotaging me, and you can't handle your part of the bargain." (2)

The spouse's expectations of the student can thus be a source of support or friction, but even when the entire family agrees to give the student full exemption from the adult role in life, it can be very hard on everyone.

These exemptions from adulthood may provide some needed relief for the M.D./Ph.D. student to study more and work harder, but at the same time they undermine the identities of the student as spouse and parent, both of which are important components of adult development (7). Some students then willingly make enormous sacrifices and withdraw from the friendships and activities of premedical days (8). The sacrifices extend to the student's family as well:

> If there are conflicts that develop between my family and the medical school, inevitably the medical school wins…. If I'm on call at the hospital, regardless of what happens at home, I'm going to be at the hospital. And that's just the way it is. (2)

The more physical sort of exemption from the adult role includes allowing the student to spend considerable time away from home (perhaps the most important exemption) and to abandon the responsibilities of cleaning bathrooms, doing laundry, shopping for groceries, and babysitting. The psychosocial sort of exemption includes disengagement from family activities and the abandonment of some markers of adulthood. Many times, allowances are made when students are too tired at the end of the day to play with the kids or talk with the spouse, when they bring their anatomy texts on family outings, when they try to memorize medications while half-heartedly doing puzzles with the kids. (I know of one professor who exempted herself from a family vacation to Europe to finish writing her book. In the preface, she expressed gratitude for their tolerance, but perhaps they were just happier not to have her and the cursed book dragging along.) Allowances are also made for the emotional consequences of chronic fatigue and stress, so that students can behave in ways not ordinarily tolerated in adults.

Tolerance of regression and instability can also be found in exemptions from other components of the adult role. Responsibility is a crucial adult characteristic, and medical students often feel compelled to break promises, such as going out to dinner with the spouse or doing something fun with the kids.

> During her husband's 110-hour work week, this spouse described her response to the call beeper's interruption of her specially prepared gourmet dinner: "Shall I scream this time? Shall I cry? Before I can choose, I instinctively bellow, 'Aaaaaaggkk,' and protest, 'I hate our lives!' Instantly I feel guilty, but I'm out of control. 'When will we ever have a normal life?' There's no time to discuss it, no time to diffuse the tension. Not even time for a fair fight. 'We'll talk about it later,' Bob promises. A quick kiss and he's gone." (9)

M.D./Ph.D. students often not only fail to contribute economically to their families but also encumber them with substantial debts, and tolerance of this failure of the student in the adult role is a deliberately calculated exemption made by the rest of the family, since it is seen as an investment in the future. And in fact this may really be a financial investment:

> Medical students and residents contemplating marriage must consider the possibility that a medical degree will be considered marital property at the time of divorce.... So those of you thinking of marriage be aware that the M.D. you're working so hard to attain will not be considered your own in the eyes of the court should you ever divorce. (10)

Medical student families often lack some other markers of the adult role, such as a home or car, adequate health insurance, disposable income, and economic security for their children. Thus while single students can opt to remain largely "nonadults," married students face a fundamental conflict with some parts of the adult role.

In the dynamics of a family system, the spouse and children adapt to the student's emotional liability. They learn when to be quiet and how to avoid arguments.

> Although some students are patient with wives who interrupt and "want to play" when they should be studying, others become peevish and irritable. One wife described her situation like this: "He studies in the living room and I usually stay in the bedroom. When I walk back and forth from one room to another, he sees me out of the corner of his eye and it bothers him. I can't make any noise puttering about the kitchen either." Other wives complain about having to lock themselves in such places as the bathroom and lament that they cannot talk on the telephone, play the television, or open squeaky doors. (11)

Some M.D./Ph.D. students explicitly endorse their withdrawal from family because their career seems to be the most important thing in their lives, and family members sometimes agree with them. One member of our local medical auxiliary was quite proud of her husband for having done nothing but study and sleep during his M-1 year, for he had actually managed to be in the top 5 percent of his class. This helps instill a sense of entitlement in the family as well as the physician. After all the trouble the student put them through, don't they have a right to enjoy a good income and the respect of the community? Consider the dilemma of the M.D./Ph.D. student offered a prestigious but low-paying postdoctoral position, or the student interested in doing more research than clinical work and thus depriving his family of many thousands of dollars in income.

Hilfiker (12) identified the sense of entitlement among physicians as one of the most serious problems in medicine today. Student physicians make enormous sacrifices and delay the benefits of adulthood, so they later feel entitled to high income and high status. The spouse who plays along and makes enormous sacrifices will in turn feel entitled to a high standard of living, and this will contribute to the stresses upon the student when making decisions about where to practice and the choice of specialty. One can reliably predict that this resident's spouse, who has willingly given him full exemption, has very high expectations for the future:

> I have no regrets about getting married and having a family.... My wife and I are very conservative and have strong family values...that's what's going to get us through. That doesn't mean she's not having a real tough time now. Everything at home is dumped on her: not just taking care of the kids and housework, but the repairs, the bills, the marketing—everything. I'm almost never available, and when I am there I mostly sleep. (4)

Women Physician-Scholars Choosing Not to Be Adults

It may seem that only male M.D./Ph.D. students choose the path of complete exemption from adulthood. Here is an example of a woman who also chose this path and put her career first in her life. She was a medical student married to another medical student and did not have children:

> I decided that for once in my life I was not going to be handicapped by running the household. I wanted to go for it, just like a man. I did not think I was capable of being both an intern and a person, and I had to be an intern. I think this attitude kept me from going crazy, because it eliminated all potential conflict. I expected no free time, so an afternoon off was a bonus. I did not expect to see my husband, so if we both happened to be home it was a party. My friends were fellow interns, so I never lacked for company. Getting the job done was all that was important. (13)

Other women tacitly accept for themselves the traditional bachelor role by postponing (often reluctantly) any plans for marriage or children.]

> A lot of my friends think that I am really lucky to have a family and kids. Especially some of the female students, because almost all of them want to have families, but they have absolutely no idea when they'll be able to fit such a thing into their lives. (2)

This is in fact the most common way for women M.D./Ph.D. students to gain exemption from the adult role, for it is widely known that in our generally sexist society the exemptions will not be maintained if one gets married or pregnant.

Is It Possible to Have Both a Career and a Family?

An alternative pathway seeks a balance between M.D./Ph.D. training and family life. It is instructive to focus on women students, because our culture often cruelly forces this conflict to arise in their professional lives. Consider this quote:

> Most fundamentally, the woman professional must face a conflict in the hierarchies of status priorities in Western society. For women, the obligations attached to family statuses are first priority, while for men the role demands deriving from the occupational status ordinarily override all others. The woman's duties as a mother override most other role obligations, her duties as a wife are second, and other status obligations are a poor third. (14)

Role boundaries have softened a bit recently for both men and women, but it seems that women feel this conflict more intensely than men. Most women M.D./Ph.D. students, whether they accept an old or new construction of the family, feel fundamentally uncomfortable with the implicit demand that they make a total commitment to medicine.

> A lot of the time when I am able to be home, I simply don't have the physical energy to respond to my husband and children in ways that I should. That is, men can be in this position, but they don't feel like they are not being good husbands. (2)

What must medical students do to find a balance between training and family? Conflicts in the family can be minimized by lowering one's career expectations and making deliberate efforts to participate in family life (i.e., to reject the lure of total exemption). One medical student addressed her academic performance:

> I know that if I hadn't had a family I probably could have been in the top 10 percent of my class. I've got the ability to do that, but I have other priorities. I've hit a compromise. My academic standards are going to have to be a little bit lower so that I can accommodate my family. (2)

M.D./Ph.D. students who choose to do this are all too aware that undesirable consequences such as lower salaries and fewer choice residencies will be the necessary result of suboptimal academic performance. However, the time and energy released by this strategy can be put to good use in the family. Examples of intentional participation in family life range from forcing oneself to share in housework and child care to getting pregnant during training.

The latter option, of course, is a very public statement that one values family life, and it will typically bring the student into conflict with M.D./Ph.D. programs as they are presently structured. One medical student described a rather brutal institutional response to her pregnancy:

> You know, you have no commitment to medicine, you're not really interested in doing this, you're diverting your energy.... And one person told me I had better begin seriously thinking real hard about having an abortion. And he said he didn't think women should be in medicine, and that they were always going off and doing things like this. (2)

The physician who made the latter remark was certainly sexist, but he also reveals some intense antipathy of academia in general toward family values. One can easily imagine that his reaction toward a male student requesting paternal leave would be equally abusive.

Women medical students seem to make the most use of this strategy of maintaining family life, and their growing numbers in medical school may result in some pressure for M.D./Ph.D. programs to meet student needs more fully, as suggested explicitly by this third-year student:

> I think as more and more women get into medical school, it is going to become more and more responsive to the needs of students generally. I think of the women students I know that have kids. They don't do what the single students do in terms of putting in the hours. I know single men who would stay a whole week in a hospital and not go home at night. But when you have children, and you feel you have a right to have children, then you say, "Look, I won't do that." Women who end up doing well in medicine and refusing to do those kinds of things will demonstrate that things can be done differently. As far as clerkships go, women will, and are, making a big difference because they are unwilling to be pushed around as much. (2)

Why Bother to Have a Family at All?

People work very hard to have families because they are very useful: They can be reliable sources of support, companionship, and personal growth. Also, the spouse has personal needs for support, companionship, and growth, and it just isn't fair to ignore them. Last, children really do need their parents, both of them, including the father (5). Neglecting children in favor of a career will eventually cost the person, the family, and society in general very dearly.

What benefit might family experience have for the student physician working in the clinic? In the present system of medical training, most of the clinical experience is obtained from poor and minority patients at university, charity, and VA hospitals. The students from white, middle-class families (the largest portion of the typical M.D./Ph.D. program) do not readily identify with these patients, and the stresses of training encourage strong negative attitudes. It becomes relatively easy for students to blame their patients for most of their own problems just because they are different. (Unfortunately, attending physicians and residents often provide ample support for these cynical attitudes.) It thus becomes easier to accept the status quo, which gives doctors substantially more power than patients, and to ignore and minimize the patients' concerns.

Family experience can modulate this socialization either in a positive or a negative fashion. In families where the student has accepted full exemption and become disengaged, some inappropriate values can be transferred from the hospital to the family. For example, the sense of entitlement many physicians have (12) may justify demands for complete authority at home, although authoritarian child-rearing styles are generally associated with negative outcomes (3). Similarly, the family's sympathy for the stress on students may make them too tolerant and actually encourage regressive behavior, such as tantrums or breaking promises, and this in turn encourages the infantile behavior of some respected academic physicians in the operating room or on the ward. How can a student have respect or compassion for patients when such feelings have been made invalid within the family, even if only as a strategy that is considered necessary for surviving medical school? In turn, all of this can take a devastating toll on the family.

On the other hand, students who remain engaged in family life will have a broader identification with patients because of their own experiences. Most of them will have taken an ill spouse or child to a doctor and endured the fear about what's going to happen, the self-blame for a child's accident, and the humiliation of doctors telling you it was unnecessary to bother them with such trivial problems. At some point, every medical student has an encounter with what I call the "that coulda been me" patient; that is, a sad case in which the patient's age, sex, and lifestyle have an uncanny similarity to the student's. This experience can break through the crusty denial of medical school and allow a student to stand in a patient's shoes for once, but quite often the student closes off the experience out of self-defense and gains little from it. I believe that a continued series of "that could have been me," "that could have been my spouse," or "that could have been my kid" patients will prevent the M.D./Ph.D. student from becoming a hermetically sealed automaton, fully insulated from the experiences, feelings, and concerns of patients.

When is this identification with patients likely to occur? Informally, I have observed it in a variety of situations. Medical students with children at home may become rattled when operating on a one-year-old boy, or have nightmares about their aging parents when working with debilitated geriatric patients, or become almost neurotic about bringing home the infectious agents they see in a pediatrics clinic.

One M.D./Ph.D. friend of mine became quite angry with a parent who had caused a serious head injury by dropping his infant son. A complete medical response to this unlucky child should have included not just management of the injury and anger toward the incompetent parents but also some compassion and understanding. Guilt and shame can sometimes cause far worse wounds than physical trauma, and the parent's response to these emotions can later inflict still more harm on the child. It is unfortunate when the medical staff reinforces this guilt and ultimately compounds the trauma.

My friend is not a parent himself, and I believe his inexperience with children led to harsh judgment of the father's carelessness. Most parents (including myself) realize how very close we have come to being in that father's predicament. Anyone who has made hundreds of trips up and down stairs carrying a baby has a private knowledge of the many small stumbles and lapses in attention, which can remain private only when no misfortune comes of them. Indeed, the power of William Kennedy's novel *Ironweed* arises from the ability of most readers to personally recognize the terror in those few seconds when a drunken father lets his infant child slip to the floor. In this sense, the medical student can benefit from having a family and thus sharing in the broader experience of patients.

Another example of sharing in the broader experience of patients is from Suzanne Trupin:

> Bearing a child does make an obstetrician more empathetic. The banalities of heartburn, hemorrhoids and maternity clothes become topics of great interest and extended conversation. To this day I quote what I learned as an expectant mother—none of which was covered in medical school or residency. But empathy can bring pain—a lesson I had to be retaught. After the birth of my second child, the first patient I delivered when I returned to work was the 26-year-old receptionist of a colleague. She delivered a Down's Syndrome child. I almost couldn't bear to tell her, and that night I think I cried as much as she did. (15)

The Price of Not Supporting Family Life

Let's consider what happens when medical training fails to support family life. Even when the spouse accepts 100 percent of the housekeeping, child care, and income earning, family and personal problems can converge and become overwhelming. When this happens, students rarely ask for help from the medical school administration or faculty—it is generally their last resort. But why would students be reluctant to ask for help, especially when explicitly encouraged to do so in policy statements and student handbooks? It is because they know that physicians place a high value on "keeping it all together." In the hospital, this "macho" attitude may have some value, but it encourages students to deny the emotional needs of their children and spouse, as well as their own. This is an unmarried surgery resident:

> Some of the guys are having a lot of second thoughts. They're faced either with quitting the field or heading for separation and divorce. (4)

(Academic surgery programs have notorious reputations for breaking up families.) Note that a third option, that the training program could provide some relief for these families, was apparently not considered by the residents. The result is that sometimes families crack apart under the stress, as this ex-wife poignantly reveals:

> I…taught his little girl to admire her daddy and understand that his growing absence was necessary to help other children who were less fortunate. And she endured. A little 4-year-old girl who was known by the hospital switchboard operators on a first-name basis. A 4-year-old who dreamed of becoming a nurse, in hopes of seeing her daddy more. A child who loved the precious few hours every other Sunday with her daddy, hours often spent taking off his three-day old socks and placing pillows under his head while mommy tried to feed him in bed because he was too exhausted to sit at the kitchen table. My husband will complete his residency in June—11 years of training counting medical school. He will, I am sure, make great strides in his field. Perhaps he will remember a few of the things his family endured for his chosen professional goal. The attorney who is handling the separation informs me that the starting salaries are quite high in my husband's subspecialty. I remember the loans I gladly signed during the years of training to supplement his income, to pay the rent. Child support is assured to be more than adequate, the attorney says, but because I am now in law school, my future earnings will preclude "rehabilitative" maintenance. My "rehabilitation" will involve a mending of my heart, I tell this attorney. We made it through medical school and most of residency. We coped for a long time, in our different ways. His patients should be grateful. Their bright young surgeon has been skillfully trained but selfishly possessed by a system that forgets that behind many good residents are their families, waiting. (16)

It's true that medical training programs have made some accommodations to students with families (e.g., allowing medical student couples to enter the match together). But consider the problems that still remain, such as one described by a woman resident married to another resident:

> I realize now how much easier things would be without Tommy…. If my husband has to go in at night and I get a call I can't handle by phone, I go a little crazy trying to find someone to take Tommy in the middle of the night…. I wish I had more time to spend with Tommy, but…he's better off spending good parts of the day away from me. Anyway, he seems to be doing fine. (4)

This resident basically feels helpless to change her situation and is actively engaged in denial and rationalization to protect herself from the painful truth about what is actually happening to her family. Inflexible M.D./Ph.D. training programs that refuse to recognize the personal needs of their students can cause great harm, and it is unfortunate that some students feel compelled to drop out of their programs rather than risk the welfare of their families (e.g., 4 and 17).

Conclusion

A review article by McCue in *The New England Journal of Medicine* summarizes my perspective on the effects of M.D./Ph.D. education on the health of families: "Retreat from family life is probably the most common adaption to the demands of medical practice. A progressive emotional separation from family life in the early years of practice becomes a de facto divorce." (1) That result, of course, can be expanded to de facto divorce and child abandonment. Even when the M.D./Ph.D. student intentionally becomes disengaged, perhaps even knowing that it will hurt the entire family, the spouse and children are rarely aware of the high price they will pay. In other words, this constitutes a Faustian bargain by the M.D./Ph.D. student, and it certainly violates the consent of other family members.

Perhaps one could argue that the Faustian bargain is justified by the genius and productivity of M.D./Ph.D.s. Two quotes from Sir Peter Medawar, the eminent immunologist and Nobel laureate, amply illustrate that credit for his enormous success should be shared with others who had been close to him, and one suspects that, with all his famed humility, it was not the famous scientist who got burned worst in the end.

> I had thought, when I was a boy, that I should be a good father, one who wisely and kindly guided my children, shaping their minds and morals by imperceptible degrees. My performance fell so far short of the ambitions that I was an outstandingly rotten father and neglected them disgracefully.... My neglect was due to my total preoccupation with research in the laboratory, writing, or delivering one or other of the very many lectures I was repeatedly asked for. (18)
>
> Jean...has relieved me, all our married life, of duties and chores that might hinder the prosecution of scientific research.... Jean has looked after them, and almost everything else of a tiresome or distracting nature. (18)

Let me summarize the choices with regard to family life during medical training, each of which can be adopted by either male or female students:

1. Don't have a family, and don't be an adult. This offers the advan tages of full exemption from adulthood, and nobody else will get hurt. For M.D./Ph.D. students, it's a very long time to wait, however, and I suspect that "giving one's all" to medicine may warp one's adult development.
2. Have a family, and don't be an adult. You get full exemption, so you can devote yourself completely to your career, plus you may get the support of your spouse and kids. Most important, your spouse will have to take on extra responsibilities that you shirk, your children will miss you, and the people closest to you may be hurt by your neglect of them.
3. Have a family, and be an adult. This means swimming against the tide in medical school and residency, but you will get to participate

in family life without hurting your family. The major drawback is the inability to perform competitively during training. This will make getting tenure more difficult, for example, and may result in many thousands of dollars in lost income.

4. Don't have a family, and be an adult. This allows one to retain a high level of self-esteem and productivity without hurting anyone. As one might expect, however, it can be a lonely choice and it seems to be rarely chosen.

It is ironic that nearly two decades later, Carolyn Crawford's (19) discussion of women medical students and their needs illustrates how little has changed to support the family life of M.D./Ph.D. students. She recommended shorter work schedules during training so that students could have reasonable amounts of contact with their family. She also argued for the development of new training programs that are supportive of parenthood (e.g., by allowing flexible or part-time tracks, providing child care while students are on call, and allowing parental leave. Today, one would ask that leave be provided for fathers as well as mothers, and for adoptions as well as births.) She called for sick-leave time for the care of dependents, so that students do not have to feign their own illness to take care of sick kids. And she asked that the family be provided some relief from the chronic stress of financial insecurity and inadequate health insurance.

Some of these recommendations are already being put in place, such as shorter hours during residency, but I am afraid that I am rather cynical about these changes. Legal concerns motivated the shorter work week. Chronically unfilled residency slots stimulated some competition for students, including good family benefits. General economic changes in medicine now allow some physicians to choose regular hours with reasonable call schedules in HMO and "doc-in-a-box" facilities. I do not believe that the medical training system did these things out of compassion for the families of physician-scholars; it still basically ignores its relationship to family life and has yet done little to support it.

References

1. McCue, "The Effects of Stress on Physicians and Their Medical Practice," *The New England Journal of Medicine,* 306 (1982): 458–63.
2. R. S. Broadhead, *The Private Lives and Professional Identity of Medical Students* (New Brunswick, N.H.: Transaction, 1983).
3. C. N. Ruble, A. S. Fleming, L. S. Hackel and C. Stangor, "Changes in Marital Relationships During the Transition to First Time Motherhood: Effects of Violated Expectations Concerning Distribution of Labor," *Journal of Personality and Social Psychology* 55 (1988): 78–87.
4. R. L. Cohen, *House Officer: Becoming a Medical Specialist* (New York: Planu, 1988).
5. R. D. Parke, "Social Development in Infancy: A 25 Year Perspective," in *Advances in Child Behavior and Development*, Vol. 22, ed. H. Reese

(Orlando, Fla: Academic Press, in press).

6. M. Scheinkman, "Graduate Student Marriages: An Organizational/ Interactional View," *Family Process* 27 (1988): 351–68
7. S. M. Dornbusch, P. L. Ritter, P. H. Leiderman and D. F. Roberts, "The Relationship of Parenting Style to Adolescent School Performance," *Child Development* 58 (1987): 1244–57.
8. M. Shapiro, *Getting Doctored* (Kitchener, Ontario: Between the Lines, 1978).
9. P. Love, "The Wild Ride of a Medical Marriage," *Focus on the Family Physician* 1 (1989): 1–3.
10. A. Kenworthy, "Letter: Divorce and the M.D. Degree," *The New Physician* (July–August 1988): 5.
11. R. H. Coombs, "The Medical Marriage," in *Psychosocial Aspects of Medical Training*, ed. R. H. Coombs and C. E. Vincent (Springfield, Ill.: Thomas, 1971).
12. D. Hilfiker, *Healing the Wounds* (New York, N.Y.: Penguin, 1985).
13. T. Martin, *How to Survive Medical School* (New York, N.Y.: Holt, Rinehart, & Winston, 1983).
14. C. F. Epstein, *Woman's Place* (Berkeley: University of California Press, 1971).
15. S. Trupin, "When the Obstetrician Gets Pregnant," in *Inside Doctoring*, ed. R. H. Coombs, D. S. May and G. W. Small (New York, N.Y.: Praeger, 1986).
16. Anonymous, "The Goal," in *Inside Doctoring*, ed. R. H. Coombs, D. S. May and G. W. Small (New York, N.Y.: Praeger, 1986).
17. M. Harrison, *A Woman in Residence* (New York, N.Y.: Penguin, 1982).
18. P. Medawar, *Memoir of a Thinking Radish* (Oxford: Oxford University Press, 1986).
19. C. S. Crawford, "Today's Women in Medicine," *The New Physician* 21

PART III
CONCLUSION

The titles of the two chapters that comprise Part III directly describe their contents. Clearly, perhaps blatantly, prescriptive, these chapters draw on all the arguments—those with and those without supporting data—presented in Chapter 1 through Chapter 18.

19

Recommendations on the Education of Physician-Scholars

Harold M. Swartz and Diane L. Gottheil with DeWitt C. Baldwin, Jr., George Cahill, Jr., Leon Eisenberg, Paul A. Hattis, Benjamin Horowitz, Arthur Kleinman, Thomas Meikle, Jr., Hamilton Smith, and August G. Swanson

- The Need for Physician-Scholars/Leaders
- Programs to Educate the Kinds and Numbers of Physician-Scholars/Leaders Needed
- Programs in Medical Humanities and Social Sciences
- Directors and Administrators of Programs to Educate Physician-Scholars
- The Physician-Scholar and the Physician-Leader
- The Relationship between Clinical Expertise and Physician Scholarship/ Leadership
- Students and Recent Graduates of Programs to Educate Physician-Scholars
- Critical Issues Perceived by Students in Training Programs for Physician-Scholars/Leaders

This chapter presents an overview of the presentations and discussions that took place at the Symposium on the Education of Physician-Scholars in the Health Care System referred to in the preface and of the impressionistic conclusions that can be drawn from the proceedings. It then provides brief summaries of conclusions and recommendations reached at five workshops attended by different symposium participants as recorded by workshop facilitators.

For several years, increasing concern has been expressed about the recruitment of adequate numbers of young physicians into careers focusing on research, teaching, and public service. Concern has also been expressed as to the ability of physician-scholar programs to meet the current and future needs of the health care system, particularly the need for physicians with expertise in areas outside the usual biomedical disciplines.

The specific and deliberate preparation of physicians for scholarship and leadership is desirable, although the pathways to leadership positions and the needs that leaders must fulfill are so varied that preparatory programs in this area will be more open ended for individuals and for areas of responsibility. Because many of the desirable attributes of leadership can be taught and learned, there should be more emphasis on them in the medical schools and residencies that seek to prepare their graduates for leadership positions. While not all leaders will be scholars, the quality of leadership is likely to be enhanced by a genuine understanding of the research process. Similarly, not all physician-scholars will enter formal leadership positions, but their expertise makes them highly eligible for such positions, and some preparation is therefore desirable.

Physicians interested in scholarly/leadership careers are very attractive to organizations interested in recruiting them at each stage of their development: as medical students, residents, or fellows, and later as faculty, researchers, and/or administrators. However, it is crucial to improve the communication of information on general and specific career opportunities to students and prospective students. Medical schools, for example, are increasingly interested in attracting students who wish to pursue combined degrees, and at some schools the range of disciplines in which graduate studies can be conducted is often much wider than students realize. Similarly, many residencies are especially interested in applicants who seek to pursue academic careers and may be willing to provide the flexibility needed to help young physicians reach their goals. In addition, academic medical centers, governmental agencies, and industry place a high value on the recruitment of physicians with strong research backgrounds and/or interest and training in policy, administration, and the like. It is, however, difficult to attract sufficient numbers of the best students into academic and related careers, partly because they are unaware of the opportunities in such careers, although, as will be noted, there are also some formidable financial and structural barriers to these careers.

The demands of research and clinical care often conflict. The interrelated questions— How can physicians achieve appropriate clinical competence in the educational phase of their careers? and, How can they blend clinical and research efforts in their actual careers?—are germane regardless of the stage at which they receive their research education. In many ways, the situation is getting more rather than less complex because of the increasing competition for research funding, the increased sophistication needed to conduct research, the many sources of pressure on academicians to be clinically active, and the likelihood that third parties will increase their scrutiny of the clinical preparation and current competence of clinicians for purposes of reimbursement and/or medical-legal coverage.

Several solutions would resolve at least some aspects of these problems. It is essential that various segments of the medical community recognize in both words and deeds some of the conflicts that can result from simultaneous requirements for high levels of clinical and research competence; in some situations, a narrower competence in one area should be accepted without loss of stature to the individual. The concept of the "triple threat"—leading clinician, bench researcher, and teacher—is an impossibility for most or all very talented physicians, so criteria for appointments and promotions should be based on more realistic expectations. The classical clinician-scholar-teacher model should still be the ideal toward which the system strives, but the minimally acceptable level appears to be board certification in a subspecialty and continued active participation in clinical care.

There are two apparently successful programs in which people with a Ph.D. are given specifically designed courses to make them more familiar with clinical aspects of medicine. A more extensive clinical preparation for individuals whose research and other professional activities would not involve the direct care of patients was proposed in the context of a modified medical school curriculum that leads to an M.D. but restricted qualification for clinical practice. Other courses of action include having research-oriented physicians pursue relatively narrow, highly focused practices directly related to their research and having clinicians interested in research serve as part of a team that includes individuals with more extensive research experience. There is a strong need for some individuals with high levels of understanding of both clinical medicine and research that is not limited to the traditional biomedical areas.

In many research areas, to stay at the cutting edge of knowledge and to remain competitive for external research support, graduates need to remain active in research during at least part of their residency. On the other hand, it can be essential for future physician-scholars to have full, undiluted clinical residencies. Parallel concerns and contradictory positions have been expressed about physicians who received their principal research education during or after the residency. The incompatibilities of various viewpoints may be further complicated by changes from outside academic medicine that may make the attainment of specialty and subspecialty certification and evidence of high clinical activity prerequisites for reimbursement and medical-legal coverage. Despite these unresolved issues, it is desirable to consider the postgraduate phases of the careers of young physician-scholars to try to optimize opportunities to enhance productivity and personal satisfaction. Many of the residency programs that are the most academically prestigious are increasingly seeking out the graduates of M.D./Ph.D. programs and are prepared to modify their residencies accordingly. A systematic program at Washington University in St. Louis has been initiated to provide such a pathway.

The later steps in the development of physician-scholars should be structured in ways that enable them to continue to participate sufficiently in research through the fellowship and early faculty phases of their careers. The importance and feasibility of extending the career pathway to this phase are illustrated by a program at Johns Hopkins University that enables young clinical faculty, selected competitively, to have 70 percent or more time fully freed up for research for at least two years. The program requires that participants prepare proposals for external support, and it appears to be working very well, as indicated by its popularity and by the success rate of participants in obtaining competitive external research funding. Although such programs are relatively expensive, they appear to be desirable if individuals and society are to obtain full benefits from the investments in the education of physicians for scholarly careers.

The role of the specialty boards in this context is crucial. The current requirements of some specialties almost rule out the participation of highly qualified researchers by calling for a long period of time in strictly clinical pursuits. On the other hand, some specialty boards have been modifying their requirements to facilitate the participation of graduates of M.D./Ph.D. programs and other young physicians with similar interests in scholarly careers. These boards have developed a number of options to allow for participation in meaningful levels of research during the residencies.

Physician-scholars are especially needed and have special opportunities in nontraditional areas, including the social sciences, humanities, and physical sciences. Very important ongoing developments in these areas affect virtually all aspects of medicine. The need exists in industry as well as in academia and government. Some of the most interesting and important problems in modern medicine may be approached most effectively by means of these "nontraditional" disciplines. As with disciplines more traditionally associated with medicine, it is no longer possible for most individuals to become sufficiently expert in these areas by informal and unstructured pathways. A number of programs educate M.D./Ph.D. students in these areas and are very attractive to many of the brightest students; the largest such programs are at the University of Illinois at Urbana-Champaign, the University of Chicago, and Harvard University. Some programs enable physicians at early or midcareer to pursue formal education in these areas; the most prominent are sponsored by the Robert Wood Johnson Foundation (Clinical Scholars and Health Policy Fellows) and the Pew Foundation.

While M.D./Ph.D. programs will likely continue to have a very significant and expanding role in the preparation of physician-scholars, it is essential that there continue to be multiple points of entry for these careers. Some students are not prepared to make a commitment to such careers when applying to medical school, and there are advantages to obtaining the principal research education after the primary clinical education.

The Medical Scientist Training Program (MSTP) of the National Institute of General Medicine is likely to continue to be a dominant force in supporting M.D./Ph.D. programs, but even at the twenty-nine schools with this type of funding, it covers, on the average, less than two-thirds of the total expenditures to support M.D./Ph.D. students. Furthermore, about seventy other medical schools have M.D./Ph.D. programs without direct support from NIH. While a majority of the latter are small, they are often considered very important by the schools and receive considerable support. Some large non-MSTP programs have as many as 130 students (University of Illinois at Urbana-Champaign).

The underrepresentation of minorities and women appears to be even greater in educational programs aimed at the development of physician-scholars/leaders than in medicine generally. Efforts to deal with this problem are necessary if these groups are eventually to have full representation in the medical community and if all potential sources of outstanding candidates are to be fully tapped.

More and better data on all aspects of the education of physician-scholars are needed. The gaps in information include the size and quality of the pool of individuals interested in such careers; the number and type of positions available in the various types of program; the outcomes of various types of program for the education of physician-scholars; the identity and characteristics of residencies that are especially applicable for and interested in such individuals; and the potential needs and roles for such individuals throughout the health care system.

Because the health care system has undergone considerable change in the recent past, data on the previous outcomes of programs need to be applied with caution to current and future situations.

From the information provided in this collection, we may draw the following conclusions:

1. There is a significant level of interest in the subject, and it is important to academia, government, and industry.
2. Informal or formal organizations should be formed to deal with specific aspects of the subject, including an organization representing students in M.D./Ph.D. programs, one for directors of M.D./Ph.D. programs, and another for programs to educate physician-scholars in the social sciences and humanities.
3. The physician-scholar career path has great promise in terms of both its potential attractiveness to the best and brightest students and its ability to fulfill society's need for leaders.
4. The research component of the education of physician-scholars needs to be rigorous and comparable to that of the best Ph.D. programs.
5. The undergraduate clinical education of physician-scholars needs to be rigorous and comparable to that of the best M.D. programs. Although physician-scholars are likely to spend less time in purely clinical aspects of medicine, it is desirable for them to have an excellent basic understanding of clinical medicine.
6. Although M.D./Ph.D. programs will play increasingly important roles, it is essential to retain multiple points of entry into this type of career.
7. Many of the most urgent current problems in the development of physician-scholars involve the educational sequences and requirements for students pursuing scholarly careers.
8. More consideration and study should be given to the stresses on students in these long and demanding educational programs that cross two cultures.
9. Additional financial support for students and programs is needed to recruit adequate numbers of appropriately prepared physician-scholars/leaders. It remains a principal task of the academic medical community to make the need and rationale for such support widely known.
10. There are needs and opportunities for more physicians to be educated at the cutting edge in the social sciences and humanities. Federal initiatives are required to accomplish this; they should be modeled after the MSTP but not diminish support for the MSTP.
11. There must be systematic and objective gathering, analyses, and dissemination of data on all aspects of this subject, ranging from the characteristics of the pool of students available for this career path through the evaluation of outcomes of the educational programs and the needs of and opportunities for the graduates.
12. It is desirable to convene meetings on this topic periodically.
13. The implementation of some of these recommendations should be pursued under the auspices of appropriate national organizations, such

as the National Institutes of Health and the Association of American Medical Colleges.

Many of the problems identified here are potentially solvable because the solutions are under the control of the academic health care community. A few require contributions from governmental agencies or other sources of new financial support, but most call only for leadership and commitment to the goal of preparing physician-scholars who can provide the leadership needed for the twenty-first century.

The Need for Physician-Scholars/Leaders

August G. Swanson

We estimate a need in the range of 2,000 physician-scholars/leaders per year for the foreseeable future, or 12 percent of the output of our medical schools. The normal historical output just to replenish our faculties is in the range of 7 percent. The need to train more physician-scientists reflects the general demand for scholarship to keep the United States from slipping to second-class status. Furthermore, the industrialization of biotechnology will greatly increase the demand for physician-scientists.

The exact number of physician-scholars needed and their mix cannot be estimated precisely, but it is clear that there will be a continuing demand for medical scholars, ranging from fundamental biomedical scientists at one end of the spectrum to medical policy analysts at the other. In between, we need medical humanists and social scientists devoted to studies of health services. A corollary is the need to incorporate into the medical curriculum some courses, instruction, and examples of the medical humanities and medical social sciences as they affect our society.

There should be an effort to reach out to the high school and college populations, particularly to underrepresented minorities, to stimulate interest in academic and scientific careers. To do this, we need medical school faculties willing to reach out to schools, social groups, and institutions within their communities. We cannot effectively reach high schools from the national level, but each medical school can reach a good number of secondary (and even primary) schools within its community and stimulate students in those institutions to think of scientific and biomedical careers. Medical schools should also form consortia directed toward reaching the liberal arts colleges to encourage the best and brightest students to consider physician-scientist careers.

All medical schools should recognize the need to nurture scholarly attitudes in all their students. Programs directed toward educating medical scholars have a particular responsibility to provide the best possible advice and guidance for their students as they progress through their educational programs into careers.

We must secure some combination of private and public resources to provide substantial and reliable support for the education of physician-scholars. The funding should come from several sources, including the Medical Scientist Training Program, locally sponsored M.D./Ph.D. programs, and postdoctoral experiences for M.D.s. Opportunities for midcareer physicians to become involved in scholarly activity based upon their experiences in the real world should be included. The education of medical humanists and medical social scientists should be funded by mechanisms similar to those used for funding physician-scientists in our current system. The Robert Wood Johnson and Pew Trust programs should be complimented on their programs, which have led the way in developing physician-scientists and physicians engaged in health research and health policy. These foundations should continue their programs.

Programs to Educate the Kinds and Numbers of Physician-Scholars/Leaders Needed

DeWitt C. Baldwin, Jr.

What is unique about M.D./Ph.D. programs is their potential for developing highly qualified persons with a broad view and perspective on both medicine and science. At the same time, scholars and leaders, as well as scholar-leaders, have come from a variety of pathways and programs. It is possible for a person to become a physician-scholar without going through a formal program, but such a pathway is generally inefficient and expensive in time and money and can leave lacunae in knowledge and skills.

Programs don't necessarily create leaders, although good programs tend to produce leaders because they recruit more potential leaders. Career pathways and training requirements are much less clear for physician-leaders than for physician-scholars, partly because of the disparate goals for leadership by physicians. Many leaders currently come from scholarly backgrounds but often do not have the requisite knowledge and skills to maximize the effectiveness of their leadership, administration, and management. Professional degrees may offer physicians a potential pathway for gaining such knowledge and skills. It is highly desirable, but not absolutely necessary, for physician-leaders to be scholars.

Specific elements necessary to a good training program include:

1. Substantive courses in the basic scientific discipline, including strong research and methodological elements
2. Regular research seminars for trainees, including both internal and external presentations
3. An introductory orientation to or survey of all the elements and dimensions of the program
4. A clear, though flexible, sequence of educational and training experiences
5. An opportunity for extensive peer and faculty interaction around issues of research, training, and socialization
6. A scientific mentoring system
7. An operational monitoring system
8. A strong organizational structure and administration, including a "nurturing" person to support and smooth the way for students

9. A program for the follow-up of trainees after they complete the program
10. Better communication and integration of administrative units
11. Multiple potential points of entry into the program
12. Appropriate role models and mentors in the respective fields or disciplines
13. A program segment on the ethics and morality of science
14. The flexibility and opportunity for independent intellectual and research exploration.

Also needed to enhance the development of programs are:
1. A listing of all M.D./Ph.D. programs
2. More effective communication with premedical institutions concerning these opportunities
3. Better integration of premedical courses with those in medical and graduate school, to allow greater freedom and flexibility to students.

Additional issues include the following:
1. Are professional programs (law, business, etc.) scholarly? This may be true only if these fields include extensive research training and foster scholarly productivity.
2. Training programs have a responsibility to help trainees continue their career development with enough support to enable them to get started (money, space, time). One objective of such programs should be to enable the trainee to conceptualize definable, "do-able" projects.
3. Physician-scholars need seasoning and development. There is a danger that bright, capable people are being "called" or "pushed" to "get ahead" too fast for their own best development.
4. Much true scholarly development occurs *after* the training program (M.D./Ph.D. or other), so such programs should focus on thorough preparation for future development.

Programs in Medical Humanities and Social Sciences
Arthur Kleinman and Leon Eisenberg

There is an increasing need for M.D./Ph.D. training in the medical humanities and social sciences. Given the astonishing array of social and moral problems in medicine, it is simply illogical and counterproductive *not* to have major M.D./Ph.D. training programs in these areas. The justification for it is as straightforward as that for training in molecular biology.

Is there a special role for M.D./Ph.D.s, as opposed to Ph.D.s, in the medical humanities and social sciences? After all, many medical sociologists, medical anthropologists, and medical historians do not have an M.D. Indeed, there is a special role for the M.D./Ph.D. as a mediator between these two professional groups. There is also a role for the M.D./Ph.D. in the general university. A course taught by an M.D./Ph.D. at Harvard University has 270 undergraduate students and is the seventh largest in the college. There is a role for teaching and research on medicine in the humanities and social sciences; the M.D./Ph.D. in these areas can contribute to that.

One must distinguish M.D./Ph.D.s from M.D./attorneys or M.D./M.B.A.s. The M.D./Ph.D. is a research degree; even when M.D./Ph.D.s do affect policy, their central interest is the generation of new knowledge. A range of individuals in the health policy arena need not have a Ph.D. degree; an M.A. in a policy area or a law degree may be more appropriate for policy work.

There are a limited number of role models. That puts students who are combining medicine with a field in the humanities or social sciences in a pioneering role, which takes courage. The candidates for the medical humanities and medical social sciences M.D./Ph.D. tracks are every bit as outstanding as those in the biological sciences. We need not worry about recruitment if we create the opportunity.

Another issue is institutionalization, including what Max Weber would have called "the institutionalization of charisma" and we might call the institutionalization of genius and creativity. That is, the physicians who first obtained postgraduate training in the humanities or social sciences were few in number; their relationships with their teachers were close mentoring relationships. As programs have developed, as whole fields have enlarged, the university has become a multiversity, an immense multiversity. Many graduate students feel like factory workers.

The most serious obstacle is budgetary. It is simply unacceptable *not* to have federal funding for M.D./Ph.D. programs in the social sciences and humanities parallel to those in the natural sciences. Some programs have attracted foundation support, but most faculty in this area have been under the high stress of having to piece together their own programs with minimal funding at a time of tremendous pressure on the departments in the humanities and social sciences, which already have limiting funding constraints.

Directors and Administrators of Programs to Educate Physician-Scholars

Hamilton Smith

In most programs, applicants are interviewed from September through March. The interviewing process for each applicant is often extensive, spanning a day or more, with numerous faculty (and, in some cases, student) interviewers drawn from the graduate disciplines as well as the medical sector. Many programs attempt to do in-depth recruiting at this stage. The procedures for selecting students to be admitted vary greatly from one program to another. Quite a few schools permit an MSTP committee to admit students to the programs, whereas other schools have been more conservative, allowing the medical admissions committee to retain that power.

As March rolls around, most programs have accepted a number of applicants and enter the final stage of recruiting, which extends into June. Some schools have finished the process, while others are continuing to interview and do not make their announcements on funding and acceptance until rather late, sometimes into late April. Consequently, there is a lot of "director anxiety," but apparently less among the applicants. The asynchrony among the schools' admission processes has been a problem. A major problem for the director is late acceptances and withdrawal from programs, thus potentially leaving empty slots with no applicants to fill them.

A "matching" program, which would presumably achieve the optimum satisfaction for both the applicant and the institution, has been proposed in the past, but a number of programs continue to resist the idea. Some problems with this approach arise when the size of the applicant pool does not correspond to the number of available positions. Another source of difficulties is the need for student couples to end up at the same institution. In addition, we know from the residency situation that under-the-table deals complicate the matching process. Until someone has prepared a specific proposal that meets these concerns, matching is not going to be considered seriously by most schools.

It would be desirable to adopt a uniform timetable in lieu of a matching program. This timetable would have to be agreed to by the twenty-nine MSTP schools, and by as many others as possible. The timetable would perhaps establish some beginning and end to the process in an attempt to synchronize it a bit more.

M.D./Ph.D. students in the MSTPs and other biomedically oriented disciplines are considerably better off than those in the social sciences and humanities in regard to funding. A number of programs around the country are without external funding, and many of these support their students through clinical earnings that are funneled, via the dean, into the program. This may be a particularly good source, because in the medical school environment the clinical departments are about the only money-making operation.

Almost universally, programs integrate clinical studies with research, but in most cases the integration is rather loose. The Ph.D. studies ought, as much as possible, to be undertaken in an uninterrupted block of time at least once a student gets into the research years. The standard breakdown is 2-3-2: two years of medical school, then three or so years of research, followed by two years of clinical work. In some cases the clinical activities take less than two years and the research time is increased. A few schools encourage students to begin with Ph.D. work to establish a mentor and initiate a research connection, go on to medical school work (especially in the basic sciences), and then, to various extents, integrate the two curricula. Other schools feel that completing a year of clinical work, actual clinical rotations, before starting the Ph.D. is desirable. One can find virtually any arrangement and degree of integration in the programs across the country. Most tend to be reasonably flexible and allow some tailoring of the curriculum for individual students.

Another common mechanism for integration is an annual meeting and/or get-togethers of the students during the year. Students in the research years are separated in time and place from those in the clinical or basic medical science portion of their training. A common activity in the program brings the students together and gives them a certain amount of identity with the program.

Most schools use a variety of mechanisms to advise students; these range from assigning an advisor during the medical years to having a Ph.D. committee oversee the progress of research and deal with problems. Obviously, the mentor plays a major role in advising. A possibly unrecognized but significant source of advising is senior students in the program who inform younger students of the best labs, various course options, and so forth. Programs have evolved various mechanisms to allow students to interact with role models.

How does one deal with a student who wants to change mentors in midstream? Usually the graduate program director deals with this, although MSTP directors come into play as well.

In many schools, the establishment of an MSTP or other M.D./Ph.D. program has had a positive effect on both the medical and the graduate curriculum: it upgrades or broadens it.

Information is badly needed on both the input and output sides of the equation. On the input side, we clearly need to know more about the total national applicant pool for M.D./Ph.D. programs. Such information could possibly be obtained through the AAMC. Pertinent questions include, What fraction of that pool obtains a place in school and actually matriculates? and, What is the quality of the matriculant pool as opposed to that of the nonmatriculant pool? This information can help us determine whether programs could be expanded while maintaining quality. On the output side of the equation, we should study the fate of MSTP graduates dating back to about 1964, when the MSTPs began. We need to determine the fraction of graduates doing research, the fraction of their time spent in research, the kinds of positions held, and some measure of their productivity (such as success on R01 grants). We should compile an on-line computer information resource, or possibly a catalog, that would contain descriptions of residency programs catering specifically to the M.D./Ph.D. graduates. It is to be hoped that such programs would give credit for the research years or would make research opportunities available in addition to the clinical work.

The Physician-Scholar and the Physician-Leader

Thomas Meikle, Jr.

The challenges of delivering comprehensive health care require strong leadership. Effective medical leaders should come from many different backgrounds, including scholarly careers such as those developed by combined degree programs. While not all leaders of the health care system need be scholars and not all scholars need be leaders, physician-scholars should be strongly encouraged to pursue leadership activities appropriate to their interest and levels of development.

Skills developed in a scholarly career (such as discipline, problem solving, critical thinking, and decision making) may enhance the effectiveness of the health care leader. However, without diluting or extending the present combined degree programs, the development of other leadership skills also needs to be incorporated in these programs.

Although leaders seem to be fundamentally self-selected, combined degree programs can nurture trainees' leadership interests and talents, especially by reinforcing the development of their interpersonal skills and by providing opportunities for them to practice leadership (for example, by serving on faculty committees and student-faculty committees).

Physician-scholar programs should be strengthened by providing organized experiences dealing with issues related to medical ethics and health policy. Scholars should also be made aware that the acquisition of management skills may be essential to effective leadership.

To produce scholarly leaders prepared to address the broad range of issues affecting research and the health care system, federal agencies and private foundations should provide additional funds to develop advanced combined degree programs in nontraditional disciplines as well as the natural sciences.

Physician-scholar programs have serious shortages of minorities. Despite the long-range deficiencies of secondary education, vigorous renewed efforts are needed to recruit qualified college students and medical students from underrepresented minority groups to pursue careers as physician-scholars and leaders in the health care system.

A detailed data base on combined degree programs and their graduates is needed and should be established by a governmental agency (such as the National Institutes of Health) or a private organization (such as the Association of the American Medical Colleges). These data should be generally available for use by other organizations to conduct independent evaluations of combined degree programs, including the characteristics of students and their careers.

The Relationship between Clinical Expertise and Physician Scholarship/ Leadership

George Cahill, Jr.

The clinical and research perspectives provided by the M.D./Ph.D. offer a tremendous breadth of intellectual biomedical pursuit. Even those individuals who get an M.D./Ph.D. and never do an internship but instead go straight into a basic science department have had their total scope broadened by this exposure to patients and disease. Therefore, although very few people are likely to pursue an M.D./Ph.D. program followed directly by a full-time research position, this pathway is to be encouraged. However, most M.D./Ph.D.s should go through clinical training, at least to the PGY-1, because in most states that serves as a kind of a "union card" to get a medical license and "caps" their clinical exposure from medical school. Yet, as they go through clinical education, they need to remain committed to the life of scholarship and not always think, "Since I have that M.D. union card, I can always go out and practice." In other words, the clinical qualification should not seduce them away from their dedication to doing a really hard and thorough academic job and getting the Ph.D. with as much rigor as would a Ph.D. not in the M.D./Ph.D. track.

Similarly, there is often a need to obtain board certification in a specialty. To get accreditization, clinics and hospitals have to have a certain number of board-qualified staff members; likewise, in government, one gets an increase in salary simply if one is board-qualified. Finally, malpractice fees are frequently based on board qualification. To keep options open and go into a clinic, even part time to generate some clinical income and/or remain clinically current, is a very practical reason to become board certified. But as mentioned before, one should not deviate from the commitment to hard science.

It is almost totally impossible for an individual in primary clinical medicine to do a physician's job properly and continue to be a bench scientist. In other words, one cannot be current with a clinical practice (maintain recertification boards, attend rounds, etc.), stay at bench science, and still be at the cutting edge of both, particularly in a "wet" laboratory science. There are, of course, some exceptions, but these are extremely rare. So the old-style "triple threat"—teacher, researcher, and clinician—is a vanishing species.

One can maintain a presence in a clinical field if that area is closely related to the wet lab science. A person who is working on the isolation of a gene, for example, could participate effectively in a clinic caring for patients with the disease associated with it. In fact, the best situation for clinical research exists when one can bridge the gap from basic science to the bedside, and that breadth of knowledge and responsibility is highly desirable and must be encouraged. But again, it is hard for one individual to do. That kind of research will be more successful when there is effective teamwork, with either M.D./Ph.D.s or pure Ph.D.s worrying about the fundamental, wet side of science.

A major economic crunch is coming. The national product expenditure in health has increased by about 1 percent per year over the past two or three years and is up to 12 percent now. That can't continue. It has to be resolved, and academically qualified people must take leading roles in the solution to this dilemma. A physician whose background is in law or policy can be as much an academic as one who can clone a gene; the same intensity of thought goes into those processes. Therefore, we should encourage people with training in law, economics, public policy, and ethics to enter programs of the M.D./Ph.D. type because they are the ones who will guide the nation in these issues. These areas should be approached with the same academic stringency that we now devote to the study of the structure of a promoter for a gene.

Many people are forced to carry out some degree of patient care to earn the money to allow them to remain in the lab, or else they have good friends in their department who earn the clinical money for their support. This tends to dilute one's academic productivity, but it's a grim reality. As the third-party payment cutbacks occur for patient care, research won't be supported on clinical income anymore.

Students and Recent Graduates of Programs to Educate Physician-Scholars

Paul A. Hattis and Benjamin Horowitz

Many students or recent graduates of M.D./Ph.D. programs are anxious or uncertain about the career track they plan to follow, which is not surprising, given their limited "world experience" and the changes facing health care today.

This angst is often magnified for those not pursuing a course of study in the traditional basic medical sciences or not training at a "traditional" academic health sciences center.

While cellular and molecular research occupy a traditional and fundamental role in solving numerous medical problems, the contributions of many other academic fields are necessary. Indeed, it is essential that scholarship and leadership in health care be defined in such a way as to encompass careers in bench research; clinical research; health services research; community health practice and advocacy for reducing disparities in health status among the poor, minorities, and other medically needy populations; and other forms of public service (to name just a few leadership arenas). We cannot be reductionist about the methods of leadership and scholarship. Our final gauge for what is legitimate and therefore to be supported must be outcome, productivity, and ultimately the health of our society.

The challenge to physician-scholars of the future is not to make the mistakes of their predecessors but rather to spend more time during the formative training years and beyond discussing these issues and actively working together to make certain that such a broad health agenda is carried out.

Young physician-scholars from biochemists to anthropologists have shown considerable interest in developing a regularly and widely distributed newsletter that might at some point grow into a journal. A computer network would also be valuable. These media would serve the following purposes:

1. Young physician-scholars can begin to create a sense of community amongst themselves.
2. Information concerning programs and other opportunities can be shared and cataloged.
3. Common hurdles and difficulties can be articulated and possible solutions explored. Given the pioneering nature of the programs and the relative lack of mobility of students in such programs, this larger perspective on the opportunities, difficulties, and simply the general condition of physician-scholars is especially valuable.
4. This formal communication would be an excellent resource for program directors and others concerned with supporting physician-scholar programs.

Critical Issues Perceived by Students in Training Programs for Physician-Scholars/Leaders

Arthur Kleinman

Guaranteed, stable funding is needed. To accomplish this might require seeking nontraditional as well as traditional sources of funding.

There is a need for follow-up studies of a more detailed kind, both quantitative and qualitative, of M.D./Ph.D. careers. There should also be a clearinghouse to make that knowledge (not just the data but also short biographies of people's careers and lives) generally available. The information should include pathways toward less traditional future jobs (e.g., nonacademic and nonuniversity). It is important to provide not just role models but also job models and lifestyle models and advice. There is real utility to having peer-to-peer communications as well as having a student affairs structure that provides programmatic attention to the issue of expectations for future jobs.

It is important to be flexible and provide a supportive environment to integrate M.D./Ph.D. students into academic environments. Some mechanisms for promoting integration are:

1. Annual meetings and conferences
2. Clear, understandable definitions of what is expected of the M.D./Ph.D. student
3. Ongoing contact with the medical school when students are in graduate school, and with the graduate school when they are in the medical setting
4. Awareness of the difficulties and tensions involved in transition, particularly from laboratory and field research settings into the clinic. A number of methods are effective in reducing the anxiety about transition (which actually seems to go much better than students fear it might go), such as having clinical mentors provide bridging clinical experiences on evenings or weekends and having peer-to-peer advice.

Outcome is important and should be measured in several ways, but it isn't the only means of assessing success. Success should also be measured by what is happening to students while they are in these programs; an iterative process of measurement would allow the refinement of both sides of the combined degree program. It is valuable to learn from successes, and there have been some long-term successes. The experiences of successful programs should teach us not only about the people who move through them but also about any mechanisms that could be transferred elsewhere. Other components of outcome might include the effect on the whole medical school program of the presence of medical students who are coming out of graduate training and thereby enriching the medical education of all students.

It is important to recognize and deal effectively with students' insecurity. Three questions capture students' concerns: What is my place? What expectations are there of me? and, How do things in this program work? These tie very closely to the value of ensuring some kind of intellectual community for students. This could be put into terms of an ecology of intellectual community that brings students in, gives them a sense of centeredness, and advocates for them. For example, the requirements for the fourth year of medical school might be refashioned more appropriately by that kind of community.

We strongly recommend support for a national communication network (a student-run newsletter, computer-based network, or whatever).

20

The Current Status of Education for Physician-Scholars: Summary and Implications

Harold M. Swartz and Diane L. Gottheil

The preparation of physicians for scholarship and leadership in the health care system is a field that conveys the overall impression of immense importance, growth, and potential. The great promise of programs to prepare physician-scholars lies in the importance of the medical and social problems that need to be solved, the increasing development of powerful means to analyze and solve these problems, professional and public awareness of the importance of solving these problems, and the interest of our best and brightest students in the problems and their solutions.

The rate of progress is being limited by a number of factors, but many of these are quite within the control of the academic medical community. Many of the limiting factors are similar to those that affect other parts of the health care system. The rapid growth of the technical and conceptual potential of medicine, combined with the great changes that have occurred in the relation between medicine and society and in the sources and methods of financing health care, have resulted in a system that is far from equilibrium and in which, inevitably, changing circumstances and needs are not automatically optimized or even, sometimes, recognized.

But, as has often been noted, such rapid and profound changes also offer excellent opportunities for innovation if the needs can be discerned accurately and communicated convincingly. One area that is in greatest need of change is our method of educating physician-scholars. It is also critical that we provide appropriate and more clearly delineated career paths and offer the guidance and support that students need to pursue them. These problems can and should be solved by the efforts of the academic medical community.

Other problems, especially in financing career paths from the initial educational steps through to the application of knowledge and skills by physician-scholars, will require the involvement of many other parts of society. Nevertheless, the academic medical community must make the case for the need to find solutions and help provide feasible means to deal with the principal financial problems.

Any and all of these changes would be greatly facilitated by more reliable data on the needs, programs, available personnel, etc., than are currently extant. Measures necessary to obtain the needed data, to plan effective courses of action, and to obtain the necessary support to implement plans will require the active participation of many segments of society—the private sector, government agencies (including some that are not usually associated with the education of physician-scholars), foundations, and various not-for-profit medically related organizations—in a cooperative effort with academic medicine. The good news, as reflected in the 1989 symposium, is that people are not only interested, but willing to participate. The best news is that when they are informed sufficiently, our best and brightest students are very interested in these careers, and if we don't put too many obstacles in their way, they will succeed in spite of us!

Specific Recommendations

In order to proceed as rapidly and effectively as possible, we suggest the following steps. These were developed from numerous sources, especially the many thoughtful talks and discussions at the symposium and various previously published position papers that provide specific and general recommendations (1, 2). The syntheses and presentation of the recommendations in their present form, however, with whatever defects or lack of clarity they may have, should be noted as the sole responsibility of the authors.

We have divided the recommendations into three types, based on what is likely to be required for implementation. The first set of recommendations could be implemented almost immediately without a major new effort or a national consensus. The second consists of recommendations for the development of new data sets; these will require the support of appropriate organizations. The third set of recommendations calls for changes that will require a new consensus and/or substantial outside financial support and other resources such as the establishment of new programs or organizations. In framing these recommendations, we attempt to 1) indicate specifically *what* we think should be done; 2) provide a brief resume of *why* it should be done (the rest of the book provides much more detailed rationales); 3) indicate *how* these goals might be accomplished. We feel more confident in our ability to articulate the *what* and the *why* than the *how*!!

Recommendations That Do Not Require More Data or a New National Consensus

1. <u>Data and experience in developing, managing, and evaluating programs to educate physician-scholars should be shared.</u>

This information should be shared among and gathered from not only M.D./Ph.D. programs, but also programs in which the primary research education occurs during or after residencies. Although programs may differ significantly at different institutions and at different points in the educational and career paths of the students, there is substantial common ground as well because the graduates are likely to pursue similar types of careers. Most programs are relatively small and/or new; to minimize the need for newer programs to "reinvent the wheel" and to enable all programs to obtain the full benefit of the experience of the various other programs, it is vital to pool and share information. By sharing information about existing programs, we can facilitate the development of program models and new initiatives. It is also important to disseminate information about nontraditional approaches to the education of physician-scholars.

One of the recommendations emanating from the symposium was that the directors and administrators of programs for the educational preparation of physician-scholars should form an organization that would hold periodic meetings, produce newsletters, and sponsor other activities to facilitate the exchange of information. Many informal comments made during and after the symposium indicate that face-to-face contact is useful. The time and expense required for national meetings, such as the symposium itself, may make it difficult for these to occur frequently, but regional meetings and a national newsletter could serve similar purposes. The occasional gatherings of the MSTP directors have already provided opportunities for information sharing among their M.D./Ph.D. programs. In addition to serving as a method of communication among members, an organization of program directors could have a key role in communication to prospective applicants and to potential employers of the graduates of various programs. Such an organization would also provide a reasonable means to achieve some aspects of the following recommendations.

2. <u>Information on opportunities afforded by dual degrees or research training should be disseminated</u>.

The effective dissemination of information is essential to permit the graduates of dual-degree or other research education programs to make appropriate choices for the next phase of their careers. The most critical information for graduates of M.D./Ph.D. programs relates to the types of options available for residencies and/or postdoctoral fellowships. This information should include material on individual programs as well as overviews of the potential career paths toward which the various programs are directed. The availability of this information is likely to stimulate development of new and expansion of existing programs, as the need for them and the pool of prospective participants become better known. The dissemination of information may have a synergistic effect: As more such residencies become available, the demand for them will increase and, in turn, increase the pool of desirable students.

All individuals who have completed their primary educational phases (research and clinical) also need widely available and comprehensive information on the options and opportunities they must consider as they take the next crucial steps toward becoming productive and stable faculty members or the equivalent in other areas. In general, at this point of their development, most physicians are not prepared to take on the full load of a faculty member and simultaneously compete for external research funding. Some institutions have transition programs to aid in this important next step (see Chapter 13), and it would be very useful for information on such programs to be disseminated, both to recruit participants and to serve as models for other institutions, encouraging the development of similar approaches. A number of programs for research support and career development are available from government, industry, foundations, and other health-related institutions; again, the dissemination of information on these programs may not only be useful per se but also stimulate the development of other similar programs.

Although all these programs attempt to disseminate their own information, these individual efforts have apparently been insufficient: Comments from both potential applicants and program directors indicate profound gaps in the knowledge of existing programs. It should be feasible systematically and thoroughly to collect and disseminate material either through an existing organization such as the AAMC or through a new organization such as that proposed for program directors or for students.

3. The admissions processes of the various programs should be coordinated.

One beneficial measure, for applicants and programs alike, would be the adoption of common dates for some or all of the various phases of the admissions processes, along with other measures to coordinate admissions. A common calendar can be implemented most straightforwardly by M.D./Ph.D. programs, which are tied to the academic calendar, but other types of programs can adopt coordinated procedures as well. It is especially important for programs to coordinate the time they notify students whether they have been placed on the primary admissions list or a waiting (alternate) list, or denied admission. They should also agree on an associated date by which applicants need to respond to the original offers of admission. This is not a recommendation for a full matching program analogous to that used for clinical residencies; while such an approach would have some advantages, it cannot be implemented at this time (as was indicated clearly in discussions at the symposium). A coordinated admissions process would necessarily be implemented voluntarily and the associated ground rules developed by the programs with input from participants.

This type of coordination would enable programs to make full use of their available assets (for example, positions at times go unfilled because of late withdrawals by candidates who accept late offers from a preferred program) and allow applicants to plan appropriately without unnecessary anxiety and uncertainty. It would also be desirable to develop uniform application packets, such as that sponsored by the AAMC for the medical school admission process, to enable applicants to obtain the necessary supporting documents as effectively and efficiently as possible. This might be especially helpful in getting relevant and useful letters of recommendation from faculty with whom applicants have worked. It would be desirable to integrate into this process a centralized, accessible source of information to advise potential applicants and their advisors of the existence of formal programs to educate physician-scholars.

Again, the most feasible mechanism to achieve this recommendation may be the formation of an appropriate organization in which all programs can participate.

4. Interaction among students in the various programs should be facilitated and promoted.

Except at the sites of the very largest programs, and probably even at those, combined degree students and young physicians in research education are usually subject to needs and demands that are not very well known by many of those with whom they interact. They face even greater challenges than their apparent peers, who are usually pursuing only clinical or research education. Consequently, they have limited access to information and support that applies directly to them, while the input they do receive assumes that they are pursuing more unidimensional paths.

The most straightforward and probably most effective approach is the formation of a national organization for students in programs for the education of physician-scholars. During the symposium, both students and faculty expressed strong support for this approach. Such an organization would allow students to enhance the quality of their lives by sharing information on problems, possible solutions, and opportunities for near-term and long-term career options. It could also help recruit excellent students into these programs by making the career of physician-scholars more visible and fostering a better understanding of the potential of such careers. An initial step toward the formation of such an organization has occurred with the publication of a student newsletter entitled *Doctor/Doctor.*

5. <u>Existing models should be used to develop and enhance existing or planned programs</u>.

It is immediately feasible for individual medical schools and residencies to initiate very positive changes in programs to educate physician-scholars/leaders, using existing knowledge and communications that are being developed and shared. Each school and residency program should examine the available information and use the experience of other programs to improve itself. The possible areas of improvement include enhanced recruitment of the appropriate types of students or residents; expansion into disciplines outside the traditional departments; increased coordination and cooperation with graduate programs and research mentors; and development of administrative structures specifically designed to provide academic, personal, and financial support for students in combined degree programs and residents in research-oriented programs. Similarly, medical schools and other institutions should become familiar with existing programs and ideas to facilitate the transition of their graduates to full faculty status (or the equivalent in other types of institutions) and adopt, adapt, or develop these strategies to fit the needs and capabilities of their institution.

The rationale for individual programs to take these steps at this time is that a number of apparently effective programs are presently using novel approaches; that is, policies and procedures not typically used in other programs. These "models" should be closely scrutinized and, where applicable, applied to the home institution. An aggressive adaptation of such approaches should further test their validity and facilitate their development. Some approaches that might be adopted more widely include the development of a residency specifically focused on graduates of M.D./Ph.D. programs (Washington University in St. Louis); a program to facilitate the transition from fellow to junior faculty (Johns

Hopkins); support for M.D./Ph.D. students at state institutions through research and teaching assistantships in graduate departments during some or all of medical school as well as graduate studies, combined with a policy of allowing students to begin their studies in their graduate departments (University of Illinois at Urbana-Champaign); and the expansion of classes exclusively for M.D./Ph.D. students to compensate for the potential loss of tuition from waivers for combined degree students, thus overcoming a critical barrier at private medical schools (Dartmouth).

These approaches will necessarily be implemented on an individualized basis at each institution, taking into account its needs and the financial and political realities it faces. Information from other programs should be available by direct contacts and perhaps through the organizations that have been suggested in the previous recommendations.

Recommendations for the Collection and Dissemination of New Data

There is a clear consensus both in the literature and among the symposium participants that the data required to proceed rationally and effectively on a number of issues or problems are inadequate or entirely absent. We recommend that the following actions be taken immediately to obtain the necessary data sets.

1. <u>The characteristics of the pool of applicants should be determined</u>.

Several types of information on the pool of applicants are needed. The first and perhaps the most elementary step in the information-gathering process is to determine how many individuals are currently applying to existing programs of various types. This information would provide answers to some important questions, such as whether the current pool of applicants for M.D./Ph.D. programs is adequate for the existing slots and whether an expansion of the number of places without an increase in the pool would be likely to lower the quality of the matriculants. This data set would also provide information on the number of programs to which applicants apply. Additionally, it would be very useful to include information on the academic records of the applicants and on their research experience. These data could be collected by cooperative efforts of existing programs through organizations that they develop, or by the efforts of an existing central organization such as the AAMC or the Institute of Medicine.

It would also be very desirable to obtain data that would indicate whether the current pool of applicants could be enlarged. That is, are there individuals whose academic credentials and personal career preferences are compatible with enrollment in programs to educate physician-scholars but who are not applying to such programs? This data set should also include items to help determine why these qualified individuals are not applying. There are some indications that a large pool of such potential applicants exists. For example, when we began to mail information on the Medical Scholars Program to a subset of individuals who had taken the MCAT exam and whose majors were not in the typical biological sciences,* there was a substantial increase in the number of applicants

*The subset was also restricted to persons in this group who scored above an average of 9 on the MCAT.

to the program. Many of these applicants indicated that they had not known of M.D./Ph.D. programs in nontraditional areas or of potential careers combining medicine and one of these fields. Programs of all types (i.e., M.D./Ph.D., postresidency research education, and midcareer fellowships) have anecdotally reported similar observations, but it is not at all clear whether this potential pool is significant or how potential applicants might be better informed about available opportunities. It would also be very desirable to learn why well-qualified individuals who *do* know about such programs decide not to apply for them or decline offers of admission. There are abundant theories and speculations on this matter but few substantial sets of data.

At the college undergraduate level, it would be useful to extend data collection beyond surveys of applicants to medical schools because there may be a substantial pool of applicants to graduate schools who would apply to combined degree programs if they were aware of the opportunities. This may be especially likely for students whose area of graduate study is outside the typical biomedical core of disciplines. Similarly, data on programs at the post-M.D. level should be collected from representative samples of all medical students and residents; some of these data are available from existing surveys by the AAMC. Data to be collected should include responses to descriptions of the whole range of career options in industry, government, and academic medicine, open to physician-scholars. Data on the potential expanded pool of applicants would probably need to be collected by a central body such as the AAMC and have a source of financing, because of the effort that it would take to carry out such a survey effectively.

2. Comprehensive data on opportunities for research education should be obtained and published.

A lack of information on opportunities is often a significant barrier for potential entrants into the field. Such information could be invaluable for those who have decided on a scholarly career but don't know where to go, as well as for those who might consider this path if they are made aware of the range of opportunities. Qualified individuals are often unaware of the option to be a physician-scholar, especially in less traditional areas. Not only students entering medical schools, but even graduates of medical schools and residencies often lack information on opportunities for initial rigorous research preparation.

Similarly, individuals who have completed an M.D./Ph.D. or a postdoctoral educational program often lack information on the opportunities available to them. It would be extremely helpful, both for their psychological well-being and their career development, for these individuals to have an accurate and comprehensive listing of their options at this phase of their career. There are many more programs, sources of support, and specifically designed positions for these graduates than many of them realize—and existing opportunities would be likely to expand more rapidly if there was a higher demand for them. One of the most frustrating and wasteful aspects of the current system is the number of students who complete an excellent M.D./Ph.D. or postdoctoral research program and then, because of a lack of knowledge of opportunities, take positions that do not enable them to build effectively on their background.

The sort of comprehensive directory envisioned here probably needs to be developed and maintained by a national organization such as the AAMC. Organizations such as those proposed for students and program directors could, however, play key roles in obtaining the information for these directories and might be effective alternative sources for publishing and maintaining them. The potential demand for and usefulness of such directories have been illustrated by the numerous inquiries for information on programs that our office has received after hosting the symposium.

3. Data should be collected on outcomes of the various programs, including trends over time.

Data on outcomes should include information on the different approaches that have been used, such as M.D./Ph.D. programs, postresidency traineeships, postresidency research fellowships, and midcareer fellowships, and also on physician-scholars who did not participate in formal programs. It would also be very useful to try to relate the outcomes of the various approaches to the specific types of programs—for instance, MSTPs as compared with other M.D./Ph.D. programs. It is essential for the data on outcomes to include evaluations of the amount *and quality* of the various activities (research, teaching, leadership positions, and so on) of the program graduates. Reasonable prudence must be used, however, in the interpretation and extrapolation of these data, because of the rapid changes that are occurring in both the programs that prepare the physician-scholars and the health care system in which they work.

Considerable data already exist on some of these aspects, as summarized in Chapter 3. There are, however, great gaps in the data in terms of the programs that are covered and various aspects of the outcomes.

Because much of the available data relate to NIH-sponsored programs, and because of the continued strong role played by NIH in the support of research education, it is essential for NIH to play a prominent role in attempts to obtain systematic and comprehensive information on outcomes. It is also essential for non-NIH programs to be covered as fully as possible; therefore, other organizations will probably also need to be involved in these efforts. The National Academy of Science, Institute of Medicine, AAMC, and the Howard Hughes Research Institute are currently the most prominent organizations in this field, and some combination of them would seem to be the appropriate source for the study and its financing.

4. The numbers of existing physician-scholars and recent trends in these numbers should be determined.

These data are needed in order to determine the need for physician-scholars and the fields in which they are needed. (Such data, of course, will not provide all the information needed on this topic, because the career paths for physician-scholars are changing rapidly as new areas are developed and the demands in existing areas change with the rapid shifts in the health care system and the nature of academic medicine.) They need to include information from industry and government as well as from academic medicine. The latter will be easier to obtain because of the AAMC's ongoing data collection on the faculty of medical schools, but considerable effort will be needed to determine the faculty's actual level of research activity. Studies conducted in departments of internal medicine indicate that a minority of the faculty have active research programs (2). It would be desirable to obtain similar data in other disciplines; a common assumption is that the level of research involvement is highest in internal medicine, but it would be useful to validate this. Some specialties, such as pediatrics, have been increasing their efforts to have more significant involvement in research, especially at the level of residency and postresidency. Data on trends will be as important as data on current levels because it appears that the attitude toward research activities is changing in some disciplines, in and out of academia.

The methods to obtain these data, with the exception of some of the data on faculty in medical schools, are not clear. The information available on opportunities in other sectors is relatively poor, but it would be useful to have it available for planning purposes and for the guidance of students. For example, during the symposium, several participants from the private sector indicated that they place a high value on recruiting physicians with advanced research training in a variety of disciplines, including nontraditional areas; these opportunities appeared to surprise many of the participants from academia. In addition to data on the number and type of positions for physician-scholars, it would also be useful to have information on the *perceptions* of potential applicants and their advisors. One possible approach to collecting the data would be to integrate these inquiries into the ongoing collaborative activities of the National Research Council and the Institute of Medicine to collect information on manpower needs in biomedical and behavioral sciences (3). These federally mandated studies have generally not included data focused on physicians or on research activities outside the specified areas, but it would seem desirable to use their expertise and ongoing activities to do so.

5. <u>Data should be gathered on existing needs for physician-scholars, and future needs should be projected</u>.

In the long run, to guide intelligent planning at a national level and to make potential applicants aware of opportunities, information must be developed on the projected needs for physician-scholars. The National Academy of Science already has a mandate to provide such data for biomedical scientists in general and has some information that relates directly to physicians, but these efforts only provide a start toward meeting the full needs (3). More focused projections must specifically address the need for physician-scholars and extend into all fields of education preparation: the social sciences, humanities, and physical sciences as well as the biomedical sciences. These projections should include data on the opportunities in the private sector, not-for-profit sector, and government as well as academia.

For the projections to be more accurate, they need to be viewed in conjunction with the nature of careers of physician-scholars in academia and elsewhere. The needs and opportunities in academia are likely to continue to be numerically dominant, but they cannot be forecast accurately without more explicit consideration of the role of research for academic physicians. As noted in Chapter 1, there are significant differences between the "ideal," in which all academic physicians carry out research, and the reality of their activities. Indeed, it is becoming clear that it is impractical and probably undesirable to expect this, in view of the limited financial resources and the technical and intellectual requirements for effective research at this time. There is a great need for meaningful discussion leading to a consensus on the role of research for academic physicians, including clear differentiation of career paths that do not require active research and other paths that enable physicians to spend sufficient time in research to be effective. Only then will it be feasible to make more accurate predictions of the manpower needs for physician-researchers in academia.

In order to fulfill this recommendation, several national organizations, such as the AAMC, NIH, and interests representing industry, must take concerted action. The logical organization to carry out such an endeavor is the Institute of Medicine (IOM), which is already involved in the projects to estimate the needs for biomedical manpower and in convening groups to discuss various policy issues.

6. Data should be gathered on the personal and financial characteristics and stresses of students in the various educational programs.

While there have been a number of essays on these subjects, including some in this book, the actual data are sparse and incomplete. Some of the characteristics of existing programs and plans to modify and improve them are based on assumptions about the financial and personal needs of the students that usually seem quite logical and reasonable, but are seldom supported by adequate data and could certainly be wrong in some important respects.

We recommend that a comprehensive study of these characteristics be undertaken. It should cover the principal types of programs: traditional M.D./Ph.D. programs with NIH support; other M.D./Ph.D. programs, including those in nontraditional areas and in sites where research is not as prominent as in the MSTP-supported programs; postresidency traineeships; postresidency fellowships; and midcareer fellowships. The design and execution of these studies should be entrusted to appropriately qualified social scientists.

A number of organizations, including the AMA, AAMC, IOM, and NIH, might sponsor and/or supervise such studies. If an organization of the directors of M.D./Ph.D. programs and other programs to educate physician-scholars is formed, it could play an important role in establishing such a study. Several foundations might be logical sponsors of these studies.

Recommendations That Will Require a New Consensus

1. The educational aspects of postgraduate pathways should be optimized from the completion of primary research training to the acquisition of tenured faculty positions (or the equivalent in other sectors).

It is crucial to develop a consensus on the accepted pathways for careers of physician-scholars in order to provide guidance for students and administrators/ directors. Once a consensus has been reached, a set of guidelines can be created that would delineate recommended standard pathways to facilitate the development of appropriate educational and professional opportunities, direct students (and their advisors) toward appropriate choices, and provide legitimization for comprehensive career paths that will produce effective physician-scholars. These guidelines should not, however, be presented as rigid rules, since there is no definitive evidence to demonstrate what pathways are most effective. Many sets of guidelines already exist *de facto* but are usually not well known, not explicit, and/or mutually contradictory. The NIH mechanisms of support for the various stages of development of physician-scholars described in Chapter 13 afford an excellent example of a comprehensive pathway aimed at the development of excellent, independent physician-scholars. But there is limited knowledge of these NIH paths; they are accorded differing degrees of availability and emphasis at the various component institutes of NIH; and there is no consensus on the desirability and feasibility of such extensive and expensive paths.

The proposed guidelines should address the need for continuity in the research and clinical development of the physician-scholar, extending through to the attainment of tenured positions on the faculty of medical schools or the equivalent in other settings. They should also take into account the different pathways and various emphases that careers can take, providing specific variations where appropriate. Specifically, they should at a minimum differentiate between paths with emphasis on bench research, clinically based research, and health services research.

Academic medicine should take the lead in establishing these guidelines in view of its preeminent role as the educator of physicians and also as the largest employer of physician-scholars. It is, however, essential that all relevant segments of society be involved, including industry, government, professional organizations, and not-for-profit entities. The AAMC is the logical organization to convene the appropriate groups to discuss this issue and attempt to reach a consensus; the IOM would be a desirable alternative or collaborative group.

2. Explicit criteria for effective educational programs should be developed for physician-scholars at the various principal levels (M.D./Ph.D., residency-associated research training, midcareer training programs, and programs in the social sciences or humanities).

The development of educational programs for physician-scholars has become an attractive and often prestigious endeavor. While this level of interest is highly desirable, it does have the potential for undesirable results such as the development of lower quality or unneeded programs. For these reasons, it is recommended that appropriate bodies establish criteria of effectiveness for programs that prepare physicians for research. The force of these guidelines should lie in their logic and widespread acceptance rather than in any formal accreditation procedure. They should address issues such as the appropriate research environment, the role of formal courses, minimum program length, and the role of mentors. Different but related guidelines should be established for M.D./Ph.D. programs in the biomedical sciences, M.D./Ph.D. programs in the social sciences and humanities, programs in which the primary research education occurs after the M.D., and midcareer fellowship programs.

These guidelines should be drawn up under the auspices of a central recognized entity such as the AAMC or IOM by committees that represent the viewpoints of the spectrum of individuals and interests in the subject. Separate committees or subcommittees should be assigned to the various areas. Input to the committees should include perspectives from students and prospective employers.

3. <u>An explicit and vigorous effort should be undertaken to establish more programs for the education of physician-scholars in the social sciences and humanities</u>.

These programs should be developed with the same care and rigor as programs in the biomedical sciences. Their sites should have a critical mass of appropriate mentors and teachers, as well as vigorous programs in the preparation of physician-scholars in the biomedical disciplines, to enrich the experience of both types of students. There should be close cooperation between well-established scholars in the social sciences and humanities and academic medicine. These criteria should restrict such programs to a limited number of sites. Entry should be possible at both the M.D./Ph.D. level and after (or during) residencies, and adequate financial support should be available to all students.

We suggest that this recommendation be fulfilled through the efforts of a special task force formed through the auspices of organizations such as the AAMC, IOM, and AMA. This task force should gather data on the need for physician-scholars in the social sciences and humanities as well as the opportunities in these areas and set guidelines for the establishment of programs. They could also provide sources of consultation for institutions considering the establishment of educational programs in these areas.

4. <u>A systematic effort should be undertaken to expand educational opportunities for prospective physician-scholars in the physical sciences (e.g., engineering, computer science, physics) and less traditional biomedical sciences such as nutrition and biophysics</u>.

Because these areas do not tend to be well represented in medical schools, there will usually need to be a close connection between the medical school and the traditional university in order to have sufficient rigor and critical mass. This will inevitably limit the number of sites where these programs can be established. As in the other disciplines, entrance should be permitted both in concert with medical school and during or after residency. Close association, preferably full integration, with educational programs for physician-scholars in other disciplines is highly desirable.

These programs should be established by the expansion of existing, more traditional programs at suitable sites. Similar criteria for admission, financial support, and so on, should be used. Appropriate faculty from the physical sciences should be brought into the administrative structure for the entire educational program for physician-scholars.

5. Common application and selection processes should be formalized.

This measure is intended to further the changes recommended in Chapter 19. To achieve the full potential of the research education programs, these arrangements should evolve into formal matching programs analogous to those currently used for residencies. This degree of formalization will require significant time and effort to ensure that the needs of the students and programs are fully considered. This should facilitate the entrance of students into the programs that are optimal for them. The current situation, in which applications to all programs are handled entirely independently by each institution, results in excessive uncertainty and unnecessary and duplicative efforts by the applicants, additional work and/or less appropriate letters by faculty who provide recommendations, and logistical problems for the administrators of the programs as they strive to fill their available slots with the most suitable students.

These recommendations would probably be best implemented by the programs themselves under the auspices of the proposed organization of program directors. Alternatively, an organization such as the AAMC could provide the necessary coordination.

6. Stable and adequate financing should be made available from entry into this career track to appointment as tenured faculty or the equivalent.

The need and rationale for this recommendation seem clear. If we are to attract "the best and the brightest," we need to provide pathways that do not involve excessive financial sacrifices and uncertainties. Even if all the financial problems in the educational pathways are resolved, the nature of these careers will still involve high degrees of uncertainty and stress related to both financial matters and success in scholarly endeavors.

The needs in this area are widely recognized within academia and some segments of government and the private sector, but so far efforts to obtain the necessary support have fallen short. It seems essential that a more systematic, comprehensive, and persistent approach be made to resolve this issue more satisfactorily, an approach that would include the development of mechanisms for supporting preparation in less traditional areas such as the social and physical sciences. We believe that the needs of and opportunities for society provide compelling arguments for financing the education of physician-scholars. The critical step is to marshal and present the arguments adequately and to the appropriate audience.

We recommend the appointment of a special task force under the auspices of the Institute of Medicine to collect the appropriate data and arguments and then to plan a long-term strategy to bring the message to government and industry, stressing the favorable cost/benefit ratio of these expenditures. To be effective, the task force must involve all the pertinent segments of the health care system and secure a consensus that this is an item of highest priority. The plans that are developed should take into account the successful involvement of nongovernmental sources (e.g., foundations such as the Howard Hughes Medical Institute; individuals such as Ross Perot, who has provided support for the M.D./Ph.D. program at Southwestern in Dallas; and consortiums such as the Life and Health Insurance Medical Research Fund) and look for ways to expand these sources. Additional sources of financial support in the federal government should also be considered. For example, the federal government spends approximately 800 billion per year on the delivery of health care through Medicare, Medicaid, and other programs—it might be a very reasonable and effective investment for these same agencies to support the education of physician-scholars in the social sciences and humanities because these individuals are likely to be key factors in the development of more efficient and more effective ways to deliver health care.

7. Problems arising from the ideal of the "triple threat" and associated myths must be resolved.

The general approach recommended is to tailor the amount of clinical training and expertise to the particular needs for the individual's career and explicitly abandon the goal of having most academic physicians be genuine leading researchers *and* fully active clinicians *and* fully active teachers. This is a crucial aspect of the whole problem of ensuring the availability of adequate numbers of well-prepared physician-scholars, and it is well within the control of the academic medical community. The now unattainable "ideal" of the triple-threat physician-scholar is a creation of the academic medical community and, although the process will be painful and will take some time to accomplish, that same community can also dispense with it. The rewards of doing this can be considerable, because it will allow the development of appropriate and feasible career paths that will be more attractive to bright young students and less frustrating for everyone throughout their careers. The changes in what individuals actually do will be much smaller than the changes in what they are expected to do, because the difficulty of a real "triple-threat" career has been obvious for some time. What is needed is the recognition that one can be a legitimate academic physician without strong and current clinical activity—and, reciprocally, the understanding that one can legitimately be involved in clinical research without the full preparation for research typical of a Ph.D. or the equivalent (such clinical researchers will need to work as part of a team).

For these changes to be implemented, the requirements of some specialty boards may need to be modified, if those specialties are to have significant numbers of well-educated physician-researchers. It may also be necessary to consider how changes in the preparation of research-oriented physicians may affect requirements for third-party reimbursement for clinical care. It is recommended that appropriate organizations within academic medicine pursue these problems directly.

In Table 20.1, we summarize our recommendations for education and activities in research and clinical medicine for various types of career paths. Our assumption is that it will continue to be increasingly difficult to carry out meaningful research without a high level of expertise in the appropriate research

Table 20.1. Recommendations for Clinical and Research Education and Ongoing Activities for Different Types of Physician-Scholars.

Type	Research Education*	Clinical Education†	Ongoing Research Activities	Ongoing Clinical Activities
ditional physician-scientist	Ph.D. or ≥ yrs	1-4 yrs	≥ 70%	≤ 30%
ntraditional physician-olar, with 70% strong versity base	≤ 30%	Ph.D. or ≥ 3 yrs		1-4 yrs ≥
alth services researcher	Ph.D. or ≥ 3 yrs	2-4 yrs	≥ 50%	≤ 50%
nical investigator, heavily % involved in research	≥ 30%	Ph.D. or ≥ yrs		≥ 3 yrs ≥
nical investigator, member of earch team‡	1-3 yrs	≥ 3 yrs	≥ 10%	≥ 70%
nical pharmacologist		≥ 2 yrs	≥ 3 yrs	≥ 30% ≥ 30%
ysician-leader without mary research activity		≥ 1 yr	≥ 3 yrs	NANA

*Associated relevant coursework in the basic areas underlying the primary research discipline.
†M.D., in an approved residency; ≥ 3 years assumes board certification. It is likely that with ongoing clinical activities of ≥ 30% this period will be extended to achieve certification in a subspecialty.
‡Ideally, this amount of research activity should be the minimal expectation for any full-time member of the faculty of a medical center.

techniques and an understanding of the research process. Therefore, for all physicians who will have roles as principal investigators, we strongly recommend that the basic research education be the equivalent of a rigorous Ph.D. It is likely to become increasingly useful for the individual to earn an actual Ph.D., because this will provide a widely recognized credential that can be related to the experience of most people in the field who are not physicians. With the exception of physicians whose principal research activities will be based on direct clinical involvement, we do not view a full residency as a requirement for an effective research-oriented career. It is quite possible, however, that other factors such as reimbursement requirements or the conventions for appointments and advancements in the institution will make board certification desirable, even if it is not directly needed for the career. The appropriate solution may be to design for these individuals focused residencies that provide excellent general principles of clinical medicine but also allow a significant part of the time to be spent in realresearch endeavors; the physician-investigator track in internal medicine is an example of such an approach, although it has not always been used to the best advantage.

We strongly recommend the adoption of a somewhat analogous attitude toward physicians whose primary activities will be in the direct delivery of clinical care. Many of these physicians will be able to function effectively as members of a research team without investing the time and effort required to earn a Ph.D. or the equivalent. Further, even if they do receive such an education, they will probably not be able to keep up the activities needed to remain at the forefront of research in their field. It makes more sense for us to recognize this and formulate educational programs that will enable them to participate effectively in research by a team approach. These investigators need to have an excellent understanding of the research process and knowledge in relevant skills such as statistics, epidemiology, and clinical pharmacology. They do need to complete full clinical residencies and probably subspecialization fellowships as well in many cases.

8. Special opportunities and tracks should be developed for underrepresented minorities.

It is unlikely that optimal progress will be made in the development and application of new concepts in the health care system without the full involvement of all segments of society. For underrepresented minorities to provide much better input, they need to participate to an appropriate degree in the leadership of medicine that generates new knowledge and new policies. This is necessary both for the unique contributions that these groups can offer and for the leadership role models they must provide before minorities can hope to participate fully in the whole range of positions in the health care system. Also, of course, simple justice requires that we strive toward such goals. To implement these goals, we must pay specific attention to the development of physician-scholars from these groups. Both in ongoing efforts and in more specifically targeted new efforts, we need to recruit the best and the brightest of the minority populations into pathways designed to prepare them to be physician-scholars. Some immediate progress could be made by having existing programs actively recruit applicants from underrepresented minorities and then, as necessary, provide them with opportunities to catch up with their colleagues who have enjoyed fuller opportunities. In particular, minority applicants are less likely to have had an opportunity to work with researchers doing cutting edge investigations, and they are also less likely to have come from environments in which such career aspirations are highly regarded. Therefore, it is also necessary to develop opportunities and programs at much earlier stages in the students' educational programs.

Recommended Components of Programs to Prepare Physician-Scholars

To supplement and expand the preceding recommendations, we offer the following specific descriptions of what we conceive to be critical elements of ideal programs to prepare physician-scholars. We first consider combined degree programs and then, more briefly, additional aspects that are especially pertinent when the research education occurs during or after the residency.

An Ideal Combined Degree Program to Prepare Physician-Scholars

1. Administrative aspects.

A number of administrative factors can greatly enhance the functioning of the program, and, conversely, can impede development if they are neglected or not put into practice. One of the most important elements in the success of a program is the willingness of its institution to acknowledge it as a high priority. Combined degree programs are costly, in both monetary and human terms, and they clearly deviate from most of the "main" and "traditional" activities of their institutions. They are therefore potentially vulnerable to criticism from many quarters and require clear statements and reassurances of their priority if they are to endure in periods of institutional stress.

A separate identity can also be a very positive feature of a combined degree program because, while it may appear similar in its components to the graduate or medical school programs, it has some important real differences that are not readily appreciated. A separate administration would help to reinforce these differences. This administration should have close connections to the graduate as well as the medical components of the program. Because the graduate components are often concerned about being dominated by the medical components, it is helpful for the program to have identifiable physical facilities that are clearly not an intrinsic part of the medical school.

Combined degree programs have many special administrative problems and requirements; they must therefore have an adequate administrative staff to serve the needs of the students, faculty, and administration associated with the program. Again, it is desirable that these staff have an identity that is not too closely tied with the medical school. The director of the program should ideally be an M.D./Ph.D. and have an active research program. There should also be a highly involved advisory committee of relevant faculty and administrators to provide both additional guidance and a core of informed supporters, especially in the medical school.

There should be a sufficient number of students to provide a coherent peer group. The stresses of M.D./Ph.D. programs and their differences from other programs are such that the students need to have peers with whom to interact; otherwise they may become abnormal medical and/or graduate students rather than normal M.D./Ph.D. students.

2. Academic aspects.

The program must have a strong commitment to high-quality education in both the graduate field and clinical medicine. Such a commitment is needed if students are to have the education—and the attitudes and expectations—they require to succeed. The faculty should control the academic aspects, principally through existing mechanisms in graduate and medical components. The development of new and different educational components for the M.D./Ph.D. students should be done with care and wide consultation to avoid adopting unproductive alternatives and antagonizing faculty who perceive a potential dilution of academic rigor. It is desirable to look for opportunities within the existing curricula where increased flexibility can be introduced and appropriate credit given for work in the other discipline.

The areas of graduate study that are available should include the complete spectrum of disciplines in which the institution has academic strength; study in these areas can and should involve the regular departments of the general university whenever this is feasible. The thesis research topics pursued within the departments should be completely open, without regard to their relationship to medicine. It should be emphasized to faculty and students that the main reason for undertaking the graduate study is to learn how to do high-quality research; when these students graduate, they will be in an excellent position to relate their capabilities to medical problems, and they should not compromise their educational opportunities at this stage with a premature emphasis on medical relevance. It is also very desirable for the student to choose a thesis topic that is a principal interest of the thesis advisor. There is a temptation, especially with faculty who do not work frequently with medical students, to give the student additional leeway in the selection of the thesis topic even if it lies outside the main theme of the advisor's research; in our experience, this frequently leads to unnecessary problems and tension when limitations in time or support occur and the advisor is forced to choose between continuing to support research outside his or her main efforts or to decrease support to the student. The most important factor for students, of course, is to work with thesis research supervisors who have excellent scholarly records and current high levels of research activity.

3. Programmatic aspects.

There should be a high degree of flexibility in integrating the scheduling of the two curricula, with control of choices vested in the students and their advisors. We feel that there are many advantages in having students begin their studies in the graduate discipline in order to achieve maximum progress in their scholarly development during the program and to develop the strongest support mechanisms, academically, personally, and financially. (In fact, in the program at the University of Illinois at Urbana-Champaign, the only scheduling option that the students and their advisors do not control is the requirement to begin the M.D./Ph.D. studies in the graduate discipline.)

Explicit attention should be paid to mechanisms to promote continuing interactions among students in the program. There should be a regular seminar series aimed specifically at the needs and interests of combined degree students, which can help students communicate with one another as well as broaden their education. There should also be an annual retreat for all students in the program, with sessions for scholarly activity, career development, and personal issues.

The seminar series and the retreat, and perhaps also special minicourses, should include topics of particular pertinence to the students, including overviews of the organization and philosophy of academic medicine, ethics in clinical medicine and research, the nature of the health care system, statistical concepts especially related to studying human populations, and the peer review system.

Efforts should be aimed at the systematic development of leadership capabilities. This aspect of the program should include discussions of the philosophy and analysis of leadership, specific instruction in skills that are usually necessary for effective leadership, and opportunities to take on leadership roles and tasks within the program and the school.

It is essential for students to have extensive advising on career goals and opportunities, as well as possible career paths, with discussion of the advantages and disadvantages of the various options. The advising should include explicit consideration of ways to alter career paths if the initial choice turns out to be inappropriate for the needs of the student. It is especially important for advisors to stress the various ways in which the careers of M.D./Ph.D.s are different from those of other medical school graduates. The existing system of choosing residencies, and so on, is necessarily geared toward conventional medical school graduates, and it is quite easy for new M.D./Ph.D.s to emulate their traditional classmates in choosing the next steps in their careers. At this point, however, it is essential that M.D./Ph.D.s choose residencies or postdoctoral programs with a very specific view toward enhancing and developing their careers as physician-scholars. It is the job of the advisor to facilitate this decision process.

4. Appropriate student characteristics.

The most important characteristic of an M.D./Ph.D. student is a commitment to a scholarly career. It is unlikely that a student can really make an informed decision on such a commitment without having realistic experience in research before entering the combined degree program. This is not always possible for some applicants, but if they are accepted into the program, they should be required to become involved in research immediately. Another essential characteristic is a high potential for academic accomplishments. This is not always apparent, especially on the basis of the academic record of the applicant. We have found that the most valuable indicators of research potential are the recommendations of advisors with whom the student has done research.

5. Financial aspects.

In order to achieve the full potential of the educational experience, students in M.D./Ph.D. programs should be provided with guaranteed support for all their years in the program, at levels that are comparable to the best-supported graduate programs at the institution. The dependability of the support is probably at least as important as the level of support. It is also highly desirable that funds be available to support travel to pertinent meetings approximately every two years. While most of the latter funds will be made available through the student's faculty advisor or department, it is important for all students in the program to have the opportunity to attend meetings because of the importance of these experiences in their development as physician-scholars.

An Ideal Program for the Education of Physician-Scholars (Without Extensive Prior Research Experience) During or After Residency

The general philosophical approach of such a program should be analogous to that of the M.D./Ph.D. programs. Essentially all areas of study, including the biological, physical, and social sciences, and the humanities, should be approached in a similar manner. It is important that the salary be similar to other postresidency opportunities so that the decision to pursue this option is not made on the basis of financial factors.

The research environment is probably the most important element of these educational programs. At this stage of their careers, young physicians usually need to be in a research-intensive environment with high-quality research being pursued by numerous individuals, usually including significant numbers of Ph.D. researchers, in order to provide a critical mass of researchers. The presence of a regular Ph.D. education being carried out in the same setting is a valuable aspect of the ideal environment, ensuring that young physicians will have experience with the traditions and perspectives of this important group of colleagues. It should also help them carry out real research projects at this critical stage of their careers.

The program should require that students place a clear priority on research activities, with 90 percent or more time committed to research and graduate education, and a minimum commitment of two-and-a-half years (longer is preferable). Students should be required to produce a research product that is comparable to that of a Ph.D. thesis in a high-quality university program. They should also have an opportunity to earn a Ph.D. and be encouraged to do so. It is very desirable to offer the structured learning of key elements of the research topic and/or methodology; many faculty in internal medicine departments considered the lack of such an opportunity a major deficiency in their research training programs (2). Most M.D. respondents felt, in retrospect, that it would be better to have had more formal instruction in mathematics and statistics, research techniques, and the basic sciences. Some opportunities to continue clinical skills and perspectives are desirable as long as these do not impinge on the priority of the research.

The program should also include seminars focused on the special needs of physicians who are obtaining an education in research. These seminars should include a systematic introduction into the process for formulating research and getting it funded by competitive mechanisms. They should also consider topics such as ethics in research and the organization of research funding agencies.

Following the primary research education, the student should continue intensive research involvement that provides the equivalent of a postdoctoral fellowship. This is essential for the graduates to complete the development of their research skills and, ultimately, compete successfully for research funding.

Summary

In summary, regardless of sequencing or subject area, an ideal overall program should include a period of full-time research education (a Ph.D. or three years of full-time research education, including appropriate systematic instruction); a postdoctoral experience of at least two years (for M.D.s who receive their primary research education during or after their residency, this is in addition to that educational experience); and, after appointment to a faculty position or its equivalent, an internally supported transition period of approximately two years in which more than 50 percent of their activities are in research. The available data indicate that it takes an average of twenty-four months from the completion of a postdoctoral fellowship to the successful funding of an independent grant; as part of the program, the individual would therefore be expected to compete successfully for external funding as a principal investigator during this period. Levey and colleagues (2) have recommended a similar program, although they did not necessarily include a separate period of initial research education. Finally, it is essential that, as faculty members, graduates continue to spend more than 33 percent of their time in active research.

References

1. S. Thier, "Clinical Investigation in the 1980's: Perspective from the Medical Schools," *Clinical Research* 28 (September 1980): 248-51.
2. G. S. Levey, C. R. Sherman, N. O. Gentile et al., "Postdoctoral Research Training of Full-Time Faculty in Academic Departments of Medicine," *Annals of Internal Medicine* (1988): 414-18.
3. Committee on Biomedical and Behavioral Research Personnel, National Research Council, *Biomedical and Behavioral Research Scientists: Their Training and Supply. Vol. I: Findings* (Washington, D.C.: National Academy Press, 1989).

LIST OF CONTRIBUTORS

Irwin M. Arias, M.D., Professor and Chairman, Department of Physiology, Professor of Medicine, Tufts University School of Medicine

William M. Awad, Jr., M.D., Ph.D., Professor of Medicine and of Biochemistry and Molecular Biology, University of Miami School of Medicine

David Babbott, M.D., Professor, Department of Medicine, University of Vermont, College of Medicine

Joe G. Baker, Ph.D., Science/Engineering Education Division, Oak Ridge Institute for Science and Education

DeWitt C. Baldwin, Jr., M.D., Division of Medical Education Research and Information, American Medical Association

James E. Black, M.D., Ph.D., Resident, Department of Psychiatry, University of Utah School of Medicine

George Cahill, Jr., M.D., Vice President, Scientific Training and Development, Howard Hughes Medical Institute

Leon Eisenberg, M.D., Chair, Department of Social Medicine and Health Policy, Harvard University Medical School

R. Mark Evans, Ph.D., Science Advisor, Consumer Affairs, American Medical Association, and Science Editor, American Medical Television

Godfrey S. Getz, M.D., Ph.D., Donald M. Pritzker Professor and Chairman, Department of Pathology, University of Chicago Pritzker School of Medicine

Phillip Gorden, M.D., Director, National Institute of Diabetes and Digestive and Kidney Diseases, National Institutes of Health

Diane L. Gottheil, Ph.D., Associate Director, Medical Scholars Program, Assistant Professor, Medical Humanities and Social Sciences Program, University of Illinois College of Medicine at Urbana-Champaign

Paul A. Hattis, M.D., J.D., Associate Director, Internal Medicine Residency Program, Carney Hospital, Community Oriented Primary Care Program

William R. Hendee, Ph.D., Senior Associate Dean of Research and Vice President for Technology, Medical College of Wisconsin

Benjamin Horowitz, M.D./Ph.D. student, University of Illinois College of Medicine at Urbana-Champaign and Department of Educational Policy Studies, University of Illinois at Urbana-Champaign

Frances Degen Horowitz, Ph.D., President of the Graduate School, City University of New York

Ruth L. Kirschstein, M.D., Director, National Institute of General Medical Sciences, National Institutes of Health

Arthur Kleinman, M.D., Professor of Medical Anthropology and Psychiatry, Harvard Medical School

Gerald Levey, M.D., Professor and Chairman, Department of Medicine, University of Pittsburgh School of Medicine

Jerod M. Loeb, Ph.D., Assistant Vice President for Science and Technology, American Medical Association

Robert McGinnis, Ph.D., Professor, Department of Sociology, Cornell University

Thomas Meikle, Jr., M.D., President, Josiah Macy, Jr., Foundation

Robert G. Petersdorf, M.D., President, Association of American Medical Colleges

Charles H. Rodgers, Ph.D., Manpower Program Director, Division of Kidney, Urologic and Hematologic Diseases, National Institute of Diabetes and Digestive and Kidney Diseases

Beverley D. Rowley, Ph.D., Director, Department of Data Systems, American Medical Association

Roberta Siegel, M.A., Assistant to the Director, University of Chicago Program in Medicine, Arts, and the Social Sciences

Hamilton Smith, M.D., Professor of Molecular Biology and Genetics, Director, Medical Scientist Training Program, The Johns Hopkins University School of Medicine

Gary E. Striker, M.D., Director, Division of Kidney, Urologic and Hematologic Diseases, National Institute of Diabetes and Digestive and Kidney Diseases, National Institutes of Health

August G. Swanson, M.D., Vice President, Division of Academic Affairs, Association of American Medical Colleges (retired)

Harold M. Swartz, M.D., Ph.D., Director, Educational Programs, Center for the Evaluative Clinical Sciences, Dartmouth Medical School

Sheila O'Leary Weaver, M.S., Department of Medical Biostatistics, University of Vermont College of Medicine

Stanley Yachnin, M.D., Professor, Department of Medicine, Director, University of Chicago Program in Medicine, Arts, and the Social Sciences

REGISTRY OF M.D./PH.D. AND OTHER COMBINED DEGREE PROGRAMS IN MEDICINE

This registry was compiled by the Medical Scholars Program, University of Illinois College of Medicine at Urbana-Champaign in October, 1990, and updated in June, 1993.

University of Alabama School of Medicine
Frank M. Griffin, Jr., M.D., Director
M.D./Ph.D. Training Program
University of Alabama at Birmingham
University Station, MEB 605
Birmingham, AL 35294
205/934-4092
Other contact: Valerie Webster, Program Coordinator.

University of South Alabama College of Medicine
Edwin R. Hughes, M.D., Director
Medical Scientist Training Program
307 University Blvd., CSAB 341
Mobile, AL 36688
205/460-6153
Other contact: Marilyn Rosson, Secretary.

University of Arizona College of Medicine
John D. Palmer, M.D., Ph.D., Director
Medical Scientist Training Program
Health Sciences Center
Tucson, AZ 85724
602/626-4491

University of Arkansas College of Medicine
Dr. Jay H. Menna, Director
Combined M.D./Ph.D. Program
4301 West Markham Street
Little Rock, AR 72205
501/686-5350

University of California, Berkeley/ San Francisco
Henrik Blum, M.D., Interim Director
UCB-UCSF Joint Medical Program
570 University Hall
Berkeley, CA 94720
Other contact: Ronnie London, Student Affairs Officer.

University of California, Davis, School of Medicine
Donal A. Walsh, Ph.D., Program Director
M.D./PH.D. Program
MSI-A, Room 2427
Davis, CA 95616
916/752-7213
Other contact: Barbara Sutton, Administrative Assistant.

University of California, Irvine, California College of Medicine
Alan L. Goldin, M.D., Ph.D., Director
Medical Scientist Program
Microbiology and Molecular Genetics
College of Medicine
Irvine, CA 92717-4025
714/856-5264
714/856-8598 (FAX)
Other contact: Mirtha Nodal-Barthold, Program Coordinator.

University of California, Los Angeles, School of Medicine
Stanley G. Korenman, M.D., Director
Medical Scientist Training Program
8-250 Factor Building
10833 Le Conte Avenue
Los Angeles, CA 90024-7041
310/794-1817
310/794-1819 (FAX)
Other contact: Alice del Rosario, Program Administrator.

University of California, San Diego, School of Medicine
Paul A. Insel, M.D., Director
Medical Scientist Training Program
9500 Gilman Drive - 0606
La Jolla, CA 92093-0606
619/534-0689
800/925-8704
Other contact: Kathleen Sexton, Program Assistant.

University of California, San Francisco, School of Medicine
David R. Cox, M.D., Ph.D., Director
Medical Scientist Training Program
505 Parnassus Avenue 1082-M
Box 0210
San Francisco, CA 94143
415/467-4423
Other contact: Jana Marie Toutolmin, Program Administrator.

Loma Linda University School of Medicine
Dr. W. B. Rippon, Director
Medical Scientist Program
Loma Linda, CA 92350
714/824-4528
Other contact: Dr. A. Zuccarelli, Program Coordinator.

University of Southern California School of Medicine
Richard N. Bergman, Ph.D., Director
M.D./Ph.D. Program
1975 Zonal Avenue, KAM 300
Los Angeles, CA 90033
213/224-7891
Other contact: Sandra Mosteller, Administrator.

Stanford University School of Medicine
David A. Clayton, M.D., Director
Medical Scientist Training Program
Room X205
Medical School Office Building
Stanford, CA 94305
415/723-6176
Other contact: Edward Mocarski, Assistant Program Director; Marjorie Weesner, Administrative Assistant.

University of Colorado School of Medicine
Margaret C. Neville, Ph.D., Director
Medical Scientist Training Program
4200 E. Ninth Avenue,
Campus Box C240
Denver, CO 80262
303/270-8230
Other contact: Sarah Dempsey, Coordinator.

University of Connecticut School of Medicine
Dr. Thiruchandura Rajan, Director
Combined M.D./Ph.D. Degree Program
Graduate Student Affairs Office
Farmington, CT 06032
203/679-3150
Other contact: Cathi Koehler-Cote, Administrator, Graduate Student Office; Keat Sanford, Director of Admission, Medical School.

Yale University School of Medicine
James D. Jamieson, M.D., Ph.D., Director
M.D./Ph.D. Program
367 Cedar Street
New Haven, CT 06510
203/785-4403
203/785-3234 (FAX)
Other contact: Michael J. Caplan, M.D., Ph.D., Assistant Director; Gerald I. Shulman, M.D., Ph.D., Assistant Director; Marybeth Brandi, Program Coordinator.

George Washington University School of Medicine and Health Sciences
Robert I. Keimowitz, M.D., Director
M.D./Ph.D. Program; Honors Program
2300 Eye Street, N.W.
Ross Hall 713
Washington, DC 20037
202/994-3266

Georgetown University School of Medicine
James F. Burris, M.D., Director
M.D./Ph.D. Program
NE 120 Med-Dent Building
3900 Reservoir Road, N.W.
Washington, DC 20007
202/687-5421

Howard University College of Medicine
Associate Dean for Academic Affairs
M.D./Ph.D. Program
520 W Street, N.W.
Washington, DC 20059
202/636-6270

University of Florida College of Medicine
Richard Moyer, Ph.D., Director
M.D./Ph.D. Program
P.O. Box 100266
Gainesville, FL 32610-0166
904/392-3311
904/392-3133 (FAX)
Other contact: Dr. Mohan Raizada, Professor, Physiology; Dr. Henry Baker, Assistant Professor, Immunology/Medical Microbiology; Dr. Daniel Driscoll, Assistant Professor, Pediatric Genetics; Joyce Conners, Secretary.

University of Miami School of Medicine
Joan Stein-Streilein, Ph.D., Director
Physician Scientist Program
1600 N.W. 10th Avenue, Room 1128A
Miami, FL 33101
305/547-6851
Other contact: Sue Lucas, Coordinator; Ondina Carcia-Pons, Staff Associate; Paul Goott, Data Control Coordinator; Grace DeGasperi, Senior Staff Assistant.

Emory University School of Medicine
Robert B. Gunn, M.D., Director
M.D./Ph.D. Program
1462 Clifton Road
Atlanta, GA 30322
404/727-5676
Other contact: Dale Edmondson, Ph.D., Associate Director; Rhond Burke, Secretary.

Medical College of Georgia
Lowell M. Greenbaum, Ph.D.
Dean of Graduate Studies and
Vice President for Research
Director, M.D./Ph.D. Program
School of Graduate Studies
Augusta, GA 30912-1500
414/721-4183

University of Chicago
Nancy Schwartz, Ph.D., Director
Pediatric M.D./Ph.D. Training Program
5841 S. Maryland Avenue, Box 413
Chicago, IL 60637
312/702-1939
Other contact: Dan Pacenti, Graduate Affairs Administrator.

University of Chicago Pritzker School of Medicine
Wolfgang Epstein, M.D., Director
Medical Scientist Training Program
920 E. 58th St., Box 4
Chicago, IL 60637
312/702-9755
Other contact: Jacqueline McKissack, MSTP Administrator.

University of Chicago Program in Medicine, Arts and the Social Sciences
Stanley Yachnin, M.D., Director
1116 East 59th Street
Chicago, IL 60637
312/702-7967
Other contact: Roberta Siegel, Associate Director.

University of Health Sciences—The Chicago Medical School
Yoon Kim, M.D., Ph.D., Chair
M.D./Ph.D. Combined Degree Program Committee
3333 Green Bay Road
North Chicago, IL 60064
708/578-3230
Other contact: Kris Jones, Administrative Assistant.

University of Illinois College of Medicine at Chicago
Donald Chambers, Ph.D., Director
M.D./Ph.D. Program
P.O. Box 6998 (mc-784)
Chicago, IL 60680
312/996-7670
Other contact: Mickey Leavy, Administrative Aide.

University of Illinois College of Medicine at Urbana-Champaign
Tony G. Waldrop, Ph.D., Director
Medical Scholars Program
190 Medical Sciences Building
506 South Mathews Avenue
Urbana, IL 61801
217/333-8146

217/333-8868 (FAX)
Other contact: Diane L. Gottheil, Ph.D., Associate Director; Nora J. Few, Coordinator; Denice A. Wells, Secretary.

Loyola University of Chicago Stritch School of Medicine
Israel Hanin, Ph.D., Director
M.D./Ph.D. Program
2160 South First Avenue
Building 102; Room 3620
Maywood, IL 60153
708/216-3261
708/216-6596
Other contact: Paula Griffin, Administrative Assistant.

Northwestern University Medical School
Janardan K. Reddy, M.D., Director
M.D./Ph.D. Program
Ward Building, 9-312
303 East Chicago Avenue
Chicago, IL 60611
312/503-8901
Other contact: Virginia Harshman, Administrator.

Southern Illinois University School of Medicine
Theodore LeBlang, Professor Medical Jurisprudence
M.D./J.D. Dual Degree Program
Department of Medical Humanities
P.O. Box 19230
Springfield, IL 62794-0362
217/782-9362

W. Eugene Basanta, Associate Professor of Law
Lesar Law Building
Southern Illinois University
School of Law
Carbondale, IL 62901-7804
618/536-7711

Indiana University School of Medicine
Catherine G. Palmer, Ph.D., Director
Combined Degree Committee
1120 South Drive
Indianapolis, IN 46202-5113
317/274-5273
Other contact: Kelly Forrestal, Secretary.

University of Iowa College of Medicine
Robert E. Fellows, M.D., Ph.D., Director
Medical Scientist Training Program
5-660 Bowen Science Building
Iowa City, IA 52242
319/335-7830
Other contact: William Johnson, Ph.D., Associate Director; Janet A. Schlechte, M.D., Associate Director for Clinical Studies; Richard Potter, Program Assistant.

University of Kansas Medical Center
A. L. Chapman, Ph.D., Coordinator
M.D./Ph.D. Program
3901 Rainbow Blvd.
Kansas City, KS 66160-7700
913/588-5242
Other contact: Richard Clancy, Ph.D., Chair, M.D./Ph.D. Advisory Committee; Joseph Bast, Ph.D., Associate Dean, Graduate Studies and Research.

University of Kentucky College of Medicine
Thomas V. Getchell, Ph.D., Director
M.D./Ph.D. Program Director
A. B. Chandler Medical Center
800 Rose Street
Lexington, KY 40536-0084
606/233-6589
Other contact: H. David Wilson, M.D., Associate Director; Jayne Middleton, Ed.D., Associate Dean, Education.

Louisiana State University School of Medicine in New Orleans
Marilyn Zimny, Ph.D.
Acting Dean
School of Graduate Studies
433 Bolivar Street
New Orleans, LA 70112-2223
504/568-4804

Louisiana State University School of Medicine in Shreveport
William A. Sodeman, Jr., M.D.
M.D./Ph.D. Program
1501 Kings Highway
P.O. Box 33932
Shreveport, LA 71130-3932
318/674-5240

Tulane University School of Medicine
Combined Degree Programs
Office of Student Affairs
1430 Tulane Avenue
New Orleans, LA 70112
504/558-5331

Johns Hopkins University School of Medicine
Stephen Desiderio, M.D., Ph.D., Director
M.D./Ph.D. Program
725 North Wolfe Street
Baltimore, MD 21205
410/955-8543
Other contact: Dana L. Baker, Administrator; Thomasine D. Williams, Secretary.

University of Maryland School of Medicine
Marshall L. Rennels, Ph.D., Director
M.D./Ph.D. Program
655 West Baltimore Street
Baltimore, MD 21201
301/328-7478

Boston University School of Medicine
Carl Franzblau, Ph.D., Director
Combined M.D./Ph.D. Degree Program
80 East Concord Street
Boston, MA 02118
617/638-5120
Other contact: Selwyn A. Broitman, Ph.D., Program Coordinator; Lorraine M. Josef, Associate Director, Administration.

Harvard Medical School
Bernardo Nadel-Ginard, M.D., Ph.D., Director
M.D./Ph.D. Program
260 Longwood Avenue
Boston, MA 02115
617/432-0991
617/432-2791 (FAX)
Other contact: Linda Burnley, Administrative Director; Robert Sawtell, Financial Administrative Assistant; Molly Lanzarotta, Special Projects Coordinator; Jennifer DeAngelo, Administrative Coordinator.

Harvard University—Massachusetts Institute of Technology, Division of Health Sciences and Technology
Roger G. Mark, M.D., Co-Director
Richard S. Kitz, M.D., Co-Director
HST/M.D. Program
Room E25-519
77 Massachusetts Avenue
Cambridge, MA 02139
617/253-7818
Other contact: Walter Abelmann, M.D., CHM Curriculum Committee; Keiko Oh, Administrative Officer.

University of Massachusetts Medical School
Robert E. Humphreys, M.D., Ph.D., Director
M.D./Ph.D. Program in Medical Sciences
55 Lake Avenue North
Worcester, MA 01655
508/856-4135
Other contact: Thomas B. Miller, Jr., Ph.D., Dean, Graduate School of Biomedical Science; Linda E. Dexter, Director, Office of Graduate Studies.

Tufts University School of Medicine
Markley H. Bryer, M.D., M.P.H., Director
Combined M.D./M.P.H. Program
136 Harrison Avenue
Boston, MA 02111
617/956-6565
Other contact: Deborah Dean, Associate Director.

Tufts University/Sackler School of Graduate Biomedical Sciences
Dr. James F. Dice, Director
M.D./Ph.D. Program
Department of Physiology

Tufts University School of Medicine
136 Harrison Avenue
Boston, MA 02111
617/956-0407
Other contact: Louis Lasagna, M.D., Dean; Peggy Newell, Assistant Dean.

Michigan State University College of Human Medicine
Lynda J. Farquhar, Ph.D., Director
Medical Scientist Training & Graduate Studies Program
A101 East Fee Hall
East Lansing, MI 48824
517/353-8856
Other contact: Loren Bieber, Ph.D., Associate Dean/Research.

Michigan State University College of Osteopathic Medicine
Veronica M. Maher, Ph.D.
J. Justin McCormick, Ph.D.
Program Directors
Medical Scientist Training Program
West Fee Hall
East Lansing, MI 48824
517/353-7785

University of Michigan Medical School
Roderick Nairn, Ph.D., Director
Medical Scientist Training Program
7310 Medical Science I, 0624
Ann Arbor, MI 48109-0624
313/764-6176
Other contact: Carole McCollister, Contact; Betty Whitlock, Secretary.

Wayne State University School of Medicine
George Dambach, Ph.D.
Assistant Dean for Research & Graduate Programs
540 East Canfield Avenue
Detroit, MI 48201
313/577-1455

University of Mississippi Medical Center
Ben H. Douglas, Ph.D., Director
Graduate Programs in the Medical Sciences
2500 North State Street
Jackson, MS 39216-4505
601/984-1195

Mayo Graduate School/Mayo Medical School
David E. Clapham, M.D., Ph.D., Director
M.D./Ph.D. Program
200 First Street, S.W.
Rochester, MN 55905
507/284-5881
Other contact: Catharine J. Chellgren, Administrative Assistant.

University of Minnesota
Martin Dworkin, Ph.D., Director
Combined M.D./Ph.D.
Box 293 UMHC, 3-111 Owre Hall
420 Delaware St. S.E.
Minneapolis, MN 55455
612/625-3680
Other contact: Dana Clark, Executive Secretary, Coordinator; Margaret Hostetter, M.D., Co-Director.

University of Missouri—Columbia School of Medicine
Herbert S. Goldberg, Ph.D., Director
M.D./Ph.D. Program
MA2-3 Medical Sciences Building
Columbia, MO 65212
314/882-1566
Other contact: Ted Grosharg, Associate Dean, Student Affairs; Robert McCollum, Assistant Dean, Student Affairs.

St. Louis University School of Medicine
Clifford Bellone, Ph.D., Director
M.D./Ph.D. Program
1402 South Grand Boulevard
Department of Microbiology
St. Louis, MO 63104
314/577-8105
Other contact: Vincent A. Chiappinelli, Ph.D., Associate Professor; Andrew L. Lechner, Associate Professor; William S. Sly, M.D., Chairman/Professor; Daniel L. Tolbert, Ph.D., Professor.

Washington University School of Medicine
Carl Frieden, Ph.D., Director
Medical Scientist Training Program
660 South Euclid Ave.
Campus Box 8033
St. Louis, MO 63110
314/362-7190
Other contact: Elliot Elson, Ph.D., Co-MSTP Director; Barbara Fox, Assistant MSTP Director; Ann Miles, Secretary.

Creighton University Medical School
William L. Pancoe, Ph.D.
Director, M.D./Ph.D. Program
California at 24th Street
Omaha, NE 68178
402/280-2905

University of Nebraska College of Medicine
C. Kirk Phares, Ph.D.
Associate Dean for Research and Development
Director, M.D./Ph.D. Program
600 S. 42nd Street
Omaha, NE 68198-6545
402/559-4506
402/559-4148 (FAX)

University of Nevada School of Medicine
David P. Westfall, Ph.D., Director
M.D./Ph.D. Program
Room 146 Howard Building
Reno, NV 89557
702/784-6956

Dartmouth University
Harold M. Swartz, M.D., Ph.D.
M.D./Ph.D. Program
Dartmouth Medical School
HB7250, 308 Strasenburgh Hall
Hanover, NH 03755-3863
603/650-1754

UMDNJ-New Jersey Medical School
Michael Small, Ph.D., Director
M.D./Ph.D. Program
185 South Orange Avenue
Newark, NJ 07103
201/456-6016
201/456-6035 (FAX)
Other contact: Lawrence A. Feldman, Ph.D., Senior Associate Dean for Education; Willie Mae Coram, Ph.D., Assistant Dean, Graduate School of Biomedical Sciences.

Albany Medical College
David A. Lawrence, Ph.D., Director
M.D./Ph.D. Program
47 New Scotland Avenue
Albany, NY 12208
518/445-5175

Albert Einstein College of Medicine of Yeshiva University
Betty A. Diamond, M.D., Director
Medical Scientist Training Program
1300 Morris Park Avenue
Bronx, NY 10461
212/430-4081
Other contact: Cecile A. Brown, Administrator; Elaine Bezold, Program Coordinator; Sandra Shames, Program Secretary.

Columbia University College of Physicians and Surgeons
David Schachter, M.D., Director
M.D./Ph.D. Program
630 West 168th Street
New York, NY 10032
212/305-4028
Other contact: Joan R. Popovitch, Program Coordinator.

Tri-Institutional M.D./Ph.D. Program (Cornell University Medical College and Graduate School of Medical Sciences, The Rockefeller University, Sloan-Kettering Institute)
Carl Nathan, M.D., Director
1300 York Avenue
New York, NY 10021
212/746-6023
Other contact: Sheila Krauss, Program Coordinator.

Mount Sinai School of Medicine of the City University of New York
Terry Ann Krulwich, Ph.D., Director
Medical Scientist Training Program
Box 1022, Mt. Sinai, 1 G. Levy Place

New York, NY 10029
212/241-6546
Other contact: Robert Desnick, M.D., Ph.D., Associate Program Director; Jack P. Green, M.D., Ph.D., Associate Program Director; Debra Schlesinger, M.P.A., Administrator.

New York Medical College
Karl P. Adler, M.D., Co-Director
Charles E. Ford, Ph.D., Co-Director
M.D./Ph.D. Program
Sunshine Cottage
Valhalla, NY 10595
914/993-4500

New York University School of Medicine
David D. Sabatini, M.D., Ph.D., Director
Medical Scientist Training Program
550 First Avenue
New York, NY 10016
212/340-5353
Other contact: Gert Kreibich, Ph.D., Deputy Director; James Salzer, M.D., Ph.D., Associate Director; Robert Schneider, Ph.D., Associate Director.

University of Rochester School of Medicine & Dentistry
George N. Abraham, M.D., Director
Medical Scientist Training Program
601 Elmwood Avenue, Box 706
Rochester, NY 14642
716/275-2891
Other contact: Richard Satran, M.D., Associate Dean/Medical Admissions; Marilyn A. Graver, Administrator.

State University of New York Health Science Center at Brooklyn College of Medicine
Harriet P. Bernheimer, Ph.D.
Chair, M.D./Ph.D. Program
450 Clarkson Avenue, Box 41
Brooklyn, NY 11203
718/270-1155
Other contact: Edward Throckmorton, Admissions Officer, Graduate School.

State University of New York at Buffalo, School of Medicine and Biomedical Sciences
Jerome A. Roth, Ph.D., Director,
MSTP, Office of Medical Education
35 CFS Addition
Buffalo, NY 14214
716/831-3236

State University of New York at Stony Brook, Health Sciences Center
Paul A. Fisher, M.D., Ph.D. Director
Medical Scientist Training Program
School of Medicine
Stony Brook, NY 11794-8651
516/444-3067
Other contact: Gail Wolf, Program Administrator.

State University of New York Health Science Center at Syracuse
Alexander Bortoff, Ph.D., Co-chair
Charles J. Hodge, Jr., M.D., Co-chair
M.D./Ph.D. Program
750 East Adams Street
Syracuse, NY 13210
315/464-4538
315/464-4544 (FAX)

Duke University School of Medicine
Salvatore V. Pizzo, M.D., Ph.D., Director
Medical Scientist Training Program
Duke University Medical Center
P.O. Box 3005
Durham, NC 27710
919/684-2412
Other contact: Douglas Anthony, M.D., Ph.D., Associate Director; Patricia O. Burks, Administrative Assistant.

University of North Carolina at Chapel Hill School of Medicine
Robert A. Eisenberg, M.D., Director
M.D./Ph.D. Program
923 FLOB, CB 7280
Chapel Hill, NC 27514-7280
919/966-4191
Other contact: Wendy S. Dower, Secretary.

University of North Dakota School of Medicine
Thomas E. Norris, Ph.D.
Executive Associate Dean for
Academic Affairs & Research
501 N. Columbia Road
Grand Forks, ND 58203
701/777-2515

Case Western Reserve University School of Medicine
Leslie T. Webster, Jr., M.D., Director
Medical Scientist Training Program
2119 Abington Road
Cleveland, OH 44106
216/368-3404
Other contact: Felicite Katz, Program Coordinator; Janice G. Douglas, M.D. Program Coordinator.

University of Cincinnati College of Medicine
Judith A. K. Harmony, Ph.D.,
Co-Director
James J. Nordlund, M.D., Co-Director
M.D./Ph.D. Program
231 Bethesda Avenue
Cincinnati, OH 45267-0592
513/558-2379
Other contact: Terri A. Berning, Secretary.

Medical College of Ohio
Lewis B. Morrow, M.D.
Director, M.D./Ph.D. Program
Acting Vice President for Academic Affairs
Caller Service No. 10008
Toledo, OH 43699
419/381-4243
Other contact: Peter J. Goldblatt, M.D., Dean, Graduate College.

Northeastern Ohio Universities College of Medicine
Gary D. Niehaus, Ph.D., Director
M.D./Ph.D. Program
4209 State Route 44
P.O. Box 95
Rootstown, OH 44272
216/325-2511
Other contact: Kitty Reedy, Secretary.

The Ohio State University College of Medicine
Branford T. Stokes, Ph.D., Director
Medical Scientist Training Program
244 Meiling Hall
370 West 9th Avenue
Columbus, OH 43210-1238
614/293-4819
Other contact: Joan Allen, Secretary.

University of Oklahoma College of Medicine
John Harley, M.D., Director
M.D./Ph.D. Program
P.O. Box 26901
Oklahoma City, OK 73190
405/271-7768
Other contact: Sally Murphy, Special Projects Coordinator; Nancy Hall, Assistant Dean for Admissions.

Oregon Health Sciences University School of Medicine
Kathleen Richardson, Ph.D., Chair
M.D./Ph.D. Program
3181 S.W. Sam Jackson Park Road
Portland, OR 97201
503/494-7557

Hahnemann University School of Medicine
Stephen R. Max, Ph.D., Dean,
Graduate School and
Vice President for Research
Carole Long, Ph.D., Director
M.D./Ph.D. Program
Broad & Vine, Mail Stop 480
Philadelphia, PA 19102-1192
215/762-1909
215/246-5731 (FAX)

Jefferson Medical College of Thomas Jefferson University
Robert S. Blacklow, M.D.
Director, The Delaware/Jefferson
Medical Scholars Program
1025 Walnut Street
Philadelphia, PA 19107

Jefferson Medical College of Thomas Jefferson University
Jussi Saukkonen, M.D., Director
Gibbons Scholars M.D./Ph.D. Program

1020 Locust Street, M 63
Philadelphia, PA 19106
215/928-8986
Other contact: Thomas Butler, Ph.D., Academic Director; Jill M. Pasternak, M.A., Coordinator.

The Medical College of Pennsylvania
Pat R. Levitt, Ph.D., Director
M.D./Ph.D. Program
2900 Queen Lane
Philadelphia, PA 19129
215/991-8570
Other contact: Kathleen Golden, Administrator.

Pennsylvania State University College of Medicine
Mary K. Howett, Ph.D.
M.D./Ph.D. Program
M. S. Hershey Medical Center
Box 850
Hershey, PA 17033
717/531-8755
Other contact: Katherine Q. Vanderav, M.Ed., Director of Student Affairs.

University of Pennsylvania School of Medicine
Jerome F. Strauss, III, M.D., Ph.D.
Director, Combined Degree Program
Suite 100 Medical Education Building
Philadelphia, PA 19104-6087
215/898-8025
Other contact: Liesel Baker, Assistant Director; Michael Prystowsky, M.D., Ph.D., Associate Director.

University of Pittsburgh/School of Medicine/Carnegie Mellon University
Joseph M. R. Furman, M.D., Ph.D.
Assistant Dean, M.D./Ph.D. Program
Alan Magee Scaife Hall of the Health Professions
Pittsburgh, PA 15261
412/648-2324
Other contact: Margaret L. Fiori, Program Administrator.

Temple University School of Medicine
Peter N. Walsh, M.D., Ph.D.
Director, M.D./Ph.D. Program
3400 North Broad Street
Philadelphia, PA 19140
215/221-4375
Other contact: Patricia Pileggi, Administrative Assistant; Sheila Booker, Secretary.

Brown University Program in Medicine
Nelson Fausto, M.D., Director
M.D./Ph.D. Program
97 Waterman Street
Providence, RI 02912
401/863-3119
Other contact: Natalie Pacheco, Senior Academic Secretary.

Medical University of South Carolina
Perry V. Halushka, M.D., Ph.D., Director
Medical Scientist Training Program
College of Graduate Studies/College of Medicine
171 Ashley Avenue
Charleston, SC 29425
803/792-1253 or 800/277-0111
803/792-0816 (FAX)
Other contact: Susan Higerd, Administrative Assistant.

University of South Carolina School of Medicine
Dr. James Buggy, Director
Biomedical Sciences Graduate Program
Office of Research and Graduate Studies
Columbia, SC 29208
803/733-3100
Other contact: Mary Sue Poole, Graduate Program Coordinator; Santley Fowler, Senior Associate Dean for Research and Graduate Studies.

University of Tennessee, Memphis, College of Medicine
David M. Mirvis, M.D., Director
M.D./Ph.D. Program
800 Madison Avenue
Memphis, TN 38163
901/528-5826

Vanderbilt University School of Medicine
Daryl K. Granner, M.D.
Director, M.D./Ph.D. Program
21st Avenue South, D-3300 MCN
Nashville, TN 37087-2104
615/322-7004
Other contact: Ellen Carter, Program Coordinator.

Baylor College of Medicine
C. Thomas Caskey, M.D., Director
Medical Scientist Training Program
One Baylor Plaza
Houston, TX 77030
713/798-6613
713/798-6325 (FAX)
Other contact: Drita P. Almeida, Senior Administrative Assistant.

Texas A&M University College of Medicine
John M. Quarles, Ph.D., Director
M.D./Ph.D. in Basic Medical Science
Joe Reynolds Medical Building
147 Medical Sciences Building
College Station, TX 77843
409/845-1358
Other contact: George Chiou, Associate Dean for Research & Graduate Studies; Elda Ortiz, Administrative Assistant.

Texas Tech University Health Sciences Center, School of Medicine
Kenneth L. Barker, Ph.D., Director
M.D./Ph.D. Medical Scientist Program
3601 4th Street
Lubbock, TX 79430
806/743-2556
Other contact: Karen H. Rolan, Executive Assistant to Vice President; James Chappell, M.D., Associate Dean for Clinical Affairs; Nancy Tarwarter, Manager, Academic Affairs.

University of Texas Southwestern Medical School
Dr. Jean D. Wilson, Director
Medical Scientist Training Program
5323 Harry Hines Boulevard
Dallas, TX 75235-8853
800/468-MSTP
Other contact: Dr. Rodney Ulane, Associate Dean; Dr. Donald Kennedy, Associate Director; Darlene Reynolds, Administrative Assistant.

University of Texas Medical Branch at Galveston
James E. Blankenship, Ph.D., Director
M.D./Ph.D. Combined Degree Program
5.108 Administration Building
Galveston, TX 77555-0132
409/772-2665
Other contact: Bettye Moore, Administrative Associate.

University of Texas Medical School at Houston
Peter J. A. Davies, M.D., Ph.D., Director
M.D./Ph.D. Program
P.O. Box 20708
Houston, TX 77225
713/792-5550
Other contact: Paul Darlington, Ph.D., Associate Director; Doris Thornton, M.Ed., Coordinator.

Eastern Virginia Medical School of the Medical College of Hampton Roads
Robert McCombs, Ph.D., Co-Director
Executive Associate Dean
P.O. Box 1980
Norfolk, VA 23501
804/446-5805
Other contact: William J. Cooke, Ph.D., Associate Dean of Research; Peggy Horton, Assistant Administrator.

Keith Carson, Ph.D., Co-Director
Director, Biomedical Sciences Program
Department of Biology
Old Dominion University
Norfolk, VA 23524
804/683-3595

Virginia Commonwealth University Medical College of Virginia
Dr. Jack L. Haar, Director
M.D./Ph.D. Program
School of Medicine
1101 East Marshall Street
MCV Station, Box 709

Richmond, VA 23298-0001
804/786-7491

University of Virginia School of Medicine
Steven L. Gonias, M.D., Ph.D., Director
Medical Scientist Training Program
Box 214, Old Medical School
Charlottesville, VA 22908
804/924-9192
Other contact: Susan Frasier, Director, Graduate Studies.

University of Washington School of Medicine
Lawrence A. Loeb, M.D., Ph.D., Director
Medical Scientist Training Program
Seattle, WA 98195
206/543-6015
Other contact: Peter S. Rabinovitch, M.D., Ph.D., Associate Director; Marjorie Ross, Program Assistant; Mary Whiting, Secretary.

Marshall University School of Medicine
Carla A. Gruetter, Ph.D., Director
Biomedical Sciences
1542 Spring Valley Drive
Huntington, WV 25755-9310
304/696-7326
Other contact: Gary Rankin, Ph.D., Associate Dean; Marlene Chaffin, Administrative Aide.

West Virginia University School of Medicine
Diana Beattie, Director
M.D./Ph.D. Medical Scientist Program
Morgantown, WV 26506
304/293-7522

Medical College of Wisconsin
Sidney E. Grossberg, M.D., Director
John P. Kampine, M.D., Ph.D., Co-Director
Medical Scientist Training Program
8701 Watertown Plank Road
Milwaukee, WI 53226
414/257-8253
Other contact: K. Joanne Benes, Administrative Associate.

University of Wisconsin Medical School
John F. Fallon, Co-Director
Deane Mosher, Co-Director
Millard Susman, Co-Director
M.D./Ph.D. Integrated Program
1300 University Avenue
Madison, WI 53706
608/263-7311
Other contact: Jeanne O'Brien, Program Assistant.

McGill University Faculty of Medicine
Dr. A. Tenenhouse
M.D./Ph.D. Combined Program
McIntyre Medical Building, 6th floor
3655 Drummond, Dean's Office
Montreal, Quebec H3G 1Y6 Canada
514/937-6011, Ext. 410
Other contact: Danielle Lefebre, Administrative Secretary.

University of Toronto Faculty of Medicine
Dr. Mel Silverman, Director
M.D./Ph.D. Program
Medical Science Building, Room 7226
Toronto, Ontario M5S 1A8 Canada
416/978-7189

Please add my name to your mailing list:

name:______________________________ date:__________

____

street:______________________________ phone:__________

city:______________ state:__________ zip:__________

Areas of interest:______________________________

____

Comments and suggestions:______________________________

____

____

Please send an information package to:

name:______________________________ date:__________

____

street address:______________________________ phone:__________

city:______________ state:__________ zip:__________

college, group, or organization:______________________________

area of interest:______________________________

____

For information and orders, please call:

800-634-4365

BETZ PUBLISHING COMPANY, INC.
P O Box 1745 - Rockville MD 20849

NO POSTAGE
NECESSARY
IF MAILED
IN THE
UNITED STATES

BUSINESS REPLY MAIL

FIRST CLASS MAIL PERMIT NO. 2073 ROCKVILLE, MD

POSTAGE WILL BE PAID BY ADDRESSEE

BETZ Publishing Company, Inc.
P.O. Box 1745
Rockville, Maryland 20849-9947

BETZ Publishing Company, Inc.
P.O. Box 1745
Rockville, Maryland 20849-9947
301-340-0030 - 800-634-4365